Promoting Entrepreneurship to Reduce Graduate Unemployment

Isaac Wasswa Katono
Uganda Christian University, Uganda

IGI Global
PUBLISHER of TIMELY KNOWLEDGE

A volume in the Advances in Higher Education and Professional Development (AHEPD) Book Series

Published in the United States of America by
IGI Global
Business Science Reference (an imprint of IGI Global)
701 E. Chocolate Avenue
Hershey PA, USA 17033
Tel: 717-533-8845
Fax: 717-533-8661
E-mail: cust@igi-global.com
Web site: http://www.igi-global.com

Library of Congress Cataloging-in-Publication Data

Names: Katono, Isaac Wasswa, 1956- editor.
Title: Promoting entrepreneurship to reduce graduate unemployment / Isaac Wasswa Katono, editor.
Description: Hershey, PA : Business Science Reference, 2022. | Includes bibliographical references and index. | Summary: "This book features researchers from all over the world that contributed book chapters that show how different countries have guided their graduates into entrepreneurship, so it can be used as a strategy to reduce graduate unemployment"-- Provided by publisher.
Identifiers: LCCN 2021048731 (print) | LCCN 2021048732 (ebook) | ISBN 9781799895817 (hardcover) | ISBN 9781799895824 (paperback) | ISBN 9781799895831 (ebook)
Subjects: LCSH: Entrepreneurship--Vocational guidance.
Classification: LCC HB615 .P777 2022 (print) | LCC HB615 (ebook) | DDC 658.4/21023--dc23/eng/20211015
LC record available at https://lccn.loc.gov/2021048731
LC ebook record available at https://lccn.loc.gov/2021048732

This book is published in the IGI Global book series Advances in Higher Education and Professional Development (AHEPD) (ISSN: 2327-6983; eISSN: 2327-6991)

British Cataloguing in Publication Data
A Cataloguing in Publication record for this book is available from the British Library.

Advances in Higher Education and Professional Development (AHEPD) Book Series

ISSN:2327-6983
EISSN:2327-6991

MISSION

As world economies continue to shift and change in response to global financial situations, job markets have begun to demand a more highly-skilled workforce. In many industries a college degree is the minimum requirement and further educational development is expected to advance. With these current trends in mind, the **Advances in Higher Education & Professional Development (AHEPD) Book Series** provides an outlet for researchers and academics to publish their research in these areas and to distribute these works to practitioners and other researchers.

AHEPD encompasses all research dealing with higher education pedagogy, development, and curriculum design, as well as all areas of professional development, regardless of focus.

COVERAGE

- Adult Education
- Assessment in Higher Education
- Career Training
- Coaching and Mentoring
- Continuing Professional Development
- Governance in Higher Education
- Higher Education Policy
- Pedagogy of Teaching Higher Education
- Vocational Education

The Advances in Higher Education and Professional Development (AHEPD) Book Series (ISSN 2327-6983) is published by IGI Global, 701 E. Chocolate Avenue, Hershey, PA 17033-1240, USA, www.igi-global.com. This series is composed of titles available for purchase individually; each title is edited to be contextually exclusive from any other title within the series. For pricing and ordering information please visit http://www.igi-global.com/book-series/advances-higher-education-professional-development/73681. Postmaster: Send all address changes to above address.

Titles in this Series

For a list of additional titles in this series, please visit:
www.igi-global.com/book-series/advances-higher-education-professional-development/73681

Voicing Diverse Teaching Experiences, Approaches, and Perspectives in Higher Education
Wilfredo Alvarez (Utica University, USA) and Patrick S. De Walt (California State University, Fresno, USA)
Information Science Reference • © 2022 • 273pp • H/C (ISBN: 9781799890003) • US $195.00

Preparing Globally Competent Professionals and Leaders for Innovation and Sustainability
Linyuan Guo-Brennan (University of Prince Edward Island, Canada) and Michael J. Guo-Brennan (Troy University, USA)
Information Science Reference • © 2022 • 415pp • H/C (ISBN: 9781668445280) • US $195.00

Achieving Equity in Higher Education Using Empathy as a Guiding Principle
Catherine Ward (California State University, Fullerton, USA)
Information Science Reference • © 2022 • 335pp • H/C (ISBN: 9781799897460) • US $195.00

Teacher Reflections on Transitioning From K-12 to Higher Education Classrooms
Amy D. Broemmel (The University of Tennessee, Knoxville, USA) and Nora Vines (The University of Tennessee, Knoxville, USA)
Information Science Reference • © 2022 • 448pp • H/C (ISBN: 9781668434604) • US $215.00

Handbook of Research on Improving Engineering Education With the European Project Semester
Benedita Malheiro (Instituto Superior de Engenharia do Porto, Instituto Politécnico do Porto, Portugal) and Pedro Fuentes-Durá (Universitat Politècnica de València, Spain)
Engineering Science Reference • © 2022 • 390pp • H/C (ISBN: 9781668423097) • US $265.00

For an entire list of titles in this series, please visit:
www.igi-global.com/book-series/advances-higher-education-professional-development/73681

IGI Global
PUBLISHER of TIMELY KNOWLEDGE

701 East Chocolate Avenue, Hershey, PA 17033, USA
Tel: 717-533-8845 x100 • Fax: 717-533-8661
E-Mail: cust@igi-global.com • www.igi-global.com

Table of Contents

Section 4
Factors Influencing Career Choice

Detailed Table of Contents

Graduate unemployment is a growing global concern. In 2019, the International Labour Organization (ILO) estimated that more than 73 million youth aged 15–24 were unemployed, the majority of them being student graduates from higher education institutions (HEIs). With a projected population increase of 10 billion by 2050, Africa will constitute 1.4 billion people, the majority of them being young people under the age of 25. Most graduates in developing countries such as Kenya fall under this age group, thus raising concern about their ability to join gainful employment or become self-reliant after graduation. With an average unemployment rate of 7.6% in 2020, The World Bank lists the skills gap between market requirements and the current curriculum provision as an impediment to Kenya's socio-economic agenda. This finding motivates more emphasis for higher education institutions to re-think their approaches in training and skilling. As such, the need for service-learning (SL) as a complementary pedagogy to enhance skills sets among graduates is necessary.

One of the major bottlenecks of the Portuguese labor market is the level of educational attainment of the population. Despite considerable evolution over the last decades, the country is still behind the European Union average in most education indicators. In 2009, 69.2% of the population aged between 15 and 64 had less than upper secondary education, a value that is more than double the European average. Due to the measures and reforms that have been introduced, in 2019, this proportion had dropped to 47.6%. Between 2009 and 2019, self-employed persons had education levels below the average of the working population. In 2009, 79.0% had less than upper secondary education, and in 2019, this number was still at 50.6%. The human capital of the self-employed persons has significant consequences on their entrepreneurial activities. The low educational attainment level of the population has demanded extensive reforms. This chapter discusses the main policies implemented to improve educational attainment and obtain a comprehensive overview of labor market and education indicators.

This chapter interrogates the notion of youth entrepreneurship and leadership as the pathway towards dealing with youth poverty and unemployment in the context of South Africa. Entrepreneurship is gaining currency as one of the panacea for youth

and correlation and regression analysis were performed to explore the nature of relationship among the independent and dependent variables. The major finding of this study is that both the independent variables (university entrepreneurial ecosystem and entrepreneurial self-efficacy) have been found to significantly affect the dependent variable (entrepreneurial intention). Further, entrepreneurial self-efficacy has been to be a more influencing factor than the university entrepreneurial ecosystem.

Every individual wants to be self-sufficient and economically independent. Entrepreneurship is the activity of setting up a business, taking financial risks in the hope of earning profit. Entrepreneur education provides the students with the groundwork needed to start successful commercial or non-commercial businesses, create and endorse new products and processes, engage in social entrepreneurship, and serve as leaders in organizations. This study provides the basis for understanding the entrepreneurial intentions and role of education for a college student—of interest to both researchers and policymakers. The objectives of the study are to understand what graduate entrepreneurship is. The internal factors that encourage students to choose graduate entrepreneurship are entrepreneurial intentions, attitudes, and motivation of students. The external factors that motivate students to choose graduate entrepreneurship are the educational environment of colleges, interaction with existing entrepreneurs, and government policies.

The chapter discusses how a public South African university, the University of KwaZulu-Natal (UKZN), teaches student entrepreneurship through hackathons, incubation programmes, and their impact on students' entrepreneurial journeys. Data was generated from various sources such as observation from student entrepreneurship week and a series of student elevator pitches. Interviews were conducted with 12 participants comprised of UKZN alumni, public relations manager, ENACTUS member, UKZN incubation centre managers, and students. Data also supplemented with secondary data sources such as UKZN magazine Indaba. Findings suggest that hackathons are utilized to identify students' start-ups for incubation. UKZN InQuabate has the capacity as a public research university by promoting innovation, commercialization, and entrepreneurship. Universities as business incubation also support student start-up business by bringing student entrepreneurs together in a common working space.

Employability is a positive and competitive state arising out of psychological capital, career identity, and social capital. Three studies were administered as censuses, (N=205), (N=214), (N=232), from graduates undertaking a skills training programme from Uganda Skills Development Programme (USDP). Quantitative analysis shows that psycap contributed greatly to employability, and social capital contributed less to employability of the unemployed but more to the employed in 2019 and 2020. Career identity showed a negative but significant relationship to employability in 2018 and 2019 while positive and significant relationship with employability in 2020. Social capital partially mediated the relationship between psycap and employability while the same fully mediated the relationship between career identity and employability. These results emphasize the importance of social capital and psycap in enhancing the various graduates' capabilities for positive employability outcomes. The negative career identity results reflect a boundaryless career mindset which is characterized by high physical and psychological mobility.

The subject and aim of this study are to examine the problem of globalizing graduate employment/unemployment and the holistic entrepreneurship strategy against this problem in the axis of Turkey. Two types of methods were followed here: First, as a method of thought, the "deductive" path was followed, since the focus was on specific graduate unemployment instead of the general unemployment problem and the solution based solely on graduate entrepreneurship instead of general employment entrepreneurship. Secondly, as a research method, with the help of official statistical data and literature, the problem and solution (i.e., diagnosis and treatment) were described and parsed-synthesized. One of the expected results from this study is to introduce the Turkish dimension of the graduate labor market and entrepreneurship problem to the world; the other is to emphasize global cooperation to tackle the problem of graduate unemployment.

Preface

Entrepreneurship is defined in many different ways by different scholars. However, it is generally agreed that entrepreneurship is centered around the discovery and exploitation of opportunities and that entrepreneurship is context driven. Entrepreneurship is important in the economies of both developed and developing countries, particularly because businesses started by entrepreneurs provide jobs for millions of people all over the world. Further these businesses come with new products and hence stimulate competition which is eventually beneficial to society. For this and many other reasons, many countries in the world attempt to nurture an entrepreneurial culture through various policies and regulations. One such policy is the focus on entrepreneurship education both at the lower and upper levels of education in order to stem youth and graduate unemployment, which is a big problem in many parts of the world. Graduate unemployment in particular would have been mitigated, if only graduates start businesses which grow, stimulate economies and provide employment to others. However, despite massive policy and education efforts to flag graduates into entrepreneurship, there are worldwide concerns that the numbers of graduates choosing the entrepreneurship career path is not commensurate with the effort made, yet there are very few job opportunities for these graduates in the formal sector. Similarly, the choice of entrepreneurship as a career path differs greatly between different regions of the world. In East Africa for example, many graduates abhor the idea of starting a business, and find it demeaning to be associated with small business, hence graduate unemployment is high. This may not be the case in other regions of the world. This publication seeks to examine how different countries have flagged their graduates into entrepreneurship, and used it as a strategy to reduce graduate unemployment.

This book composed of 14 chapters, authored by scholars in universities from 10 different countries namely Brunei, Germany, India, Kenya, Malaysia, Nigeria, Portugal, South Africa, Turkey and Uganda. The authors are top scholars in this field and have commendable research profiles. The chapters are organised into four sections: "Skills and Training in Higher Education" (five chapters), "Entrepreneurship Programmes" (two chapters), "The University Environment" (three chapters), and

"Factors Influencing Career Choice" (four chapters). This book will be particularly useful to entrepreneurship researchers, scholars in other fields, policy makers and all those who have a bearing on graduate career choice. It is hoped that the book will stimulate interest in the fight against graduate unemployment globally, as an understanding of graduate inhibitors to entrepreneurship are brought into the limelight.

SECTION 1: SKILLS AND TRAINING IN HIGHER EDUCATION

In the chapter "Entrepreneurship as a Tool to Tackle Graduate Youth Unemployment in Developing Economies: The Role of Action-Oriented Entrepreneurship Training," Arobindu Dash and Michael M. Gielnik appreciate that many governments and policymakers seek to promote entrepreneurship to address the issue of unemployment through entrepreneurship education and training. Premised on this position, this chapter discusses STEP (Student Training for Entrepreneurial Promotion) as an action-oriented entrepreneurship training program, showing the theoretical and methodological underpinnings of STEP, how the impact of STEP unfolds over time, and the processes that happen during STEP. This chapter also covers cases where STEP has been extended to different academic settings, bringing systemic change in academic curriculums and for different target groups. Finally, this chapter discusses some common challenges when implementing STEP at partner institutions. The chapter concludes that STEP is an effective tool to tackle graduate youth unemployment in developing economies.

In the chapter "Service Learning in Higher Education Institutions (HEIs) in Kenya," Henry Kiptum Yatich notes that in developing countries such as Kenya, the ability of the youth to join gainful employment or become self-reliant after graduation is a matter of great concern. Given that The World Bank lists the skills gap between market requirements and the current curriculum provision as an impediment to Kenya's socio-economic agenda, this paper calls upon higher education institutions to re-think their approaches in training and skilling, hence the need for Service-Learning (SL) as a complementary pedagogy to enhance skills sets among graduates.

In the chapter "Bridging Into the Future Through Education," Nadia Simoes and Nuno Crespo observe that one of the major bottlenecks of the Portuguese labor market is the level of educational attainment of the population and that despite considerable evolution over the last decades, the country is still behind the European Union average in most education indicators. Since the human capital of the self-employed persons has significant consequences on their entrepreneurial activities, this chapter discusses the main policies implemented to improve educational attainment and obtain a comprehensive overview of labor market and education indicators.

In the chapter "Uprooting Poverty and Unemployment Through Youth Entrepreneurship Leadership and Skills Development," Ndwa Ndwakhulu Stephen Tshishonga examines the notion of youth entrepreneurship and leadership as the pathway towards dealing with youth poverty and unemployment in South Africa. He notes that entrepreneurship is gaining momentum as a panacea for youth unemployment and underemployment within the government circles and youth orientated organizations. The chapter argues that if youth entrepreneurship and leadership interventions are to yield desired results, young people should master technology and be innovative in developing and growing sustainable businesses. In this light, an entrepreneurial mind-set, innovative skills and competencies as well as financial and infrastructural support, are needed if young people are to make a dent on existing poverty and unemployment challenges.

In the chapter "Role of Entrepreneurship Education in Small Business Startups Among Graduates in Nigeria," Johnson Dare Adeeko and Oluwaseyitanfunmi Osunade note that Nigeria is currently going through a period of economic stagnation and unemployment among the educated and illiterate workforce is in large numbers. Tertiary institutions have reacted to this challenge by teaching students entrepreneurship courses at the undergraduate level, aimed at creating small business owners so as to reduce the dependence on white collar jobs. The authors examine the role of entrepreneurship education in small business startups among past students of the University of Ibadan (UI) who took the course on Basic Entrepreneurship Education (ETR 301). The course aimed to fill the gap between entrepreneurship education and ability to be an entrepreneur. A survey of students of the University of Ibadan students who had taken the course on entrepreneurship was conducted. The results showed that entrepreneurship education as provided through the course ETR 301 has significant influence on entrepreneurial mindset and entrepreneurial skills of university students, therefore, should be sustained.

SECTION 2: ENTREPRENEURSHIP PROGRAMS

In the chapter "Upskilling Graduates and Young Professionals Through Entrepreneurship Programmes in South Africa," Ndwa Ndwakhulu Stephen Tshishonga evaluates the youth entrepreneurship programmes aimed at upskilling and socializing both the graduates and young professionals in the world of work in this country. He notes that socio-economic exclusion and marginalization of the youth have led to growing youth unemployment, unemployability and discontent while among the graduates, unemployment has become an emerging phenomenon. This chapter therefore, argues that for youth to escape the scourge of unemployment, exclusion and marginalization, entrepreneurship coaching and mentoring as well as entrepreneurial education are imperative. The chapter underscores the need for progressive policy support, skills and mentoring programmes which should help the youth to join the mainstream economy.

In the chapter "Entrepreneurship as the Future Career of Graduates: An Assessment for the Malaysian Context and Some Policy Directions," Mohd Amirul Rafiq Abu Rahim, Rohana Jani, and Diana Abdul Wahab discuss the pertinent question: whether graduates will consider entrepreneurship as their career option in this country. The chapter explores whether entrepreneurship is aspired by young people, especially graduates, in their future careers. Aspirations and perceptions of entrepreneurial skills, support and assistance are also discussed throughout this chapter. Several practical implications and policy options in promoting entrepreneurship to graduates in Malaysia are proposed.

SECTION 3: THE UNIVERSITY ENVIRONMENT

In the chapter "Role of University Entrepreneurial Ecosystem and Entrepreneurial Self-Efficacy in Shaping Entrepreneurial Intention: A study of Indian Students," Raj Karan Gupta attempts to explore the role of the university entrepreneurial ecosystem and entrepreneurial self-efficacy in shaping entrepreneurial intention of students of higher education institutions in India. Based on a quantitative approach and a causal survey research design, the main objective of the study was to explore the relationship between the university entrepreneurial ecosystem, student entrepreneurial self-efficacy and entrepreneurial intention. Further, in this study, entrepreneurial self-efficacy has been found to be a more influencing factor than the university entrepreneurial ecosystem

In the chapter "The University Environment and Graduate Entrepreneurship: A Study of Ranchi City," Bhavna Taneja conducts a study to examine the basis for understanding the entrepreneurial intentions and role of education for a college student. The objectives of the study are to understand the internal factors which encourage students to choose graduate entrepreneurship such as attitudes and motivation of students as well as the external factors which influence students to choose the entrepreneurial career path, such as the educational environment of colleges, interaction with existing entrepreneurs, and Government policies.

In the chapter "Students' Hackathon, Universities Business Incubator, and Fourth Industrial Revolution (4IR) in a South African University," Adetola Elizabeth Oyewo and Samuel Uwem umoh, examine an incubation program at a public University in South Africa, the University of KwaZulu-Natal (UKZN). The university teaches students entrepreneurship through hackathons incubation programs, and thus the purpose of the study was to examine the impact of these activities on students' entrepreneurial journeys. Data was mainly generated from a qualitative approach, such as observations and interviews. Findings suggest that Hackathons are utilized to identify students' start-ups for incubation. Universities as business incubation also support student start-ups business by bringing student entrepreneurs together in a common working space.

SECTION 4: FACTORS INFLUENCING CAREER CHOICE

In the chapter "An Expanded Framework of Factors influencing Career Choice," Mohammad Izzuddin Mohammed Jamil notes that most studies on career choice have been based on a three-dimensional framework that is intrinsic, extrinsic and interpersonal factors. He further observes that most frameworks in the literature do not consider the public and private sectors as a variables impacting career choice. The objective of this paper is to propose a new, updated framework to studying factors influencing career choice, by including public and private sectors as dimensions as that influence career choice.

In the chapter "Entrepreneurship: Scope of Addressing Educated Unemployment in India," Badal Chandra Das and Sebak Kumar Jana, affirm the importance of a country's social and economic environment in the promotion of entrepreneurship i.e. laws, regulations, infrastructure etc. It is, therefore, necessary for each country to adopt measures to encourage people to embrace self-employment and entrepreneurship for generating gainful income and livelihood promotion. In light of the social and economic context, this paper makes an attempt to highlight the role of entrepreneurship development in combating the problem of unemployment among educated youths in India.

In the chapter "Graduate Employability in an African Country: A Study of the Potential Roles of Psychological Capital, Social Capital and Career Identity," Peter Ntale uses data from a skills training development program (The Uganda Skills Development Program) to study employability. Based on a quantitative design, he investigates the relationship between employability, psychological capital, career identity, and social capital of students in Uganda. The results emphasize the importance of social capital and psychological capital in enhancing the various graduates' capabilities for positive employability outcomes.

In the chapter "Graduate Un/Employment in Turkey: A Holistic Entrepreneurship Strategy to Increase Employment and Reduce Unemployment," İrfan Kalaycı tackles the problem of graduate unemployment in Turkey based on a deductive approach and secondary data. The purpose of the study is to examine the global graduate unemployment problem, and the holistic strategy that can be applied against this problem from the Turkish perspective. The study emphasizes global cooperation to overcome the graduate unemployment problem.

Youth and, in particular, graduate unemployment is a global phenomenon. Within these 14 chapters, the authors discuss this problem within their country contexts, thus the major objective of this book is met. This book makes a practical contribution in the entrepreneurship arena by putting together views and strategies to stem graduate unemployment. These chapters show that we need to throw the net wider, and examine what is happening in other countries. Hence this book is a good start, as more lessons have to be drawn from contexts not examined here.

Isaac Wasswa Katono
Uganda Christian University, Uganda

Acknowledgment

I would like to thank the IGI global team for all they have done in the production of this work. I would also like to thank the authors for their tireless effort in revising their work.

Many thanks go to the anonymous reviewers from various corners of the world for accepting to review these chapters. Many thanks also go to Associate Professor David Priilaid of the University of Cape Town, Professor Gert Human of Stellenbosch University, Professor Terrell Manyak of Nova South Eastern University, Professor Michael Frese of the Frese Group my mentors for the solid knowledge they imparted into me, which knowledge has resulted in the production of this work.

Lastly, I thank my wife Christine Katono, children Angela, Jimson and Sam plus friends at Uganda Christian University and in many other universities globally for all the support rendered to me. Special thanks go to Professor William Kisaalita of the University of Georgia who is an adjunct Professor at Uganda Christian University for all the help and encouragement.

Section 1

Skills and Training in Higher Education

Chapter 1
Entrepreneurship as a Tool to Tackle Graduate Youth Unemployment in Developing Economies:
The Role of Action-Oriented Entrepreneurship Training

Arobindu Dash
https://orcid.org/0000-0003-4642-512X
Leuphana University Lüneburg, Germany

Michael M. Gielnik
https://orcid.org/0000-0002-8234-4071
Leuphana University Lüneburg, Germany

ABSTRACT

Unemployment reduction is one of the grand challenges to achieve the sustainable development goals. More specifically, graduate youth unemployment is a rising concern for low and middle-income countries. Accordingly, government and policymakers seek to promote entrepreneurship to address the issue of unemployment through entrepreneurship education and training. Building on this notion, this chapter discusses STEP (student training for entrepreneurial promotion) as an action-oriented entrepreneurship training program. This chapter shows the theoretical and methodological underpinnings of STEP, how the impact of STEP unfolds over time, and the processes that happen during STEP. This chapter also covers cases where STEP has been extended to different academic settings, bringing systemic change in academic curriculums and for different target groups. Finally, this chapter discusses some common challenges when implementing STEP at partner

DOI: 10.4018/978-1-7998-9581-7.ch001

institutions. The chapter concludes that STEP is an effective tool to tackle graduate youth unemployment in developing economies.

INTRODUCTION

Unemployment is one of the most challenging issues in low and middle-income countries (Cho et al., 2012). According to the International Labor Organization database (ILO-STAT, 2021), the global unemployment rate stood at 6.4% in 2020, which is the highest unemployment rate in the last 20 years (1991-2020) (World Bank, 2021). Furthermore, the International Labor Organization (ILO, 2021) forecasted that the global unemployment rate would be over 200 million in 2022 of which the majority portion will come from low and middle-income countries. Recently, the World Economic Forum Global Risks Perception Survey (2021-2022) indicated that the problem could become even worse in the future and marked 'livelihood crises' as one of the leading societal global concerns, especially in the post-pandemic world. This 'employment and livelihood crisis' is the second most worsened factor since the start of the COVID-19 crisis, and it is the second most critical threat in the short-term (next two years) and fourth most critical threat in the medium-term (next two to five years) (World Economic Forum, 2022).

It is important to note that the unemployment rate is high even among the highly educated youth in low- and middle-income countries. Indeed, youth with tertiary education are more likely to be unemployed compared to youth with only a basic educational level in 82% of low-income countries, 70% of lower-middle-income countries, 31% of upper-middle-income countries, and only 16% of developed countries (Gammarano, 2020). The causes of youth unemployment in low- and middle-income countries are multi-dimensional including individual, cultural, social, and political factors. An individual factor is, for example, the fact that university graduates' priority is on being wage-employed although the job opportunities are limited. Consequently, university graduates wait for a long time after their graduation for employment instead of pursuing an alternative career, for example as an entrepreneur (Oyugi, 2014; Plattner et al., 2009). A cultural factor is that patriarchal views decrease the likelihood of females being employed, especially in the Middle East and Southern Asia (Kabeer, 2016). Social factors deal with, for example, the demographic structure of low and middle-income countries, which is becoming youth intensive. The cumulative labor market entry rate is higher than the availability of jobs and the limited employment scope cannot mitigate the high demand for youth employment (Bloom et al., 2003; Drummond et al., 2014). Finally, a political factor is, for example, corruption within government institutions, which leads to an increase in unemployment (Bouzid, 2016).

An important part of the solution to tackle the issue of unemployment in general and among the youth, in particular, is entrepreneurship (United Nations, 2015). Indeed, entrepreneurship is a driver of economic growth and job creation (Ayyagari et al., 2014; van Praag & Versloot, 2007). Accordingly, promoting entrepreneurship has become a major policy issue around the world. Governments influence the macro context, such as improving the access to financial capital and ease of doing business, reducing entry regulations, and facilitating entrepreneurial eco-systems (Audretsch, 2004; De Mel et al., 2009; Klapper et al., 2009; Welter, 2011). For example, the government in Uganda initiated the 'Youth Livelihood Programme' (YLP) to support the unemployed youth in terms of skill development, livelihood support, and institutional support. From 2014 to 2018, the government in Uganda invested UGX 265 billion (US$71 million) under this program and within the first three years, it has helped to create 114,471 jobs for youth (Makumbi, 2018). Furthermore, offering entrepreneurship education and training has been widely adopted as an effective approach toward promoting entrepreneurship (Valerio et al., 2014). Over the last couple of years, governments, private sectors, international organizations, and universities have provided different entrepreneurship education and training programs across the world.

Government-led entrepreneurship training programs have the potential to make a large-scale impact on unemployment reduction. To reduce unemployment, governments usually develop curricula and train instructors to implement entrepreneurship education and training, provide funding, and launch an entrepreneurship education and training program through public-private partnerships (Cho & Honorati, 2013; Farstad, 2002). For example, Tunisia's government launched a program called 'Business Plan Thesis Competition' to promote entrepreneurship among university graduates in 2009–10 (Premand et al., 2012). Similarly, the Vietnam Chamber of Commerce and Industry (VCCI) in partnership with the International Labour Organization (ILO) implemented the 'Start and Improve Your Business (SIYB)' program in Vietnam from 1998 to 2004 (Majurin, 2014). Universities also incorporated entrepreneurship education and training in their curriculum to reduce graduate youth unemployment. For example, a study found that 91% of higher education institutions offer an entrepreneurship course in sub-Saharan Africa (Kabongo & Okpara, 2010).

However, traditional entrepreneurship education and training programs are oftentimes insufficiently tailored to the participants' needs, lack a focus on developing participants' entrepreneurial mindset, and are theoretical and teacher-centered (Robb et al., 2014). So, governments, academics, and policymakers have to think beyond traditional strategies for building graduate entrepreneurial mindsets. In this regard, research showed that action-oriented interventions are particularly effective in fostering entrepreneurship and business creation (Campos et al., 2017; Frese et al.,

2016; Pick et al., 2010). The objective of this chapter is to present the evidence and mechanisms of a specific action-oriented entrepreneurship training program—the Student Training for Entrepreneurial Promotion (STEP)—that is an effective tool to tackle graduate youth unemployment in developing economies. STEP has shown promising results in developing entrepreneurial mindsets and business creation among young adults (Gielnik et al., 2015; Melyoki & Gielnik, 2020). STEP is an entrepreneurship training program that is action-oriented, evidence-based, locally embedded, and scientifically evaluated. In this chapter, we focus on STEP and not on other interventions, such as the personal initiative training (Frese et al., 1996; Glaub et al., 2014; Campos et al., 2017), BizWorld (Huber et al., 2012), Business Plan Thesis Competition (Premand et al., 2012), or Junior Achievement Company (Oosterbeek et al., 2010), because STEP is explicitly designed for young adults, it works in different educational settings, and there is substantial evidence of its effectiveness over the last decade in low middle-income countries (Frese et al., 2016; Gielnik et al., 2015).

CONCEPTUAL FRAMEWORK

We discuss STEP and its objectives, the content and underlying theoretical background as well as the results of the randomized controlled trials (RCTs) to assess the impact of STEP for developing entrepreneurial mindsets, business, and job creation among youth (see Figure 1). Furthermore, we discuss the psychological mechanisms of developing entrepreneurial mindsets that explain why STEP is effective. These mechanisms include action-regulatory factors (e.g., goal intentions, self-efficacy, and action planning), passion, and coping with capital constraints. We also discuss findings from a qualitative study that has shown additional pathways through which STEP is effective. Furthermore, we present the results from studies examining the processes during training (such as entrepreneurial learning and error mastery orientation, the feedback loop of the opportunity development process, the development of passion over time, and the dynamics of self-efficacy). These studies provide detailed insights into how the positive effects of STEP unfold in the course of the training program and help to promote business and job creation in the long term. Furthermore, this chapter covers the applicability and institutionalization of STEP in different academic settings worldwide (such as traditional higher education institutions, vocational training institutions, and secondary schools) to reduce unemployment among youth in low- and middle-income countries. Finally, we present conclusions and challenges in future implementations of STEP and related entrepreneurship education and training programs.

Figure 1.

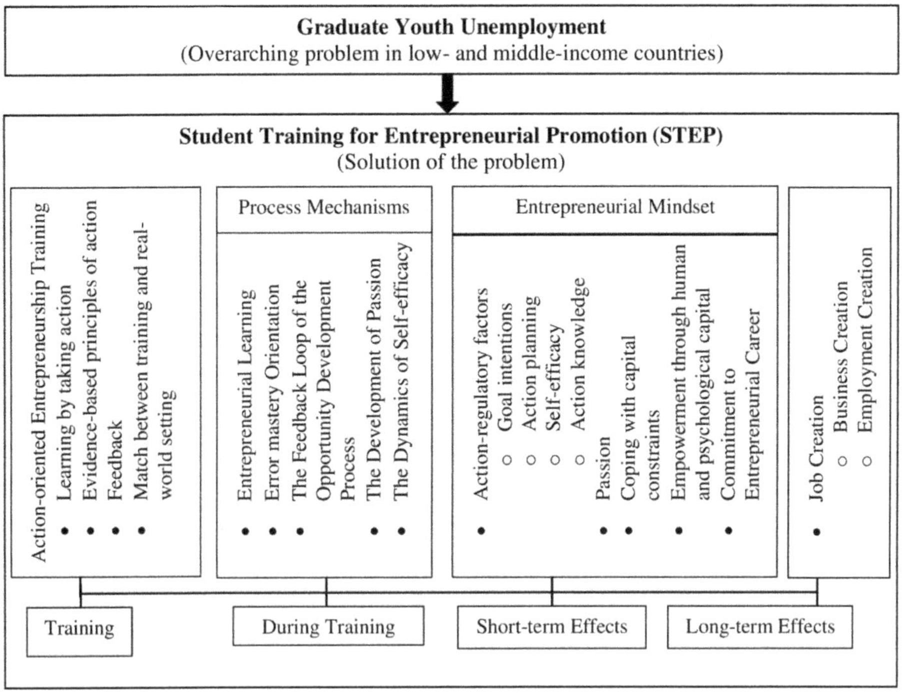

THEORETICAL AND METHODOLOGICAL FOUNDATION OF STEP

STEP is an action-oriented entrepreneurship training program during which students learn practical skills in entrepreneurship and develop an entrepreneurial mindset over a period of 12 weeks. STEP involves 12 weekly sessions of three hours, which are facilitated by a certified STEP trainer. The theoretical foundation of STEP is action regulation theory (Frese, 2009; Frese & Zapf, 1994). Action regulation theory proposes four core principles according to which action-oriented training programs should be designed: learning by taking action, teaching evidence-based principles of action, feedback, and matching training and real-world setting (cf., Gielnik & Frese, 2013; Gielnik et al., 2015). In the following, we describe the four principles as they are used in STEP.

In STEP, students *learn by taking action*. The students engage in real entrepreneurial actions and start a real micro-business during the 12 weeks of the training program. Thus, STEP expands the learning space beyond the classroom and gives the students the space to actively develop their real new business opportunities. To this end, the students form entrepreneurial teams in the first session and engage in the whole entrepreneurial process. The entrepreneurial teams identify a business opportunity, acquire the necessary equipment, produce a product or service, and introduce it into the market. Importantly, the entrepreneurial teams develop a real product or service and sell it to real customers. Accordingly, STEP is not a simulation but provides real entrepreneurial experiences resulting in learning experiences that can be successfully transferred to settings outside the training context. To facilitate the process, the students receive a small amount of starting capital (approx. 100 USD) that they repay—if possible—at the end of the program (the repayment rate varies across projects, but is usually 90% or higher). In the process of developing, producing, and selling a real product or service, the students learn entrepreneurial skills, develop entrepreneurial self-efficacy, i.e. confidence in their capabilities to succeed in entrepreneurship, and understand that overcoming setbacks and failure is part of the process.

Students learn *evidence-based action principles* during the 12 sessions of the training program. STEP is evidence-based with regard to its content and teaching approach. Evidence-based means that practices in a field are science-informed and based on the best evidence. Regarding its content, STEP builds on scientific findings and adopts a multi-disciplinary approach. STEP includes business skills and puts a strong focus on psychological skills to provide students with an entrepreneurial mindset to take action, innovate, and persevere. STEP covers 12 modules relevant to starting and managing a new venture: identifying business opportunities, taking action, marketing, strategic management, managing finances, overcoming barriers, accounting, business planning, finding starting capital, and registering the business. In each module, the students learn the content based on action-principles. Action-principles are guidelines ("rules-of-thumb") derived from scientific knowledge. For example, the module on taking action teaches action principles derived from action regulation theory about how to develop action plans in the form of specifying when, where, and how to engage in action. Action principles are a fast and effective route to gain knowledge and skills to succeed in entrepreneurship. In addition, STEP uses an evidence-based teaching approach based on active learning. The students take control by implementing their business opportunities. During the weekly sessions, the students work on exercises that specifically refer to the teams' real businesses they start during the program (e.g., developing a marketing strategy), they present their results and progress in the class and receive positive and negative feedback from the trainer and their fellow students.

Feedback (positive and negative) is an important element in STEP training. When students discuss and present their team's current status and future directions, the trainers give them feedback. Positive feedback (e.g., having been successful in assembling the raw materials for their desired businesses) reinforces students' behavior either for repeating the behavior or moving to the next. Furthermore, trainers provide negative feedback (e.g., having failed to assemble the raw materials for their desired businesses) in a constructive way. This feedback highlights the discrepancy between students' current performance and their goals. The discrepancy has a motivating function and provides information about areas of possible improvement. Furthermore, STEP emphasizes students' self-feedback (e.g., own assessment regarding their task accomplishment and goal achievement) and peer feedback (e.g., feedback from team members and other students).

In STEP, there is a match between *training tasks and real-world tasks*. Students perform real entrepreneurial activities to start and manage their businesses during the 12 weeks of the training program. The match facilitates training transfer. The idea is that STEP works as a foundation stage and entrepreneurial start-up activities are the replication and generalization of activities performed during training.

Local Implementation of STEP

STEP is locally embedded. So far, STEP has been implemented in twelve countries at more than twenty institutions across the three continents of Africa, Asia, and America. The past ten years have demonstrated that STEP can be successfully scaled and replicated across a variety of contexts and regions across the globe to reduce graduate youth unemployment. STEP is implemented in close cooperation with the STEP team and local partner institutions. STEP prioritizes the capacity building of host institutions so that they can take an active part in the preparation, project management, delivery, and evaluation of STEP without external support, and comply with the STEP quality standards. Thus, the partner institutions take ownership right from the start, which is important to ensure the long-term sustainability of the implementation. Furthermore, the process involves STEP master trainers and a three-day train-the-trainer workshop (TTT) at the partner institution. The TTT is the key element to ensure that STEP is implemented according to the quality standards and its central elements of being action-orientated, evidence-based, feedback-focused, and the similarity between training and real-world tasks.

After successful completion of the TTT, the lecturers (usually a team of six to twelve lecturers from the partner universities) become certified STEP trainers and give the STEP training to their students. Thus, STEP is taught by local trainers from the partner institution and accordingly, the partner institution gains the capacity to offer STEP by themselves. Additionally, the local trainers know the environment and they use their examples that fit the local context, which further adds to the effectiveness of STEP. Usually, the process to fully implement STEP at a partner institution and integrate STEP into the curriculum takes three years and involves several TTTs and workshops to support the process. The TTT is conducted by

STEP master trainers. The training to become a STEP master trainer is a process, which usually takes two years. The process includes conducting STEP as a certified STEP trainer (minimum three times), taking part in TTTs as an assistant trainer, conducting TTTs as a lead trainer, and completing theoretical work on the STEP training to obtain a comprehensive theoretical understanding of STEP in addition to the practical understanding.

THE IMPACT ASSESSMENT STUDIES OF STEP

The objects of STEP are promoting students' entrepreneurial mindsets as well as increasing their rate of business creation and job creation (employing others). Indeed, more than thirty studies have shown that STEP significantly increases students' entrepreneurial mindsets, the rate of business creation, as well as job creation in the training group compared to a control group. In this way, STEP is creating an impact to reduce graduate youth unemployment in low- and middle-income countries. To assess the impact, we use randomized controlled trials (RCTs). We assign students who applied for the training to the experimental (training group) or control (no training) group based on a random process. We collect data before STEP (baseline; T1) and just after STEP (T2) to assess the short-term impact of STEP on students' entrepreneurial mindset. Furthermore, we collect data one year (T3) and two years after STEP (T4) to assess the long-term impact on students' performance in terms of business creation and job creation.

The impact assessment studies provided evidence that STEP enhances students' entrepreneurial mindset in terms of a strong entrepreneurial motivation to engage in entrepreneurial action (Gielnik et al., 2015). The students understand that entrepreneurship is a viable and feasible career option. Furthermore, the students develop a never-give-up attitude and learn to overcome setbacks and barriers, such as constraints in financial capital (Bischoff et al., 2020; Melyoki & Gielnik, 2020). These changes in students' entrepreneurial mindset explain why the students create more businesses one year after STEP and create more jobs two years after STEP in comparison to a control group (Frese et al., 2016). This evidence shows that action-oriented entrepreneurship training is effective to reduce graduate youth unemployment through business and job creation in developing economies.

THE MECHANISMS UNDERLYING THE POSITIVE IMPACT OF STEP

Action-Regulatory Factors

Entrepreneurial action is one of the key drivers of entrepreneurial success (e.g., business creation, job creation, business success). Accordingly, STEP emphasizes initiating entrepreneurial action. In the first impact assessment study, Gielnik et al. (2015) built on action regulation theory to develop a theoretical model about action regulatory factors that facilitate action. The factors are entrepreneurial goal intentions, entrepreneurial action planning, entrepreneurial self-efficacy, and action knowledge. Entrepreneurial goal intentions refer to the students' willingness to engage in business creation. Entrepreneurial action planning refers to students' planning for business creation. Entrepreneurial self-efficacy captures students' beliefs in their competencies. Action knowledge refers to the cognitive schema about the principles and causal processes (including anticipated outcomes and consequences) of entrepreneurial actions. The evaluation study demonstrated that these factors facilitate entrepreneurial actions, which in turn predicted business creation one year after training (Gielnik et al., 2015).

Passion

Passion is an important construct in the entrepreneurial process. Entrepreneurial passion refers to an intense positive feeling towards entrepreneurial actions that are central to people's identity (Cardon et al., 2009). Entrepreneurial passion motivates entrepreneurs to work hard and to remain persistent and dedicated towards their entrepreneurial actions (Cardon et al., 2009; Vallerand et al., 2003). Building on this notion, Gielnik et al. (2017) investigated the role of passion in explaining the long-term effects of STEP on business creation. Furthermore, they examined how to maintain passion over time. The maintenance of passion is particularly relevant because the transfer literature showed that motivational constructs, such as passion, tend to decline over time after training (Blume et al., 2010). Gielnik et al. (2017) hypothesized and found that entrepreneurial self-efficacy is a critical factor to boost and maintain passion over time. They concluded that a feeling of mastery, a key aspect of entrepreneurial self-efficacy, is crucial to remain passionate when engaging in entrepreneurship. Maintaining passion over time then predicted business creation two years after training. Interestingly, passion immediately after training did not predict business creation, suggesting that passion after training is rather a 'flickering flame', and that passion needs to be developed and sustained over time to exert a motivating function.

Coping with Capital Constraints

Resource constraints, especially financial constraints, are one of the major barriers to entrepreneurship and business creation in developing economies (Chliova et al., 2015; Khavul, 2010; Naudé et al., 2008). Government, policymakers, and academics have a common understanding that access to finance is the main solution for overcoming this barrier to promote business creation. However, the effect of capital constraints on business creation varies across studies, and research showed that entrepreneurial ability and experiences are helpful to navigate the financial constraints in business venturing (Chandler & Hanks, 1998; De Mel et al., 2008; Naudé et al., 2008). Building on this notion, Bischoff and colleagues (2020) extended the theoretical understanding by showing that entrepreneurship training can influence the effect of capital constraints on business creation. In two studies, they found that STEP substantially weakened the negative effect of financial constraints on business creation. The underlying mechanism to explain the effect was that STEP developed financial mental models. Accordingly, providing training is an equally effective means to overcome capital constraints as providing financial capital. Furthermore, it is more sustainable because entrepreneurs still have the mental model even when a business fails and the financial capital is expended.

Additional Factors from Qualitative Research

With substantial evidence of the positive impact of STEP from quantitative studies, qualitative findings have recently opened a new avenue of understanding the effectiveness of STEP. Human and psychological capital are assets for entrepreneurship. In a qualitative study, Melyoki and Gielnik (2020) found that STEP boosts students' human capital, such as knowledge, skills, experiences, as well as their psychological capital, such as confidence, which ultimately acts as an 'empowerment' condition for students. This feeling of empowerment helps students to think about entrepreneurship as a new career perspective. Consequently, they develop a commitment towards the entrepreneurial career path, realize that entrepreneurship is doable, and understand that only little starting capital is necessary to start a business. These insights from the qualitative study show a new avenue regarding how the effects of STEP unfold over time. Previous research has shown that entrepreneurship training works through cognitive and motivational factors such as action-regulatory factors (Gielnik et al., 2015), passion (Gielnik, et al., 2017), and mental models (Bischoff et al., 2020). The qualitative study provides new process mechanisms of training effects, such as empowerment and a shift in perspective that entrepreneurship is a viable and doable career option.

Processes during STEP

Previously, we focused on the effects of STEP on short- and long-term outcomes. We explored how the effects unfold over time after training. Now, we will discuss the processes during training that explain the effectiveness of STEP. Specifically, we discuss error mastery orientation and entrepreneurial learning (Funken et al., 2020), feedback loops of the opportunity development process (Eller, et al., in press), entrepreneurial passion (Lex et al., in press), and entrepreneurial self-efficacy (Gielnik et al., 2020).

Entrepreneurship scholars noted that problems are a gift for entrepreneurs because they are a means for learning and development. However, problems do not necessarily translate into blessings for entrepreneurs because associated negative emotions and dysfunctional cognitive appraisals may act as barriers to learning from the problem. In this line, Funken and colleagues (2020) found that error mastery orientation is critical to understand when entrepreneurs turn problems into opportunities for learning. High error mastery orientation involves a positive attitude toward errors and a belief that errors serve a positive function. People with high error mastery orientation consider errors as inevitable and they strive to maximize the positive consequences from problems. In contrast, low error mastery orientation implies that people have a stiff focus on inhibiting negative consequences and find no scope to benefit from the negative experiences. People with low error mastery orientation perceive problems negatively and experience strain when problems occur instead of considering it as a learning opportunity. Building on this notion, Funken et al. (2020) argued that error mastery orientation is a boundary condition that determines, like a switch, whether problems will be good or bad for learning. People with high error mastery orientation give more attention, invest more cognitive processing, and consider problems as an opportunity for learning. In contrast, people with low error mastery orientation reflect less on the problem and experience negative emotions, which drain cognitive resources and consequently, hinder learning from problems. Therefore, problems have a positive impact on learning in case of high error mastery orientation but a negative impact if error mastery orientation is low. The findings supported the reasoning, indicating to replace the traditional thought of 'fail fast, fail often' with a new one 'learn fast, learn often'. Furthermore, Funken et al. (2020) showed that problems could ultimately lead to venture progress through learning in case of high error mastery orientation. This study provides interesting insights into the boundary conditions of the training method of STEP, which involves taking action and dealing with problems. Students high in error mastery orientation are more likely to learn and make progress during STEP than students low in error mastery orientation.

The study by Eller et al. (in press) also examined processes during STEP and examined the feedback loop of the opportunity development process. Feedback plays a significant role in the opportunity development process, because it helps students to shape and improve their business models. Drawing from action regulation theory (Zacher & Frese, 2018), Eller et al. (in press) argued that the opportunity development process is a recursive process consisting of changes in the business opportunity, goals, performance, and feedback. Feedback then leads to changes in the business opportunity starting the cycle anew. Thus, feedback shapes the business opportunities. Eller and colleagues (in press) found that this feedback loop evolves in a cyclic fashion where error mastery orientation and monitoring act as two boundary conditions influencing how the cyclical effects unfold over time. Specifically, high error mastery orientation strengthens the relationship between changes in business opportunities and goals. The reasoning is that team members with high error mastery orientation acknowledge that changes are necessary and have a positive function for venture development. Further, monitoring strengthens the negative relationship between performance and feedback. The reasoning is that team members with high monitoring continuously evaluate their performance and understand when changes are or are not required. When they perform better, they need less feedback as no or little change is required. However, in case of low monitoring, the effect of performance on feedback is weak as teams are not assessing their performance and do not understand when feedback is or is not necessary. In conclusion, how business opportunities develop over time depends on feedback that the participants gather as well as their error mastery orientation and monitoring to make progress in the opportunity development process. Furthermore, Eller et al. (in press) demonstrated that making progress in the opportunity development process during training influenced participants' entrepreneurial goal intentions after training and ultimately their business creation one year after the training program.

Another study by Lex et al. (in press) asked the question of how passion develops during entrepreneurship training. In the previous section, we discussed the role of passion in entrepreneurship training transfer, that is after training (Gielnik et al., 2017). The study by Lex et al. (in press) shifted the perspective to the development of passion during training. Lex et al. (in press) argued that Vallerand et al.'s (2003) and Cardon et al.'s (2009) theories of passion incorporate two key elements of passion, positive feelings and identity centrality. Incorporating these two elements, Lex and colleagues (in press) developed a theoretical model which shows that entrepreneurial passion develops over time and acts as a predictor and outcome of entrepreneurial self-efficacy and performance. Specifically, they showed that entrepreneurial performance positively influences positive feelings of entrepreneurial passion over shorter time periods and identity centrality of entrepreneurial passion over longer time periods. Accordingly, different time horizons play a significant role in the development of passion. Furthermore, Lex et al. (in press) showed that entrepreneurial self-efficacy mediates the relationship between performance and passion. This study added new insights into the development of passion by disentangling the elements of passion and demonstrating that the underlying process resulting in changes in positive feelings and identity centrality is similar as both elements are affected by performance and entrepreneurial self-efficacy. However, the time horizon over which these effects occur is different. The effects unfold faster for positive feelings and slower for identity centrality. Furthermore, this study also provided evidence that the relationships between passion, entrepreneurial self-efficacy, and performance are reciprocal, instead of unidirectional.

Finally, the study by Gielnik et al. (2020) examined the question why some students are able to translate their entrepreneurial intentions to actions whereas others are not. Findings showed that students' self-efficacy plays an important role. However, it is not only their absolute level of self-efficacy but also their variability in self-efficacy over time that influences their likelihood of taking action and creating a new business. Gielnik et al. (2020) showed that self-efficacy is not static but changes dynamically over time. Gielnik et al. (2020) used a sophisticated research design and examined students' self-efficacy during as well as after STEP. The variability and average in self-efficacy during training influence business ownership one year after training. Furthermore, Gielnik and colleagues (2020) showed that the relationship between entrepreneurial self-efficacy after training and business ownership has an inverted u-shape, such that there is a tipping point at around 90% beyond which the positive effect of self-efficacy becomes negative. Their findings are in line with their reasoning that the probability of being a business owner depends on the threshold range of entrepreneurial self-efficacy. The absolute threshold point should be above 66% and the terminal threshold point should be below 100% of confidence to maximize students' motivation. Variability in and the inverted u-shape relationship between self-efficacy and business creation reflect similar underlying mechanisms that contribute to students' motivation. Experiencing high self-efficacy is important to form intentions and initiate actions. At the same time, experiencing dips in self-efficacy and levels below the maximum of 100% is important to perceive a discrepancy between the current state and the desired state. This discrepancy prompts investing additional effort to achieve the goal. Thus, experiencing ups and downs in self-efficacy, or in other words experiencing a level that is high but not too high is most beneficial for students' motivation and performance in entrepreneurship.

THE APPLICABILITY OF STEP IN DIFFERENT SETTINGS

STEP has been mainly implemented at universities. However, implementing entrepreneurship training at institutions other than the higher education systems is important for two reasons. First, entrepreneurship scholars argued that entrepreneurship education should be implemented from early education to introduce students early in their lives to the idea of pursuing an entrepreneurial career (Huber et al., 2014). Second, not everyone has access to higher education systems, especially in low and middle-income countries. Consequently, entrepreneurship training should be offered at additional institutions, such as secondary schools and vocational training institutions. Following this reasoning, STEP was extended to secondary schools and vocational training institutes.

Secondary School Application

Recently, the concept of STEP was extended to student teachers who were trained in the concept of STEP and used it to teach students at secondary schools. In total, more than 450 student teachers trained 800 secondary school students. The short- and long-term evaluations showed significant effects: STEP was effective in increasing students' entrepreneurial motivation and behavior, demonstrating the potential of STEP for an effective approach to teach entrepreneurship at various educational levels. Indeed, such studies are important because they demonstrate how future teachers can be trained during their studies at university to become effective entrepreneurship trainers.

Application in Vocational Training Institutes

Vocational training is an overarching concept in developing economies for the promotion of entrepreneurship. However, are only technical skills enough for being entrepreneurs? To address this question, Gielnik and colleagues (2016) implemented STEP at a Vocational Training Institute in Uganda. The study showed that STEP promoted entrepreneurial behaviors in terms of business opportunity identification and entrepreneurial actions in the training group having both entrepreneurial and technical skills compared to a control group having only technical skills. Furthermore, researchers and academics find it difficult to incorporate practical training into vocational training curriculum because of setting the benchmark for the credit system and for standardizing grading (Rasmussen & Sorheim, 2006; Souitaris et al., 2007). In addition, it is a challenge to implement the training in the long term because of high administrative hurdles and a lack of financial support. Facing these challenges, the study by Gielnik and colleagues (2016) provides a best-practice approach demonstrating how action-oriented training could be incorporated in vocational training settings.

INSTITUTIONALIZATION AND EXTENSION OF STEP

Usually, the implementation of STEP happens in a three-year project. In the first year, the partner university is introduced to the concept of STEP, local trainers are trained in a train-the-trainer workshop, and the local trainers implement STEP for the first time. In the second year, the partner institution continues to offer STEP and start managing the process by themselves. In the third year, they take charge of conducting the training program and including STEP in their regular academic curriculum. In this section, we want to present six exemplary cases that represent different types of educational institutions and levels to demonstrate systemic change in the academic curriculum because of STEP. This shows different pathways to reduce graduate youth unemployment in low- and middle-income countries.

Makerere University Business School (MUBS) in Kampala, Uganda, adopted STEP and created the Michael Frese Business Creation Program at their Innovation, Incubation and Entrepreneurship Centre (IIEC) to promote entrepreneurial capacities. Furthermore, at the level of youth in the informal sector, the IIEC partners with MTN Uganda, the largest telecom company, to support jua-kali youth (youth with micro businesses) to improve and scale their businesses. This happens under the "Youth Empowerment Services" program. In addition, due to the COVID-19 pandemic, the IIEC arranged a special program called "Start Your Business" based on STEP. In this program, IIEC facilitates STEP to undergraduate students and secondary school pupils who are waiting to join university. Finally, MUBS provided STEP to youth who had dropped out of school in the Eastern part of Uganda, and they worked with the National Social Security Fund (NSSF) of Uganda and FAO Uganda to offer entrepreneurship training.

At the university level, Bicol University in the Philippines implemented STEP for the first time in 2015. After the positive evaluation of STEP, Bicol University uses the program as the standard course ("Entrepreneurial Mind Class") for teaching entrepreneurship. The course runs at all colleges as a mandatory course at varying levels per program for all undergraduate students. So far, more than 7,000 students have participated in STEP at Bicol University. This case demonstrates the successful long-term institutionalization of STEP at the university level.

At the level of vocational training, the Nakawa Vocational Training Institute (NVTI) in Kampala, Uganda, implemented STEP in 2013. STEP replaced the former curriculum that was adopted from UNIDO (United Nations Industrial Development Organization). The colleagues at NVTI reported that they realized that STEP offers a promising program because it is more practical and has a strong impact on their students' entrepreneurial mindset. Based on the results of the evaluation study, they decided to replace the old program. Since then STEP runs as a mandatory course for all their students. It is important to note that NVTI adapted STEP to their specific requirements. After a cohort of students has attended STEP, the students pass on their businesses to the next cohort of students to ensure continuity of the businesses and the program. The case of NVTI demonstrates that it is possible to implement STEP into vocational training settings when the training institutions are proactive and take necessary responsibility, maintain the conceptual core of the STEP (action-orientation), and tailor STEP to their specific needs.

At the level of youth education, the Kenyatta University (Nairobi, Kenya) created a new project called STEP4Y (STEP for youth), acquired third-party funding by their own, and used its capacities to support youth in the counties. The goal of STEP4Y is to empower youth and provide them with entrepreneurial skills that broaden their career perspectives even if the youth do not have access to university education. STEP4Y was piloted in the Kiambu county in cooperation with the Kenya National Commission for UNESCO (KNATCOM), Kenyatta University, the County Government of Kiambu, and the Youth Enterprise Development Fund. STEP4Y is targeted at out of school youth to address the issue of high unemployment among this marginalized group of young people. STEP4Y is now offered by Kenyatta University in various counties in Kenya.

At the university level, Mount Kenya University (MKU) in Thika, Kenya, implements STEP since 2018. MKU extends STEP into four priority areas such as STEP for undergraduate students, STEP for youth, STEP for professional services, and STEP for practitioners. Firstly, MKU is using STEP as a co-curriculum activity for undergraduate students from different undergraduate levels especially from the second year to final year students. Secondly, in collaboration with Kenyatta University and the Kenya National Commission for UNESCO, MKU implemented STEP for youth programs. So far, MKU provided in-person STEP to two counties (e.g. Kiambu and Isiolo), and between June 2020 and April 2021, to four counties (e.g., Nairobi, Kajiado, Busia, and Bungoma) that benefitted from an online STEP for the youth program. Most importantly, this online platform has doubled its annual training capacity compared to in-person training. Thirdly, MKU established the Graduate Enterprise Academy (GEA) where certified STEP trainers provide professional services for entrepreneurial promotion on a regular basis. Finally, current entrepreneurs who are MKU alumni and have been trained as STEP trainers serve as practitioners to develop entrepreneurial skills in their communities.

Finally, Uganda Christian University (UCU) at Mukono, Uganda, is regularly using STEP at the bachelor level since 2014 for their course "Advanced Entrepreneurship". They are facilitating university-wide STEP training, especially for non-business students. UCU also extended STEP to the bird tourism promotion sector through funding support from the Private Sector Foundation Uganda (PSFU) and used STEP modules, such as opportunity identification and registering a business, to teach students in entrepreneurship.

DIVERSIFICATION OF STEP

STEP is extremely flexible. We developed a version of STEP to train 500 illiterate female farmers in Mozambique in a project in cooperation with the World Bank. Preliminary results demonstrated that this version of STEP is also effective in this context. Similarly, we used STEP to train youth in Afghanistan with a focus on social community projects and educate young politicians in Kenya to provide a more profound understanding of entrepreneurship and how to promote it. We, the STEP team, are currently running a project with the World Bank to implement STEP and train 2,000 unemployed young adults and university graduates in the Democratic Republic of Congo. In cooperation with the World Bank, we also extend our project to Burkina Faso and Niger. Thus, STEP benefits a diverse group of people and promotes entrepreneurship beyond the original goal of creating business and jobs by fostering initiatives to support the community and social projects. These multi-dimensional projects make a social impact by reducing persisting youth unemployment in developing economies.

CHALLENGES FOR STEP

There are several challenges when implementing STEP. First, maintaining the quality standards is one of the critical challenges of STEP. To have an impact, STEP uses core principles derived from action regulation theory (i.e., active learning, action principles, feedback and similarity between training and real-world condition). When the partner institutions begin to implement STEP independent of the support of the STEP team, it is of critical importance that the trainers keep these core principles in mind when teaching STEP. Therefore, the STEP team conducts refresher workshops with the trainers to maintain a high level of quality. Secondly, trainer quality is an important factor for the impact of STEP. To address this issue, trainers are selected after the train-the-trainer workshop based on their performance during the workshop. Thirdly, institutions are oftentimes teacher-centered and have a preconceived idea that lectures are sufficient for entrepreneurial learning, whereas STEP is learner-centered putting a focus on action and interaction. Accordingly, institutions sometimes try to eliminate the practical part of STEP, for example due to budget limitations.

However, the action-oriented part of STEP is most critical for the positive impact on business and job creation. Hence, anything that restricts the action orientation of STEP needs to be avoided (e.g. shortening the training period, canceling starting capital, teaching only the content without the real experience of starting a business).

The commitment and ownership of partner institutions to take necessary responsibility is also critical for the successful long-term implementation and institutionalization of STEP. Accordingly, partner institutions need a committed and motivated coordinator or team of coordinators from different hierarchical levels. Coordinators need to monitor the program, evaluate the trainers, plan future implementations, generate a recycle-based start-up capital system, and arrange regular refresher workshops. Indeed, our experience shows that a change of coordinators is a critical event that jeopardizes the institutionalization of STEP.

Finally, STEP has incorporated giving seed money (approximately 100 USD in local currency) to the participants to start a business during training, and students are encouraged to pay it back after the training period. That is why it requires some investment from the partner institution or third-party funding. It is important to note that STEP creates value by promoting business and job creation. Therefore, these investments might eventually pay off in the long run. This is particularly the case as most of the seed capital is repaid by the training participants and can be used for future cohorts.

CONCLUSION

The theoretical and methodological underpinnings give STEP a unique position in entrepreneurship education and training. So far, more than 11,000 students across more than 30 projects have completed STEP. The scientific evaluation of these projects demonstrated that STEP can promote entrepreneurship in both the short- and long-term. Specifically, STEP boosts entrepreneurial mindsets, business creation, and job creation. Furthermore, STEP has been continuously extended to address the needs of different target groups. Therefore, we can conclude that STEP as an action-oriented entrepreneurship training program is a successful tool to promote entrepreneurship and ultimately tackle graduate youth unemployment in developing economies.

REFERENCES

Audretsch, D. B. (2004). Sustaining innovation and growth: Public policy support for entrepreneurship. *Industry and Innovation, 11*(3), 167–191. doi:10.1080/1366271042000265366

Ayyagari, M., Demirguc-Kunt, A., & Maksimovic, V. (2014). Who creates jobs in developing countries? *Small Business Economics, 43*(1), 75–99. doi:10.100711187-014-9549-5

Bischoff, K. M., Gielnik, M. M., & Frese, M. (2020). When capital does not matter: How entrepreneurship training buffers the negative effect of capital constraints on business creation. *Strategic Entrepreneurship Journal, 14*(3), 369–395. doi:10.1002ej.1364

Bloom, D., Canning, D., & Sevilla, J. (2003). *The demographic dividend: A new perspective on the economic consequences of population change*. Rand Corporation. doi:10.7249/MR1274

Blume, B. D., Ford, J. K., Baldwin, T. T., & Huang, J. L. (2010). Transfer of training: A meta-analytic review. *Journal of Management, 36*(4), 1065–1105. doi:10.1177/0149206309352880

Bouzid, B. N. (2016). Dynamic relationship between corruption and youth unemployment: empirical evidences from a system GMM approach. *World Bank Policy Research Working Paper*, (7842). https://openknowledge.worldbank.org/handle/10986/25158

Campos, F., Frese, M., Goldstein, M., Iacovone, L., Johnson, H. C., McKenzie, D., & Mensmann, M. (2017). Teaching personal initiative beats traditional training in boosting small business in West Africa. *Science, 357*(6357), 1287–1290. doi:10.1126cience.aan5329 PMID:28935805

Cardon, M. S., Wincent, J., Singh, J., & Drnovsek, M. (2009). The nature and experience of entrepreneurial passion. *Academy of Management Review, 34*(3), 511–532. doi:10.5465/amr.2009.40633190

Chandler, G. N., & Hanks, S. H. (1998). An examination of the substitutability of founders human and financial capital in emerging business ventures. *Journal of Business Venturing, 13*(5), 353–369. doi:10.1016/S0883-9026(97)00034-7

Chliova, M., Brinckmann, J., & Rosenbusch, N. (2015). Is microcredit a blessing for the poor? A meta-analysis examining development outcomes and contextual considerations. *Journal of Business Venturing, 30*(3), 467–487. doi:10.1016/j.jbusvent.2014.10.003

Cho, Y., Margolis, D. N., Newhouse, D., & Robalino, D. A. (2012). *Labor Markets in Low and Middle-Income Countries: Trends and Implications for Social Protection and Labor Policies*. https://openknowledge.worldbank.org/bitstream/handle/10986/13550/676130NWP012070Box367885B00PUBLIC0.pdf;sequence=1

De Mel, S., McKenzie, D., & Woodruff, C. (2008). Returns to capital in microenterprises: Evidence from a field experiment. *The Quarterly Journal of Economics, 123*(4), 1329–1372. doi:10.1162/qjec.2008.123.4.1329

De Mel, S., McKenzie, D. J., & Woodruff, C. (2009). Measuring microenterprise profits: Must we ask how the sausage is made? *Journal of Development Economics, 88*(1), 19–31. doi:10.1016/j.jdeveco.2008.01.007

Drummond, M. P., Thakoor, V., & Yu, S. (2014). *Africa rising: harnessing the demographic dividend*. International Monetary Fund.

Eller, F. J., Gielnik, M. M., Yeves, J., Alvarado, Y. C., & Guerrero, O. A. (in press). Adjusting the Sails: Investigating the Feedback Loop of the Opportunity Development Process in Entrepreneurship Training. *Academy of Management Learning & Education*. doi:10.5465/amle.2020.0041

Farstad, H. (2002). *Integrated entrepreneurship education in Botswana, Uganda and Kenya. World Bank*. National Institute of Technology.

Frese, M. (2009). *Toward a psychology of entrepreneurship: An action theory perspective*. Now Publishers Inc.

Frese, M., Gielnik, M. M., & Mensmann, M. (2016). Psychological training for entrepreneurs to take action: Contributing to poverty reduction in developing countries. *Current Directions in Psychological Science, 25*(3), 196–202. doi:10.1177/0963721416636957

Frese, M., Kring, W., Soose, A., & Zempel, J. (1996). Personal initiative at work: Differences between East and West Germany. *Academy of Management Journal, 39*(1), 37–63.

Frese, M., & Zapf, D. (1994). Action as the core of work psychology: A German approach. Handbook of Industrial and Organizational Psychology, 4(2), 271-340.

Funken, R., Gielnik, M. M., & Foo, M. D. (2020). How can problems be turned into something good? The role of entrepreneurial learning and error mastery orientation. *Entrepreneurship Theory and Practice*, *44*(2), 315–338. doi:10.1177/1042258718801600

Gammarano, R. (2020, August 18). Education pays off, but you have to be patient. *ILO STAT spotlight on work statistics*. https://ilostat.ilo.org/education-pays-off-but-you-have-to-be-patient/

Gielnik, M. M., Bledow, R., & Stark, M. S. (2020). A dynamic account of self-efficacy in entrepreneurship. *The Journal of Applied Psychology*, *105*(5), 487–505. doi:10.1037/apl0000451 PMID:31535872

Gielnik, M. M., & Frese, M. (2013). Entrepreneurship and poverty reduction: Applying IO psychology to microbusiness and entrepreneurship in developing countries. In J. Olson-Buchanan, L. Koppes Bryan, & L. Foster Thompson (Eds.), *Using I-O Psychology for the Greater Good: Helping those who Help Others* (pp. 394–438). Routledge, Taylor and Francis.

Gielnik, M. M., Frese, M., Bischoff, K. M., Muhangi, G., & Omoo, F. (2016). Positive impact of entrepreneurship training on entrepreneurial behavior in a vocational training setting. *Africa Journal of Management*, *2*(3), 330–348. doi:10.1080/23322373.2016.1206804

Gielnik, M. M., Frese, M., Kahara-Kawuki, A., Wasswa Katono, I., Kyejjusa, S., Ngoma, M., Munene, J., Namatovu-Dawa, R., Nansubuga, F., Orobia, L., Oyugi, J., Sejjaaka, S., Sserwanga, A., Walter, T., Bischoff, K. M., & Dlugosch, T. J. (2015). Action and action-regulation in entrepreneurship: Evaluating a student training for promoting entrepreneurship. *Academy of Management Learning & Education*, *14*(1), 69–94. doi:10.5465/amle.2012.0107

Gielnik, M. M., Uy, M. A., Funken, R., & Bischoff, K. M. (2017). Boosting and sustaining passion: A long-term perspective on the effects of entrepreneurship training. *Journal of Business Venturing*, *32*(3), 334–353. doi:10.1016/j.jbusvent.2017.02.003

Glaub, M. E., Frese, M., Fischer, S., & Hoppe, M. (2014). Increasing personal initiative in small business managers or owners leads to entrepreneurial success: A theory-based controlled randomized field intervention for evidence-based management. *Academy of Management Learning & Education*, *13*(3), 354–379. doi:10.5465/amle.2013.0234

Goppers, K., & Cuong, M. T. (2007). *Business training for entrepreneurs in Vietnam: An evaluation of the Sida-supported Start and Improve Your Business (SIYB) project*. Sida. https://www.ilo.org/wcmsp5/groups/public/---ed_emp/---emp_ent/---ifp_seed/documents/publication/wcms_143285.pdf

Huber, L. R., Sloof, R., & Van Praag, M. (2014). The effect of early entrepreneurship education: Evidence from a field experiment. *European Economic Review*, *72*, 76–97. doi:10.1016/j.euroecorev.2014.09.002

International Labour Office. (2020). *Global Employment Trends for Youth 2020: Technology and the future of jobs*. International Labour Office. https://www.ilo.org/wcmsp5/groups/public/---dgreports/---dcomm/---publ/documents/publication/wcms_737648.pdf

International Labour Office. (2021). *World Employment and Social Outlook: Trends 2021*. International Labour Office. https://www.ilo.org/wcmsp5/groups/public/---dgreports/---dcomm/---publ/documents/publication/wcms_795453.pdf

Kabeer, N. (2016). Gender equality, economic growth, and women's agency: The "endless variety" and "monotonous similarity" of patriarchal constraints. *Feminist Economics*, *22*(1), 295–321. doi:10.1080/13545701.2015.1090009

Kabongo, J. D., & Okpara, J. O. (2010). Entrepreneurship education in sub-Saharan African universities. *International Journal of Entrepreneurial Behaviour & Research*, *16*(4), 296–308. doi:10.1108/13552551011054499

Khavul, S. (2010). Microfinance: Creating opportunities for the poor? *The Academy of Management Perspectives*, *24*(3), 58–72. doi:10.5465/AMP.2010.52842951

Klapper, L., Lewin, A., & Delgado, J. M. (2009). *The impact of the business environment on the business creation process* (Policy Research Working Paper 4937). Washington, DC: The World Bank.

Lex, M., Gielnik, M. M., Spitzmuller, M., Jacob, G. H., & Frese, M. (in press). How passion in entrepreneurship develops over time: A self-regulation perspective. *Entrepreneurship Theory and Practice*. doi:10.1177/1042258720929894

Majurin, E. (2014). *Start and improve your business: Implementation guide*. ILO. https://www.ilo.org/wcmsp5/groups/public/---ed_emp/---emp_ent/---ifp_seed/documents/publication/wcms_315262.pdf

Makumbi, R. (2018). Uganda's national youth policy and job creation for youth. In S. Ayele, D. Glover, & M. Oosterom (Eds.), *Youth Employment and the Private Sector in Africa* (pp. 45–54). IDS Bulletin. doi:10.19088/1968-2018.173

Melyoki, L. L., & Gielnik, M. M. (2020). How action-oriented entrepreneurship training transforms university students into entrepreneurs: Insights from a qualitative study. *Journal of Small Business and Entrepreneurship*, 1–28. doi:10.1080/08276331.2020.1832831

Minniti, M. (2008). The role of government policy on entrepreneurial activity: Productive, unproductive, or destructive? *Entrepreneurship Theory and Practice*, *32*(5), 779–790. doi:10.1111/j.1540-6520.2008.00255.x

Naude, W., Gries, T., Wood, E., & Meintjies, A. (2008). Regional determinants of entrepreneurial start-ups in a developing country. *Entrepreneurship and Regional Development*, *20*(2), 111–124. doi:10.1080/08985620701631498

Oosterbeek, H., Van Praag, M., & Ijsselstein, A. (2010). The impact of entrepreneurship education on entrepreneurship skills and motivation. *European Economic Review*, *54*(3), 442–454. doi:10.1016/j.euroecorev.2009.08.002

Oyugi, J. L. (2014). Effectiveness of the methods of teaching entrepreneurship courses to developing self-efficacy and intention among university students in Uganda. *International Journal of Social Sciences and Entrepreneurship*, *1*(11), 491–513.

Pick, S., de Weiss, S. P., & Sirkin, J. (2010). *Breaking the poverty cycle: The human basis for sustainable development*. Oxford University Press. doi:10.1093/acprof:oso/9780195383164.001.0001

Plattner, I. E., Lechaena, M., Mmolawa, W., & Mzingwane, B. (2009). Are university students psychologically ready for entrepreneurship? A Botswana study. *African Journal of Business Management*, *3*(7), 305–310.

Premand, P., Brodmann, S., Almeida, R., Grun, R., & Barouni, M. (2012). Entrepreneurship training and self-employment among university graduates: Evidence from a randomized trial in Tunisia. *World Bank Policy Research Working Paper*, (6285). https://www.econstor.eu/bitstream/10419/69343/1/733736653.pdf

Premand, P., Brodmann, S., Almeida, R., Grun, R., & Barouni, M. (2012). *Entrepreneurship training and self-employment among university graduates. Evidence from a randomized trial in Tunisia* (Research Working Paper 6285). Washington, DC: The World Bank.

Rasmussen, E. A., & Sørheim, R. (2006). Action-based entrepreneurship education. *Technovation*, *26*(2), 185–194. doi:10.1016/j.technovation.2005.06.012

Robb, A., Valerio, A., & Parton, B. (Eds.). (2014). Entrepreneurship education and training: insights from Ghana, Kenya, and Mozambique. The World Bank. doi:10.1596/978-1-4648-0278-2

Souitaris, V., Zerbinati, S., & Al-Laham, A. (2007). Do entrepreneurship programmes raise entrepreneurial intention of science and engineering students? The effect of learning, inspiration and resources. *Journal of Business Venturing*, *22*(4), 566–591. doi:10.1016/j.jbusvent.2006.05.002

United Nations. (2015). *Transforming our world: the 2030 agenda for sustainable development.* New York: United Nations, Department of Economic and Social Affairs. Resolution adopted by the General Assembly on 25 September 2015. https://sustainabledevelopment.un.org/post2015/transformingourworld

Valerio, A., Parton, B., & Robb, A. (2014). *Entrepreneurship education and training programs around the world: Dimensions for success*. The World Bank. doi:10.1596/978-1-4648-0202-7

Vallerand, R. J., Blanchard, C., Mageau, G. A., Koestner, R., Ratelle, C., Léonard, M., Gagné, M., & Marsolais, J. (2003). Les passions de l'ame: On obsessive and harmonious passion. *Journal of Personality and Social Psychology*, *85*(4), 756–767. doi:10.1037/0022-3514.85.4.756 PMID:14561128

Van Praag, C. M., & Versloot, P. H. (2007). What is the value of entrepreneurship? A review of recent research. *Small Business Economics*, *29*(4), 351–382. doi:10.100711187-007-9074-x

Welter, F. (2011). Contextualizing entrepreneurship—Conceptual challenges and ways forward. *Entrepreneurship Theory and Practice*, *35*(1), 165–184. doi:10.1111/j.1540-6520.2010.00427.x

World Bank. (2021, June 15). *Unemployment, total (% of total labor force) (modeled ILO estimate)*. International Labour Organization, ILOSTAT database. https://data.worldbank.org/indicator/SL.UEM.TOTL.ZS

World Economic Forum. (2022). *The Global Risks Report 2022* (17th ed.). https://www3.weforum.org/docs/WEF_The_Global_Risks_Report_2022.pdf

Chapter 2
Promoting Entrepreneurship to Reduce Graduate Unemployment:
Service-Learning in Higher Education Institutions, Kenya

Henry Kiptum Yatich
https://orcid.org/0000-0002-7887-1549
Mount Kenya University, Kenya

ABSTRACT

Graduate unemployment is a growing global concern. In 2019, the International Labour Organization (ILO) estimated that more than 73 million youth aged 15–24 were unemployed, the majority of them being student graduates from higher education institutions (HEIs). With a projected population increase of 10 billion by 2050, Africa will constitute 1.4 billion people, the majority of them being young people under the age of 25. Most graduates in developing countries such as Kenya fall under this age group, thus raising concern about their ability to join gainful employment or become self-reliant after graduation. With an average unemployment rate of 7.6% in 2020, The World Bank lists the skills gap between market requirements and the current curriculum provision as an impediment to Kenya's socio-economic agenda. This finding motivates more emphasis for higher education institutions to re-think their approaches in training and skilling. As such, the need for service-learning (SL) as a complementary pedagogy to enhance skills sets among graduates is necessary.

DOI: 10.4018/978-1-7998-9581-7.ch002

INTRODUCTION

The role of universities in nurturing the service-learning ecosystem is crucial in developing competitive graduates, self-efficacy, and intentions of graduates. Universities can promote a service-based learning ecosystem by realigning their core mandates of the curriculum to contribute to research and knowledge dissemination among communities and firms. The labor market in Kenya is faced with a myriad of problems that require the apex institutions to provide solutions. Youth unemployment is one of the major challenges of our times that universities can address. Youth unemployment accounts for 60% of jobless in Africa, thus raising the concern of the need to examine ways and strategies to reduce unemployment especially among the youth (World Bank Group, 2020). Universities can address this challenge by developing a service-learning ecosystem that not only improves graduate employability but also creates entrepreneurs who in turn create jobs. However, efforts to develop a service-learning ecosystem require collaboration from different stakeholders where universities should take up the leading role.

The contribution of universities in developing a service-learning ecosystem is crucial. Universities play an important role in providing service-learning (SL) and setting the appropriate learning context. This will enhance the Self-Efficacy (SE) of learners by inspiring their willingness to venture into communities and firms, identifying and seizing opportunities within the entire labor market and economy. It is necessary to design and package the right SL pedagogy that is in tandem with high labor market needs. The appropriate training methods would result in producing graduates with high belief in their ability to venture and prosper, thus would address unemployment, lead to more job opportunities, support livelihoods, deter engagement in social ills, and lead to economic growth and improved standard of living. However, universities in Kenya are yet to embrace this approach, and there is no comprehensive framework for service learning, hence the need to develop synergy among the various stakeholders that interact with higher education institutions. A service-learning ecosystem has been adopted by many countries as a panacea in strategy in building the practice experience among learners. Service-learning is now recognized as an established field of study, and some international, regional, national, and local actors are taking part in it. It is considered to have the ability to harness early learners' aspirations and to equip them with practical skills (Setiawan, 2014).

It should be noted that there has been rapid university expansion in Kenya, mainly through the conversion of colleges into universities. This has impacted the curriculum delivered because although the government wishes to train more science and technology graduates, in practice the biggest growth in public universities has been in arts, humanities, and social science degrees (and most public universities offer the same range) (Hall, 2017). Both students and employers feel that universities are not preparing students with employability skills (Mukhwana, Oure, Too, and Some, 2016). Federation of Kenya Employers (2018) noted that some students aspire to be self-employed and that there were few opportunities within existing degree courses to develop business start-up skills or to access internships in the blue-collar and informal sectors, in addition to the mismatch between training and labor market needs.

51% of companies surveyed by the Federation of Kenya Employers in 2018 felt that most graduates don't have the right competencies to perform on jobs without gaining further experience or training, thus contributing to graduate unemployment in Kenya. Graduates were found to be enrolled in low-skilled positions such as watchmen, messengers, drivers, and clerical officers (replacing those qualified with diplomas or certificates). Federation of Kenya Employers

(2018a) shares that inadequate training of college graduates has led to the displacement of college-educated young people from roles they might have occupied and to concerns about over qualification, underemployment, and skills mismatching.

This phenomenon is affirmed by Coursera (an online training organization) that, unemployment among university graduates remains a challenge in Africa considering the 2020 global skills index report showing that skills proficiency is critical for socio-economic development across nations. This has been manifested in lower employment rates, lower income inequality, and higher per capita GDP. Europe is the most skilled region according to the finding (Coursera, 2020). Coursera report shows that the youth between 19-25 years are the most affected, and it is considered that majority of university graduates fall under this category, thus constituting one of the highest numbers of the unemployed youth group (Coursera, 2020). The proposition of service-learning strategy is opined to mitigate albeit with some significant level of success, improvement of skill sets among graduates, thus contributing success in entering the labor market or providing the trainee with the adequate skill for idea generation or business start-up.

Service-learning (SL) is a pedagogical technique to enable learners actively participate in communities and organizations by applying knowledge gained to resolve practical challenges and consequently, improve their practical experiences, which can lead to the competitive potential for employment or entrepreneurial ventures (Le Grange, 2007; Clayton, Bringle, & Hatcher, 2013).

Service-learning allows students to engage in activities that address community and organization needs, while at the same time promoting students learning and development (Jacoby, 1996. P.5). Howard (2001) states that civic engagements and reflection are the key elements that distinguish service learning from internships. It includes research projects that are developed in partnership with communities or organizations and leads to problem-solving while providing the much-needed practical application for the student. This is in addition to enabling the student to network and showcase their abilities and skills sets, relevant for the labor market and self-reliance. SL provides a platform for a symbiotic relationship between society, organizations, students, and higher education institutions by bridging the gap between theory and practice through its key components of service to the community, reflection, and experiential learning. This is opined to be one of the panacea to graduate unemployment which is one of the major challenges of our times.

GRADUATE UNEMPLOYMENT IN KENYA

Unemployment remains a political and economic challenge in the 21st century. Globally, all leaders and citizens ought to recognize the significance of education to alleviate unemployment and as a unifying force that brings together individuals from diverse cultures, religions, economies, and beliefs to discuss matters affecting modern life and chart a better future. The fundamental question is how to initiate and build novel collaboration between industry, civil society, and tertiary education to improve the skills needed by industry while creating opportunities for self-employment and promoting national economic development.

Kenya as an economy has witnessed a persistent mismatch of appropriate skills required by labor market actors in addition to, not developing competent graduates who can venture into self-employment. According to the World Bank (2016) and Federation of Kenya Employers (FKE) (2018), Kenya ranks among the countries with the highest unemployment rate among the youth. The report notes that one of the essential ingredients in the education sector is the quality of skills and education. FKE notes that employers in Kenya incur costly burdens of training fresh graduates and this has increased the costs of business, reduced productivity, and delay output because new workers take a long period to familiarize themselves with work processes and expectations. FKE further notes that over 70% of fresh graduates have to undergo refresher courses to understand and deliver on the requirements of the workplace (FKE, 2018). Kenya Institute for Public Policy Research and Analysis (KIPPRA) observes that there exists a relatively high level of unemployment within the East African Community (EAC). This is attributed largely to shortages of professionals and a mismatch of training/education skills. Kenya National Bureau of Statistics (KNBS) in its Economic Survey 2018 showed university graduates formed a big percentage of the unemployed group of 15-19 years standing at 55.4% while those of ages 20-24 years stood at 19.2% (KNBS, 2018). This gives an average unemployment rate of university graduates who form a bulk of this group (15-24 years) at 37.2%. Further, KIPPRA in their findings acknowledged the existence of mismatch in university training and the needs of the labor and entrepreneurial market (KIPPRA, 2017). KIPPRA in particular observed that institutions of higher learning in Kenya were offering training that emphasized academic qualification at the expense of specific practical skills and competencies required by the labor market or the economy at large.

There is a need for innovative strategies for training university students to enhance employability in the labor market in addition to imparting skills for self-employment. As such, the author proposes service-learning as a complementary approach to promote practical skills and enhance the throughput of graduate absorption both by labor market actors and for self-reliance. It is the authors believe that adoption of service-learning as a measure to promote practical skill acquisition is key among higher education service providers. SL is a novel idea among institutions of higher learning in Kenya, and its practice is considered to have gained traction in European universities of applied sciences, where learners are embedded in organizations and communities, to provide service while at the same time improving their practical skills. Service-learning has the potential of linking students to communities, and industries where they can be problem solvers to their needs and challenges. In addition, it promotes practice-based training, idea generation, and endear students to potential employers, thus making them more competitive in the strides to reduce graduate unemployment in Kenya.

This chapter seeks to examine how service-learning can inspire practical skill acquisition among undergraduate students in Kenya as a strategy for inspiring entrepreneurial ventures, creating competitive graduates, and thus reducing unemployment among HEI graduates.

GRADUATE TRAINING IN HEIS IN KENYA

Graduate training in HEIs in Kenya is primarily traditional. It encompasses, lecture method, lab sessions, and industrial attachment or teaching practice for teachers at the end or in between the course. It is differing in some universities but the process remains the same. Some institutions have some arrangements with specific organizations such as National Industrial Training Authority (NITA) for paid internship opportunities after graduation, but owing to the high number of graduates, the majority of graduates are left out due to limited opportunities. This is also compounded by 49% of new graduates from Kenyan universities who are not adequately prepared for the labor market (British Council, 2016). In addition, it is important to note that as late as 2020, the highest proportion of unemployment reported by the Kenya National Bureau of Statistics (KNBS) in its 3rd quarter report of 2020, stood at 11.6% for 18-34 years old (KNBS, 2020). This group of youth aged 18-34 are both continuing and graduates of HE and TVET. As such, there is a need for a concerted effort by all HEIs to implement strategies that can offer additional practical skills to graduates as they exit training institutions.

The introduction of a competency-based curriculum (CBC) in 2017 by Kenya's Ministry of Education is envisaged to be the panacea to perennial problems of the real and perceived disconnect between the 8-4-4 system and the labor market needs. At the same time (2017), there was bilateral discussion among Kenya government officers and some European nations to adopt the universities of applies science model (UAS) in Kenya. The UAS model emphasizes close working relationships with industry and labor market actors, to integrate teaching and practice. In Kenya, this is deeply rooted in programs in medical and health science fields. Other programs of study such as social sciences depend solely on industrial attachment which is considered inadequate to produce competent graduates going by the FKE report of 2018. Almost all players in Kenya such as ILO, FKE, CUE, British Council among others agree that the link between education training and industry is weak in Kenya, resulting in job mismatch with labor market needs. HE sector in Kenya is considered to be planning for review of curriculums in anticipation of the CBC candidates who are likely to join the HE/TVET institutions in 2029/2030. In doing so, service-learning can be a strategic measure that if implemented, can reduce the disconnect between theory and practice while at the same time, assisting societal organizations to solve emerging issues and challenges.

In Kenya, economic, political, and social-cultural factors are likely to make individuals more successful at starting new ventures. University students are graduating with inadequate practical skills thus calling for higher education institutions to re-examine their curriculum offering (Federation of Kenya Employers, 2018). These factors influence the setting up of a conducive student-centered environment, learning facilities, and enabling resources such as incubators. A conducive learning environment that integrates service-learning would encourage interrogation of contemporary issues to articulate issues in communities, firms, and society which keeps on changing. Exposing learnings to practical-based training forms a context in which entrepreneurial opportunities can arise or are built. The ability to identify these dynamisms is a crucial milestone in developing a service-learning ecosystem. However, universities do not operate on an island and thus collaboration with other stakeholders in shaping the service-learning strategy is necessary. The key stakeholders in developing an entrepreneurship ecosystem are academia, community organizations, industry, and policymakers. Nevertheless, Mascarenhas, Marques, Galvao, and Santos, (2017) found that there exist collaboration obstacles in terms of divergent attitudes between universities and industries which brings about a disconnect between academic and business systems. Universities have higher bureaucracy, inertia, and inefficiency than the industry (Lehrer, Nell & Gaerber, 2009). Such evidence provides an impetus for the adoption of service-learning as a complementary approach in training higher education students. Empirical studies on service-learning in Africa show that learning and development among learners are influenced by challenges affecting higher education, hence the need for institutions of higher learning in Kenya to consider the adoption of service-learning (VanLeeuwen, Weeks, and Guo-Brennan, 2017).

SERVICE-LEARNING ECOSYSTEM IN KENYA

Service-learning in Kenya is considered a new idea, especially in higher education institutions. Some of the approaches enumerated by (Eyler, Giles, Stenson, and Gray, 2001)) in which SL is conducted are;

- **Pure service-learning** (sending students into communities to serve as volunteers or engaged citizens)
- **Discipline-based service-learning courses** (sending students into communities throughout the semester, where they reflect on their experiences using the course content as a source in analyzing and understanding community challenges or issues).
- **Problem-based service-learning courses** (sending students in teams to communities and organizations where they respond to their challenges as "consultants" working for a "client."
- **Capstone courses** (where courses are designed for majors and minors in a given discipline. As such, students are requested to draw upon knowledge obtained in their course work and combine it with relevant service work in the community to explore new ideas that can enhance their understanding of the discipline.
- **Service internships** (they mirror traditional internships where students work between 10 to 20 hours a week in a community setting. At the end of the exercise, students are expected to produce ideas and solutions that are of value to the community or organization.
- **Undergraduate community**-based action research (this is a novel approach and involves action research. Students work closely with university staff members to learn research methodology while continuing to serve as advocates for important community issues.

Organizations advancing the SL idea in Kenya are limited to non-governmental organizations such as Edu-Africa are the pioneers, Strathmore University, and Association of International Schools in Africa (AISA). Edu-Africa runs a service-learning program at Brackenhurst Botanic Garden for two weeks or longer at a fee.

This is one of their many programs which they run across the continent (Kenya, Tanzania, South Africa, Zimbabwe, and Zambia). The Brackenhurst program involves learners who are willing to gain practical skills through supporting local communities around the indigenous forest to identify sustainable human settlements and agricultural systems. This is done by modeling ideas together with community members. This project is very interactive and includes practical activities, design thinking exercises, lectures, discussions groups that bring together both the learners and local community members (https://edu-africa.com). Edu-Africa believes that service learning is key in developing learners' practical competence and stimulating idea generation through community support. In doing so, students are exposed to real work experiences and the opportunity to network with communities in meaningful service while strengthening their skills and gaining rich life experiences. Edu-Africa has partnered with strategic community institutions such as Maasai Mara Conservancies (Income Generation; Education and Outreach; Infrastructure and Water), Primary Education Development initiatives.

At Strathmore university business school, service-learning is embedded in the curriculum as a strategy to integrate community service into the student learning process to enrich their learning experience. In addition, it inculcates civic responsibility and promotes solutions identification to community challenges (Barreneche, 2011). At the university, It is a curriculum requirement for learners to undergo 225 hours of community service-learning program. Students in groups are placed in institutions around Nairobi wherein in 2021 four students were placed at Hospital hill primary school. The learners participated with teachers and the young learners to better the learning environment for the pupils and teachers. On the university student's part, they were able to acquire effective communication, teaching, and interactive skills as bachelor of commerce students at the university. In addition to bettering the learning environment, the students during their interactions with the pupils at Hospital hill primary school highlighted environmental conservation as one of the key lessons learned through the SL program (Hinga, 2021). They noted that through close interaction and teamwork they were made aware that humans are the problem when it comes to global warming and they were able to come up with the "Go Green Initiative" as a solution for the primary school. The Go Green Initiative enabled the student participants and the pupils to plant various fruit trees around Hill School primary school.

Strathmore University seems to follow in the footsteps of students in the School of Business at George Washington University (GW) where a problem-based service-learning approach is adopted. George Washington University is located within communities with a high number of global policymakers and institutions to enable students access for SL opportunities (Umpleby and Levkov, 2008). At GW, students work in teams of three to five students to improve the functioning of identified organizations. The students use the knowledge and methods acquired from the classroom and literature and together with specific staff in an organization they work to improve some aspects of the organization. It is on the same premise that Mount Kenya University (MKU) (2021) in Kenya has started a roll-out of SL adopting the problem-based service-Learning courses in 2022. The program is a transfer measure under the university business linkages pillar (UBL) a DAAD program sponsored under African Centre for Career Enhancement and Skills Support (ACCESS) project. The program entails working with organizations within the university with students in groups of 4, working as consultants for the firms are selected. This includes business firms and community initiatives by the county government. Through this initiative, the students work with the "client" by mutually sharing a particular problem or need. The students then draw upon their classroom knowledge and make recommendations to the organization or community attached to in developing a solution to the identified challenge. The university also leverages the existing partnership with African International Foundation for Educational Excellence (AIFEE), the USA to utilize their sites for service-learning initiatives in Kenya.

The Kenya Institute of Curriculum Development (KICD) has also embraced service-learning in 2019 as the first component of implementing the Competence-Based Curriculum (CBC) in secondary schools. The objective of KICD is to ensure learners are equipped with skills to enable them to use their talents when out of school to turn problems into solutions in their communities (Onyango and Langat, 2019). In as much as this is offered at the secondary level of education, its implementation has been a challenge owing to low capacity building and resource support.

The problem-based service-learning course is considered an appropriate approach that gives rise to the ability that students can work with businesses firms, local and national government agencies, learning institutions, and non–profit organizations (Eyler, et al. 2001). This approach allows students to work in any organization regardless of discipline or specialization and the result benefits both parties involved. To students, it will promote the acquisition of practical skills thus preparing them better for the labor market and self-reliance.

YOUTH UNEMPLOYMENT AND SL ECOSYSTEM IN KENYA

The role of higher education in Kenya is to nurture a conducive ecosystem that is crucial in developing the practical competencies and intentions of graduates. Universities can develop such an ecosystem by realigning their theory and practice among learners. As such, they enable knowledge dissemination and service to communities while ensuring learners gain the much-needed experiences. Service-learning, therefore, enables learners to expand their opportunities, while developing their relationship-building skills. This is attained as a result of working closely with field supervisors and partnering institutions. Due to regular feedback, learners can brainstorm, discuss and seek guidance and advice (Kathuri-Ogola et al., 2015).

In Kenya's higher education sector, the need for quality education should inculcate adequate preparation of the youth in anticipating their future roles in society and communities (Pacho, 2019). Quality education should motivate the learner to engage in genuine reflection and action, to enhance learner participation rather than being observers. This is in addition to preparing the youth for their future roles in society. In doing this, it empowers the learner to challenge dominant worldviews, enhance knowledge creation among communities, connect learning with the realities, and instill a passion for social justice (Apple, 1993). Service learning if fully adopted in Kenya's HEIs, can lead to responsible citizens and enable societal transformation by inculcating civic responsibility. Through reflective learning, SL integrates theory and practice while consciously promoting the learner's experience (Moon, 2013).

The contemporary world is faced with a myriad of problems that require Kenya's HEIs to provide practical and tailor-made solutions. Youth unemployment is one of the major challenges of our times that universities can address. Youth unemployment accounts for a high percentage of jobless graduates in Africa, universities are required to address this challenge by developing a service-learning ecosystem that not only improves graduate employability but also creates entrepreneurs who in turn create jobs (World Bank Group, 2020). However, efforts to develop a service-learning ecosystem require collaboration from different stakeholders where universities should take up the leading role.

The contribution of universities in developing a service-learning ecosystem is crucial. Universities play an important role in providing SL opportunities for their learners and setting the appropriate learning context. Service-learning is paramount in enhancing entrepreneurship self-Efficacy (ESE) of learners by inspiring idea generation and willingness to venture into self-employment, by identifying and seizing opportunities in the economy, while interacting with communities or organizations. High levels of service-learning are likely to result in innovation and opportunity recognition among learners and can be exploited for greater prosperity both for labor market absorption and entrepreneurial opportunities. It is necessary to design and package the right SL pedagogy that is in tandem with high labor market needs and curriculum expectations (Mukhwana et al., 2016; Federation of Kenya Employers, 2018). The appropriate training methods would result in producing graduates with high belief in their ability to venture and prosper in entrepreneurship or higher absorption by labor market actors, thus addressing unemployment, creating more job opportunities, supporting livelihoods, deter engagement in social ills, and leading to economic growth and improved standard of living. However, universities in Kenya are yet to embrace fully service-learning pedagogy since there is no comprehensive framework for a service-learning ecosystem (Hermanto and Suryanto, 2017). There is a need to develop synergy among the various stakeholders that interact with service learning to foster an entrepreneurial spirit among learners enrolled in the program.

Service-learning is an instructional method that has been adopted by many countries as a panacea in promoting self-employment and producing competent graduates who meet employers' expectations. SL is now recognized as an established field of consideration, and some international, regional, national, and local actors are taking part in it. It is practiced mostly at the basic level of training in Kenya, as envisaged in the CBC curriculum (KICD, 2019). Kenyan Institute of Curriculum Development (KICD) considers SL as a form of experiential education that enables learners to apply their knowledge and skills to community challenges to drive solution identification while instilling practical experience among learners.

SL is perceived to have the ability to harness early entrepreneurial aspirations and develop new venture creation potential for the future benefit of communities or organizations. It is also expected to develop an entrepreneurial mindset and intention among students and to equip them with knowledge and skills to be entrepreneurs (Setiawan, 2014). This has resulted in SL emerging with the expectation of producing more and better-equipped individuals. Service-learning can bring about much enthusiasm with associated outcomes such as economic growth, innovation commercialization, and job creation among HEI graduates. The contribution of SL in developing the graduate experiences is therefore important, but there is a need to address the curriculum content, context, and trainer's capacity which when combined forms a strong SL ecosystem.

In Kenya, learning in HEIs takes place along traditional pathways. The major training approaches used to teach students in universities are mostly traditional methods, albeit with a little integration of technology. Traditional methods include; lectures, discussions, questions, and answers (Maritz, 2013). Traditional methods have the advantage of being the most commonly used form of delivering the curriculum. The disadvantages of traditional methods are that they are passive and less effective in inñuencing practical skill acquisition and reduce entrepreneurial attributes (Mwasalwiba, 2012). Taatila, (2010) posited that theoretical content should not necessarily lead to traditional teaching methods. The practical aspect and creative process of embedding entrepreneurial attitudes should lead to the adoption of SL as a complementary method of instruction to traditional approaches (Maritz, 2013). Service-learning is a multifaceted discipline that requires a concerted effort of external actors both within and outside learning institutions in the HEI sector in Kenya.

Experiential learning or non-traditional methods is a process whereby knowledge is created through reñection on doing. SL therefore can make learners initiate discoveries and experiments using their ðrst-hand classroom knowledge instead of hearing or reading about others' experiences (Tomczak et al., 2011). The students in this approach act as active researchers and co-researcher among student teams and industry or community supervisors and members. It treats the student as a constructor and not as a consumer of knowledge that has been planned by the facilitator. The aims of service-learning; to encourage active participation, to develop oneself, connect new knowledge to experiences, to acquire skills in handling and solving problematic situations, develop research skills, cooperating in teams, accept the responsibility of presenting work to the class, and giving and receiving feedback (Clayton et al., 2013). Service-learning enables learners to work in teams (team-based learning), prepare poster plans and presentation sessions, thus promoting project-based learning, blended learning, active and collaborative learning. It increases educational experiences, mentoring, action learning, student-centered learning among students involved. Service-learning coupled with the right context is important in raising the quality of Kenyan graduates and is applicable across the globe.

A training environment that possesses the right contextual factors can foster service-learning. Maritz (2013), points out that training context is the conditions and circumstances that are relevant and contribute to the full meaning of quality training. As such, service-learning can be considered as an excellent pedagogical strategy for enhancing the quality of higher education in Kenya (Bringle and Hatcher, 2007)

The industry too has its obstacles. To begin with, there is the challenge of knowledge absorption capacity. Cruz-Gonzalez, Lopez-Saez, Navas- Lopez, and Delgado-Verde (2014) have pointed out to cognitive dissonance in the acquisition of external knowledge and its assimilation in the industry requires concerted effort of all partners in the training chain and network. The situation has been contributed to by low activities in Research and Development (R&D) departments. Esquinas, Hermandez, and Andia (2016) observed that there are few firms with robust R & D and sometimes the task of formalizing the linkage between private investors and universities is difficult. These challenges can be overcome by the removal of impediments, increased interaction in the National Innovation System (NIS), provision of resources, and development of the required infrastructure.

In Kenya's institutions of higher learning, entrepreneurship training is offered as a common unit to undergraduate students. However, this has not remedied the need for practical exposure, hence the proposal for HEIs to adopt service-learning pedagogy.

SERVICE-LEARNING BENEFITS

Service-learning is considered an approach that promotes active teaching and learning and benefits both the learners, communities, industry and training institutions. It impacts a sense of citizenship, acquisition of practical skills and offers solutions (service) to the partnering institution. As such, it links academia with local organizations. Consequently, it ensures the graduate is adequately prepared for the job market and self-employment (Butin, 2010; UNESCO, 2010; Zentner, 2011). Service-learning enables the learner to work on real organization problems that make academic learning worthwhile. It enhanced the learner's practical skills, self-worth, and promotes idea generation through critical thinking and application (Kenya Institute of Curriculum Development, 2017). Additionally, service-learning promotes active participation during the learning process, a key ingredient for a competence-based curriculum in Kenya, Further, it develops responsible citizens, who appreciate the value of product differentiation in their attitude towards becoming competitive employees as well as for self-reliance. Given the high rate of youth unemployment in Kenya, service-learning can improve graduate employability and hence increase their chances of being absorbed by employers in addition to becoming entrepreneurs.

IMPLEMENTATION MODEL FOR SL MODELS

The development of a partnership model should be anchored on the core mandate of universities. The first model ventilates on the three key functions of universities which are; training, research, and community outreach or dissemination while indicating how each of them can be leveraged to promote service-learning strategy. The interactions between the three functions of universities are depicted in Figure 1.

The model shows that the ultimate goal of quality training is the dissemination of knowledge and research findings to the community while promoting requisite skills for self-reliance and meeting labor market needs. It demonstrates how universities can leverage service-learning pedagogy to enhance practical skills which can be employed for transformative research and the establishment of innovative enterprises.

The model indicates that universities can develop a service-learning ecosystem by providing an experiential learning environment in partnership with industry (community organizations and firms). This can be done by setting up a conducive student-centered environment, appropriate learning facilities, strengthening university-business linkages (UBL), and enabling resources such as business parks and innovation incubators. The model further indicates that universities should engage themselves in action-oriented research that promotes discovery, inventions, and innovative pedagogies such as service learning. Universities' output to the

Figure 1. Role of universities in developing an entrepreneurship service-learning ecosystem
Source: Author (2022).

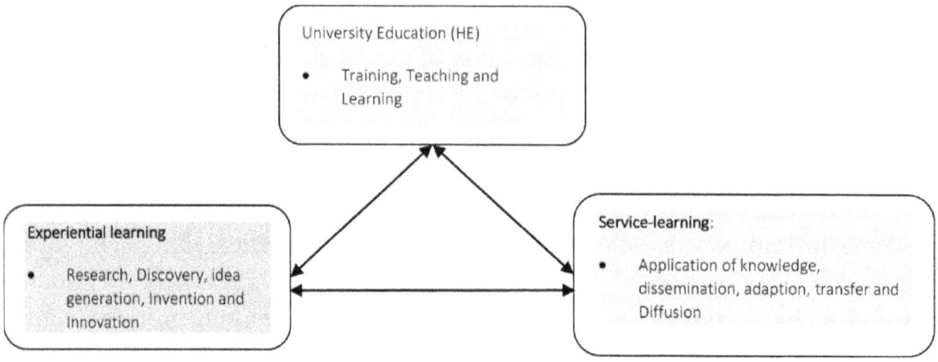

society should inspire confidence to generate enterprises that leverage technology to bring about innovation performance, improved industry competitiveness, inclusive economic participation, and ultimately sustainable development. The output of revamped university problem-based service-learning ecosystem can be illustrated in the second model.

The model is an improvement of the triple helix model which depicts the association of universities, government, and industry (communities and organizations). This is shown in Figure 2.

The model indicates that Universities are expected to create an enabling environment where communities and firms participate in knowledge generation through interactive problem-solving approaches in the real world. The students' entrepreneurial intentions and efficacy will also be raised in such as system. The government is pivotal in developing policies and the requisite regulatory framework for both universities, community organizations, and the industry. Development and

Figure 2. Outcome of entrepreneurship service-learning ecosystem
Source: Author (2022).

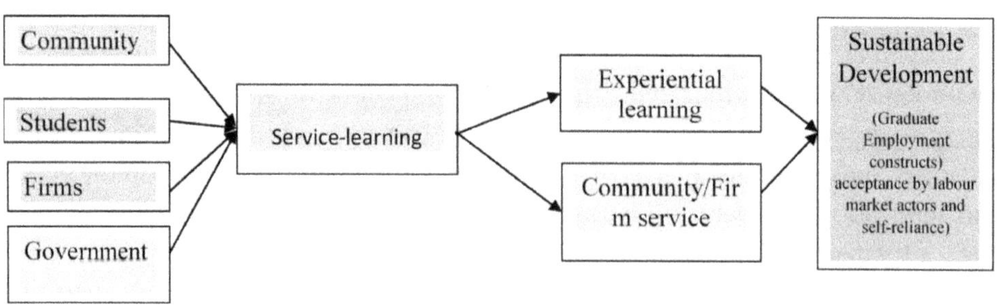

strategic partners are also important in supporting the initiatives of the universities, community organizations, industry, and government especially in setting up the required infrastructure such as incubation center opportunities. This will lead to the development of enterprises that will churn out innovative product that addresses the problems of unemployment among HEIs graduates.

The framework for the service-learning ecosystem process can be implemented using the framework shown in Figure 3.

Figure 3. SL process model
Source; Author, (2022)

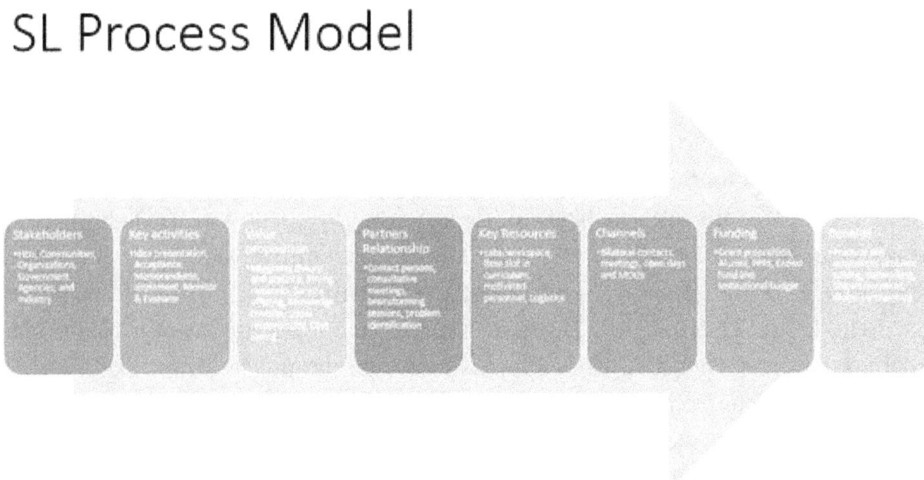

The framework enumerates the stakeholders, resource requirements, channels, partners relationship, cost structures, and benefits. Their interaction forms the service-learning ecosystem. The more robust and intense networking within the system, the better the service-learning system and hence improved output. Service-learning implementation requires continuous monitoring and elimination of deviations, with the ultimate goal of achieving the learning outcomes. This can be done while minimizing the variability of the process. Such a method ensures that the program delivers on the learning outcomes. To remain efficient, and sustainable, HEIs should seek synergetic partnerships with organizations and communities to ensure minimization of costs, meet learning outcomes, and efficient utilization of resources.

CONCLUSION

We live in the 21st Century, where labor market demands, socio-economic and political trends continue to exert pressure on the need for new qualifications and competencies to all players in education spheres. The need for these qualifications and competencies are driven by households changing needs and lifestyles, firms' needs for competitiveness, governments' need for citizen service, and other social institutions. Consequently, TVET and HEIs institutions, therefore, have no option, but to progressively adapt to these dynamic demands.

Service-learning is a pedagogical method in higher education that has become noticeable in Kenya but not well embraced. Institutions of higher learning are continuously searching for avenues to assist students to bridge the gap between practice and theory. This entails collaboration with firms and communities in most disciplines. Through the use of service-learning as an instructional method and the findings of notable scholars, communities, and institutions of higher learning since it has the potential of offering increased learning outcomes in the programs where practical skills are emphasized. Research by Pribbenow (2005) shows that there is an increased positive effect on students' cognitive skills and academic motivation (Clayton, Bringle, Senor, Huq, and Morrison, 2010). It should be noted that Bringle and Hatcher (1995) affirm that service-learning is not a traditional volunteering endeavor because it reinforces academic learning goals and experiences while strengthening communities and organizations. As such, learners who engage in SL can integrate theory with practice and develop reflective practical skills (Behar-Horenstein et al., 2016). Service-learning has the opportunity to increase communal and shared academic and instructional approaches (Flecky and Gitlow, 2009). Flecky and Gitlow (2009) further state that service-learning stimulates competencies related to service-learning and encompasses facets of citizenship, entrepreneurship, leadership, life skills, communication skills, and research skills. This, therefore, places service-learning as a fundamental pillar that augments the field of a competency-based approach to curriculum (CBC) development, where the emphasis is placed on the outcome of the learning process with lesson content and more of competencies and skills.

It should not be lost that, higher education institutions remain the catalyst for socio-economic growth and prosperity, and this may explain why developed and developing nations continue to put more emphasis on the training of their graduates

The author believes that as champions of continuous improvement, both HEIs and TVETs in Kenya should aim at a multifaceted approach in integrating practice-based competencies in the development and continuous review of curriculums to inculcate approaches that promote practice-based learning, akin to the universities of applied sciences model. Program curriculums should also be tailored for distinct economic activities. To further the service-learning cause, there is a need for government agencies, HEIs, Industry partners, and relevant entities to constantly consider each other as stakeholders in the training process if the labor market is to receive quality and competent graduates as well as create opportunities for self-reliance. In this case, the author proposes a problem-based service-learning approach among higher education institutions in Kenya and possibly across other training institutions locally, regionally and globally.

REFERENCES

Apple, M. W. (2014). *Official knowledge: Democratic education in a conservative age*. Routledge. doi:10.4324/9780203814383

Barreneche, G. I. (2011). Language learners as teachers: Integrating service-learning and the advanced language course. *Hispania*, 103–120.

Bringle, R. G., & Hatcher, J. A. (1995). *A service-learning curriculum for faculty*. Academic Press.

Butin, D. (2010). *Service-learning in theory and practice: The future of community engagement in higher education*. Springer. doi:10.1057/9780230106154

Clayton, P. H., Bringle, R. G., & Hatcher, J. A. (2013). *Research on service learning: Conceptual frameworks and assessment, Vol. 2B: Communities, institutions, and partnerships. Stylus.*

Clayton, P. H., Bringle, R. G., Senor, B., Huq, J., & Morrison, M. (2010). Differentiating and assessing relationships in service-learning and civic engagement: Exploitative, transactional, or transformational. *Michigan Journal of Community Service Learning*, *16*(2), 5–21.

Coursera. (2020). *Global Skills Index 2020*. www.coursera.org/gsi

Cruz-González, J., López-Sáez, P., Navas-López, J. E., & Delgado-Verde, M. (2014). Directions of external knowledge search: Investigating their different impact on firm performance in high-technology industries. *Journal of Knowledge Management*, *18*(5), 847–866. doi:10.1108/JKM-06-2014-0243

Dörner, N., Morhart, F., Gassmann, O., & Tomczak, T. (2011). Inter-institutional collaboration for new integrative teaching programs. *On the Horizon*, *19*(3), 217–225. doi:10.1108/10748121111163922

Eyler, J., Giles, D. E., Jr., Stenson, C. M., & Gray, C. J. (2001). At a glance: What we know about the effects of service-learning on college students, faculty, institutions and communities. *Higher Education.* 139. https://digitalcommons.unomaha.edu/slcehighered/139

Federation of Kenya Employers. (2018a). *Skills Mismatch Survey*. Retrieved from: https://www.fke-kenya.org/

Fernández-Esquinas, M., Merchán-Hernández, C., & Valmaseda-Andía, O. (2016). How effective are interface organizations in the promotion of university-industry links? Evidence from a regional innovation system. *European Journal of Innovation Management, 19*(3), 424–442. doi:10.1108/EJIM-07-2013-0068

Flecky, K., & Gitlow, L. (2009). *Service-Learning in Occupational Therapy Education: Philosophy & Practice*. Jones & Bartlett Publishers.

Hall, S. (2017). *Youth employment in Kenya.* British Council. Retrieved from: https://www.britishcouncil.co.ke/

Hermanto, B., & Suryanto, S. E. (2017). Entrepreneurship ecosystem policy in Indonesia. *Mediterranean Journal of Social Sciences, 8*(1), 110–110. doi:10.5901/mjss.2017.v8n1p110

Hinga, J. (2021, May 10). *Service-based learning: Going beyond academics.* Strathmore University Business School. Retrieved February 1, 2022, from https://sbs.strathmore.edu/service-based-learning-going-beyond-academics/

Howard, J. (2001). *Michigan journal of community service learning. In Service-learning Course Design Workbook.* OCSL Press.

ILO. (2019). *Skills and jobs mismatches in low- and middle-income countries.* https://www.ilo.org/

Jacoby, B. (1996). Service-learning in higher education: concepts and practices. Jossey-Bass Publishers.

Kariba, F. (2020, July 30). *The burgeoning Africa youth population: Potential or challenge?* Cities Alliance. Retrieved January 31, 2022, from https://www.citiesalliance.org/newsroom/news/cities-alliance-news/%C2%A0burgeoning-africa-youth-population-potential-or-challenge%C2%A0

Kathuri-Ogola, L., VanLeeuwen, C., Kabaria-Muriithi, J., Weeks, L. E., Kieru, J., & Ndayala, P. (2015). Supervision challenges encountered during Kenyan university students' practicum attachment. *Journal of Education and Practice, 6*(17), 111–117.

Kenya Institute of Curriculum Development. (2017). *Basic education curriculum framework*. KICD.

Kenya Institute of Curriculum Development. (2019). *Popular sides on CBC*. https://kicd.ac.ke/cbc-materials/popular-slides-on-cbc/

KIfPPRaA. (2017). Kenya Economic Report 2017" Sustaining Kenya's Economic Development by Deepening and Expanding Economic Integration in the Region. Kenya Institute for Public Policy Research and Analysis Nairobi.

KNBS. (2018). Economic survey 2018. *Kenya National Bureau of Statistics*.

KNBS. (2020, Nov.). *Quarterly Labour Force Report*. Author.

Le Grange, L. (2007). The'theoretical foundations' of community service-learning: From taproots to rhizomes. *Education as Change*, *11*(3), 3–13. doi:10.1080/16823200709487174

Lehrer, M., Nell, P., & Gaerber, L. (2009). A national system view of university entrepreneurism: Inferences from comparison of the German and US experience. *Research Policy*, *38*(2), 268–280. doi:10.1016/j.respol.2008.11.007

Levkov, N., & Umpleby, S. (2009). *How Service Learning is Conducted in a School of Business*. CEA Journal of Economics.

Maritz, A. (2017). Illuminating the black box of entrepreneurship education programmes: Part 2. *Education + Training*, *59*(5), 471–482. doi:10.1108/ET-02-2017-0018

Mascarenhas, C., Marques, C. S., Galvão, A. R., & Santos, G. (2017). Entrepreneurial university: towards a better understanding of past trends and future directions. *Journal of Enterprising Communities: People and Places in the Global Economy*.

Moon, J. A. (2013). *A handbook of reflective and experiential learning: Theory and practice*. Routledge. doi:10.4324/9780203416150

Mount Kenya University. (2021, July 2). *Linkages and partnership*. Mount Kenya University. Retrieved February 1, 2022, from https://www.mku.ac.ke/linkages-and-partnership/

Mukhwana, E., Oure, S., Too, J., & Some, D. K. (2016). *State ofpostgraduate research training in Kenya*. Commission for University Education. Discussion Paper 02.

Mwasalwiba, E. S. (2012). Entrepreneurship education: A review of its objectives, teaching methods, and impact indicators. *IEEE Engineering Management Review*, *40*(2), 72–94. doi:10.1109/EMR.2012.6210519

Onyango, A., & Langat, D. (2019, July 2). *Community service learning*. Kenya News Agency. Retrieved February 1, 2022, from https://www.kenyanews.go.ke/community-service-learning/#:~:text=Kenya%20Institute%20of%20Curriculum%20Development,Based%20Curriculum%20in%20secondary%20schools

Pacho, T. (2019). Service-learning: An innovative approach to education in Africa. *The good education and Africa's future: Concepts, issues and options*, 232-259

Pribbenow, D. A. (2005). The impact of service-learning pedagogy on faculty teaching and learning. *Michigan Journal of Community Service Learning*, *11*(2), 25–38.

Setiawan, J. L. (2014). Examining entrepreneurial self-efficacy among students. *Procedia: Social and Behavioral Sciences*, *115*, 235–242. doi:10.1016/j.sbspro.2014.02.431

UNESCO. (2010). *World Conference on Higher Education 2009*. Final Report.

VanLeeuwen, C. A., Weeks, L. E., & Guo-Brennan, L. (2017). Indigenous perspectives on community service-learning in higher education: An examination of the Kenyan context. *The International Journal of Research on Service-Learning and Community Engagement*, *5*(1), 129–143. doi:10.37333/001c.29769

World Bank. (2016). *Informal enterprises in Kenya*. World Bank.

World Bank. (2020). *Kenya overview*. https://www.worldbank.org/

Zentner, S., Nagy, F., Götz, M., & Maiberg, H. (2011). *Lernen durch Engagement. service-learning in German schools. A promising way to get youth involved–in active learning and in civic engagement*. Weinheim: Freudenberg Foundation.

Chapter 3
Bridging Into the Future Through Education

Nadia Simoes
https://orcid.org/0000-0002-4334-4482
ISCTE-Instituto Universitário de Lisboa, Portugal

Nuno Crespo
https://orcid.org/0000-0002-6546-6325
ISCTE-Instituto Universitário de Lisboa, Portugal

ABSTRACT

One of the major bottlenecks of the Portuguese labor market is the level of educational attainment of the population. Despite considerable evolution over the last decades, the country is still behind the European Union average in most education indicators. In 2009, 69.2% of the population aged between 15 and 64 had less than upper secondary education, a value that is more than double the European average. Due to the measures and reforms that have been introduced, in 2019, this proportion had dropped to 47.6%. Between 2009 and 2019, self-employed persons had education levels below the average of the working population. In 2009, 79.0% had less than upper secondary education, and in 2019, this number was still at 50.6%. The human capital of the self-employed persons has significant consequences on their entrepreneurial activities. The low educational attainment level of the population has demanded extensive reforms. This chapter discusses the main policies implemented to improve educational attainment and obtain a comprehensive overview of labor market and education indicators.

DOI: 10.4018/978-1-7998-9581-7.ch003

INTRODUCTION

Human capital has long been considered one of the most important determinants of economic growth and cross-country income differences, and in 2015 the Portuguese Prime minister recognized that the skill deficit is the most import deficit of the country. As stressed by the OECD (2015, p. 3), "skills and human capital are the bedrock upon which Portugal is building a new road to growth". In an in-depth study of the Portuguese economic growth, Veiga, Alexandre, Silva, and Arezes (2019, p. 28) illustrate the gap between Portugal and other countries, "for at least two hundred years, Portugal has had a remarkable skills gap. In 2000, with less than eight years of average schooling, the Portuguese resident had a schooling similar to that of the resident in Germany of 1930 or in Romania of 1970". Despite significant evolution over the last decades (Gouveia & Fernandes, 2017; Gouveia, Santos, & Gonçalves, 2017), the country is still behind the European Union average in most education indicators (OECD, 2015).

In 2009, 69.2% of the population aged between 15 and 64 had less than upper secondary education, which compares with 31.6% for the European Union (EU28). Due to the measures and reforms that have been introduced, in 2019, 47.6% of the Portuguese population aged 15 to 64 had less than upper secondary education and 23.8% had tertiary education, which compares to 24.9% and 29.5%, respectively, for the EU28. For the entire period, self-employed persons had education levels below the average of the working population. In 2009, 79.0% had less than upper secondary education. In 2019, despite some improvement, this number was still at 50.6%. The size and composition of the human capital of the self-employed persons have consequences in the size-class and volume of business of their firms. For that reason, in 2018, 96.2% of the Portuguese firms employed fewer than 10 workers (Statistics Portugal, 2020). At the firm-level, this issue has two types of consequences: (i) entrepreneurs with lower levels of educational attainment engage, on average, in economic activities characterized by less complexity (and less value added); (ii) the lack of qualifications of the workforce introduces constraints in the ability of firms to perform.

Obviously, it is important to have programs to promote entrepreneurship, but in a country with these characteristics qualifications must continue to be a top priority. In recent decades most national and international reports addressing the competitiveness of the Portuguese economy have highlighted the importance of increasing qualifications. For example, in the Memorandum of Understanding that Portugal signed in 2011 with the European Central Bank, the European Commission, and the International Monetary Fund it is stated that "the Government will continue action to tackle low education attainment and early school leaving and to improve the quality of secondary education and vocational education and training, with a view to increase efficiency in the education sector, raise the quality of human capital and facilitate labour market matching".

The XXI Constitutional Government of Portugal (established in November 2015 as a Socialist Party minority government supported by an agreement celebrated with the Left Bloc, the Portuguese Communist Party, and the Ecologist Party "The Greens") considered that the issues related to the system of education and vocational training were critical. Two main objectives were set: tackling school dropout and investing in lifelong learning opportunities. The actions carried out since the end of 2015 (by that Government and the subsequent one, established in 2019, also of the Socialist Party) were comprehensive. This chapter discusses the main policies introduced in the most recent period to improve educational attainment and produce a comprehensive overview of labor market and education indicators concerning the skills of employers and employees. A comparison with selected European countries is also made.

The chapter is organized as follows. Section 2 explores the link between entrepreneurship and skills. Section 3 presents recent actions to promote educational attainment in Portugal. Section 4 discusses the dynamics of education and labor market outcomes. Section 5 concludes.

SKILLS AND ENTREPRENEURSHIP

Entrepreneurship is a hot topic in academic research, with an increasing number of publications per year, and due to its multifaceted nature, receives contributions from several scientific areas. One relevant research question concerns the determinants of entrepreneurship entry and success. Factors that affect these variables are grouped into three categories: national, regional, and individual-level. The human capital (including education and experience) of the entrepreneur is one of the most important individual-level determinants (Unger, Rauch, Frese & Rosenbusch, 2011; Simoes, Crespo, & Moreira, 2016; Mamabolo & Myres, 2020). The literature on the influence of education on self-employment points to mixed directions. Individuals with more education are more likely to find paid employment opportunities (Van der Sluis, Van Praag & Vijverberg, 2008); and simultaneously they have better tools for identifying business opportunities and are better equipped for developing their businesses. In addition, if we take into account the heterogeneity that is inherent to the individuals that are self-employed, another layer of complexity comes into play. Some studies suggest the existence of a non-linear impact on the selection toward self-employment, which can be explained by the fact that those that have less education are more likely to make the transition by necessity (Von Greiff, 2009), while those with more education are more opportunity-driven. As summarized by von Bloh, Mandakovic, Apablaza, Amorós, & Sternberg, 2020 (p. 2012-2013), "Opportunity-based entrepreneurship (OPP) covers entrepreneurial activities started voluntarily in order to gain more income or independence. In [sic] the other hand, necessity-based entrepreneurial activity (NEC) is the creation of a new business out of need, when no other appropriate employment is available to the individual in the formal job market".

Moving the focus of analysis from general to specific human capital, the influence of the experience accumulated in particular industries or markets positively affects the entry into entrepreneurship (e.g., Evans & Leighton, 1989; Poschke, 2013). This type of knowledge endows individuals with better tools for identifying business opportunities, a better network of contacts (suppliers, clients, potential employees), and more possibilities to access funding. In addition, having previous self-employment experience also increases the likelihood of starting new ventures (Eliasson & Westlund, 2013), especially if these have been developed as full-time employment.

A disruptive line of reasoning was established by Lazear (2005). This study introduced a model of occupational choice between paid employment and entrepreneurship in which the focus is put on the balance of the human capital portfolio (in opposition to the dominant perspective that puts the focus on the level of human capital). In this model, "because the entrepreneur must bring together many resources, he or she must have knowledge, at least at a basic level, of a large number of business areas. An entrepreneur must possess the ability to combine talents and manage those of others" (Lazear, 2005, p. 650). Therefore, the entrepreneur is a jack-of-all-trades. On the other hand, in the case of paid employment, it is specialization that is required and rewarded. An important proposition derived from this model relates the complexity of the production process and the supply of entrepreneurs. The basic idea is that while some production processes are simple, others are much more complex, requiring solid knowledge in many areas. Therefore, the ability of an individual to become an entrepreneur decreases with this degree of complexity (expressed in a larger number of specific skills).

Mamabolo and Myres (2020) have recently published a survey on skills and the entrepreneurial process and conclude that studies on entrepreneurship usually follow a single-phase rather than a multi-phase approach. Nevertheless, "examining skills at the different entrepreneurial phases shows that the importance and complexity of skills change across the phases. These findings suggest that skills are not static, as their importance and complexity change across the entrepreneurial phases" (Mamabolo & Myres, 2020, p. 57).

RECENT REFORMS AND ACTIONS TO PROMOTE EDUCATIONAL ATTAINMENT IN PORTUGAL

The Government established in November 2015 as a Socialist Party minority government set two key objectives for education: (i) tackling school dropout, thereby seeking a higher percentage of young people finishing secondary education; and (ii) investing in lifelong learning opportunities. The same Party won the elections in 2019 and pursued the continuity of the core policies. The main interventions can be divided into three main levels: (i) basic education; (ii) secondary education; (iii) adult learning.

Regarding basic education, taking the recommendations of international organizations such as the OECD (OECD, 2017) into consideration, the strategy aims to reduce very early school leaving. To that end several measures were adopted including fewer students per class, more diversity in the learning contents, more support for students with lower performance, identification of core competencies, increased social action mechanisms, and the end of vocational training in this level of education. In secondary education, the emphasis concerns vocational education and training (VET). The major goal was to reach 50% of students finishing secondary education coming from VET pathways. In order to reach this goal, an extensive revision of the structure of the Portuguese Education System is underway. Finally, aiming to promote the education attainment levels among the adult population, the government launched the Qualifica Program.

Given the focus of the current chapter, we concentrate our discussion on four areas: the efforts developed to assure the labor market relevance of VET; the initiatives taken to improve the quality of VET; work-based learning; and adult learning.

Actions to Ensure the Labor Market Relevance of VET

There are several mechanisms at play in Portugal to ensure the labor market relevance of VET. Most of these are associated with the initiatives of the National Agency for Qualification and Vocational Education and Training (ANQEP). This Agency was created in 2012 and has played an important role in developing mechanisms to ensure the adequacy between skills demand and supply.

The Sectoral Advisory Councils for Qualification

The National Catalog of Qualifications (*Catálogo Nacional de Qualificações*, CNQ) was created in 2007 and requires continuous updating. This process is the responsibility of ANQEP, being important to emphasize the existence of several mechanisms to assure the alignment between the contents and labor market needs.

The Sectoral Advisory Councils for Qualification (*Conselhos Sectoriais para a Qualificação*, CSQ) play a critical role at this level identifying the updates that are required in the CNQ. In more specific terms, these Councils have four objectives: (i) identify the dynamics in each sector; (ii) identify the skills needed to respond to the changes diagnosed in the sector; (iii) provide feedback on the proposals to change the CNQ; (iv) present recommendations about the design of each qualification.

System for Anticipating Skills Needs

For many years the Portuguese education and vocational training system was not prepared to anticipate labor market needs (Pedroso, 2011; Araújo, 2017). Probably the most important reason for that is the existence of several structural problems in the education field, making the response of the system to labor market needs a non-priority. Following extensive reforms, it has become possible to address additional concerns.

A central mechanism to guarantee an adequate match between skills demand and supply is the System for Anticipating Skills Needs (Sistema de Antecipação de Necessidades de Qualificações, SANQ). This system answers to the problem of having to decide on the supply of training opportunities in a context characterized by two opposite trends: the steady increase of the number of institutions offering VET courses (Azevedo, 2014), and the decreasing number of students due to demographic reasons.

The SANQ is a strategic vector of the National Qualifications System (Sistema Nacional de Qualificações, SNQ). The system is managed by ANQEP with the participation of the social partners, Public Employment Services, Agency for Development and Cohesion, and technical support from the International Labor Organization. The main goals of the SANQ include: (i) analyzing the economic outlook and labor market conditions in order to foresee the demand of skills (short and medium term); (ii) producing recommendations about key priority skills of levels 2, 4, and 5 of the National Qualifications Framework, which should be taken into consideration in the process of managing the supply of skills; (iii) making suggestions about qualifications that will be in high demand in the future.

In a recent assessment concerning the implementation of the National Reform Program 2016-2020, the independent Economic and Social Council (CES, 2018, p. 59) recognizes the importance of the SANQ, affirming that "there is the need to assure the balance between short-term training needs with a broader perspective that takes into consideration a long-term view and the expectations of all actors involved".

The Qualifica Passport

The National Catalog of Qualifications (*Catálogo Nacional de Qualificações*, CNQ) was created in 2007 and requires continuous updating. This process is the responsibility of ANQEP, being important to emphasize the existence of several mechanisms to assure the alignment between the contents and labor market needs. The Sectoral Advisory Councils for Qualification (*Conselhos Sectoriais para a Qualificação*, CSQ) play a critical role at this level identifying the updates that are required in the CNQ. In more specific terms, these Councils have four objectives: (i) identify the dynamics in each sector; (ii) identify the skills needed to respond to the changes diagnosed in the sector; (iii) provide feedback on the proposals to change the CNQ; (iv) present recommendations about the design of each qualification.

Actions to Improve the Quality of VET

Several actions were recently taken to improve the quality of VET. The recommendation of 18 June 2009 of the European Parliament and of the Council concerning the establishment of a European Quality Assurance Reference Framework for Vocational Education and Training (Recommendation 2009/C 155/01) was a challenge to the Member States in which VET-providers are more delayed in having robust quality systems. Portugal belongs to this group and was able to benefit the most with this process. Following this recommendation, the Decree-Law no. 92/2014 establishes that: (i) vocational schools should implement quality assurance systems in line with the EQAVET framework; (ii) ANQEP would be responsible not only for promoting, monitoring, and supporting the implementation of quality assurance systems assessing the results obtained by students in VET but also by certifying VET-providers as holding EQAVET systems. ANQEP designated this initiative as "Quality Assurance in Vocational Education and Training".

The following transversal criteria were established for assessing the degree of alignment with the EQAVET Framework in the conformity verification process: (i) having a culture of guarantee and improvement of quality; (ii) participation of the stakeholders in the quality assurance and improvement cycle. The other criteria relate to specific phases of the process. The recognition that the quality assurance system of the VET-provider is aligned with EQAVET results in the award of a certification. ANQEP has also developed a set of actions to educate the VET-providers about compliance with the framework.

One of the critical benefits of the EQAVET framework is that it allows the country to have a system with systematic reporting, analysis, and discussion of evidence concerning a set of indicators to focus on: (i) completion rates of the courses; (ii) placement of graduates; (iii) occupation of graduates; (iv) employers' satisfaction with

VET-graduates. This information gives an overall picture about the results that are being achieved by VET-operators. In addition, the authorities managing the network of training offers know the employability by education path, the assessment that employers make of the graduates they recruit, and if there is demand for the skills they acquired or, on the contrary, recruitment is occurring outside the training area.

Work-Based Learning and Apprenticeship Opportunities

Regarding young people, the possibility of choosing a VET program emerges mainly in upper-secondary education and includes the following possibilities:

1. Education and training programs for young people.
2. Professional programs.
3. Apprenticeship programs.
4. Specialized artistic programs.
5. Vocational programs.
6. Technological specialization programs.

The pathways for adults include, among others:

1. Programs of Training in Basic Skills;
2. Adult education and training programs, the main type of programs for adults;
3. Certified modular training;
4. Prior learning processes, recognized within Qualifica Centers;
5. Technological Specialization Programs.

Since these programs are developed for adults (in most cases with previous experience), the relevance of work-based learning is lower. This type of learning is provided in the case of professional adult education and training programs varying between 120 and 210 hours directed at those who do not have experience in the area of the course.

Adult Learning

The Government's commitment to adult education is reflected in the Qualifica Program, launched in March 2017. The main objective of the program is to contribute to the up-skilling of the adult population, a key feature in which Portugal continues to lag behind other European countries. The Qualifica Program focuses on: (i) the attainment of qualifications; (ii) assuring that the qualifications acquired are able to improve the employability of adults; (iii) adapting the supply of training opportunities to the needs of the labor market, incorporating regional diversity. Taking the year of 2020 as reference, the following goals were established: (i) to ensure that 50% of the active adult population completes secondary education; (ii) to ensure that 15% of adults participate in lifelong learning (and 25% in 2025); (iii) to contribute to the achievement of 40% of graduates from higher education in the 30-34 year age group.

These goals are mainly addressed through two instruments: the National Credit System for Vocational Education and Training and the Qualifica Passport (discussed above). In turn, the National Credit System incorporates the principles of the European Credit System for Vocational Education and Training (ECVET) and gives credit points to: (i) qualifications of the National Qualification Catalog; (ii) other qualifications included in the Information and Management System of the Education and Training Offer.

THE RECENT DYNAMICS OF EDUCATION AND LABOR MARKET OUTCOMES

One of the major bottlenecks of the Portuguese labor market is the level of educational attainment of the population. In 2009, despite the policy efforts undertaken in the years before, 69.2% of the population have less than primary, primary and lower secondary education (ISCED levels 0-2), while at the European level this group represented only 31.6% (Figure 1). This was the highest value among all countries in the European Union (EU28: 24.9%; lowest value was for the Czech Republic: 15.2%). In 2009, the national early school dropout rate was 30.9%, which compares with 14.2% for the EU28 (Figure 2). This was the highest value among European countries (thereby explaining the lower levels of educational attainment).

Portugal was able to develop a strong convergence trend toward the European average. In 2019 th0e percentage of adults holding ISCED levels 0-2 dropped 21.6 p.p. to 47.6% (in this period of time only Malta presented a similar performance, decreasing the percentage by 19.8 p.p. to 42.2%). Despite this evolution, Portugal was still the country with the second highest proportion of individuals with only this level of educational attainment (nearly twice the average of the EU28). The national early school dropout rate fell by 20 p.p. to 10.6%, making Portugal the country with the greatest improvement in this area (followed by Spain with -14 p.p. in this indicator). Although starting in the beginning of the period with similar values, in 2011/2012 the two countries began to diverge and Portugal was able to achieve a greater decline in dropout rates. To a great extent, the reforms described in Section 3 sought to tackle this problem at primary and secondary education.

The outlook for the country concerning tertiary education is slightly better. In 2009, 13.1% of the Portuguese population had higher education (with Romania,

Figure 1. Population aged 15-64 with less than primary, primary and lower secondary education
Source: Eurostat

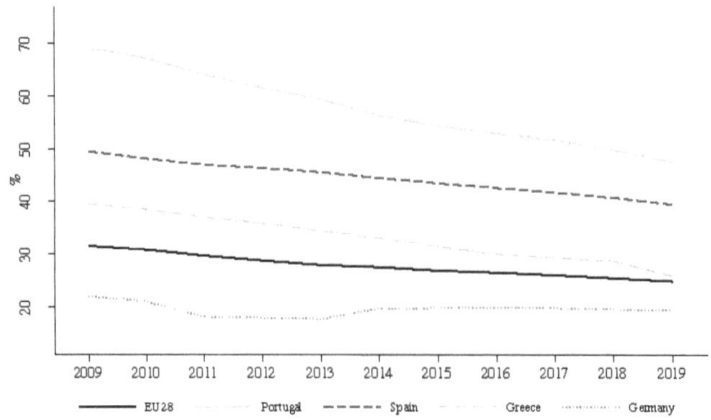

Malta, and Italy presenting lower values), which compares to an average of 22% at the European level (Figure 3). By the end of the decade adult population with higher

Figure 2. Early leavers from education and training - Percentage of the population aged 18-24 with at most lower secondary education and not in further education or training
Source: Eurostat

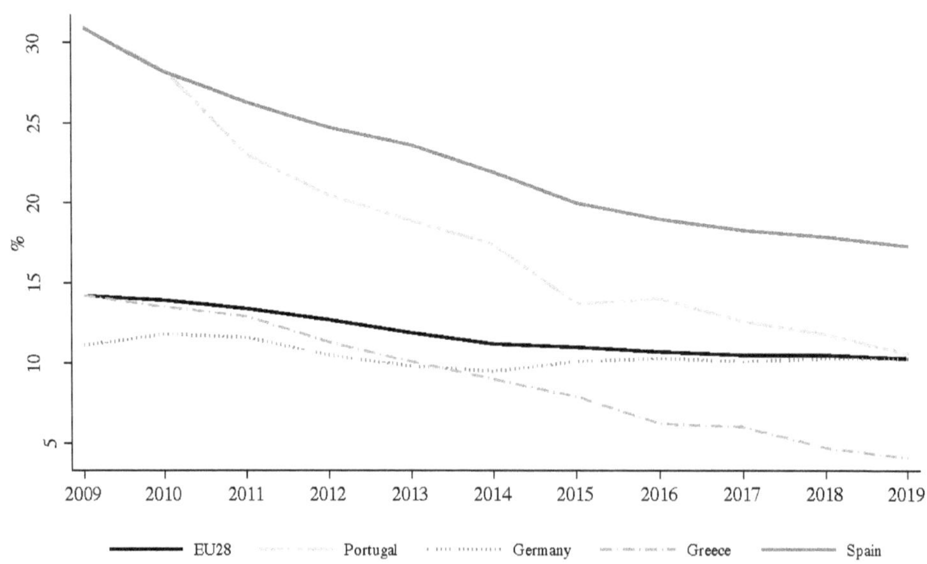

Figure 3. Population aged 15-64 with tertiary education
Source: Eurostat

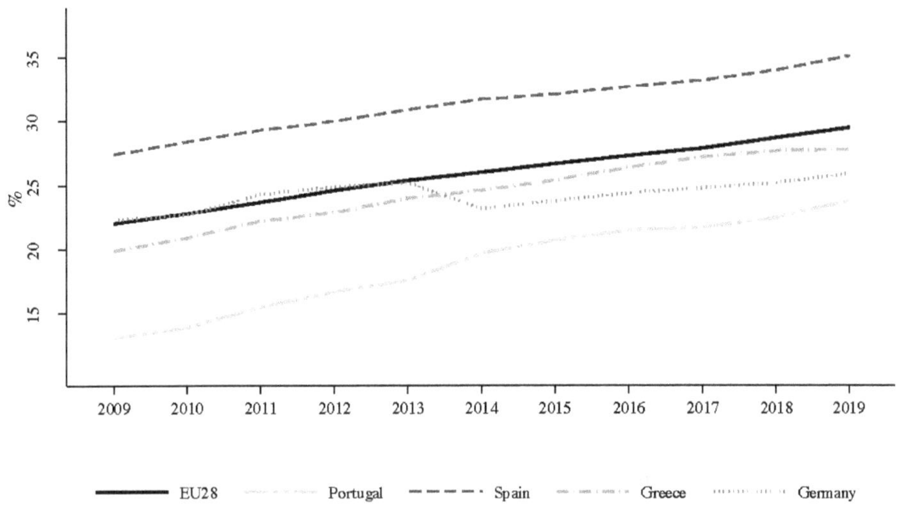

education in Portugal had increased to 23.8% (a value that is now above Slovakia, Romania, Hungary, the Czech Republic, Italy, and Croatia).

The educational attainment level of the population is important for several reasons. Let us start by stressing the strong link found in empirical analysis between education and activity rates. As years of schooling increase, individuals are less likely to be in inactivity (Figure 4). For the period of 2009 until 2019 the activity rate for males increased from 73.7% for those having at most lower secondary education, to 78.8% for upper secondary education, and 89.8% for tertiary education (for females these rates are 44.3%, 69.5%, and 84.5%, respectively). Policies aimed at raising the average level of qualifications will therefore influence activity rates and indirectly affect the employment rates and the composition of employment.

Qualifications have a strong impact on labor productivity and the growth of *per capita* income. Although there was some convergence, in 2009 labor productivity in Portugal remained below the European average (Figure 5), and stood at only 79.8% of the reference value of the EU27_2020. Despite the efforts carried out during this last decade, the situation of the country has deteriorated, dropping to 74.9% in 2019. This means that the growth rate of this variable was slower than what other countries were able to achieve (Productivity Council, 2019). As highlighted by Alves (2017, p. 137), "Portugal is experiencing a larger slowdown of productivity growth than the one occurring in advanced economies (…). Reasons for this slowdown and

Figure 4. Activity rates by gender, age groups, and highest level of education attained (%)
Source: Eurostat

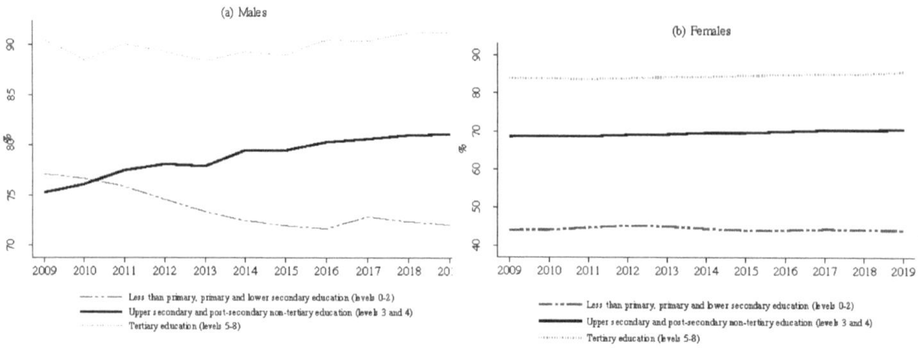

divergence with developed economies since the mid-1990s are associated with an increasing misallocation of capital, labour and skills both at a sectorial and firm level". Labor productivity gains, along with wage adjustments, are key determinants of the national cost competitiveness, which is crucial to determine the ability of domestic firms to respond to the increasing global competition (Alexandre et al., 2017). This is an especially important dimension for firms in the sector of tradable goods. The performance of these firms has a direct effect on employment levels.

At the end of 2019 the National Association of Portuguese Firms (Associação Empresarial de Portugal, AEP) issued a report highlighting the importance of skills for the productivity of the Portuguese firms. According to their arguments, skills are important but the contents taught by education providers are a critical dimension to take into consideration (an issue targeted by the initiatives described in Section 3.1). Following this line of reasoning, Veiga et al. (2019, p. 35) stress that "vocational secondary and post-secondary education will play a key role in providing answers to companies seeking intermediate technical staff with appropriate training for their needs. Thus, the objective of reaching a proportion of 50% of secondary school students enrolled in double-certified vocational education modalities, enrolled in Portugal 2020, is not only ambitious, but also desirable". In that direction, the actions implemented to assure the labor market relevance of VET are welcomed by the different stakeholders.

According to the strategic report produced by the National Strategic Reference Framework in 2012, "when compared to the EU average, the Portuguese economy is over-specialized in low value-added, low knowledge-intensive and internal market-oriented sectors in both manufacturing and services. This specialization

Figure 5. Labor productivity per person employed and hours worked (EU27_2020=100)
Source: Eurostat

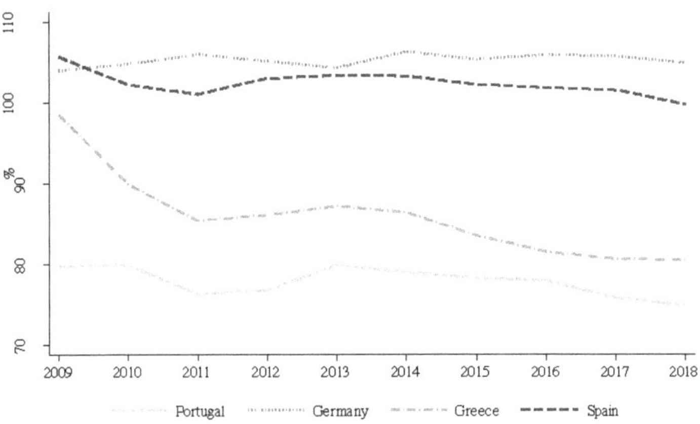

profile strongly penalizes the growth prospects of the Portuguese economy" (QREN, 2012, p. 38).

Over the last decade, paid employment increased its relative importance in total employment (from 78.9% to 83.4%). This evolution was mainly explained by a steady decrease in the number of own account workers. Nevertheless, self-employment with no employees is usually perceived as a precarious labor market situation. When the Portuguese economy entered a more favorable phase of the business cycle, a significant proportion of individuals under these conditions were able to shift toward paid employment. The share of employers in overall employment remained stable, varying between 4.75% in 2017 and 5.27% in 2013. The evolution was similar for both genders. The main difference is that women are more represented in paid employment than men are. Nevertheless, this follows a pattern that can be found in other countries too: "men have traditionally been more likely than women to start new businesses" (Global Entrepreneurship Monitor, 2020, p. 55). The relative stability found in the self-employment rate is in line with previous international surveys showing that in Portugal between 70% and 75% of entrepreneurial activities are opportunity-driven (Eurobarometer, 2012; Eurofound, 2017).

When we consider the occupational status, a very concerning fact becomes clear: the skills deficit is more pronounced among the self-employed than in the case of employees. In 2009, 79.0% of the self-employed persons had at most lower secondary education, which compares with 62.4% for employees. In both cases, for the EU28 the comparable values were 26.7% and 21.3%, respectively. Also at the European level, employees present a higher attainment level but the difference in

Table 1. Distribution of employment according to occupational status

	Overall			Males			Females		
	Employees	Own account workers	Employers	Employees	Own account workers	Employers	Employees	Own account workers	Employers
2011	78.9%	15.9%	5.2%	74.9%	17.9%	7.2%	83.4%	13.6%	3.0%
2012	78.4%	16.5%	5.1%	74.2%	19.1%	6.7%	83.0%	13.7%	3.3%
2013	78.6%	16.2%	5.3%	74.3%	18.6%	7.1%	83.2%	13.5%	3.3%
2014	80.7%	14.1%	5.2%	76.1%	16.8%	7.2%	85.7%	11.2%	3.1%
2015	82.0%	13.2%	4.8%	77.6%	15.7%	6.7%	86.6%	10.6%	2.8%
2016	82.8%	12.5%	4.8%	78.6%	15.1%	6.4%	87.2%	9.8%	3.1%
2017	83.4%	11.8%	4.8%	79.3%	14.2%	6.5%	87.8%	9.3%	3.0%
2018	83.7%	11.4%	4.9%	79.7%	13.8%	6.5%	87.9%	9.0%	3.1%
2019	83.4%	11.7%	4.9%	79.5%	14.0%	6.5%	87.5%	9.3%	3.2%

Source: National Statistics

the share of both groups is much smaller than in Portugal. There was a convergence when the analysis is developed for the year of 2019, although the self-employed with ISCED levels 0-2 still represent 50.6%. The lack of skills in management positions has strong implications at the firm level. Table 3 shows that in 2018, 96.3% of the overall number of firms had fewer than 10 workers, and that this percentage has shown a positive trend since 2009. In addition, it is also important to stress that the number of firms with more than 250 employees is only 994.

Using data for the Portuguese economy, Alexandre et al. (2017) analyze the relationship between the average schooling of managers and the average schooling of workers within the company and verify a high correlation between them. "Considering that the productivity of companies depends on the qualification of employees, our results suggest that companies with more qualified managers may be more productive, either because these qualifications allow for efficiency gains at the organization level or because they will tend to hire more qualified workers" (Alexandre et al., 2017, p. 114). Therefore, the study suggests that the investment in the opportunities for adult learning should be reinforced.

The participation of the population in lifelong learning is below the average of other Member States (Figure 6). Nevertheless, there has been significant convergence. In 2009, 6.4% of the population aged 25-64 participated in education and training over the four weeks prior to the survey (at the European level the average rate was 9.5%). In 2019, this proportion had increased to 10.5%, becoming closer to the objectives described in Section 3.4.

Table 2. Distribution of employment according to occupational status and educational attainment

	2009		2019	
	EU28	PT	EU28	PT
Employees				
Less than primary, primary and lower secondary education	21.3%	62.4%	16.1%	39.8%
Upper secondary and post-secondary non-tertiary education	50.1%	19.5%	47.8%	30.8%
Tertiary education	28.6%	18.2%	36.1%	29.3%
Self-employed persons				
Less than primary, primary and lower secondary education	26.7%	79.0%	19.1%	50.6%
Upper secondary and post-secondary non-tertiary education	45.8%	10.3%	43.9%	23.5%
Tertiary education	27.6%	10.7%	37.0%	25.8%

Source: National Statistics

CONCLUSION

An analysis of the available evidence allows us to draw two important conclusions: (i) there is an improvement of most indicators regarding the education of the population, and (ii) there is still a considerable gap in comparison to other Member States. Therefore, this area should continue to be a top priority in the political agenda.

For many years the policies have put a great emphasis on the quantitative dimension of the progress to be achieved. However, this approach has placed a less than desirable emphasis on: (i) the need for greater investment in the development of a framework to promote a better match between the demand and supply of skills; and (ii) the quality of the training offered. As described in this chapter, over this decade there has been a shift in the dominant approach. The creation of the National Agency for Qualification and Vocational Education and Training (ANQEP) was a very

Table 3. Distribution of firms according to the employment size class

	2009		2018	
	No.	%	No.	%
Total	1,199,843	100.0%	1,278,164	100.0%
Fewer than 10 employees	1,150,380	95.9%	1,229,939	96.2%
10 - 49 employees	42,667	3.6%	40,963	3.2%
50 - 249 employees	5,947	0.5%	6,268	0.5%
More than 250 employees	849	0.1%	994	0.1%

Source: National Statistics

Figure 6. Life-long learning (adult participation in education and training) - Percentage of the population aged 25-64 participating in education and training over the four weeks prior to the survey
Source: Eurostat

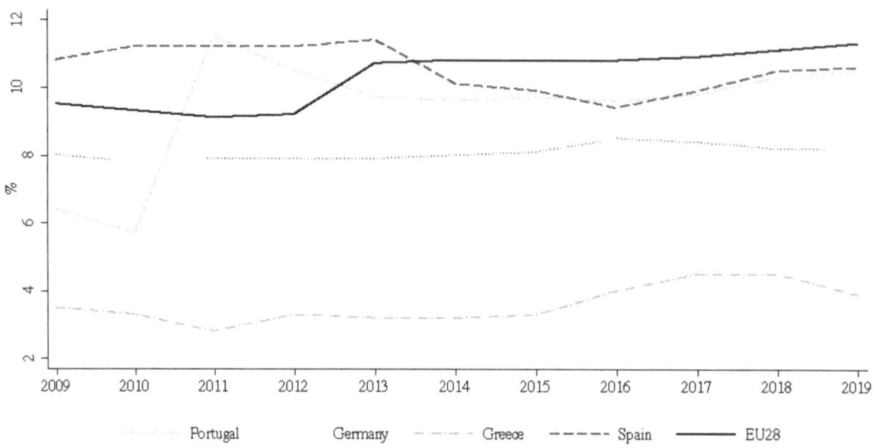

positive effort in that direction. In this chapter we have seen measures and initiatives to develop the institutional framework in order to guarantee the necessary means to assess and monitor the quality of the training being offered and to promote a closer alignment between the contents of the programs and labor market needs. In addition, there has also been a reform in VET pathways. The greater number of opportunities that young people and adults have access to in order to finish secondary education through this type of program can be an effective solution to reduce dropout rates and at the same time supply the economy with human resources possessing skills that are closer to what firms need in a variety of occupations.

International institutions such as the OECD and the European Commission have acknowledged this progress of the Portuguese Education System. Nevertheless, these types of policy take time to produce results that are captured through education and labor market statistics.

As a final remark, there is one critical issue related to this strategic commitment with vocational education and training that raises concerns in several discussions related to this topic: the mechanisms for financing these activities. Until now, these have depended heavily on European funds. In the future, when this type of funding is significantly reduced or even ceases to exist, alternative funding models will have to be found.

REFERENCES

Alexandre, F., Bação, P., Carreira, C., Cerejeira, J., Loureiro, G., Martins, A., & Portela, M. (2017). *Investimento empresarial e o crescimento da economia portuguesa*. Fundação Calouste Gulbenkian.

Alves, R. (2017). Portugal: A paradox in productivity. International Productivity Monitor. *Centre for the Study of Living Standards*, *32*, 137–160.

Araújo, S. (2017). *Raising skills in Portugal*. OECD Economics Department Working Papers, No. 1405. OECD Publishing.

Azevedo, J. (2014). *Ensino profissional em Portugal, 1989-2014: os primeiros vinte e cinco anos de uma viagem que trouxe o ensino profissional da periferia para o centro das políticas educativas*. Mimeo.

CES. (2018). *Parecer do CES sobre o Programa Nacional de Reformas 2018 (PNR 2018)*. Conselho Económico e Social.

DGERT. (2016). *Vocational education and training in Europe: Portugal*. CEDEFOP Refernet VET in Europe reports.

Eliasson, K., & Westlund, H. (2013). Attributes influencing self-employment propensity in urban and rural Sweden. *The Annals of Regional Science*, *50*(2), 479–514. doi:10.100700168-012-0501-9

Eurobarometer. (2012). *Entrepreneurship Survey of the EU*. Flash EB Series 354.

Eurofound. (2017). *Sixth European Working Conditions Survey – Update*. Eurofound.

Evans, D., & Leighton, L. (1989). Some empirical aspects of entrepreneurship. *The American Economic Review*, *79*, 519–535.

GEM. (2020). *Global Entrepreneurship Monitor 2019-2020*. London: Global Entrepreneurship Research Association.

Gouveia & Fernandes. (2017). *Structural reforms and long-term growth – a model based analysis*. Article GPEARI 05/2017.

Gouveia, A., Santos, S., & Gonçalves, I. (2017). *The impact of structural reforms on productivity: the role of the distance to the technological frontier*. OECD Productivity Working Papers, 2017-08. Paris: OECD Publishing.

Lazear, E. (2005). Entrepreneurship. *Journal of Labor Economics*, *23*(4), 649–680. doi:10.1086/491605

Mamabolo, A., & Myres, K. (2020). A systematic literature review of skills required in the different phases of the entrepreneurial process. *Small Enterprise Research, 27*(1), 39–63. doi:10.1080/13215906.2020.1730230

OECD. (2015). *OECD Skills strategy diagnostic report: Portugal 2015*. OECD Publishing.

OECD. (2017). *OECD Economic Surveys: Portugal*. OECD Publishing.

Pedroso, P. (2011). *Análise Prospectiva da Evolução Sectorial em Portugal*. ANESPO and ANQ.

Poschke, M. (2013). Who becomes an entrepreneur? Labor market prospects and occupational choice. *Journal of Economic Dynamics & Control, 37*(3), 693–710. doi:10.1016/j.jedc.2012.11.003

Productivity Council. (2019). *A Produtividade da Economia Portuguesa*. Conselho da Produtividade.

QREN. (2012). *Relatório Estratégico 2012*. Observatório do QREN.

Simoes, N., Crespo, N., & Moreira, S. (2016). Individual determinants of self-employment entry: What do we really know? *Journal of Economic Surveys, 30*(4), 783–806. doi:10.1111/joes.12111

Statistics Portugal. (2020). *Enterprises in Portugal – 2018*. Statistics Portugal.

Unger, J. M., Rauch, A., Frese, M., & Rosenbusch, N. (2011). Human capital and entrepreneurial success: A meta-analytical review. *Journal of Business Venturing, 26*(3), 341–358. doi:10.1016/j.jbusvent.2009.09.004

Van der Sluis, J., Van Praag, M., & Vijverberg, W. (2008). Education and entrepreneurship selection and performance: A review of the empirical literature. *Journal of Economic Surveys, 22*(5), 795–841. doi:10.1111/j.1467-6419.2008.00550.x

Veiga, F., Alexandre, F., Silva, J., & Arezes, P. (2019). *Crescimento da Economia Portuguesa*. Associação Missão Crescimento.

von Bloh, J., Mandakovic, V., Apablaza, M., Amorós, J., & Sternberg, R. (2020). Transnational entrepreneurs: Opportunity or necessity driven? Empirical evidence from two dynamic economies from Latin America and Europe. *Journal of Ethnic and Migration Studies, 46*(10), 2008–2026. doi:10.1080/1369183X.2018.1559996

Von Greiff, J. (2009). Displacement and self-employment entry. *Labour Economics, 16*(5), 556–565. doi:10.1016/j.labeco.2009.02.005

Chapter 4
Uprooting Poverty and Unemployment Through Youth Entrepreneurship Leadership and Skills Development

Ndwakhulu stephen Tshishonga
University of KwaZulu-Natal, South Africa

ABSTRACT

This chapter interrogates the notion of youth entrepreneurship and leadership as the pathway towards dealing with youth poverty and unemployment in the context of South Africa. Entrepreneurship is gaining currency as one of the panacea for youth unemployment and underemployment within the government cycles and youth-orientated organizations. For youth entrepreneurship and leadership interventions to yield desired results, young people should master technology and be innovative in developing and growing sustainable businesses. It is against this that this chapter argues that through entrepreneurial mind-set together with innovative skills and competencies as well as financial and infrastructural support, young people could make a dent on existing poverty and unemployment challenges. Youth entrepreneurial organizations and projects are used to demonstrate the opportunities and challenges of using youth entrepreneurship as one of the pathways to deal with poverty and unemployment in South Africa.

INTRODUCTION

Since the dawn of democracy, various policy and programme interventions were

DOI: 10.4018/978-1-7998-9581-7.ch004

experimented in an attempt to rehabilitate young people into the democratic norms of society. Youth designated institutions such the National Development Youth Agency (NDYA) and the National Youth Service Programme (NYSP) were set up with the sole purpose of advocating youth development through harnessing the potential of young people (Mlatsheni, 2012). Outside government, various youth programmes such as Harambee Youth Employment Accelerator, The Innovation Hub, The Start-Up Programme and Competition, eKasiLabs Innovation Centers and Youth Capital (Sibanda, 2021) aimed at skilling and reskilling thereby encouraging young people to start self-employment enterprises. Through such interventions, the development of youth led enterprises have become a key priority in addressing youth underemployment and underemployment. Against all odds, this chapter argues that entrepreneurial mind-set together with innovative skills, education and competencies as well as financial and infrastructural support could enable young people to curb existing poverty and unemployment challenges. Thus, for South Africa to address youth challenges such as the high unemployment rate, a lack of skills and improved employability needs to be dealt with, Mkasi & Tamukamoyo (2016, p. 18) argue that "credible and effective youth-focused institutions" are required.

It is against this background that this chapter interrogates the notion of youth entrepreneurship and leadership as the pathway towards dealing with youth poverty and unemployment in the context of South Africa. Within the government cycles and youth orientated organizations, entrepreneurship is gaining prominence as the panacea for youth unemployment and underemployment. The chapter commenced by laying the social-economic background of youth, goes to share the theoretical exposition of youth entrepreneurship and leadership, followed by the programmes of various youth entrepreneurial programmes. It further provides the critical analysis of the programmes in terms of their opportunities and challenges encountered by young entrepreneurs in their journey to address poverty and unemployment as key challenges. The chapter finally provides the future research direction and the conclusion.

BACKGROUND

Socio-Economic Situation of Youth in South Africa

In more than two decades of South African democracy, young people's socio-economic situation has not drastically changed for them to enjoy a promised "better life for all". On the social front, youth are either disengaged or indulged in life-threating activities such as drugs and alcohol above. The reality is that apartheid did not only leave the country with a scarcity of skills and high rate of unemployment, poverty and inequality (Terreblanche, 2012), but also contributed to the perpetual challenges of slow economic growth and infrastructural decay (Burger, 2018). Historically, South African youth both in rural and urban areas have experienced and continue to experience social dislocation and alienation. Noyoo, Patel and Loffell (2006) argue that prior to 1994 the position of youth was insecure and unpredictable. The apartheid regime had no programmes for African youth as they were perceived as enemies of the state. Although the apartheid regime saw them as enemies, the outside world perceived them as heroes after the 1976 Soweto uprisings (Duncan, 2016). It is an undeniable fact that through the relentless effort and bravery of youth that South Africa gained its democracy, which is enjoyed by many in post-apartheid era (Heffernan & Nieftagodien, 2016). Despite young people's contribution to the liberation struggle, the youth are still in the majority of those mostly affected by poverty, unemployment, lack of housing and the HIV/ AIDS epidemic (Tshishonga, 2019). Poor education in basic and higher education has thwarted youth opportunities to receive good qualifications with skills and knowledge attractive to the labour market. Mismatch between the economy and education, according to Handley (2016, p. 79) produces many job seekers with low skills. This is made worse by higher education institutions who graduate a huge cohort of students with what Bhorat & Kanbur (2006, p. 6) call 'wrong kinds of tertiary qualifications' hence graduate unemployment. FMF was inclusive in its demands, free, quality and decolonized system of education (Eloff, 2017, Naidoo, 2016). The legacy of apartheid affects all young people with African youth bearing the brunt of racially oppressive and constraining policies that continue to haunt them to this day. Added to the historical legacies and new challenges in the wake of democracy, problems facing youth continue to multiply. Policies and empirical studies often portray young people as having overwhelming challenges (Mafema & Tshishonga, 2010). Predominant challenges facing these young people, especially those residing in the townships, range from poverty, youth unemployment, health related predicaments such as HIV/ AIDS to social ills in the form of alcohol and drug abuse, crime, suicide and depression (World Bank Group, 2018).

Amongst the youth, poverty and unemployment remain a perpetual challenge with young people between the ages of 15 and 24 being the most affected by this twin social-economic challenge. The relationship between unemployment and poverty is very complex in South Africa. While the unemployment rate has remained very high due to the rising rate of poverty, the poverty rate has equally remained high due to the high level of unemployment. In order to address poverty, the danger of unemployment must also be checked through a very effective employment policy process (Odeh, & Okoye, 2014). According to Okafor (2011), youth unemployment in any country is an indication of far more complex problems. South Africa has very high levels of unemployment amongst young people. In 2010, '51% of 18 to

24 year olds were unemployed by the strict definition, as compared with a national average of 25.3%; while about two-thirds of all 18 to 24 year olds who were able and available to work were unemployed by the broad definition' (Altman, Mokomane, & Wright, 2014, p. 348). In South Africa, youth are viewed as those falling within the category between 14- to 35-year-olds. The reasons categorising youth up to 35 years is based on the context of inequalities, underdevelopment and marginalisation young people suffered during the apartheid are and still enduring in the democratic dispensation (Buckley, 2017). South Africa's National Youth Policy (NYP) defines a young person as any individual between the ages of 14 and 35 years (NYP, 2015-2020) the African Youth Charter defines youth as those between the ages 15 and 35 years (NYP, 2015-2020). From these definitions, age category is the common denominator in the conceptualisation and understanding of youth as a societal cohort.

In South Africa, more than one-half of all 18 to 24 year olds live under a poverty line of R604 per month (2011 Rand) and more than two-thirds live under a poverty line of R1113 per month (Altman, Mokomane, & Wright, 2014). Poverty and unemployment go hand in hand, as demonstrated by the above fact that the working youth living above poverty-line in the poorest groups are very low. Fourie (2011) describes this as 'bi-directional causality' which is a link between unemployment and poverty. Unemployment causes poverty and poverty contributes to unemployment and its persistence (Fourie, 2011). One of the contributing factors to continued poverty and unemployment is the view that poverty persists not only because of a shortage of resources, but because some people have incompetent economic systems, or lack of natural resources, and or because poor people lack determination. Poverty is an outcome of human social relationships because, social features of relationships set the structure of economic exchange, further influencing the way in which resources are distributed (Cloete, 2015). In that regard, the manner in which people assign and allocate things of value, is dependent on how integrated and segregated their relationships are and how powerful they are in relation to one another. Therefore, youth unemployment and poverty are the outcome of an economic system that seems to exclude them from participating in economic activities (Honwana, 2013). Predominant challenges facing these young people, especially those residing in the townships, range from poverty, youth unemployment, health related predicaments such as HIV/ AIDS to social ills in the form of alcohol and drug abuse, crime, suicide and depression (World Bank Group, 2018). Thus, the legacy of apartheid affects all young people with African youth bearing the brunt of racially oppressive and constraining policies that continue to haunt them to this day (Cebekhlu, 2018). Added to the historical legacies and new challenges in the wake of democracy, problems facing youth continue to multiply.

The brutal reality is the failure of the current government, the youth have not been afforded the opportunities to develop their potential educationally and economically

(Mafema & Tshishonga, 2010). Socio-economic hardships faced by youth especially the unemployed made Cebekhulu (2018) to conclude that young people are unable to size the existing opportunities in the form of various programmes designed to empower them with skills development. Without job opportunities, qualifications and experience, young people will continue to experience socio-economic exclusion and marginalization. This situation can be made even worse by the societal perceptions that still view youth challenges as self-inflicting and require clinical rehabilitation rather than developmental and skills development and interventions as the solution. This situation is a time bomb and unless youth issues are given urgent and pragmatic attention, South Africa will again witness more social unrests and looting which took place in both Gauteng and KwaZulu-Natal provinces in the month of July 2021.

The exclusion and marginalization of young people has led to the support of youth entrepreneurship as the pathway to escape poverty and unemployment. However, considering that South African youth lack the entrepreneurial skills, absence of adequate financial resources, ability by young people to start successful businesses as well as a slow growing economy. In South Africa, the economic growth has failed to absorb the youth into the job market due to rapid urbanization, poor education, and disintegrating family structures (Mafema & Tshishonga, 2010).

YOUTH ENTREPRENEURSHIP AND LEADERSHIP

Entrepreneurship is associated with business innovative and creative ideas and endevours. From such ideas, business enterprises are developed into successful formal job creation companies. Entrepreneurship is defined as a process where entrepreneurs seize business opportunities with limited resources (Rankhumise & Venter, 2016). For Desai (2012, p. 54), entrepreneurship is the process of identifying and starting a business venture, sourcing and organizing the required resources and taking both the risks and rewards associated with the business venture. Through the practice of entrepreneurship, entrepreneurs are able to optimally apply their skills, expertise and aptitudes in developing and growing their businesses (Strydom & Niewenhuizen, 2012). Above, entrepreneurs are unique in their radical ideas to create businesses from nothing and particularly in taking risks (Costa, 2021). In essence it could be argued that entrepreneurs are path finders who can spot new business opportunities, organize businesses using their own or borrowed fund (Hossain et al., 2009). Innovative ideas centred on entrepreneurship is a catalyst for economic development and growth both in the developed and developing world (Wong, Ho & Autio, 2005), and a process of venture creation (Lackeus *et al.,* 2015).

For youth entrepreneurship and leadership interventions to yield desired results, young people should master technology and be innovative in developing and growing sustainable businesses. Entrepreneurship is associated to the work of entrepreneurs, people who according to Markley et al, (2005) create and grow an enterprise by transforming ideas into business ventures. Attempts were made by government and other NGOs through their established employment stimulus schemes and youth led programmes to provide needed labour skills and entrepreneurial education. In particular, the youth designated institutions such the National Development Youth Agency (NDYA) and the National Youth Service Programme (NYSP) were set up with the sole purpose of advocating for youth development through harnessing the potential of young people (Mlatsheni, 2012). Outside government, various youth programmes such as Harambee Youth Employment Accelerator, The Innovation Hub, The Start-Up Programme and Competition, eKasiLabs Innovation Centers and Youth Capital are aimed at skilling and encouraging young people to start self-employment enterprises. Through such interventions, the development of youth led enterprises have become a key priority in addressing youth underemployment and unemployment. This chapter argues that an entrepreneurial mind-set together with innovative skills and competencies as well as financial and infrastructural support; young people could curb existing poverty and unemployment challenges. Amongst the challenges confronting youth are high unemployment rates, a lack of skills and improved employability needs to be dealt with hence, Mkasi & Tamukamoyo (2016, p. 18) argue that credible and effective youth-focused institutions are required. Thus, mentorship could be helpful in addressing mind-set redress and should be incorporated in the entrepreneurship training and education programmes.

Youth can escape underdevelopment and the deprivation trap through economic endeavours initiated, run and managed by youth themselves. Thus, promoting youth enterprise is slowly gaining momentum as a viable economic alternative for unemployed youth (Chigunta, 2002 cited in Zuze, 2012). Considering that young people are resourceful and energetic, embarking on entrepreneurial projects beyond the common ones such as community gardening, cleaning, catering, co-operatives and so forth are imperative. The use of technology to create innovative projects in areas of security, marketing and advertisement, agriculture, ICT, recycling are funded by national and international organisations. There are increasing opportunities for formal education and training and learnerships and internships for youth empowerment as well as employment services aimed at improving job searches and job matches. Apart from these interventions, there is a promotion of entrepreneurial activities among youth in urban, rural and township areas (The Presidency, 2014).

Entrepreneurship is associated to the work of entrepreneurs, people who according to Markley et al, (2005) creates and grows an enterprise through transforming ideas into business ventures. Government through its established centres and units tried to encourage young people to market the ideas and strategies for self-employment. In particular, the youth designated institutions such the National Development Youth

Agency (NDYA) and the National Youth Service Programme (NYSP) were set up with the sole purpose of advocating youth development through harnessing the potential of young people (Mlatsheni, 2012).

According to Marinic (2016), entrepreneurship is a powerful driver of economic growth and also a source of job creation. Entrepreneurship draws people together to work in conjunction for a particular desired purpose. The state school and other institutions need to develop the foundation of entrepreneurship and enterprise especially for youth in the sense that it can secure growth and employment for the majority of youth who are not working and live below poverty line (Dufour & Jacq, 2017). Educational entrepreneurship should be founded on the basis of encouraging students to be entrepreneurs and schools, communities, public and private sectors need to be the main actors in ensuring that youth entrepreneurship thrive (Dahlstedt & Hertzberg, 2012). Another pressing fact that needs attention for youth entrepreneurship is that, there is a poor match between education and available employment opportunities, causing vast youth unemployment. According to Naong (2011), there is a mismatch between education and type of employment opportunities available in the labour market, as the result youth entrepreneurship should be revived and encouraged. The graduates and unemployed youth suffer from unemployment "because they have chosen the wrong field of study in which available jobs are rare" (Dufour, & Jacq, 2017, p. 9). While youth do not find jobs because of irrelevant choice or lack of skill and unpredicted labour market, youth entrepreneurship should be a solution. According to Gheorghe (2013), youth entrepreneurship can be an alternative source of income for the youth and can also be a way of getting experience.

YOUTH ENTERPRENEURIAL PROGRAMMES

This section deals with youth related entrepreneurial programmes such as Harambee Youth Employment Accelerator, The Innovation Hub, The Start-Up Programme and Competition, eKasiLabs Innovation Centers and Youth Capital. These programmes were established with the primary purpose of skilling and reskilling thereby encouraging young people to start self-employment enterprises.

Harambee Youth Employment Accelerator

Harambee was conceptualised as an employment accelerator, which would serve the needs of companies within their group, by recruiting, training, and placing work-ready employees especially youth in job positions that are available (Harambee, n.d). The Harambee programme is in response to problems that predominantly plagued the insurance companies in their network, as it does in many other sectors such as retail, business process outsourcing (BPO), hospitality, and financial services, namely, that they were struggling with recruiting and retaining the right demographic profile of employees for entry level positions (De Kok, 2019, p.161). Graham, & Mlatsheni (2015) adds that Harambee Youth Employment Accelerator is not-for-profit organisation reputable to quicken youth inclusion and break unemployment and poverty cycles. Addressing barriers in the labour market, Harambee provides an end-to-end, solution that is intended to change disadvantaged 18 to 28-year-old unemployed job seekers, without prior work experience, into entry level jobs (World Bank Group, 2017). Therefore, it can be argued that this programme identifies potential sectors in the South African economy where there are possible job opportunities and emphasizes the need to understand the recruitment needs of employers in those sectors.

The Innovation Hub

In the increasingly competitive, agile and fast developing business environment, there is an increasing demand on firms to be innovative in order to remain competitive. The "emerging global markets and rapid advancements in world order means markets are becoming ever more competitive", thus innovation is the way to adapt in such environs (Wu, & Eriksson-Lantz, 2017, p. 4). As a result, innovation hubs have progressively been adopted by different sectors including businesses, science firms and local governments to ensure that people are equipped for changing environments. The innovation hub fosters economic development and competitiveness in businesses (Giaccone & Longo, 2016). The Innovation Hub can be considered as a business incubator that typically charges young entrepreneurs at the very initial seed stage in exchange for its services, while updating their skills and capacity development. In support of innovators and entrepreneurs that drive and stimulate socio-economic development, the unemployment, poverty and other social illnesses are reduced (Sibanda, 2021).

The Start-Up Programme and Competition

Youth entrepreneurship development through start-up projects plays a key role in the formation of South African government policies as a result of the high poverty and unemployment rate. According to the "2014-2015 Global Entrepreneurship Monitor (GEM) report, South African youth entrepreneurship propensity is the lowest in Africa with 23.3% as compared to Malawi and Uganda with 55.2% and 55.4% respectively" (Mbuya, 2021, p. 2). The start-up programmes are meant to skill and position non-working class particular youth while significantly contributing to the creation of employment and economic development. Steenekamp, van der Merwe and Athayde (2011) indicate that it is crucial to nurture entrepreneurial skills, in early stages in order to kindle a culture of entrepreneurship among the youth population. Forrest and Jali (2012) also suggested that Start-Up Programme and competition fills the need not only to position the youth with the essential skills to be future entrepreneurs, but also to inspire them to become agent for transformation in their communities. Therefore, youth participation in such a programme can have a positive impact on social and economic development and unemployment and poverty reduction.

eKasi Labs Innovation Centers

South Africa is encountering high unemployment rate, low economic growth and a disappointing youth statistics who venture into business (Chimucheka, 2014). In light of this assertion, Chimucheka (2014) recommends that in order to stimulate economic growth, reduce youth unemployment rate and increase work opportunities, entrepreneurship education should be the focus point for the way out. The eKasiLabs programme "is an extension of The Innovation Hub's service offering which spread across the five economic corridors in Gauteng, fostering and cultivating a culture of innovation and entrepreneurship in townships", (Department of Economic Development (2019/21, p. 104). The eKasi Labs Programme is the vehicle to promote the culture of innovation and entrepreneurship in the townships in line with the innovation hub in order to expand the success of developing entrepreneurs. The eKasiLabs programme focuses on new innovative output as well as innovative entrepreneurship in communities through business development (De Beer, et al., 2017).

ANALYSIS OF YOUTH ENTREPRENEURIAL PROGRAMS

Skills Development for Youth Entrepreneurs

- **Towards developing entrepreneurial mind-set**

The changing nature of job demands throughout the world requires qualities that include adaptability, initiative and leadership, objectivity and integrity, critical thinking and judgment, and information integration (US State Department, 2014). The development systems that aims to create entrepreneurial mind-set must reflect these realities with a paradigm shift in thinking to create new programs or upgrade current ones which develop these qualities and skill sets to compete effectively with the global labour force. Currently there are more than 3.3 million students worldwide studying courses which are not related to entrepreneurship, hence the need to advantage and develop entrepreneurial mind-set (Macready & Tucker, 2011). With such a diverse array of youth attending educational institutions globally, the teaching profession must instil entrepreneurial mind-set who for more effectively trained students (Richert-Kazmierska, & Lechman, 2014).

- **Cultivating skills through entrepreneurial education**

Entrepreneurial education is in line with the idea of the Danish Foundation for Entrepreneurship (Moberg et al., 2012, p.14) which states that "content, methods and activities supporting the creation of knowledge, competencies and experiences that make it possible for students to initiate and participate in entrepreneurial value creating processes". This idea of entrepreneurial education and skills cultivation leans on acting upon opportunities and ideas that one should transform them into value, which can be financial or other. As a result, experts promote entrepreneurial education as entrepreneurship is seen as a major engine for economic growth and job creation (Lackeus, 2015). The necessity for cultivating skills through entrepreneurial education is frequently perceived as a response to the increasingly globalized, uncertain and complex world, requiring everyone in society to be gradually equipped with entrepreneurial competencies.

Placing entrepreneurial learning at the core of all education, throughout the education system (European Commission, 2013), builds on the idea that entrepreneurship can be taught (Henry, Hill and Leitch, 2005) and entrepreneurial attributes developed (Jones and Iredale, 2010). Entrepreneurial education in the context of developing entrepreneurial mind-set is therefore apparent on how to start a firm, as well as developing approaches that develop entrepreneurial mind-sets and actions (Fayolle and Klandt, 2006). Therefore, cultivating skills through education is not only about creating job opportunities but it is also about being more creative, opportunity oriented, proactive and innovative.

- **Support for young entrepreneurship**

The elimination of young entrepreneurs' problems and to prosper young entrepreneurship among society education is very important. Entrepreneurial support such as provision of skills for creativity, innovation, risk-taking and ability to understand entrepreneurial environment and entrepreneurial knowledge in terms of, fundamentals of business practices, financial literacy and opportunities (Fatoki & Chindoga, 2011). Entrepreneurship support develops attributes, expertise, and attitudes necessary for emerging entrepreneurs and increases entrepreneurship awareness as a career choice for young people. The success rate of entrepreneurship rises when entrepreneurship motivation, support, and education is delivered, and its problems are solved. The majority of young entrepreneurs believe that entrepreneurship support through education and training increase the success rate of productions dramatically (Sitoula, 2015).

Entrepreneurship support either socially or with physical resources could be a solution to various challenges regarding learning possibilities of money, procedures of management, taxation, regulations, business contacts and dealing with a fear of failure (Jakubczak, 2015). Most of the youth are detached and disconnected from the socio-business world. Without social skills and identities as well as emotional intelligence, businesses led by youth are unlikely to grow and sustained themselves (Booysen, 2017). Thus, acquiring knowledge and competencies in the complex world of entrepreneurship demand that young people obtain cognitive and emotional intelligence as well as social intelligence in order to stay afloat.

- **Self-empowerment through youth entrepreneurship**

Youth entrepreneurship is a tool that could be employed and also deployed for economic empowerment in order to arrest the growing rate of insecurity caused by poverty and unemployment (Shefiu, 2016). A thriving economy would require a greater number of young people who are self-motivated, willing and able to become entrepreneurs; who can launch and successfully develop their own ventures, and who will become inventors and innovators championing their organisations. Entrepreneurship empowers young people to build a vision for the future, and give access to exploration of new opportunities (Oviawe, 2010). Empowerment through youth entrepreneurship allows youth to explore wider opportunities and educational aspirations, adopting the skills, understanding and interest to be successful in employment and entrepreneurship.

Youth entrepreneurship empowerment "promotes innovation and development; it also encourages young people to find new solutions, ideas and ways of doing things", (Mtenga, 2013, p. 52). Moreover, self-empowerment through youth entrepreneurship creates employable skills to youth which they can apply in identifying opportunities within their surroundings and be able to use them for creating self-employment. In the entrepreneurial industry, self-empowerment is intrinsically linked to self-employment with requisite skills to take calculated risks taking into account all forms of social, economic, cultural and political capitals (Mahlobo, 2016). Apart from the programmes profiled in this chapter, Tshishonga and Matsiliza (2021) argue that young people have not taken advantage of public work programmes to gain skills and access to resources.

CHALLENGES FACSED BY YOUTH ENTREPRENEURS

- **Problems of Youth Entrepreneurship**

The most frequent encountered problems by young entrepreneurs are the acquisition of resources, premises of venture, information problems, product/service problems, timing problems, regulatory problems and organizational problems in the state of setting a new business (Van Gelderen, Thurik, & Patel, 2011). The various nature of challenges which are also geographical hardens the opportunities to effectively venture into the corridors of entrepreneurship. Gwija, Eresia-Eke, & Iwu, (2014) adds that, expensive business registration, insufficiency of good employee and lack of business management are the main stumbling blocks for young Africans in the Western Cape, South Africa.

- **Financial Problems and Barriers**

The quality of the entrepreneurship ecosystem is determined by the accessibility and diversity of financial resources. Young people who own or want to start enterprises do not have strong financial and institutional infrastructure to get loans (Er, Şahin, & Mutlu, 2015). Securing loans could be a way forward but since they do not have good financial history it is difficult for loaners to land them money. On the other hand, being reliant on loans could delay reaching of secure financing. If young entrepreneurs carry student loans, their possibility to reach secure financing becomes much harder (Schoof, 2006). Therefore, finances prove to be a challenge for young entrepreneurs.

The non-availability of financial resources remains a challenge for young people to pursue their entrepreneurial ideas and businesses. In some cases, where financial resources are available, young people lack innovative ideas, which can be funded. While some youth have no kick-start money others lack social networks to enable them to gain entrepreneurial skills and role models in the business industry. In South Africa, financial and operational environment is according to Mahlobo (2016) not supportive for entrepreneurs especially in terms of its regulations, policies and access to financial capital. Banks being the major finders of emerging businesses implies that young people cannot afford no matter how creative and innovative their ideas are.

- **Social Influences on Young Entrepreneurs**

The social approach against entrepreneurship affects the motivation of entrepreneurs. According to Hofstede (1980), some society and family structures are more inclined to entrepreneurship than others. The decisions of young people toward entrepreneurship are affected by their societal and family background which influence theirs. Bad society examples and insufficient support from personal environment can creates big problems for young entrepreneurs who might view entrepreneurship opportunity as salaried employment instead of entrepreneurship (Aslam & Hasnu, 2016). Young people do not venture into new spaces when they lack support in the business environment, they also fear failure and embarrassment hinders them from applying their entrepreneurial ideas (Fatoki & Chindoga, 2011).

The emergence of tenderpreneurship has contributed to a situation where young people have developed an attitude that job creation and wealth can come easily through government tenders. The dominance of this culture has killed the spirt of hard work and creativity when it comes to developing entrepreneurship businesses. Tenderpreneurship is the practises of kick-starting the business based on wining tenders while entrepreneurship is often driven by innovation, creativity, motivation and capacity. Amassing wealth through tenderpreneurship blinded young people from identifying business opportunities, taking risks and use their ability to use perceived opportunities into business ventures to address prevailing poverty and unemployment. In its practice sense, tenderpreneurship is that the association of business; politicians and civil servant are in collision to defraud state resources (Mabaso & Cawee, 2020). The completion to secure government contracts result into bribery and corruption (Sefalafala, 20200). Thus, popularity associated with wealth based on tenderpreneurship has culminated into social status by young people without solidi entrepreneurial education and training. Pooe, Ngcaweni & Zwane (2020) allude to the fact that poor entrepreneurial training reinforces and is reinforced by wider inequities in post-1994-economy.

- **Uprooting poverty and Unemployment through youth Entrepreneurial Businesses**

Young people cannot depend on formal education and qualifications to uproot prevailing poverty and unemployment. Ramphele (2012) and other scholars are skeptical about the status of South African educational system and its ability to equip young people and students to be skilled and competitive in the information economy. In the current situation, having qualifications and degrees is not adequate for youth and university graduates to secure employment in the world underpinned by a high demand for technological skills and competencies. Young people of all categories are therefore demanded to upskill and reskill themselves in order to navigate the work environment dictated by the Fourth Industrial Revolution and Artificial Intelligence (Marwala, 2020). This is imperative for South African youth who are still haunted by the legacy of Bantu Education manifesting through intergenerational deprivation (Tshishonga, 2019).

In order for youth to uproot unemployment and underemployment and further navigate the competitive world of work, universities are compelled to package their academic programmes based on developing creative and critical skills, emotional intelligence and competencies as well as entrepreneurial skills and education. The repertoire of skills and knowledge obtained from university will not only prepare graduates for the world of work, but also equip them with entrepreneurship mind-set and education to create their own businesses. With the growing rate of unemployed youth and graduate, programmes outlined above (Harambee Youth Employment Accelerator, The Innovation Hub, The Start-Up Programme and Competition, eKasiLabs Innovation Centers and Youth Capital) (Sibanda, 2021), will not only arm youth with necessary skills and knowledge, but also prepare them to venture into entrepreneurial world. This implies utilizing acquired entrepreneurial skills and knowledge to move away from being job seekers to innovative job creators. In this regard, the promotion and support of youth entrepreneurship remains one of the strategies government and youth-based organizations could put their creative ideas into income generating projects and businesses. Thus, exercising entrepreneurial leadership is imperative for youth initiated businesses to yield positive results. The exercise of entrepreneurial leadership for Booysen (2017) has a bearing in leading and managing available business resources and development of new businesses and wealth based on innovation.

DIRECTION FOR FUTURE REASERCH

The current study explored youth entrepreneurship as a solution towards addressing the twin challenge of poverty and unemployment among youth in South Africa. However, considering the persistence of youth unemployment, there is a need for a comprehensive study that focuses on the ingredients and incentives to promote sustainable youth run and managed entrepreneurial businesses within the provinces and across the South African borders and within the SADC region. Further studies could be instrumental in motiving young people on various strategies effective to initiate and run successful income programmes.

CONLUSION

This chapter has shared some insight on the prospects, dynamics and challenges of using youth entrepreneurship and leadership interventions as a strategy to address the scourge of youth unemployment in South Africa. It became apparent that for young people to take advantage of the limited opportunities available for them to advance their lives socially and economically, acquiring skills and knowledge relating to entrepreneurship is imperative. Considering the growing poverty and unemployment among the youth, developing entrepreneurship based o self-empowerment was found to be a powerful instrument towards releasing young people's untapped potential to be their own socio-economic liberators. This chapter profiled a few but relevant youth related entrepreneurial programmes such Harambee Youth Employment Accelerator, The Innovation Hub, The Start-Up Programme and Competition, eKasiLabs Innovation Centers and Youth Capital to demonstrate that with the right support and resources youth can be the socio-economic pathfinders. As deliberated in this chapter, these programmes were established to skill and reskilling young people in order for them to be confident in starting and managing their own self-employment enterprises to address youth poverty and unemployment.

In addition, the chapter highlighted cultivating entrepreneurial mind-set, acquiring skills and education, indispensable support, self-empowerment and finally establishment of the actual entrepreneurial business as the some ingredients for youth to succeed in running sustainable businesses. However, despite these key elements, the chapter also shed light on the challenges facing young entrepreneurs in their journey to run their businesses and eradicating poverty and unemployment in South Africa. Lastly, the chapter cautions young people about the tenderpreneurship as a panacea towards addressing prevailing poverty and unemployment challenges in South Africa.

REFERENCES

Ahlstrom, D., Chang, A. Y., & Cheung, J. S. (2019). Encouraging entrepreneurship and economic growth. *Journal of Risk and Financial Management, 12*(4), 178. doi:10.3390/jrfm12040178

Altman, M., Mokomane, Z., & Wright, G. (2014). Social security for young people amidst high poverty and unemployment: Some policy options for South Africa. *Development Southern Africa, 31*(2), 347–362. doi:10.1080/0376835X.2013.873346

Aslam, S., & Hasnu, S. A. F. (2016). Issues and constraints perceived by young entrepreneurs of Pakistan. *World Journal of Entrepreneurship, Management and Sustainable Development, 12*(1), 50–65. doi:10.1108/WJEMSD-03-2015-0015

Booysen, L. (2017). Leadership Excellence across Cultural settings. In Leadership Excellence: Perspectives from the Front Line (pp. 31-51). KR Publishing.

Buckley, S. (2017). *Conceptualisations of Youth and Implications for Policy: A Study of Four Cases in Aotearoa/New Zealand*. Te Herenga Waka – Victoria University of Wellington.

Cebekhulu, A. (2018). *Umhlaba Uyahlaba! The World is Thorny*. Reach Publishers.

Chimucheka, T. (2014). Entrepreneurship Education in South Africa. *Mediterranean Journal of Social Sciences*, *5*(2), 403–416.

Cloete, A. (2015). Youth unemployment in South Africa-a theological reflection through the lens of human dignity. *Missionalia: Southern African Journal of Mission Studies*, *43*(3), 513–525. doi:10.7832/43-3-133

Dahlstedt, M., & Hertzberg, F. (2012). Schooling entrepreneurs: Entrepreneurship, governmentality and education policy in Sweden at the turn of the millennium. *Journal of Pedagogy*, *3*(2), 242–262. doi:10.2478/v10159-012-0012-x

De Beer, J., Armstrong, C., Ellis, M., & Kraemer-Mbula, E. (2017). *A scan of South Africa's maker movement*. Open African Innovation Research Working Paper.

De Kok, M. B. (2019). *Remedying unemployment through affirmative development: The validation of the prediction model and qualitative assessment of an employment accelerator programme* (Doctoral dissertation). Stellenbosch University.

Department of Economic Development. (2019/20). *Estimates of Provincial Revenue and Expenditure*. Gauteng Provincial Treasury.

Dufour, M., & Jacq, L. (2017). *Engagement of young graduates in Entrepreneurship: Entrepreneurship*. Strategy and Business Development.

Er, B., Şahin, Y. E., & Mutlu, M. (2015). Alternative Sources of Financing for Entrepreneurs. *Present Situation and Recommendations*, *1*(1), 31–54.

European Commission. (2013). *Entrepreneurship Education: A Guide for Educators*. Author.

Fatoki, O., & Chindoga, L. (2011). An investigation into the obstacles to youth entrepreneurship in South Africa. *International Business Research*, *4*(2), 161–169. doi:10.5539/ibr.v4n2p161

Fayolle, A., Klandt, H. (2006). Issues and newness in the field of entrepreneurship education: new lenses for new practical and academic questions. *International Entrepreneurship Education*, 1-17.

Forrest, C., & Jali, P. (2012). *LED is a young person's game: youth employment and local economic development.* http://www.durban.gov.za/City_Services/Economic_Development/PSIR/Documents/Skills@ Work%20FINAL%20Vol5.pdf

Fourie, F. (2011). *The South African unemployment debate: Three worlds, three discourses?* Academic Press.

Gheorghe, N., & Georgeta, N. L. (2013). The Entrepreneurship, an Actual Challenge for the Young Graduates of Higher Education Institutions. *Ovidius University Annals, Series Economic Sciences, 13*(1).

Giaccone, S. C., & Longo, M. C. (2016). Insights on the innovation hub's design and management. *International Journal of Technology Marketing, 11*(1), 97. doi:10.1504/IJTMKT.2016.073318

Graham, L., & Mlatsheni, C. (2015). Youth unemployment in South Africa: Understanding the challenge and working on solutions. *South African Child Gauge, 2*, 51-59.

Gwija, S. A., Eresia-Eke, C., & Iwu, C. G.Chux Gervase Iwu. (2014). Challenges and Prospects of Youth Entrepreneurship Development in a Designated Community in the Western Cape, South Africa. *Journal of Economics and Behavioral Studies, 6*(1), 10–20. doi:10.22610/jebs.v6i1.465

Harambee. (n.d.). https://harambee.co.za/harambee/

Hofstede, G. (1980). Culture's Consequences: International Differences in Work-Related Values. Academic Press.

Honwana, A. (2013). *The Time of Youth; Works, social Change and Politics in Africa.* Kumarian Press.

Hossain, A., Zaman, K. N. A., & Nuseibeh, R. (2009). Factors influencing women business development in the developing countries. *The International Journal of Organizational Analysis, 17*(3), 202–224. doi:10.1108/19348830910974923

Jakubczak, J. (2015). Youth entrepreneurship barriers and role of education in their overcoming-pilot study. *Managing Intellectual capital management, and innovation for sustainable knowledge and learning and inclusive society*, 1775-1782.

Jones, B., & Iredale, N. (2010). Enterprise education as pedagogy. *Education + Training, 52*(1), 7–19. doi:10.1108/00400911011017654

Lackeus, M. (2015). *Entrepreneurship in education: What, why, when, how.* Background paper.

Mabasa, K., & Cawe, A. (2020). Introduction: The future of Black Empowerment and entrepreneurship. In Beyond Tenderpreneurship: Rethinking Black Business and Economic Empowerment (pp. 1-26). Johannesburg: Mapungubwe Institute for Strategic Reflection (MISTRA).

Macready, C., & Tucker, C. (2011). Who goes where and why: An overview and analysis of global educational mobility. In *IIE and AIFS Foundation*. Institute of International Education.

Mafema, E., & Tshishonga, N. (2010). Living on the margins: the effects of intergenerational poverty amongst youth at Cato Manor in Durban. In Contemporary Social Issues in Africa: Cases in Gaborone, Kampala and Durban (pp. 179-194). Pretoria: Africa Institute of South Africa.

Mbuya, M. J. M. (2021). Youth Entrepreneurship in South Africa: A Progress Review. Academic Press.

Meyer, D. F., & Mncayi, P. (2021). An Analysis of Underemployment among Young Graduates: The Case of a Higher Education Institution in South Africa. *Economies*, *9*(4), 196. doi:10.3390/economies9040196

Moberg, K., Stenberg, E., & Vestergaard, L. (2012). *Impact of entrepreneurship education in Denmark*. The Danish Foundation for Entrepreneurship–Young Enterprise.

Moerane, P. (2016). *A study of graduates' experience of unemployment in Durban, South Africa* (Doctoral dissertation). University of Kwa-Zulu Natal.

Mtenga, V. D. (2013). *Empowering youth through entrepreneurship skills training: The case of Makangarawe ward* (Doctoral dissertation). The Open University of Tanzania.

Naong, M. (2011). Promotion of Entrepreneurship Education - A Remedy to Graduates and Youth Unemployment – A Theoretical Perspective. *Social Sciences*, 181–189.

National Youth Policy. (2015 – 2020). We are generation 2020. We don't want a hand-out, we want a hand up! #NYP2020.

Ndinga-Kanga, M., van der Merwe, H., & Hartford, D. (2020). Forging a resilient social contract in South Africa: States and societies sustaining peace in the post-apartheid era. *Journal of Intervention and Statebuilding*, *14*(1), 22–41. doi:10.1080/17502977.2019.1706436

Netshitenzhe, J. (2021). Beating the counter-revolutionaries: South Africa's people are the ultimate defenders of democracy. *Daily Maverick*. https://www.dailymaverick.co.za/article/2021-08-02-beating-the-counter-revolutionaries-south-africas-people-are-the-ultimate-defenders-of-democracy/

Odeh, M. A., & Okoye, C. O. (2014). Poverty reduction policy and youth unemployment in Nigeria. *Public Policy and Administration Research*, *3*(4), 92–103.

Okafor, E. E. (2011). Youth unemployment and implications for stability of democracy in Nigeria. *Journal of Sustainable Development in Africa*, *13*(1), 358–373.

Oviawe, J. I. (2010). Repositioning Nigerian youths for economic empowerment through entrepreneurship education. *European Journal of Educational Studies*, *2*(2), 113–118.

Pooe, T. K., Ngcaweni, W., & Zwane, N. (2020). "Lost in Transformation"? A case study of black youth entrepreneurship in post-apartheid South Africa. In Beyond Tenderpreneurship: Rethinking Black Business and Economic Empowerment (pp. 313-335). Johannesburg: Mapungubwe Institute for Strategic Reflection (MISTRA).

Rae, D., & Woodier-Harris, N. R. (2013). How does enterprise and entrepreneurship education influence postgraduate students' career intentions in the New Era economy? *Education + Training*, *55*(8/9), 926–948. doi:10.1108/ET-07-2013-0095

Ramphele, M. (2012). *Conservations with My Sons and Daughters*. Penguin Books.

Richert-Kazmierska, A., & Lechman, E. (2014). Creating entrepreneurial mind-set. *Innocase Project*, (2012-1).

Schoof, U. (2006). *Stimulating Youth Entrepreneurship: Barriers and incentives to enterprise start-ups by young people*. Youth and Entrepreneurship. http://search.ebscohost.com/login.aspx?direct=true&db=buh&AN=48077905&site=ehost-live

Shefiu, R. (2016). Youth empowerment leveraging on entrepreneurship. *Continental. Journal of Sustainable Development*, *7*(1), 45–60.

Sibanda, M. (2021). *Nuts & Bolts: Strengthening Africa's Innovation and Entrepreneurship Ecosystems*. Tracey McDonald Publishers.

Sitoula, T. (2015). *Challenges and Prospects of Youth Entrepreneurship in Kathmandu*. https://brage.bibsys.no/xmlui/bitstream/handle/11250/2385486/Sitoula.pdf?sequence=1

Steenekamp, A. G., Van der Merwe, S. P., & Athayde, R. (2011). An investigation into youth entrepreneurship in selected South African secondary schools: An exploratory study. *Southern African Business Review*, *15*(3), 46–75.

Terreblanche, S. (2012). *Lost in Transformation: South Africa's search for a New Future since 1986*. KMM Review Publishing Company.

The Innovation Hub. (n.d.). *Innovatively Working Together To Connect All of Us*. Accessed from: https://www.theinnovationhub.com/press-room-media/media/the-innovation-hub-celebrates-south-africas-innovators-and-entrepreneurs-during-global-entreprenuership-week-nws461

Tshishonga, N. (2019). The Effects of Intergenerational Poverty and Unemployment on South African Township Youth. In J. Kurebwa (Ed.), *Participation of Young People in Governance Processes in Africa* (pp. 1–21). IGI Global. doi:10.4018/978-1-5225-9388-1.ch001

Tshishonga, N., & Matsiliza, N. S. (2021). Addressing the Twin Challenges of Poverty and Unemployment through Community Work Programmes in South Africa. *African Journal of Development Studies*, *11*(2), 217–235.

United States Education: Statistical Profile. (2014). *Nation Master*. Retrieved from: https://www.nationmaster.com/country-info/profiles/UnitedStates/Education

Van Gelderen, M., Thurik, R., & Patel, P. (2011). Encountered Problems and Outcome Status in Nascent Entrepreneurship. *Journal of Small Business Management*, *49*(1), 71–91. doi:10.1111/j.1540-627X.2010.00315.x

Wong, P. K., Ho, Y. P., & Autio, E. (2005). Entrepreneurship, innovation and economic growth: Evidence from GEM data. *Small Business Economics, 24*(3), 335–350. doi:10.100711187-005-2000-1

World Bank Group. (2017). *Harambee Youth Employment Accelerator: Solutions for Youth Employment*. https://www.s4ye.org/sites/default/files/S4YE%20Digital%20Jobs%20Case%20Study%20-%2012.%20Harambee%20Youth%20Employment%20Accelerator.pdf

Wu, K. Y., & Eriksson Lantz, C. (2017). *Building and managing an innovation hub: A case study of the challenges and opportunities faced by a Northern Swedish innovation hub*. Academic Press.

KEY TERMS AND DEFINITIONS

Entrepreneurial Leadership: A mind-set that focuses organizations on turning problems into opportunities that create economic and social value.

Entrepreneurial Mindset: An entrepreneurial mind-set is a set of skills that enable people to identify and make the most of opportunities, overcome and learn from setbacks, and succeed in a variety of settings.

Skills Development: An ability and capacity acquired through deliberate, systematic, and sustained effort to carryout complex activities involving ideas (cognitive skills), things (technical skills), and/or people (interpersonal skills).

Youth Entrepreneurship: Practical application of enterprising qualities, such as initiative, innovation, creativity, and risk-taking into the work environment (either in self-employment or employment in small start-up firms).

Youth Unemployment: Youth unemployment is the unemployment of young people, aging between 18–35 years old. An unemployed person is defined as someone who does not have a job but is actively seeking work.

Chapter 5
Role of Entrepreneurship Education in Small Business Startups Among Graduates in Nigeria

Johnson Dare Adeeko
https://orcid.org/0000-0002-8248-8809
Bamidele Olumilua University of Education, Science, and Technology, Nigeria

Oluwaseyitanfunmi Osunade
University of Ibadan, Nigeria

ABSTRACT

Nigeria is currently going through a period of economic stagnation. There is unemployment among the educated and illiterate workforce in large numbers. Tertiary institutions reacted to this challenge by teaching students entrepreneurship courses at the undergraduate level. The entrepreneurship courses offered aimed at creating small business owners so as to reduce the dependence on white collar jobs. This study examined the role of entrepreneurship education in small business startups among the past students of University of Ibadan (UI) who took the course on Basic Entrepreneurship Education (ETR 301). The course aimed to fill the gap between entrepreneurship education and ability to be an entrepreneur. Former University of Ibadan students who had taken the course on entrepreneurship were surveyed using Google Forms. The results showed that entrepreneurship education as provided through the course ETR 301 has significant influence on entrepreneurial mindset and entrepreneurial skills of university students, therefore, should be sustained.

DOI: 10.4018/978-1-7998-9581-7.ch005

INTRODUCTION

The trend in the job market is gradually moving from seeking white or blue-collar jobs to creating jobs through enterprise development. The formal sector is unable to meet the employment demands of the growing young population, as a result; millions of young Africans create jobs for themselves and others. More emphasis is also placed on skills acquisition and business development in all sections of the economy and the Nigerian government is intensifying awareness for entrepreneurship through training and financial support. Business consultants all over the country are calling for a change of mindset for the youth so that they can reduce their attention securing jobs in corporate organizations and start harnessing business opportunities in the country. (Adeyemo 2017)

However, there has been a tremendous increase in the recent decades among other countries regarding attention toward entrepreneurship, Nigeria has also witnessed and showed a significant interest in various entrepreneurship fields, both in higher educational settings, policy making and business. Accordingly, measures and mechanisms have been proposed to develop entrepreneurship in the public and private sectors as well as universities. Entrepreneurship has been recognized as the determinant or pivotal element of economic growth and development (Rebmann and Mickiewicz 2020). This is because Entrepreneurship leads to the creation of small and medium scale businesses, providing employment opportunities, income generation, uplifting of standard of living, and utilization of human, material and financial resources of a country in the right direction. Because of the importance and role of Entrepreneurship in the economy, the federal government of Nigeria through national universities commission introduced Entrepreneurship education course under general studies programmes which is mandatory for all undergraduate students in the country. It is believed that it will facilitate the development of favourable attitude towards Entrepreneurship and its education (Emmanuel and Daniya 2017)

The benefits of entrepreneurship education have been praised by both researchers and educators; nevertheless, its impact on entrepreneurial competencies and the ability to become an entrepreneur has remained largely unexplored. It is of primary importance to understand whether entrepreneurship education raises career abilities to be an entrepreneur generally. The purpose of this experimental study, therefore, is to contribute to filling this gap. Previous studies including the work of Karimi and Lans (2018) have dwelled most on entrepreneurial intentions of students but this research work moves further to correlate the number of small businesses started by students of entrepreneurship education with the entrepreneurship course they offered.

The aim of this study is to analyse the role of Entrepreneurship Education in the startup of small businesses using students of University of Ibadan, Nigeria who took the entrepreneurship course as case study. Two parameters, entrepreneurial mindset and entrepreneurial skills were used for the evaluation.

LITERATURE REVIEW

During the last decades, entrepreneurship has become an important economic and social topic as well as a well-known research topic in the world (Morris et al., 2017). Entrepreneurship is important because it leads to increased economic efficiencies, brings innovation to market, creates new jobs, and raises employment levels (Matthias Filser 2020). Most empirical studies conducted indicate that entrepreneurship can be taught and that education can foster entrepreneurship (Kuratko, 2018; Henry et al. 2019; Fejes et *al.,* 2018) which has led to a dramatic rise in the number and status of entrepreneurship programs at colleges and universities.

Entrepreneurship education focuses on the development and application of an enterprising mindset and skills in the specific contexts of setting up a new venture, developing and growing an existing business, or designing an entrepreneurial organization. It aims to produce graduates with the mindset and skills to come up with original ideas in response to identified needs and shortfalls, and the ability to act on them. In short, having an idea and making it happen (Hegarty and Porter, 2018). A small business startup is an entrepreneurial venture which is typically a new emerged, fast growing business that aims to meet a marketplace need by developing a viable business model around innovative product, service, process or a platform (Rebmann A and Mickiewicz T. 2020) Small scale enterprise constitute essential ingredients in the lubrication and development of any economy (Emmanuel and Daniyo, 2017)

Entrepreneurial mindset indicates a way of thinking about business and its opportunities that capture the benefits of uncertainty (Dhliwayo and Vuuren, 2019). According to Bahareh and Hossein (2017) in Senge's Model of Entrepreneurship, it portrays the innovative and energetic search for opportunities and facilitates actions aimed at exploiting opportunities. Establishing an entrepreneurial mindset is important to sustain the competitiveness of economic organizations and the socioeconomic lifestyle of the population through value and job creation. This importance is portrayed in the sense that it enables supporters of new ideas to establish organizations with new valuable ideas, which are resourced and developed in an encouraging and enabling culture (Thompson, 2019).

Entrepreneurial skills are the basic skills necessary to enable you start, develop, finance and succeed in your home enterprise (Adeyemo, 2017).Entrepreneurial skills include taking the initiative, intuitive decision making, making things happen, networking, identifying opportunities, creative problem solving, strategic thinking, and personal effectiveness. Entrepreneurship education extends beyond knowledge acquisition to a wide range of emotional, intellectual, social, and practical skills. Entrepreneurship education aims to produce graduates who are capable of identifying opportunities and developing ventures,

Jamieson, in the work of Raposo and Arminder (2017), developed a three-category framework for entrepreneurship education. He distinguished between education about enterprise, education for enterprise and education in enterprise, recognizing the roles that the different types of education represent. The first category deals mainly with awareness creation, and has the aim of educating students on the issues about setting up and running a business. Education for enterprise, the second category, deals more with the training of aspiring entrepreneurs for a career in self-employment with the aim of encouraging participants to set-up and run their own business. Individuals are taught the practical skills required for business management. The third category, education in enterprise, includes management training for established entrepreneurs and focuses on ensuring the expansion and development of the business.

Pioch and Dweck (2017) developed two self-theories and characteristics of entrepreneurial mindset by providing insight into the psychological (motivational) processes essential for achievement. They stated that individuals hold either an entity theory of intelligence, known as a fixed mindset or an incremental theory of intelligence, known as a growth mindset. Individuals with a fixed mindset belief that one's intelligence, abilities, talents, and attributes are permanent and unchangeable. They further infer that one's ability comes from talents rather than from their slow development of skills through learning and as such give up or decline in the face of setbacks. . Individuals with a growth mindset, on the other hand believe that one's ability and success are due to learning, that intelligence can grow and change with effort and believe in trying other approaches or seeking help when face with difficulties and tends to adopt learning goals. They concluded that most great business leaders who have been successful had a growth mindset, since building and maintaining excellent organizations in the face of constant change requires it.

Chell (2018) also reviews some of the key literature regarding the nature of entrepreneurship, noting that the knowledge, skills and abilities of entrepreneurs and innovators are many and various, but as with personality traits, they interact with situations. One implication of these observations is that, while there may be some personality traits that are associated with entrepreneurial behaviour, in principle it is possible to identify a range of entrepreneurial skills that can be learnt, practiced and improved, in turn enhancing the prospects of business survival and growth.

Some researchers have found that entrepreneurship education is positively related to opportunity recognition. Olugbola (2017) noted this in a number of empirical studies, and suggested that the increased knowledge that educated individuals hold provides them with a greater resource from which to draw links to new idea, thus creating new innovative opportunities. Cognitive skills including counterfactual thinking and analytical thinking have been identified as crucial for entrepreneurial growth especially in translating opportunity recognition into information processing ultimately leading to transforming a market opportunity into a business (Chell, 2018). Therefore, courses and workshops on tools to enhance creativity and entrepreneurial decision-making are likely to prove beneficial in facilitating the growth of small businesses.

A survey of entrepreneurship education research published between 2008 and 2009, based in leading academic journals, was conducted by Gormon and King (2017). They suggested that the central theme in the research they reviewed was the extent to which formal education can contribute to entrepreneurship. They argued that the existing empirical research published, during the time period of their review seem to suggest a consensus among researchers that entrepreneurship can be taught and that entrepreneurial attributes can be positively influenced by educational programmes. In the research work by Neneh (2017), entrepreneurship education is considered as a lifelong learning process that encourages the development of personal qualities and skills to enable the learner to survive in the world of business. A positive relationship was established between entrepreneurship education and business creation.

METHODOLOGY

The survey research design was used to determine the relationship between entrepreneurship education and small business startups among former Basic Entrepreneurship and Innovation (ETR 301) students of University of Ibadan.

The email addresses of past students were collected from the Centre for Entrepreneurship and Innovation, University of Ibadan. The study used all the email addresses provided as sample for the study. A survey instrument in digital format was designed in Google Forms with Likert scales. The questionnaire was created by the researcher and validated by the research supervisor in consultation with social science researchers. The questionnaire was administered via previous students email addresses and 167 responded to the questionnaire. Both descriptive and inferential statistics were used to analyse the data collected. Data on demographic information were analysed with simple percentage and frequency distribution table. The first hypothesis was analysed with multiple regression to establish the impact of Entrepreneurship Education on entrepreneurial mindset of students, the other hypothesis was analyzed with Spearman's rank correlation to establish the relationship between Entrepreneurship Education and entrepreneurial skills of students.

Table 1. Socio demographic characteristics of respondents

		Frequency	Percentage N=196
Gender			
	Male	99	59.3%
	Female	68	40.7%
Marital Status			
	Single	105	62.9%
	Married	62	37.7%
Age			
	15-25	55	32.9%
	26-36	74	44.3%
	37-47	32	19.2%
	48 & above	6	3.6%
Education qualification			
	Undergraduate	33	19.8%
	B.Sc.	97	58.1%
	M.Sc & above	37	22.2%

Source: Questionnaire Response (Adeeko, 2021)

RESULTS AND DISCUSSION

This is divided into two parts. The first part focused on the descriptive analysis of responses gathered using the frequency counts and percentage weights. The second part focused on the testing of hypothesis using Regression analysis and Spearman's Rank Correlation statistics.

Majority of the respondents representing 99(59.3%) are male while 68 (40.7%) are female as shown in the Table 1. The profile depicted by the demographics is representative of the expected respondents based on year of graduation and lifespan of the entrepreneurship course.

In Table 2, student's pre-knowledge before taking the entrepreneurship course is presented.

Table 3 shows the students perception of the entrepreneurship course and its potential impact.

The impact of the entrepreneurship course on the students is presented in Table 4.

Table 2. Frequency and percentage of entrepreneurial mindset and skills of students before entrepreneurship education

QUESTIONS	YES %	NO %
You had thought of setting up your own business before entrepreneurship education class	39 (23.4%)	128 (76.6%)
You had started your business before Entrepreneurship Education class	61 (35.5%)	106 (63.5%)
You had knowledge of entrepreneurial skills before Entrepreneurship Education class	71 (42.5%)	96 (57.5%)
You had orientation about self -employment before Entrepreneurship Education class?	37 (22.5%)	130 (77.8%)

Source: Questionnaire Response (Adeeko, 2021)

Hypotheses Testing

H_{01}: Entrepreneurship education has no significant effect on entrepreneurial mindset of university students.

Decision Rule: Reject **H_0**, if the p-value in the analysis of variance table is less than 5% and accept if otherwise.

Table 3. Frequency and percentage of impact of entrepreneurship education on students' entrepreneurial mindset and skills during entrepreneurship education

QUESTIONS	SD %	D %	N %	A %	SA %
Entrepreneurship Education introduces business startup ideas to students.	5	4	18	85	55
	3%	2.4%	10.8	50.9%	32.9%
Entrepreneurship Education helps in building positive entrepreneurial mindset of the students.	4	11	17	70	65
	2.4%	6.6%	10.2%	41.9%	38.9%
Entrepreneurship Education plays significant role in developing entrepreneurial skills of students.	3	8	16	80	60
	1.8%	4.8%	9.6%	47.9%	35.9%
Entrepreneurship education introduces opportunity identification process to students.	2	11	17	76	61
	1.2%	6.6%	10,2%	45.5%	36.5%
Entrepreneurship education teaches students how to develop and implement business ideas.	3	7	25	79	53
	1.8%	4.2%	15%	47.3%	31.7%
The teaching of entrepreneurship creates future and effective entrepreneurs.	2	15	20	75	55
	1.2%	9.0%	12%	44.9%	32.9%

Source: Questionnaire Response (Adeeko, 2021)

Table 4. Frequency and percentage of impact of entrepreneurship education on entrepreneurial mindset and skills of students after entrepreneurship education

QUESTION	SD %	D %	N %	A %	SA %
Entrepreneurship classes have fully prepared me for entrepreneurship career.	7	14	31	59	56
	4.2%	8.4%	18.6%	35.3%	33.5%
I started my own business due to Entrepreneurship Courses attended at the University of Ibadan.	25	29	39	36	38
	15.0%	17.4%	23.4%	21.6%	22.8%
I was taught how to scan my environment, generate ideas and identify customers' needs in entrepreneurship education class.	13	24	36	44	50
	7.8%	14.4%	21.6%	26.3%	29.9%
Entrepreneurship Education has built the confidence to be self-employed in me.	3	11	28	58	67
	1.8%	6.6%	16.8%	34.7%	40.1%

Source: Questionnaire Response (Adeeko, 2021)

Decision: Since the P-value in the ANOVA Table (***0.017***) is less than ***5%,*** we reject $\mathbf{H}_0$. Therefore, Entrepreneurship education has a significant effect on entrepreneurial mindset of university students.

$\mathbf{H}_{02}$**:** There is no significant relationship between entrepreneurship education and entrepreneurial skills of university students.

Decision rule: Reject $\mathbf{H}_0$, if p-value is less than ***0.05*** and accept if otherwise.

Decision: Since the p-value (***0.029***) of the spearman's rank correlation is less than ***0.05***, we reject $\mathbf{H}_{02}$. Therefore, there is a statistically significant relationship between entrepreneurship education and entrepreneurial skills of university students.

The estimated result showed that 23.4% of the respondents had thought of setting up their business before entrepreneurship education class while 76.6% never thought

Table 5. Analysis of variance showing effects of entrepreneurship education on students

Model	Sum of Square	Degree of freedom	Mean Square	F	Sig.
Regression	20.829	1	20.829	186.737	0.017
Residual	18.404	165	0.112		
Total	39.234	166			

Table 6. Spearman's rank correlation table

		Entrepreneurship Entrepreneurial	Education Skills
Spearman'rho	correlation coefficient	1.000	0.029
Entrepreneurship Education	Sig (2-tailed)		0.642
	Number of observation	167	167
Entrepreneurial Skills	correlation coefficient	0.029	1.000
	Sig.(2-tailed)	0.642	
	Number of observation	167	167

of setting up any business. This indicates that entrepreneurial education has positively impacted the entrepreneurial mindset of students as 76.6% of students never thought of setting up their own business until entrepreneurship class. Also, 36.5% of the respondents had started their business before entrepreneurship education class while 63.5% had not setup any business before entrepreneurship education class which indicates that the larger percentage of the respondents started their own business after attending entrepreneurship class.

Also, based on the results, 83.8% of the respondents agree that entrepreneurship education introduces business ideas and opportunity identification process to students while 5.3% disagree. This indicates a positive relationship between entrepreneurship education and entrepreneurship skills. This finding is consistent with the findings of prior studies such as Bahareh and Hossein (2017) who found that entrepreneurship education is positively related to opportunity recognition. The results also revealed that 77% of the respondents agree with the statement that the teaching of entrepreneurship education creates future and effective entrepreneurs while 13.2% disagree with the statement, this indicates a positive correlation between Entrepreneurship education and entrepreneurial effectiveness and it is supported by the work of Neneh (2017) which establish a positive relationship between entrepreneurship education and business creation. The study concluded that entrepreneurship education is a lifelong learning process that encourages the development of personal qualities and skills to enable the learner to survive in the world of business.

From the results, it has been shown that that 68.8% of the respondents agree with the statement that entrepreneurship education has fully prepared them for their entrepreneurship career while 12.6% disagree with the statement; this indicates positive effects of entrepreneurship education on the development of entrepreneurial mindset of students. This is supported by findings of Gormon and King (2017), which affirmed that entrepreneurship can be taught and that entrepreneurial attributes can be positively influenced by educational programmes. Results also showed that74.8%

of the respondents agree with the statement that entrepreneurship education has built the confidence to be self employed in them while 8.4% disagree with the statement and this indicates that entrepreneurship education has set straight the mindset of students to be self-employed. This lend support to the empirical findings Chell 2018 that taking entrepreneurship education course has positive effects on students' entrepreneurial attitude

It has also been established from the results that 44% of the respondents agree with the statement that they started their own business as a result of entrepreneurship courses attended at the University of Ibadan while 32.4% of them disagree with the statement, this indicates that larger percentage of the respondents started their own business as a result of entrepreneurship course attended. The estimated result showed that 90.1% of the respondents started their business/venture between 2009 and 2016 which fall within the scope of study while only 9.1% of the respondent did not start any business during the period of study. From the results 27% of the respondents got their business ideas and entrepreneurial skills from entrepreneurship education class, university of Ibadan while the remaining percentage was shared among the remaining five sources but entrepreneurship education had the highest percentage.

CONCLUSION

Based on the empirical investigation conducted, entrepreneurship education has a significant effect on entrepreneurial mindset of university students. There is a statistically significant relationship between entrepreneurship education and entrepreneurial skills. There is a statistically significant relationship between entrepreneurship education and emergence of students' owned entrepreneurial ventures which indicates a correlation between entrepreneurship education and small business startups among the students of entrepreneurship education. These relationships demonstrate that entrepreneurship education plays a significant role in the ability of entrepreneurship students to set up small businesses. Entrepreneurship education for university students should be sustained. Students should seize the opportunities that entrepreneurship education presents to enable them to prepare for future entrepreneurial activity and opportunity.

ACKNOWLEDGMENT

The authors appreciate the support of Centre for Entrepreneurship and Innovation, University of Ibadan for the email addresses of previous students of ETR 301 provided.

REFERENCES

Adeeko, J. D. (2017). *Role of Entrepreneurship Education in the Ability of Students to Set up*. Academic Press.

Adeyemo, S. A. (2017). *Understanding and Acquisition of Entrepreneurial Skills: A Pedagogical Re-Orientation for Classroom Teacher.* University of Lagos.

Bahareh, A. N., & Hossein, J. (2017). *Effective Approach toward Entrepreneurship*. Research paper in Senges's Learning Organization. Payame Noor University Iran.

Chell, E. (2018). Review of Skill and the Entrepreneurial Process. *International Journal of Entrepreneurial Behaviour & Research*, *19*(1), 6–31. doi:10.1108/13552551311299233

Dhiliwayyo, S., & Vuuren, V. (2019). Evolution View of Entrepreneurial Mindset Theory. *International Journal of Business and Social Science*, *10*(6). Advance online publication. doi:10.30845/ijbss.v10n6p13

Dweck, C. (2017). *Mindset: The New Psychology of Success, Self-theory, Mindset: Key Takeaways*. Stanford University.

Emmanuel, O. O., & Daniya, A. A. (2017). Development of small and Medium Scale Enterprises. *Arabian Journal of Business and Management Review.*, *1*(7), 2.

Fejes, A., Nylund, M., & Wallin, J. (2018). How do Teachers Interpret and Transform Entrepreneurship Education? *Journal of Curriculum Studies*, *51*(4), 554–566. doi: 10.1080/00220272.2018.1488998

Filser, M., Tiberius, V., Kraus, S., Zeitlhofer, T., Kailer, N., & Müller, A. (2020). Opportunity Recognition: Conversational Foundations and Pathways Ahead. *Entrepreneurship Research Journal*, *0*(0), 20200124. Advance online publication. doi:10.1515/erj-2020-0124

Gorman, G., & King, W. (2017). *Research Perspectives on Entrepreneurship Education, Enterprise Education and Education for Small Business Management*: A ten year literature review. *International Small Business Journal*, *15*(3), 56–77. doi:10.1177/0266242697153004

Hegarty, C., & Porter, S. (2018). Rediscovering Enterprise: Developing appropriate University Entrepreneurship Education. *Education + Training*, *5*.

Henry, C., Hill, F., & Leitch, C. (2019). Entrepreneurship Education and Training: Can Entrepreneurship be Taught? Part 1. *Education + Training*, *47*(2), 98–111. doi:10.1108/00400910510586524

Karimi, S., & Lans, T. (2018). Testing Relationship between Personality. *Characteristics Contextual Factors and Entrepreneurial Intentions in Developing Country*, *52*(3), 227–240. PMID:26334129

Kuratko, D. F. (2018). *Corporate Entrepreneurship: A Critical Challenge for Educators and Researchers*. SAGE Journal Author Gateway. doi:10.1177/2515127417737291

Morris. (2017). Assessing the Impact of Entrepreneurship Education Programmes: A New Methodology. *Journal of European Industrial Training*, *30*(9).

Neneh, N. B. (2017). *An Exploratory Study of Entrepreneurial Mindset in the Small and Medium Enterprise*. Department of Business Management, University of the Free State.

Olugbola, S. A. (2017). Exploring Entrepreneurial Readiness of Youth and Startup Success Components: Entrepreneurship Training as a Moderator. *Journal of Innovation and Knowledge*, *2*(3), 155–171. doi:10.1016/j.jik.2016.12.004

Pioch, S., & Dweck, C. S. (2017). Startup Intelligence: New Opportunities for Entrepreneurs of the Digital Economy Through Knowledge-Based Market Decisions. *Emerging Trends in Entrepreneurial Finance Conference*. 10.2139srn.2963682

Raposo, M., & Armida, P. (2017). *Entrepreneurship Education: Relationship between Education Entrepreneurial Activity*. University of Beira Interior.

Rebmann, A., & Mickiewicz, T. (2020). Entrepreneurship as Trust. *Foundations and Trends in Entrepreneurship*, *16*(3), 244–309. doi:10.1561/0300000088

Thompson, E. R. (2019). Individual Entrepreneurial Intent. *Construct Classification and Development of an Internationally Reliable Metric*, *33*, 65–67.

Section 2
Entrepreneurship Programs

Chapter 6
Upskilling Graduates and Young Professionals Through Entrepreneurship Programmes in South Africa

Ndwakhulu stephen Tshishonga
University of KwaZulu-Natal, South Africa

ABSTRACT

This chapter evaluates the youth entrepreneurship programmes aimed at upskilling and socialising both the graduates and young professionals in the world of work. Their socio-economic exclusion and marginalisation have led to the growing youth unemployment, unemployability, and discontent while among the graduates, the unemployment has become an emerging phenomenon. This chapter, therefore, argues that for youth to escape the scourge of unemployment, exclusion, and marginalisation, entrepreneurship coaching and mentoring as well as entrepreneurial education and mind-set are imperative. The chapter found that with progressive policy support, skills, and mentoring programmes, young people are able not only to create self-employment, but to also emerge as drivers of innovative entrepreneurial programmes. Thus, without requisite skills and access to the market, youth will continue to exist in the periphery of the mainstream economy. Case studies and secondary sources were used to analyse the opportunities and challenges faced by youth entrepreneurship programmes in South Africa.

DOI: 10.4018/978-1-7998-9581-7.ch006

INTRODUCTION

In the prevalence of youth unemployment, entrepreneurship has become a panacea. In Africa, particularly in South Africa, young people are disillusioned with no or limited prospects for securing sustainable job opportunities for themselves (Honwana, 2013; Tshishonga, 2019). The reality is that young people have been at the forefront for the liberation struggles which culminated into dismantling colonial and apartheid regimes in Africa. Their involvement did not only deprive them of their youth, but also denied them golden opportunities to advance themselves in areas of education, economics, welfare and entrepreneurship. Thus, political exclusion, which occurred during the apartheid era closed the doors for youth to engage in the economic opportunities in the democratic dispensation. It is therefore not surprising that the advent of democracy in Africa and in particular South Africa, policies and programmes have been developed with the primary aim of restoring young people's dignity and advancement of their socio-economic development. Despite these policies, youth are still among the most deprived, excluded and marginalized socially, politically and economically. Among this cohort of population, youth exclusion and marginalization manifest itself through growing poverty, unemployment, lack of educational and economic opportunities for them to lead decent lives (Netshitenzhe, 2021). Hicks & Buccus (2016) reiterated this by stating that youth population is characterized by unemployment, poor education and unsettling sense of discontent. The paradox is that nations often hail youth as the cream or the future of the nation while at the same time perpetuating anti-youth tendencies and behaviours that impede their development towards being responsible and full citizens. The disturbing reality is that the existing political opportunity structures and participation of young people have not translated into economic opportunity for them to unlock their potential (Sika, 2017). These anti-youth development tendencies and behaviors further aggravate youth underdevelopment and marginalization.

It is against this background that this chapter provides a critical evaluation of youth entrepreneurship programmes designed to upskill and socialize both the graduates and young professionals in the world of work. This chapter, therefore, argues that for youth (graduates) to escape the scourge of unemployment, exclusion and marginalisation, entrepreneurship coaching and mentoring as well as entrepreneurial education and mind-set is imperative. The quest for skilled and innovative young workforce, led the South African government to introduce various programmes directed at upskilling and training youth and graduates. Fundamental to these programme interventions is the exposure to skills set and environment that nurture innovation and entrepreneurial spirit. This chapter used existing youth entrepreneurial related programmes to showcase the potential of young people's ability to address the prevailing challenges of young unemployment and un-employability. Selected programme interventions are assessed using a) fostering the entrepreneurship mind-set, b) job creation, c) acquisition of entrepreneurial and management skills as well as the creation of innovative and entrepreneurial businesses. The chapter found that with progressive policy support, skills and mentoring programmes, young people are able not only to create self-employment, but also emerge as drivers of innovative entrepreneurial programmes. Thus, without requisite skills and access to the market, youth will continue to exist in the periphery of the mainstream economy. Secondary sources were used to analyse the opportunities and challenges faced by youth entrepreneurship programmes in South Africa. The chapter made use of youth programmes as the study methodology to extract and analyse the potential of youth entrepreneurship programmes in upskilling and socializing both the graduates and young professionals to the world of work.

BACKGROUND

Youth socio-economic exclusion and marginalization has led to growing youth unemployment, underemployment and discontent, while among the graduates, the unemployment has become an emerging phenomenon. Most affected by the triple challenges of poverty, unemployment and inequality are the youth falling within the NEET (Not in Employment, Education and Training) category. This is a cohort of young people between the ages of 15-24 years that are disgruntled (Labour Market Dynamics Report in South Africa, 2016). Of the 32,6% of unemployment rate in South Africa, the most concerning category is the youth unemployment rate of those between the ages of 15-34 years standing at 46,3% in Quarter 1 of 2021, of which, 9,3% are university graduates. This picture depicts that the youth remains the most vulnerable in the South African labour market (Quarterly Labour Force Survey (QLFS) – Q1:2021). Stats SA 2020 (2020) revealed that 32.4% of the 10.2 million youth between the ages of 15-24 years are in the NEET (Not in employment, not in education and training) cohort, of which, females have recorded the highest as compared males. These statistical reports indicate that youth unemployment is a major problem in South Africa. They also suggest that the government may not be doing enough to create sustainable job opportunities for young people (Business Tech, 2017).

The numbers portraying youth unemployment in South Africa are overwhelming and suggest an upward trend in the coming years (Ndinga-Kanga, van der Merwe and Hartford, 2020). The International Labour Organization (ILO) (2016) reported that overall, "South Africa's unemployment would rise to the 6th highest in the world by the year 2020 from its current 8th position" (Moerane, 2016, p.1). Therefore, it is with no doubt that, given the condition of South African struggling economic growth, the next decades will be critical. As an illustration, based on the government's definition of unemployment, over 60% of South Africans who are between the ages of 15 and 24 years are unemployed and most of them do not have formal education or opportunities that can give them access to employment (Meyer and Mncayi, 2021). Thus, unemployment among the youth in the African context is likely to affect a sense of confidence, self-esteem and personal agency, which are needed to participate in the labour market. The negative effect of unemployment on the well-being of unemployed youth cannot be disregarded as it affects their attitude in positioning themselves for employment opportunities. In Africa and South Africa in particular, unemployment is interwoven with challenges such as health-related predicaments such as HIV/ AIDS to social ills as alcohol and drug abuse, crime, suicide and depression (World Bank Group, 2018). The legacy of apartheid also continues to have negative effects on young people's potential to live a decent living. Accordingly, African youth endure the most racially oppressive and constraining policies and programmes that continue to undermine youth socially and economically (Cebekhulu, 2018). Added to the historical legacies and new challenges in the wake of democracy, problems facing the youth continue to multiply.

Scholars in youth and education sectors have attributed youth unemployment to the mismatch between skills demanded by the job market and the nature of the education system (Honwana, 2013, Cross & Ngandu, 2014). Moreover, Burger (2018) highlighted the mismatch between the scarcity of skills, economic growth and education system has contributed to the scourge of unemployed graduates and budging youth unemployment and un-employability. Poor and mediocre education in basic and higher education have thwarted youth opportunities to receive good qualifications with skills and knowledge attractive to the labour market (Ramphele, 2012). Thus, mismatch between the economy and education, according to Handley (2016, p. 79) produces many "job seekers with low skills". This is made worse by higher education institutions who graduate a huge cohort of students with what Bhorat & Kanbur (2006) call 'wrong kinds of tertiary qualifications' hence the graduate unemployment. The shortage of skills, especially technical skills is among the challenges facing the labour market and South Africa as a whole. An aging population of experienced professional engineers who are pre-dominantly white further worsens this challenge. This in return creates a gap in the labour market for skilled and competent professionals (Department of Public Works, 2020). Although institutions of higher education are graduating students in the technical field, lack of work experience as well as registered skilled and competency especially among previously disadvantaged technical professionals, is a hindering factor.

Challenges in Finding Skilled Personnel

Skills shortages force organizations to deliberately incorporate talent management practices and even go back to poaching and headhunting (Gundling, Caldwell, & Cvitkovich, 2016). Clearly, talent supply does not meet the current demand adequately, and that may remain a long-term challenge. The Organisation for Economic Corporation Development (OECD) Report (2018, cited in Probst & Scharffer, 2019, p. 9) revealed that "only 31% of at risk employee" (job loss through automation) received professional training in a year. With aging employees, companies face a growing lack of resources (Minneci, 2015). The developing economies, on the other hand, have a growing population that is becoming younger. Planning to replace staff near to retirement age with a new generation of talent seems necessary (Thunnissen & Van Arensbergen, 2015). The older and the younger generation have varied characteristics and expectations, making it challenging to facilitate skill transfer from one generation to another, and if it does not pose an imminent threat, aging workers needs to be tackled before it is an urgent concern. According to Probst & Scharff (2019), millions of people across Europe and the Middle East, who already have formal education, find themselves out of work. They have little chance to reintegrate unless the entire process of knowledge and skills acquisition is reengineered to target sustainable jobs (Probst & Scharffer, 2019). This challenge provides an opportunity for young previously disadvantaged technical professionals to look closely at their individual job standards, behaviours and career goals in order to ensure successful approaches in communication and talent management (Ng & Parry, 2016). The implications of high unemployment rates – especially in youths and older workers coupled with increasing job vacancies are undeniable. Another issue is that there is a large number of youths graduating from years of education that is not tied to market projections or needs (Probst and Scharff, 2020).

Deloitte (2018) warns that failure to address the mismatch is likely to intensify as the Fourth Industrial Revolution (4IR) is characterized by the marriage of physical assets and digital technologies that transforms society, economies, jobs, and people's personal lives. Deloitte (2018) argue that it is critical to prepare tomorrow's workforce for the Fourth Industrial Revolution (4IR) as most graduates lack current required skills. Thus, the 4IR demands that young people learn new skills that will render them versatile in the knowledge economy. Along the mission of developing skills for future generations, Marwala (2020) argues that higher education institutions are obliged to reskilling and training young people for the rapid changing world of technology. Thus, embracing the 4IR and Artificial intelligence related skills and competencies would require young people to tap into current trending professions such as creative industries, food technologists, 3D designers, data centre workers and care, education and health workers (World Economic Forum, 2017). This entails in the future the learning of hard and soft infrastructure, green jobs, the ICT sector as the strong job growth potential for future economic prosperity.

Interestingly, Probst and Scharff (2019:16) point to the cost of failing to upskill the population as a major problem that can compromise different elements below:

1. High percentages in NEET (Youth Not in Employment, Education or Training) –
   leading to a disenfranchised and demotivated youth;
2. vocational training inefficiencies and wasted training funds as people participate in
   knowledge or skills acquisition in the wrong domain;
3. higher unemployment insurance increasing subsidy and support costs, impacting mental health and well-being of a large segment of the population and finally
4. losses in tax base and revenue caused by vacant positions, and migration of jobs and industries to regions or countries where skilled workers are more available and impacting regional economic well-being (personal and corporate tax loss) (Probst and Scharff, 2019).

Without employment, education or training, it is obvious that these youngsters' future is doomed. In South Africa, there are almost 20 millions of young people between the ages of 15-34 falls under the NEET category. Out of these 20 million, 9.1 millions of this cohort of young people are unable to secure work hence escaping poverty and unemployment will be impossible. Failed public training system, according to Bernstein & Schirmer (2021, p. 18), makes South Africa not attractive to young people whom many of them are jobless.

Impact of Capacity Building on Young Professionals

According to Gratton (2019), upskilling is a way of learning current tasks in-depth. Gratton (2019, p. 1532) points out that 'every conceivable job will have new technologies to learn and new personal relationships to navigate as those roles fit and refit into a changing economic landscape'. Gratton (2019, p. 1532) further states that upskilling is about 'learning existing skills in newer, deeper ways and this is often required when the routine tasks of a job become automated'. Upskilling is about learning new skills in new occupations (Manyika et al., 2017). Upskilling involves training people but keeping them in the same roles instead of changing their job (Randstad). The line manager of a company identifies employees with most potential and offer then training they need to develop (Manyika et al., 2017). According to Probst and Scharff (2019) upskilling is a way in which people's capabilities are expanded to be employable and to fulfil the talents needed in a rapidly changing economy. Unlike reskilling which retrains works like steelworkers or locksmith, upskilling by contrast is a comprehensive initiative to convert applicable knowledge into productive results (Probst and Scharff, 2019).

According to O'Leary, Widener and Agarwal (2020), in the past public sector training programmes focused on the individual getting the training. However, the advent of technology has brought in new occupations hence governments are placing increasing emphasis on helping companies find the right candidates for the new jobs (O'Leary et al, 2020). This government initiative is one example of the growing focus at all levels on working with businesses to help connect them with new talent and ensure that the workforce has the skills that business needs (O'Leary et al., 2020).

The growing use of digital technologies, robotics, and artificial intelligence are expected to require a company's existing workforce to learn different skills as technology advances (O'Leary et al., 2020). According to a Joint Survey by Deloitte and MIT Sloan Management Review (2016. p.2),, about 90 percent of organizations anticipate their industries will be completely disrupted by digital trends. At the same time, 70 percent of organizations believe that their current employees will not be able to manage this disruption. However, it was also clear that some individuals were much more pro-active than others in taking advantage of these opportunities. A recent report by the World Economic Forum (2016) predicts that about 75 million jobs will be eliminated due to artificial intelligence (AI) by 2025 but about 133 million new jobs will also be created. The Report (2016) further predicts that around 54 percent of employees will need to reskill in order to take advantage of these new opportunities. Therefore, access to opportunities for learning and development is important, and to some extent these opportunities were more likely to be given to individuals showing a strong commitment to work. However, it was also clear that some individuals were much more pro-active than others in taking advantage of these opportunities.

For workers, apprenticeships may be an attractive way to earn an industry-recognized credential or degree as an alternative to a four-year, traditional university, trade school, or community college (Chankseliani et al., 2017). Apprenticeships offer workers occupational-specific training, providing a pathway into a career and higher earnings (Chankseliani et al., 2017). Although jobs remain the same, change is easily accommodated within normal patterns of learning (Barnes, Brimrose and Brown, 2006). These authors add that benefits of upskilling is that learning becomes the central component of career development. According to Barnes et al. (2006), access to opportunities for upskilling and development is important as it encourages workers to transform themselves and to believe in what they can do. These authors add that recruiting a new workforce is costly hence upskilling the existing workforce saves cost. The National skills Coalition Foundational Skills in the Service Sector Report (2019) asserts that policies that support upskilling enhance companies' investments.

Thus, businesses that invest in their workers' skills building reap dividends not only for the workers but also for the business bottom line. Barnes et al. (2006) argue that the value of learning while working helps individuals not only to keep their skills, knowledge and bring up-to-date competences while keeping a positive disposition towards learning. Companies benefit from service and workers improve their skills (Barnes et al., 2006).

Upskilling graduates and young professionals in South Africa is fundamental for improving service delivery (The South African Government News Agency, 2017). Speaking at the European Union (EU)-National School of Government (NSG) Public Service Training and Capacity Building Programme on the 19th Public Sector Trainer's Forum Conference; the former Public Service and Administration Minister Faith Muthambi acknowledged the number of the unemployed and unemployable graduates and conceded that the skills gap in the country could only be filled by upskilling young people who enter the job market (The South African Government News Agency, 2017). A study done in the United Kingdom by Pickles (2019) revealed that a better trained workforce is more efficient and productive and helps in delivering projects more effectively. Pickles (2019) further found that the public sector has realised the value of upskilling and investing in the workforce in the future. Upskilling and continuous learning also increases the chances of a long-lasting and stable workforce to help the public sector focus on continuing to deliver great services.

These programmes demonstrated again and again the value of learning while working in helping individuals, not only keep their skills, knowledge and competences up-to-date but also in helping them keep a positive disposition towards learning (Pickles, 2019). However, it was also clear that some individuals were much more pro-active than others in taking advantage of these opportunities (Pickles, 2019).

UPSKILLING PROGRAMMES FOR YOUNG PEOPLE

Apprenticeships

According to Chankseliani et al. (2017), an apprenticeship is an agreed-upon learning model that formally combines work-based training (periods of practical work experience at a workplace) with institution-based education (periods of theoretical practical education followed at a school, college, or training centre). It is regulated by a contract agreement between apprentices. Apprenticeships are available in a variety of occupations, including both traditional fields and newer ones such as mechatronics, cost estimation, computer simulation, banking, medical coding, and pharmacy operations. In all, the Department of labour Registered Apprenticeship

(RA) programme covers over a thousand occupations. According to Deloitte (2019), dual-education apprenticeship models, for example seek to ease the transition between education and the workforce by providing students/young professionals with on-the-job skills training while they complete their formal education. At a minimum, for an apprenticeship program to be registered with Department of Labour (DOL). It must combine classroom instruction with paid on-the-job training that teaches workers practical skills, and the full apprenticeship must last at least one year (Deloitte, 2019). Around the world, apprenticeships are used as a policy lever to address a wide range of social ills including youth unemployment, skill gaps, skill shortages, economic problems and social exclusion (Chankseliani et al., 2017). Apprenticeships may also reduce hiring costs by providing a streamlined channel to bring on new workers. Apprenticeships may reduce attrition by building a bond of loyalty between company and employee or by providing an opportunity for motivated young people to stay rooted in their communities (Chankseliani et al., 2017). Apprenticeships as a policy instrument are often used to combat youth unemployment concurrently, as well as creating the high-level skills. Chankseliani et al (2017) point out that apprenticeships are appealing to policymakers because they are associated by both fellow lawmakers and constituents, but the concern is that apprenticeships are often used as an 'answer' to what are mostly weakly established policy problems. Essentially, 'a policy discourse has developed in which apprenticeships have acquired the 'magic dust' characteristics that can be sprinkled on almost any problem of vocational education and training (Chankseliani et al., 2017: 73).

Candidacy Programme

The candidacy program in South Africa enrols students who have trained in the built environment business (Department of Public Works, 2017). They consist of architects, engineers, quantity surveyors, landscape planners, project and construction managers, and property evaluators (Department of Public Works, 2017). Fresh graduates from universities from the different disciplines mentioned above are not yet professionals, they are qualified applicants to go through candidacy program with the ultimate aim of being professionals (Department of Public Works, 2017).

In South Africa the requirement to become a professional, is that a candidate as to first register with the relevant professional council. The candidate goes through two, three to five or more years of work experience before being subjected to a final Council assessment (Department of Public Works, 2017). When the claimant is considered qualified, he / she is licensed and considered a professional. In 2018, the Public Works Department funded a hundred and twenty (120) professionals. As one of its signature programs, the construction Education and Training Authority has taken candidacy to ensure that historically marginalized students enrol as practitioners upon completing the programme (Department of Public Works, 2017). This will account for the vital and limited skills found in most of the built environment careers set up above (Department of Public Works, 2017). The construction Education and Training Authority is also targeting a large number of candidates who have worked for a long time and have not been able to register so that they are assisted in registering as professionals (Construction Education and Training Authority, 2019). For candidancy programme, training that helps ensure that activities are aligned with the requirements of a particular job in order to address the deficiency in construction skills Probst and Scharff (2020) and Deloitte (2019) Emuze, et al, (2015).

Workplace-Based Learning

Another method of upskilling young professionals is learning on the job. Workplace-based learning refers to any type of workplace training to provide practical on-the-job experience for the trainee (Alvarez-Galvan, 2015). According to Sajjid and Mahboob (2015), 'workplace-based learning', also termed as 'situational learning' is a learning experience which allows students to learn through supervised application of their professional roles in real workplace settings. According to Cornyn and Brewer (2018), workplace-based learning involves activities recognized by a number of words, including apprenticeships, traineeships, apprenticeships, job placements, work experience, cooperatives, and phases. According to UNESCO (2019), job-based learning refers to any form of youth or adult learning and vocational training within a business or job (Oviawe, 2018). Likewise, the International Labour Organization agrees that apprenticeships, cadetships, traineeships, and internships are workplace-based employment as they support the gap from education to youth jobs (Cornyn and Brewer, 2018).

The workplace provides a strong learning environment in which young people can learn the job-related soft and technical skills (Alvarez-Galvan, 2015). Thus, supporting local CTE/TVET/training programs through financial resources and/or technical expertise can help strengthen alternative education programs while building a talent base with the skills needed for industry (Deloitte, 2019). TVET, also known as Vocational Education and Training (VET) or Vocational Training (VT), is an avenue through which workplace-based learning can be provided (Akoojee, 2016). National governments generally regulate TVET, offered by training providers from both the public and private sectors (Oviawe, 2018). In South Africa, for example TVET lecturers undertake workplace-based learning to improve their theorisation and teaching skills (Van der Bill and Taylor, 2016). These authors further state that workplace-based learning for TVET lecturers improves their knowledge development and competencies (Oviwe, 2018). France for example has a policy on upskilling the less qualified. In order to upskill young qualified teachers, Malaysia has an industry teacher placement (Bergami, Schuller and Cheok, 2009). Workplace-based learning is considered as one of the most effective way of translating knowledge of various educational theories and principles and their application at workplace can enhance student learning and motivation, for which faculty development is much needed (Sajjad & Mahboob, 2015).

Job Rotation and Transfers

In South Africa, the government uses job rotation in upskilling young professionals. Job rotation is a practice in which workers of the same organization switch between jobs (Department of Publick Works, 2018). Employees take on new tasks for a period of time at a different job before reverting to their original position (Blakely-Gray, 2017). Over 60 per cent of employers in the construction industry now have some sort of skills acquisition program in place, from moving workers from various divisions or assignments to providing extra incentives to help and promote training (Blakely-Gray, 2017). The issue of employee retention is of great concern to business leaders in developing countries in Africa, such as Senegal, Ghana and Nigeria (Ldama & Bazza, 2015). These authors add that all organizations are configured to achieve specific goals and the most important resource for achieving the goals is the human resources (Ldama & Bazza, 2015). The factors motivate employees to remain in their jobs are essential because they affect the organization's performance. George, (2015) published a report to figure out why experts stay put in their organizations. Thus, preparation and growth are often linked to among other reasons retention of workers.

Artisans Development Programme

Artisan development is a collaborative government-private sector initiative. According to the Department of Higher Education and Training (2020), the majority of artisan training and learning takes place in the workplace. The Department of Higher Education and Training (2020) further states that it is in the workplace that apprentices get to apply theory and practice they acquired at the Skills Development Provider (SDP). The delivery of the A21 apprenticeship is incorporated into the dual systems principles applied within the South African context incorporating lessons from Dual System Apprenticeship Programme (DSAP) and Dual System Apprenticeship Pilot Project (DSPP) (Department of Higher Education and Training, 2020).

Apprentices get theoretical knowledge at colleges of technical and vocational education and training, usually before they are employed (Department of Higher Education and Training, 2020). They then contract an apprenticeship with employers which lasts three years. Once the learners have been contracted, they undergo practical and workplace training in order to prepare them for trade tests. Practical training is generally conducted by private training providers although the necessary facilities are provided by some public technical and vocational education and training colleges (Perold, 2012). It is a given fact that for both developed and developing nations to advance economically, artisans should be promoted. In the case of South Africa, training of artisans is key in dealing the challenges of unemployed graduates in particular and youth unemployment in general.

FINDINGS AND ANALYSIS

The programmes profiled above are gauged using the following criteria: a) fostering the entrepreneurship mind-set, b) job creation, c) acquisition of entrepreneurial and management skills as well as the creation of innovative and entrepreneurial businesses.

1. Fostering the entrepreneurship mind-set,

The success of the programmes introduced by government and other NGOs is depended on the attitude and the mind-set among graduates and young professionals to be innovators in finding alternative solutions to the challenges besetting them and society. Within trending mentality of entitlement and dependency syndrome, programmes such as apprenticeships, Candidacy programme, Work-based learning and Job rotation and Transfers as well as Artisans development programmes should arm them with skills and work exposure to be self-employed.

Evidence from these cases studies show that there is a need for multifaceted skills and competences for graduates and young professionals to operate in the ever-changing world of world today. Through the cultivating of resilient spirit based on entrepreneurial mind-set, the receivers of training and work exposure should be motivated to view entrepreneurship as one of the pathways towards addressing socio-economic challenges facing the youth today. Entrepreneurial orientation and mind-set could allow allows income and employment generation as well as boosting the economic growth among the young people (Costa, 2021). There is a need for developing training, coaching and mentoring as well as the training programmes for youth entrepreneurs. According to OEOD & European Union (2014), entrepreneurial mind-sets and change of attitudes of youth are key in developing entrepreneurs. In this regards, Probst and Scharff (2019) argue that for companies, reskilling and upskilling strategies are critical if they are to find the skilled work force they need and to contribute to socially responsible approaches to the future of work. For policy-makers, reskilling and retraining the existing workforce are essential levers to fuel future economic growth, enhance societal resilience in the face of technological

Table 1.

	Programme	Skills and Knowledge	Mind-set
1	Apprenticeships	- workers practical skills - Institutional-based training - Specialisation in mechatronics, 4IR skills	- Motivation - Education is not adequate without concrete experience
2	Candidacy programme	- Consolidate built environment skills - Eg. architects, engineers, quantity surveyors, landscape planners, project and construction managers, and property evaluators - Professional skills and knowledge	- Experiential learning - Disciplines
3	Work-based learning	- Workplace training - On-the-job experience for the trainees - Placements in vocational training - Technical and vocational training	- Work exposure
4	Job rotation and Transfers	- Job rotation in upskilling young professionals	- Motivated employees - skill labour-power
5	Artisans development programmes	- Artisans training and learning - Integrating theory into practice - Technical and vocational educational and training	- Self -employment mind-set

Source: Author's analysis

change and pave the way for future-ready education systems for the next generation of workers (Probst and Sharff, 2019). In addition, there is a disconnection between education and the required skills in the workplace. The emergency of the fourth industrial revolution calls for the know-how, knowledge and expertise of technologies (World Economic Forum, 2016). Aubert-Tarby, Escobar and Rayna (2018) state that technological change will impact growth and creation of employment, lack of skills, training and gaps between the sexes. Consequently, skills and resources are needed for the fourth industrial revolution. The Economic Forum (2016) reports that technological transition would have an effect on jobs growth and development, skills shortages, training and gender differences. The fourth Industrial Revolution therefore requires skills and resources (World Economic Forum, 2016). These skills can be acquired through retraining, work placements and structured mentoring of young people.

Job Creation through Entrepreneurial Interventions

Entrepreneurship is centred on the generation of new and innovative ideas pertaining to business and job creation. Tshishonga (2021) posits that entrepreneurship is important as the driver of economic growth and job creation in South Africa.

Although skills and resources are necessary, creative entrepreneurs are tested on the basis of their ability to create businesses out of nothing. The success or failure of entrepreneurship depends on the skills and competency of an entrepreneur. In essence, this differentiates an entrepreneur from other business people by displaying entrepreneurial intelligence that seize the opportunity for value creation out of a new or existing business (Petty et al. (2012). Fundamental to entrepreneur is taking risks pertaining to investing in business opportunities based on the feasibility and viability of the idea (Rankhumise & Venter, 2016). Successful entrepreneurs are distinguished by their features such as 1) skills, expertise and aptitudes, 2) personal characteristics, 3) ability to take risks, 40 need for achievement, 50 commitment to the business, 6) perseverance, 6) good personal relationships, 7) involvement in the business and 8) knowledge of functional management (Strydom & Niewenhuizen, 2012, p. 28). Youth entrepreneurial programmes profiled do not only inspire graduates and young people for self-empowerment to start their entrepreneurial enterprises, buts also anchored entrepreneurship is the backbone of the local economic development at local level. It further reiterated scholars who advocated entrepreneurship as the driver of innovation, generates wealth and creates jobs thereby improving the living standards of the unemployed youth and people at large (Altinay, Madanoglu, Daniele, & Lashley, 2012).

Innovation is key to the life of an entrepreneur hence it is economy entrepreneurial ventures are according Kelley, Singer & Herrington (2012), opportunity based. The programmes outlined above can only skill and expose youth to the world of work, but the jest is on how the acquired skills and knowledge are used to start and run sustainable business for job creation. With the government especially in the Public Works Department, the current situation is desperate as the majority of technical experience, qualified and professional registered engineers are aging (Department of Public Works, 2017). The lack of young professional engineers and the shortage of technical staff with experience exacerbate the technical skill deficiency (Department of Public Works, 2017). The lack of technical young professionals within the National Department of Public Works and Infrastructure (NDPWI) undermines the Department's efforts to execute its infrastructure development mandate.

Acquisition of Entrepreneurial and Management Skills and Education

However, motivation and right attitude are adequate for youth to translate their ideas into successful entrepreneurs businesses without formal entrepreneurial education. This implies that companies and individual youth should invest in entrepreneurial education in order to obtain relevant skills and knowledge to be productive or to create successful businesses. In the case of government department, skilled and competent professionals are handy in providing quality work and fast track work in progress (Department of Public Works, 2017). As such, upskilling is a way where an organisation puts emphasis on investing training programmes to help employees to develop new abilities and reduce skills gaps (International Labour Organisation, 2019). Artisans and all types of engineers are important and needed in the department due to the shortages in these skills (Department of Public Works, 2017). It is thus important to upskill previously disadvantaged technical professionals in order to meet demand and fill the gap being left by the aging population of white professionals in engineering, artisan, town planning fields and many other skills shortages (Department of Public Works, 2017). South Africa, for example has invested in upskilling its workforce and adjusting its training strategies through the Ministry of Higher Education (World Economic Forum, 2020). In this instance, the training by service providers has to take into consideration the skills demanded by the 4IR and artificial intelligence.

Creation of Innovative and Entrepreneurial Businesses

Entrepreneurship is all about skills self-empowerment and its test is on the creation of innovative and entrepreneurial businesses that managed and sustained by graduates and young professionals themselves. Both graduates and professionals in their line of training have received basic skills and competencies for them to create businesses. These businesses in essence should be the driver for young people towards self-employments and integrate skills and institutional exposure through programmes such as Apprenticeships, Candidacy Programme, Work-based learning, Job rotation and Transfers and finally the Artisans development programmes. These programmes are designed to cater for graduates and professionals in different fields hence, the optimal utilisation of the acquired skills are relevant for start-ups. These programmes are linked to self-empowerment where human capital is developed and training and opportunities provided for young people could unlock their entrepreneurial potential. Khoza (2013) adds that knowledge, communication and teamwork are key features towards self-empowerment in the entrepreneurship sector. Graduates and young professionals created business could range from those involved public-private sector, income, survival informal to temporary self-employed and micro-medium entrepreneurial ventures.

Youth unemployment and unemployed graduates (Cross & Ngandu, 2014) should not be the only reasons for establishing entrepreneurial ventures, but also the business networks and innovative ideas that can be experimented into good sustainable businesses. Key the sustainability of entrepreneurial businesses as highlighted by Khoza (2013) depended on broad-based support from customers, suppliers, shareholders and regulators.

Figure 1. Classification of income-generating activities and types of business
Source: *Osses & Molenaar, 1989 in OECD & European Union, 2014, p. 18*

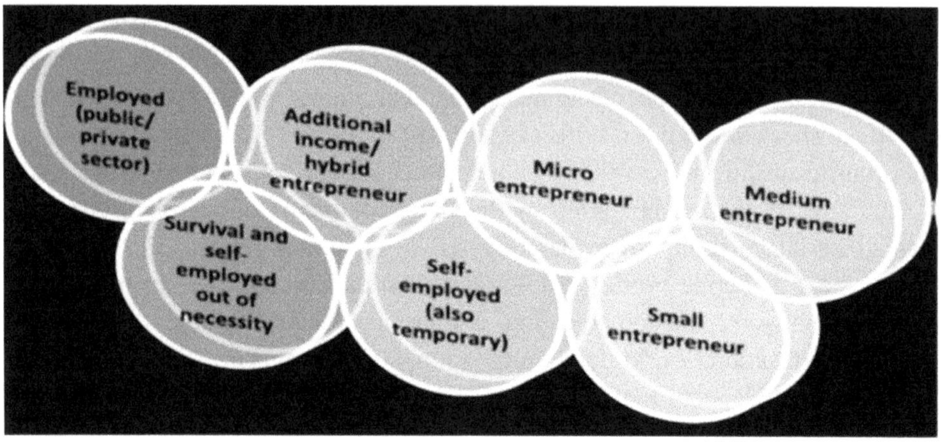

Challenges Faced Graduates and Young Professional Entrepreneurs

Socio-economic challenges faced by both graduates and youth in general are enormous. Young unemployment and the growing scourge of unemployed graduates coupled with poverty, skills deficits, low educational qualifications and education are among the gravitating challenges. These growing challenges are further aggravated by the slow growing economy and the mismatch between education system and labour market (Mlathseni, 2012), even those young people exposed to skills training in various programmes, the hostile labour environment discourages them to seek either jobs or use acquired skills for self-employment. Their socio-economic exclusion and marginalisation have led to the growing youth unemployment, un-employability and discontent while among the graduates; the unemployment has become an emerging phenomenon. In an attempt to address the problems of youth unemployment and unemployed graduates, Qwesha (2020, p. 6) proposed a "two-pronged strategy". In this strategy support is given for businesses owned by people and secondly, government providing incentives to support young people's employment within the business sector or government departments.

DIRECTION FOR FUTURE RESEARCH

Based on these deliberations, there is need for an integrated and compressive research to investigate how these entrepreneurial programmes have imparted skills and knowledge that graduate and young professional could use to establish their own sustainable businesses in South Africa. This research should take into account the trends in the economy and needed skills required to work in the 4IR and artificial intelligence environment.

CONCLUSION

This chapter has demonstrated that upskilling through capacity building of graduates and young professionals in government departments and organisations could be instrumental in boosting their skill set competencies for employability or self-employability. In the situation where there is a mismatch between labour skills and experiences, upskilling programmes is could improve the skilled labour and develop new talents among both graduates and young professionals in South Africa. Upskilling can further improve the effectiveness of graduates, young professional themselves and organisations employing them. It is clear that institutional capacity building does not exist in isolation, but would require sustainable relationships among experienced staff, young professionals, the community and individuals. In this context, capacity building remains key for all youth organisations to enable the development and fulfilment of their respective missions and visions.

In this chapter, upskilling young people has proven to ensure young people become better entrepreneurs and eventually create employment opportunities for other young people. Thus, upskilling young people in the workforce particularly those in industry and technology has become critical. Many young people join industries with theory and without practical skills that are needed in the workplace hence the need to upskill them and make them better employees. For young people especially the unemployed graduates and young professionals to gain skills, technical knowledge and competencies, upskilling programmes should be well-coordinated, well-resourced to promote youth entrepreneurship in South Africa. This chapter therefore recommends an intersectoral approach towards reskilling and upskilling of young graduates and professionals.

REFERENCES

Ahlstrom, D., Chang, A. Y., & Cheung, J. S. (2019). Encouraging entrepreneurship and economic growth. *Journal of Risk and Financial Management*, *12*(4), 178.

Altinay, L., Madanoglu, M., Daniele, R., & Lashley, C. (2012). The influence of family tradition and psychological traits on entrepreneurial intention. *International Journal of Hospitality Management, 31*(2), 489–499.

Alvarez-Galvan, J. (2015). *Organization for Economic Co-operation and Development review of vocational education and training: Skills beyond school review of Egypt. OECD. Accessed from* https://read.oecd-ilibrary.org/education/a-skills-beyond-school-review-ofegypt_9789264209626-en#page1

Aubert-Taby, C., Escobar, O. R., & Rayna, T. (2018). *The impact of technological change on employment: The case of press digitalisation. Technological Forecasting and Social Change. Elsevier. Accessed from* www.sciencedirect.com/science//article/abs/pii/S0040162

Barnes, S. A., Bimrose, J., & Brown, A. (2006). *Older workers' careers: upskilling, reskilling and transitions*. Academic Press.

Bergami, R., Schüller, A., & Cheok, J. (2009). Building bridges through industry placements: Perceptions from Malaysian academics. *Journal of the Worldwide Forum on Education and Culture, 1*(1), 50–61.

Bhorat, H., & Kanbur, S. R. (Eds.). (2006). *Poverty and policy in post-apartheid South Africa*. HSRC press.

Blakely-Gary, R. (2017). *Addressing the skills shortage in the construction sector.* https://probuildermag.co.uk/features/addressing-skills-shortage-construction-sector

Buckley, S. (2017). *Conceptualisations of Youth and Implications for Policy: A Study of Four Cases in Aotearoa/New Zealand.* Te Herenga Waka – Victoria University of Wellington.

Burger, P. (2018). *Getting It Right: A New Economy for South Africa*. Review Publishing Company Ltd.

Busetto, L., Wick, W., & Gumbinger, C. (2020). How to use and assess qualitative research methods. *Neurol. Res. Pract., 2*, 14.

Business Tech. (2021). *Youth still find it difficult to secure jobs in South Africa.* http://www.statssa.gov.za/?p=14415

Cebekhulu, A. (2018). *Umhlaba Uyahlaba! The World is Thorny. Wandabeck.* Reach publishers.

Chankseliani, M., Keep, E., & Wilde, S. (2017). *People and Policy: A comprehensive study of apprenticeship across eight national contexts (Study)*. University of Oxford.

Construction Education and Training Authority. (2019). https://static.pmg.org.za/CETA_APP_2019_2020.pdf

Cornyn, P., & Brewer, L. (2018). *Does workplace learning facilitate transitions to decent work?* ILO, Employment Working Paper (242). Accessed from: https://www.ilo.org/employment/Whatwedo/Publications/workingpapers/WCMS_635797/lang--en/index.htm.

Cross, C., & Ngandu, S. (2014). Youth unemployment dynamics in the labour market of the periphery. In State of the Nation (2014). South Africa 1994-2014: A twenty-year review (pp. 198-222). Cape Town: HSRC Press.

Deloitte & Aspen Institute. (2018). *A Guide to Upskilling America's Frontline Workers*. https://assets.aspeninstitute.org/content/uploads/2018/03/Upskilling_Employer_Handbook_042015.pdf

Department of Higher Education and Training. (2020). *Apprenticeship of the 21st Century A1. Department of Higher Education and Training*. Government Printers.

Department of Public Works. (2017). *Capacity Building Programme*. http://www.publicworks.gov.za/prof-services-new.html

Department of Public Works. (2020). *Public Works welcomes Cuban Technical Advisors*. http://www.publicworks.gov.za/prof-services-new.html

Dlamini, S., & Bimha, H. (2017). The effectiveness of youth entrepreneurship programmes in enhancing an entrepreneurial culture in Swaziland. *IOSR Journal of Research & Method in Education*, *7*(3), 73–82.

Emuze, F., van Eeden, L., & Geminiani, F. (2015). Causes and effects of building collapse: A case study in South Africa. *Proceedings CIB W099 Belfast 2015*, 408.

George, C. (2015). Retaining professional workers: What makes them stay? *Employee Relations*, *37*, 102–121. doi:10.1108/ER-10- 2013-0151

Gundling, E., Caldwell, C., & Cvitkovich, K. (2016). Global talent: Beyond outsourcing. In Advances in global leadership (pp. 353–374). http: //doi. org/doi:10.1108/S1535-120320160000009025

Handley, A. (2016). Cui Bono? A Political-Economy Assessment of 20 Years of South African Freedom. In T. Kepe, M. Levin, & B. von Lieres (Eds.), *Domain of Freedom: Justice, Citizenship and Social Change in South Africa* (pp. 61–83). UCT Press.

Hicks, J., & Buccus, I. (2016). Public participation in South Africa: Strengthening state accountability in a dominant system. In State, governance and Development in Africa (pp. 100-120). Lansdown: UCT Press.

Honwana, A. (2013). *Youth and revolution in Tunisia*. Zed Books Ltd.

Khoza, R. J. (2013). *Let Africa Lead: African Transformational Leadership for 21st Century Business*. Vezubuntu Publishing Ltd.

Krafft, C., & Rizk, R. (2021). The promise and peril of youth entrepreneurship in the Middle East and North Africa. *International Journal of Manpower*, *42*(8), 1500–1526.

Labour Market Dynamics. (2016). Labour market dynamics in South Africa. Statistics South Africa.

Ldama, J., & Bazza, M. (2015). Effect of Training and Development on Employees' Retention in Selected Commercial Banks in Adamawa State-Nigeria. *European Journal of Business and Management*, *7*(36), 96–101.

Leshilo, A., & Lethoko, M. (2017). The contribution of youth in Local Economic Development and entrepreneurship in Polokwane municipality, Limpopo Province. *Skills at Work: Theory and Practice Journal*, *8*(1), 45–58.

Manolova, T. S., Edelman, L. F., Shirokova, G., & Tsukanova, T. (2019). Youth entrepreneurship in emerging economies: Can family support help navigate institutional voids? *Journal of East-West Business*, *25*(4), 363–395.

Manyika, J., Chui, M., Miremadi, M., & Bughin, J. (2017). A future that works: AI, automation, employment, and productivity. *McKinsey Global Institute Research. Tech. Rep*, *60*, 1–135.

Meyer, D. F., & Mncayi, P. (2021). An Analysis of Underemployment among Young Graduates: The Case of a Higher Education Institution in South Africa. *Economies*, *9*(4), 196. doi:10.3390/economies9040196

Minneci, F. (2015). If there were a "highly skilled red octopus"? The case of Italian highly skilled mobility at times of crisis. *Economia e Sociologia*, *8*(3), 170–182.

Mlatsheni, C., & Leibbrandt, M. (2011). Youth unemployment in South Africa: Concepts, challenges and opportunities. *Journal of International Research and Development*, *14*, 118–126.

Moerane, P. (2016). *A study of graduates' experience of unemployment in Durban, South Africa* (Doctoral dissertation). University Of Kwa-Zulu Natal.

Ndinga-Kanga, M., van der Merwe, H., & Hartford, D. (2020). Forging a resilient social contract in South Africa: States and societies sustaining peace in the post-apartheid era. *Journal of Intervention and Statebuilding*, *14*(1), 22–41.

Netshitenzhe, J. (2021). *Beating the counter-revolutionaries: South Africa's people are the ultimate defenders of democracy*. South Africa. Daily Maverick. https://www.dailymaverick.co.za/article/2021-08-02-beating-the-counter-revolutionaries-south-africas-people-are-the-ultimate-defenders-of-democracy/

Ng, E. S., & Parry, E. (2016). Multigenerational research in human resource management. In M. R. Buckley, J. R. B. Halbesleben, & A. R. Wheeler (Eds.), *Research in personnel and human resources management* (Vol. 34, pp. 1–41). Emerald Group.

OECD & European Union. (2014). *Supporting Youth in Entrepreneurship.* Summary report of a policy development seminar organised by the OECD and the European Commission. Accessed from: http://www.oecd.org/cfe/leed/inclusive-entrepreneurship.htm

Olugbola, S. A. (2017). Exploring entrepreneurial readiness of youth and startup success components: Entrepreneurship training as a moderator. *Journal of Innovation & Knowledge*, *2*(3), 155–171.

Oviawe, J. I. (2018). Revamping Technical Vocational Education and Training through Public-Private Partnerships for Skill Development. *Makerere Journal of Higher Education*, *10*(1), 73–91.

Perold, A. F. (2012). *Negative real interest rates: The conundrum for investment and spending policies*. Academic Press.

Probst, L., & Scharff, C. (2019). *A strategy guide to upskilling. PwC's New World New Skills. Leadership, autumn 2019, 99.* https://www.strategy-business.com/feature/A-strategists-guide-to-upskilling?gko=0bb8b

Qwesha, N. (2020, Dec. 22). The challenge of youth unemployment. *Daily News*, p. 6.

Ramphele, M. (2012). *Conservations with My Sons and Daughters. Rosebank.* Penguin Books.

Sajjad, M., & Mahboob, U. (2015). Improving workplace-based learning for undergraduate medical students. *Pakistan Journal of Medical Sciences*, *31*(5), 1272.

Sika, N. (2017). *Youth Activism and Contentious Politics: Dynamics of Continuity and Change.* Cambridge University Press.

Singh, B., Verma, P., & Rao, M. K. (2016). Influence of individual and socio-cultural factors on entrepreneurial intention. *South Asian Journal of Management*, *23*(1), 33.

Statistics South Africa. (2021). *Quarterly Labour Force Survey: Quarter 1*. Statistics South Africa.

Stats, S A. (2020). Wholesale trade sales. *Statistical Release, 6141*.

Thunnissen, M., & Van Arensbergen, P. (2015). A multi-dimensional approach to talent. *Personnel Review*, *44*(2), 182–199.

Tshishonga, N. (2019). The Effects of Intergenerational Poverty and Unemployment on South African Township Youth. In J. Kurebwa (Ed.), *Participation of Young People in Governance Processes in Africa* (pp. 1–21). IGI Global.

Tshishonga, N. (2021). Economic survival: Towards balancing Financial and intellectual Act? In Higher Education, Community Engagement and Entrepreneurship in Southern Africa (pp. 66-95). Cambridge Scholars Publishing.

World Bank Group. (2018). *An Incomplete Transition: Overcoming the Legacy of Exclusion in South Africa*. UCT Press.

World Economic Forum. (2016). *The Global Competitiveness Report 2016–2021*. Accessed from: https://www.weforum.org/reports/the-global-competitiveness-report-2016-2017

World Economic Forum. (2017). *The Future of Jobs and Skills in Africa Preparing the Region for the Fourth Industrial Revolution*. https://www3.weforum.org/docs/WEF_EGW_FOJ_Africa.pdf

World Economic Forum. (2020). *Towards a reskilling revolution: A future of jobs for all*. Accessed from: http://hdl.voced.edu.au/10707/448194

ADDITIONAL READING

Coetzee, J. (2018). Strategic implications of Fintech on South African retail banks. *Suid-Afrikaanse Tydskrif vir Ekonomiese en Bestuurswetenskappe*, *21*(1), 1–11.

Fakih, A., Haimoun, N., & Kassem, M. (2020). Youth unemployment, gender and institutions during transition: Evidence from the Arab Spring. *Social Indicators Research*, *150*(1), 311–336.

Lester, S., & Costley, C. (2010). Work-based learning at higher education level: Value, practice and critique. *Studies in Higher Education*, *35*(5), 561–575.

KEY TERMS AND DEFINITIONS

Apartheid Regime: This is the type of regime that described the apartheid discriminatory political and economic system of racial segregation used by the white minority on non-whites.

Graduate: A person who has successfully completed a course of study or training, and has been awarded an undergraduate or first academic degree.

Unemployed Graduate: Graduate unemployment, or educated unemployment, is unemployment among people with an academic degree.

Young Professional: A recent graduate and skilled person whose main objectives in life include career advancement and becoming socio-economically secure.

Chapter 7
Entrepreneurship as the Future Career of Graduates:
An Assessment for the Malaysian Context and Some Policy Directions

Mohd Amirul Rafiq Abu Rahim
https://orcid.org/0000-0001-6719-6149
Universiti Malaya, Malaysia

Rohana Jani
Universiti Malaya, Malaysia

Diana Abdul Wahab
Universiti Malaya, Malaysia

ABSTRACT

Entrepreneurship is often considered as an alternative to youth and graduate unemployment, which at the same time provides more job opportunities and stimulates economic growth. Based on previous studies, the question that emerged was whether graduates will consider entrepreneurship as their career option. This chapter aims to explore whether entrepreneurship is aspired by young people, especially graduates, in their future careers. Aspirations and perceptions of entrepreneurial skills, support, and assistance are also discussed throughout this chapter. Several practical implications and policy options in promoting entrepreneurship to graduates are proposed.

DOI: 10.4018/978-1-7998-9581-7.ch007

INTRODUCTION

Since independence, the education sector in Malaysia has been vastly improved as part of its development policy. The country has produced more tertiary educated graduates with an average growth rate of 1.37%[1] and student enrolment in higher learning institutions is expected to increase further (Peng, 2020). Most of previous studies have indicated the cyclical issue of extraordinary growth on graduate output which brings another challenge in the labour market—employers continue to complain that they are unable to find graduates with the necessary skills, but at the same time, graduates also struggle to secure good and decent jobs. Therefore, this situation raises the prominent question of whether it is evident that the relationship between higher learning institutions and the labour market is weak and challenging? The graduate labour market has broader economic impact, including cyclical graduate unemployment, skills mismatch, low starting salary and slow career growth.

Concerned over the negative implications of high graduate unemployment rates, entrepreneurship is often considered as an alternative to youth and graduate unemployment, which significantly provides more job opportunities and stimulates economic growth. Based on previous studies, the question that emerged was whether graduates would like to consider entrepreneurship as an alternative career option. According to the Global Entrepreneurship Monitor (GEM)[2] quoted by The Malaysia Education Blueprint 2015-2025 (Higher Education)[3], the entrepreneurship rate in Malaysia was the lowest among the South Asian and Asia Pacific countries which participated in the survey, and the second lowest for total early stage entrepreneurial activity. Malaysia ranked last in high social prestige for successful business and ranked first in terms of dread of failure. In comparison with other nations in the region, Xavier et al. (2014) claimed Malaysia is recognised to have a low number of potential entrepreneurs—who lack confidence in their entrepreneurial abilities and have negative attitude towards entrepreneurship as a career option. Malaysia's entrepreneurial intention is half that of efficiency-driven countries, and it has the lowest degree of early-stage entrepreneurial activity in the ASEAN-6 area.

The graduate employment landscape becomes increasingly bleak as the number of graduates increases over the years which is exacerbated by current COVID-19 epidemic situation. Entrepreneurship for graduates has the potential to not only create jobs for the society and reduce labour shortages, but also to deepen their social understanding and boost their self-worth. Therefore, graduates should be guided on how to establish their own enterprise, and this is significantly explored nowadays. Entrepreneurship is a double-edged sword, meaning that entrepreneurs may gain significant rewards or suffer significant losses in the near future, especially due to the crisis. As a result, entrepreneurship education and guidance for graduates is essential to assist them in treading the path of successful entrepreneurship. However, for some time, the education policy-making has given attention on the mindset of being an employee with paid work rather than an entrepreneur. The government, particularly in the Malaysian context, has developed several policies in higher learning institutions to encourage graduates to initiate their own businesses to improve their employability. Nevertheless, these policies have some flaws which could be further reinforced. It is important to constantly enhance the policies and develop a systematic and professional incentive system to stimulate entrepreneurial mindset and interest among graduates to effectively address the transition from education to the job market.

This chapter discusses several key issues related to fostering and encouraging entrepreneurship in graduates—(i) to explore graduates' interests, aspirations and perceptional behaviour in the field of entrepreneurship; (ii) to examine the challenges arising from entrepreneurship education and mindset; (iii) to gauge measures taken by the government to encourage graduate participation in entrepreneurship; and (iv) to put forward recommendations which could be considered by the country in promoting entrepreneurship to graduates.

Methodology and Analysis

The analysis of this chapter utilises several publicly available data in Malaysia, mainly from the Labour Force Statistics of the Department of Statistics Malaysia, higher education statistics and the Graduate Tracer Study from the Ministry of Higher Education Malaysia and data from the School-to-Work Transition of Young Malaysians collected by Khazanah Research Institute Malaysia. A descriptive and trend analysis over time were used to analyse the situation in relation to the context of the study. Review of a few policy documents related to entrepreneurship development in Malaysia are also reviewed to gain understanding on the issue discussed.

BACKGROUND AND LITERATURE REVIEW

Graduate unemployment is of the utmost concern in many countries, while entrepreneurship has been the key theme in policy discourse in addressing the issue. This issue has sparked the effort of Malaysian government to transform the country into a learning-based economy, with entrepreneurship seen as a crucial component. One of the challenges is to encourage graduate students to initiate their own businesses, become job creator rather than job seeker. In general, universities are responsible for equipping graduates with entrepreneurship-related skills, so they will be able to engage independently in entrepreneurship upon graduation. Thus, it is prudent to enhance entrepreneurship education policies and related programs to attract graduates to be part of this system. Apart from rapid labour market changes, the COVID-19 pandemic has made the school-to-work transition more difficult for students and graduates (Abu Rahim & Filippi, 2021). During labour shortages, employers often reduce staffing levels by implementing 'last-in-first-out' policies (Institute for Labour Market Information and Analysis, n.d.). Moreover, the experience of persistent unemployment at a young age will compromise career prospects, incomes and well-being. These setbacks emphasise the urgent need for intervention.

Entrepreneurship education can prepare graduates for volatile and dynamic labour market due to the pandemic and rapid technological changes (Rae, 2010), at the same time enable graduates' smooth transition into the labor market through the various competencies they obtained from the program (Killingberg, Kubberød, & Blenker, 2020). The entrepreneurship programme does not prepare a graduate to start a business venture but also for value creation ventures such as social enterprise (Blenker, Korsgaard, Neergaard, & Thrane, 2011). Killingberg et al. (2020) categorized three career orientations for entrepreneurship education: (1) a traditional orientating on preparing task-performing employees, (2) preparing graduates with continuous adaptation to changes in work contexts, and (3) preparing graduates with boundaryless career where individuals construct their entrepreneurial identity.

Many studies shows that entrepreneurship education had a positive impact upon entrepreneurial outcomes (Matlay, 2008; Oosterbeek, Van Praag, & Ijsselstein, 2010; Von Graevenitz, Harhoff, & Weber, 2010). In fact, graduates from developing countries are more likely to choose entrepreneurship as their future career aspiration and that they are more positive towards entrepreneurship than their European counterparts (Davey, Plewa, & Struwig, 2011). However, there are also studies that shows student's self-assessed entrepreneurial skills does not contribute to the intention to choose entrepreneurship as their career aspirations (Oosterbeek et al., 2010). In fact, it is found that the entrepreneurship education in Malaysia does not match with student's expectation on the skills and knowledge they would get from such programs (Cheng, Chan, & Mahmood, 2009). Mixed understanding of the objectives of entrepreneurship education where one party believe that the program instills certain value added skills to increase their chances for employment, and another believe the program is to produce a graduate entrepreneur (Rahim & Chik, 2014). This is probably due to most of the educators were academics who were not given proper trainings before being given the task of teaching entrepreneurship (Rahim et al., 2015).

Entrepreneurship is widely recognised as critical for national development (Acs & Szerb, 2007), owing to its capacity for innovation and employment creation (Wennekers et al., 2010). It has become a policy priority among the majority of governments globally as evidenced by numerous measures and assistance to encourage the development of new start-ups. Women's participation in entrepreneurship and the gig economy has expanded in recent years in line with this growth is hailed as a boon for women, with the proportion of self-employed women increased by 8% since 2010 (from 11.6% in 2010 to 19.5% in 2018) (Chung, 2019) —increased female labour force participation and rapid growth in technology through improved internet access and connectivity.

Graduate Labour Market Characteristics in Malaysia – At a Glance[4]

This subsection discusses labour market trends and the education landscape in Malaysia. As mentioned, the supply of highly educated labour is more than in the previous days of post-independence. The Malaysian government has maintained economic stability and ensured that it does not deviate too far from full employment— through the responsibility to the education sector, which produces a more competent and productive workforce. Figure 1 clearly shows that the development of educational attainment of the workforce in Malaysia was dominated by both secondary and tertiary education levels, which constituted about more than 80% of its total labour force. Tertiary education has become the main exit point for youth in the age group of 25 to 34 years, and is a necessary condition for securing good employment prospects, reflecting higher graduate labour force participation rate. As shown in Figure 2, the graduate labour force participation rate in Malaysia was higher for the younger workforces, aged between 25 to 44 years.

Tertiary education provides an infinite number of opportunities for social mobility and economic development. However, the majority of middle-income nations encounter a quality conundrum, with substantial resources spent on tertiary education but no significant improvement in the quality and persistent skill mismatches (World Bank, 2021). Recent statistics on the graduate unemployment rate are depicted in Figure 3. It is obvious that the total graduate unemployment rate exceeded the overall unemployment rate. The figure for 2020 indicated higher unemployment rates, which was equivalent to the overall unemployment rate.

The world was alarmed by the unexpected COVID-19 crisis in 2020, resultingin Malaysia experiencing its worst economic crisis since 1998. The enactment of several Movement Control Orders (MCOs) aimed at curbing the spread of COVID-19 resulted in a surge in job losses and an increase in the unemployment rate of 200 thousand to 718.1 thousand by 2020. Competition for employment among graduates became more difficult due to the increasing number of unemployed individuals who lost their jobs during the pandemic (Department of Statistics Malaysia, 2021a). This suggests that recent graduates are most severely hit by the current pandemic situation in terms of unemployment – the problem which has coexisted over the years but is emphasized in the present crisis. In 2020, Malaysian unemployment

Figure 1. Labour force based on educational attainment in Malaysia from 1982-2011
*Note: *Second quarter 2021*
Source: Department of Statistics Malaysia (2021a, 2021b)

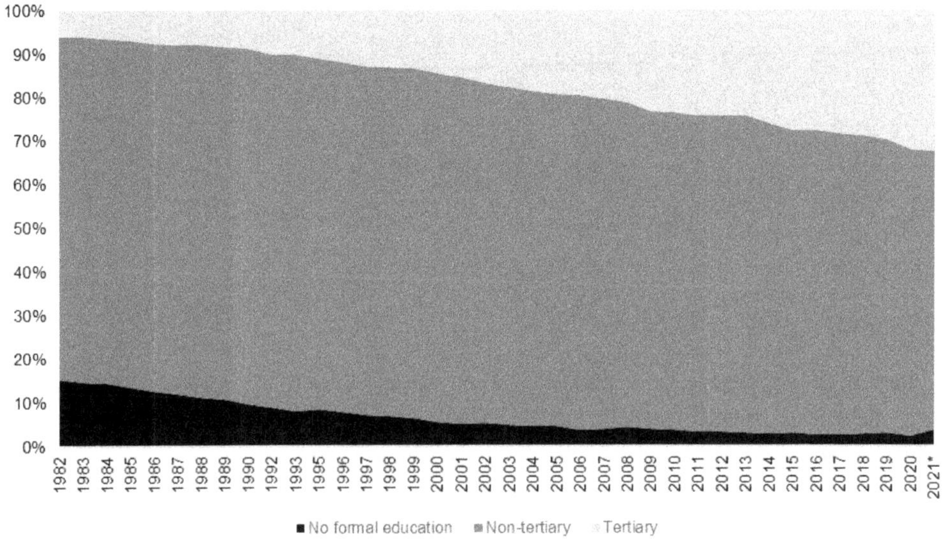

soared to alarming levels, reaching a 27-year high unlike anything seen in recent memory since 1993. The Labour Market Review by the Department of Statistics

Figure 2. Graduates labour force participation rate according to age group in Malaysia from 2016-2020
Source: Department of Statistics Malaysia (2021a)

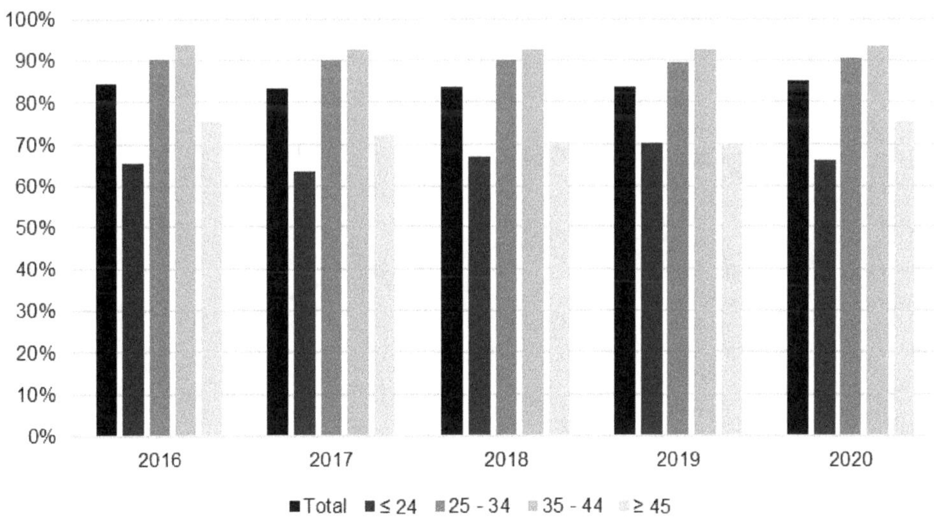

Figure 3. Overall and graduate unemployment rate from 2016-2020
Source: Department of Statistics Malaysia (2021a)

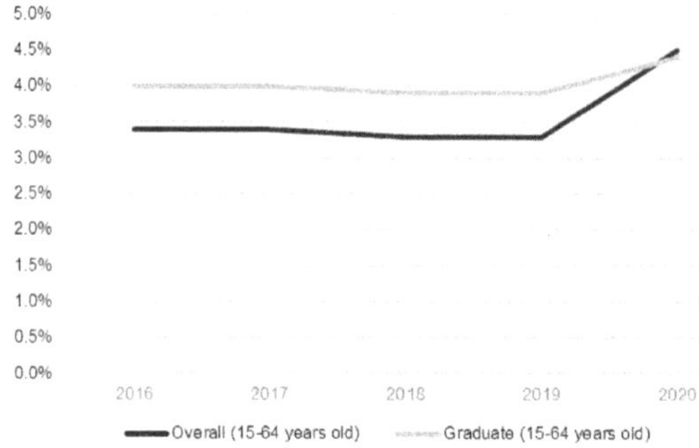

Malaysia (DOS) for the first quarter of 2021 indicated unemployment rate of 4.8%, demonstrating no discernible improvement from a similar rate in the fourth quarter of 2020 (Department of Statistics Malaysia, 2021d). The alarming disparity between the national average and the youth unemployment rate (aged15-24 years old) also did not improve, stagnating at levels nearly three times higher in the fourth quarter of 2020 and in the first quarter of 2021. It can be reasonably expect ed that the unemployment rate will escalate in the second half of 2021 due to the implementation of the third nationwide lockdown (MCO 3.0) since June 1, 2021. The challenges in the graduate labour market are nothing new - graduate unemployment has persisted over the years. As can be seen from Figure 4, despite reaching almost all-time full employment figure, graduates constitute about one-third of the total unemployed in Malaysia since the 2011. In fact, due to the unprecedented COVID-19 crisis, unemployment figures in Malaysia have breached full employment rates of 4% for almost three decades, for the first time in 2020.

Figure 4. Percentage of unemployed people based on educational attainment in Malaysia from 1982-2020
Source: Department of Statistics Malaysia (2021d)

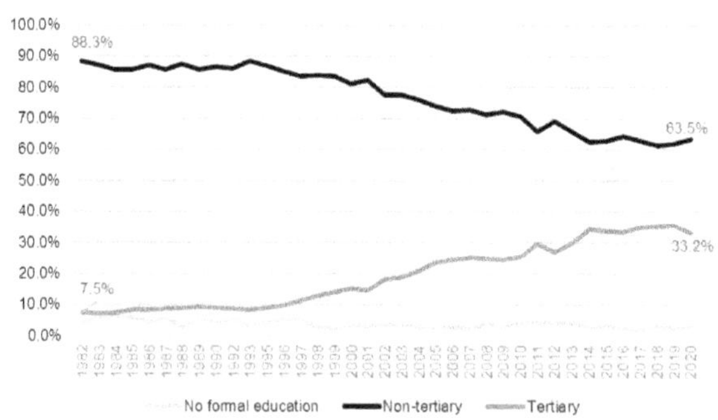

Figure 5. Employed graduates according to skill levels
Source: Department of Statistics Malaysia (2021a)

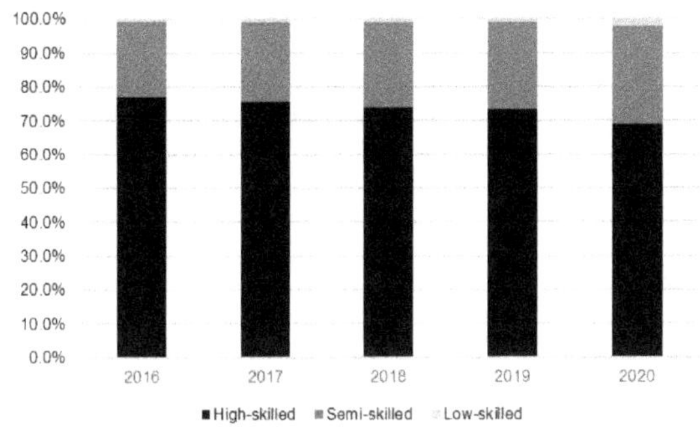

In Figure 5, it was seen that graduate employment has been focused on high-skilled occupations which are typically defined as occupation owned by Diploma holders and above. Less than 80% of graduates worked in a graduate-type occupations[5] and the trends decreased gradually from 77.1% in 2016 to 68.8% in 2020. This phenomenon also persists among new graduates. Data from the Graduate Tracer Study[6] indicated that the higher learning institutions have produced around 250 thousand to 300 thousand new graduates each year with high employability rates of more than 80.0% (Figure 6).

Figure 6. Graduate output and employability in Malaysia from 2010-2020
Source: Ministry of Higher Education Malaysia (various years), Authors' calculations

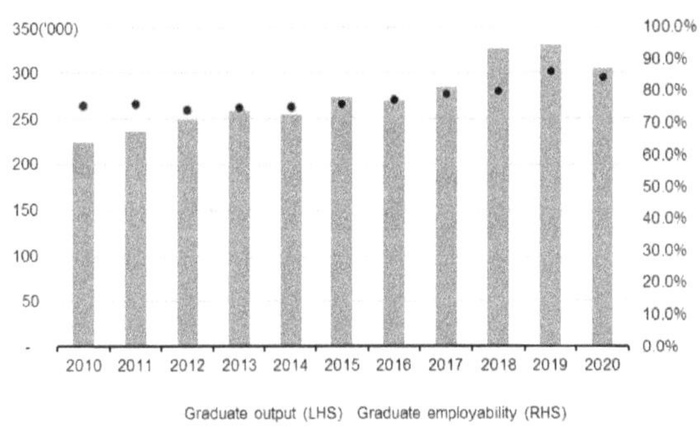

As shown in Figure 7, the number of new graduates employed in non-highly-skilled jobs constituted about a third of total graduates. In many countries, popular discourse about the relationship between higher education and the labour market is summed up by a frequently asked question: Is *the country producing too many?* The rapid expansion of tertiary-educated workforce across many countries raises the

Figure 7. Graduates worked at semi- and low-skilled levels in Malaysia from 2010-2019
Source: Ministry of Higher Education Malaysia (various years), Authors' calculations

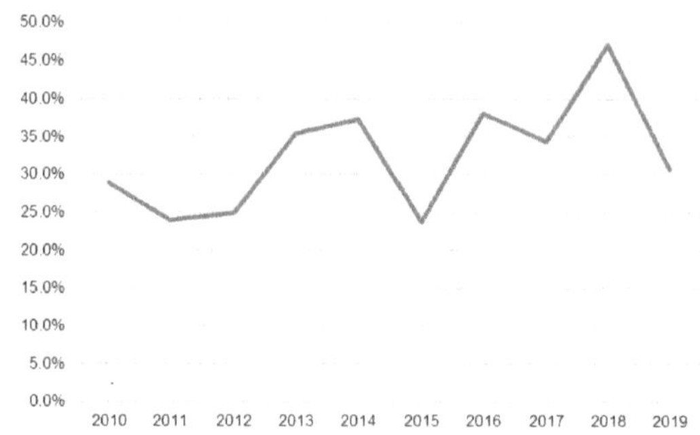

possibility of education and occupation mismatches—the case of 'overeducation' and 'undereducation'. This pertinent question is also accompanied by a contentious debate, in which expansionary and skeptical viewpoints coexist with the relationship between supply and demand, and the ability of labour market to absorb them. Concerned about the possibility of a surplus of graduates, initial emphasis was focused on the whereabouts of graduates in occupations which were not considered common for higher-education graduates. Surveys of employers and graduates were conducted to determine how many graduates were not employed in accordance with their educational level based on relevant perceptions.[7] Previous studies have generally demonstrated that traditional graduate employment has not expanded at the same rate as the number of graduates in recent decades, hence it has been persistently debated as to whether this resulted in high proportion of "overeducated" graduates and the gap between demand and supply was too small. Given the persistence of graduate unemployment and skills mismatch (particularly overeducation), the government has made graduate entrepreneurship as part of the solution. The next section discusses the progress of entrepreneurship in Malaysia, particularly among the graduates whether it can be achieved by the country as targeted. Hence, this will be a benchmark to the government efforts for graduate entrepreneurship-related policies.

PROGRESS SO FAR – ARE WE THERE YET?

This section discusses the progress of graduate entrepreneurship involvement that Malaysia has achieved so far. Graduate unemployment has always been a priority agenda of the Ministry of Higher Education Malaysia (New Straits Times, 2021). Several measures have been taken to curb the graduate unemployment rate in

Figure 8. Employed persons based on employment status in Malaysia from 1982-2020
Source: Department of Statistics Malaysia (2021d)

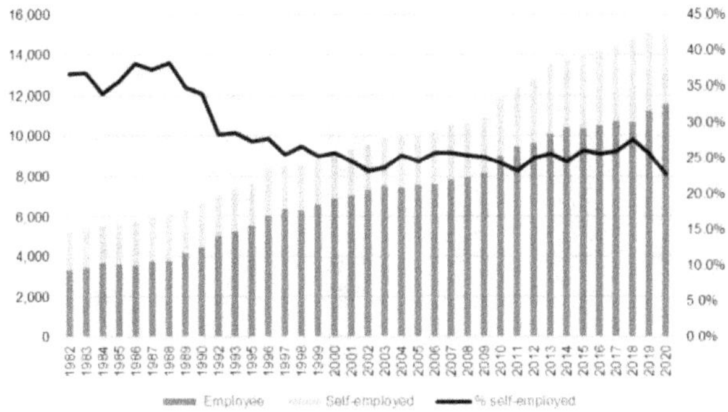

Malaysia, especially during the current COVID-19 crisis.[8] This subsection assesses various measures taken by the government to encourage graduate participation in entrepreneurship. The main question to be discussed is whether graduate considers entrepreneurship as an alternative career option. Using the dataset available for Malaysia, the discussion is divided into two parts: i) aspirations of youth and graduates about their jobs and lives, and ii) possible disengages between youth aspirations and the reality of employment—where their preference and aspirations do not match the reality.

A time-series data on the total employed persons based on employment status by the Department of Statistics (Department of Statistics Malaysia, 2021e) indicated that the percentage of the self-employed[9] workforce has declined since 1982 from 36.7% to 22.7%. As shown in Figure 8, the workforce in Malaysia's is predominantly wage earner (employee). The same dataset also indicated that the number of self-employed graduate workforce was relatively low in 2018 (15.8%) (Figure 9). A recent study by Khazanah Research Institute (2020) noted that there were positive changes in the employment share of self-account workers, and The School-to-Work Transition of Young Malaysians survey (SWTS) also found that more respondents went for informal and non-standard type of employment. While non-standard employment offers more opportunities, it may have negative consequences on youth. Gig employment, freelance work outsourced online via transactional platforms and crowd work are all rapidly expanding, offering flexible employment alternatives but with restricted access to labour and social protection, as well as increased work-related stress due to job instability and inconsistent incomes. According to SWTS, the youth are optimistic to develop job opportunities associated with the Internet of Things. It also identified a large number of young workers in such non-standard employment, as well as informal self-employed workers and contributing

Figure 9. Employed graduates based on employment status
*Note: *Self-employed includes employer, self-account worker and unpaid family worker*
Source: Department of Statistics Malaysia (2021a); Authors' calculations

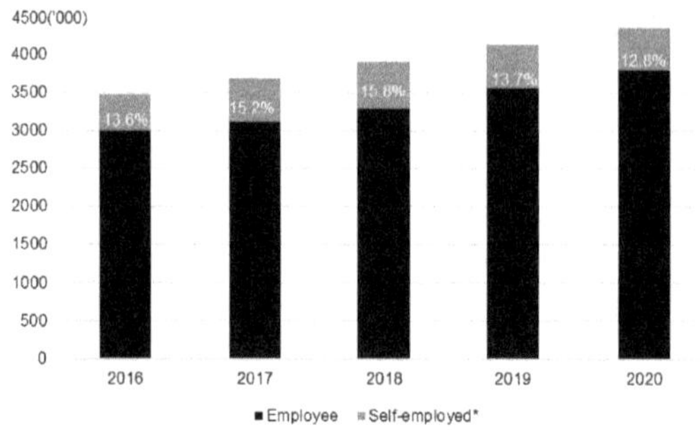

family workers, who earn low wages, have low productivity, and frequently work in hazardous conditions.

The first national representative dataset of SWTS showed a similar pattern among the younger workforce (Khazanah Research Institute, 2018). As can be seen in Figure 10, less than 20% were self-employed while the rest were wage earners. The result also indicated that self-employed workers were dominated by those without tertiary educational qualification. Moreover, the report discovered that only 20% of job seekers indicated a preference for creating their own jobs through business ownership. Apparently, the young workforce did not value entrepreneurial skills, and became less interested to initiate their own businesses. From Table 1, the perceived usefulness of skills and competencies by young workers consider to secure good jobs was slightly different from those identified by the other groups of young people covered in the SWTS. Young workers rated "creative and analytical thinking" as most useful, followed by "communication skills" and "honest and hardworking". Young people still in the education system and job seekers ranked "communication skills" above "creative and analytical thinking"; they also put greater emphasis on "English language proficiency" than young workers. Indeed, the survey found that young workers were unaware of government incentives and support for SMEs, with very few young entrepreneurs reporting receiving assistance from the government. Thus, it is quite clear that based on the information provided, entrepreneurship is not given much attention by young people, especially graduates. Nevertheless, there is an avenue for policy discourse to improve aspirations so that enterpreneurship is not seen as a secondary option for career paths.

Figure 10. Employment status of young workers in 2018
Source: Khazanah Research Institute (2018), Authors' calculations

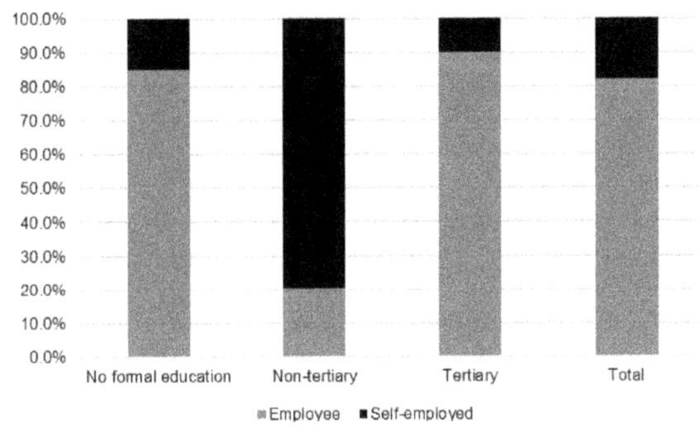

Table 1. Perceived usefulness competencies and skills for a good job for different groups of youth

Most useful soft skill	Young Workers	Job seeker	Tertiary education youth	Upper secondary youth
Creative and analytical thinking	22.6	22.3	24.8	21.2
English language proficiency	4.9	7.2	6.4	6.8
Communication skills	19.7	22.8	28.1	25.8
Teamwork skills	5.5	5.5	5.0	3.0
Entrepreneurship	3.0	3.0	3.2	2.1
Organisational adaptability	12.0	11.0	10.2	7.9
Ability to get along with people	4.2	4.7	4.0	5.9
Knowledge of the business world	3.6	3.1	2.9	3.5
Being honest and hardworking	18.1	13.2	9.6	18.0
Other	6.4	7.3	5.8	5.9
Total	100.0	100.0	100.0	100.0

Source: Khazanah Research Institute (2018), Authors' calculations

Measures to Encourage Graduate Participation in Entrepreneurship

Recognizing the value of entrepreneurship to communities and individuals, as well as its contribution to the economy, the government has laid great emphasis commencing with the New Economic Policy (1971-1990), National Development Policy (1990-2000), National Vision Policy (2001-2010), and New Economic

Model (2011-2020). Entrepreneurship is also a key component of 40 policies/ master plans/action plans/national programs of different ministries and agencies. Numerous implementing agencies also have promoted entrepreneurship. These initiatives undoubtedly demonstrate the government's commitment to this sector and its participants.

The process of cultivating an entrepreneurship culture in the education sector in Malaysia has been going for a long time. The National Education Policy (Ministry of Education Malaysia, 2015; Ministry of Higher Education Malaysia, 2013) emphasised on entrepreneurship mindset and education for students in primary, secondary and higher learning institutions. The Ministry of Education, for example, has implemented programs aimed at cultivating entrepreneurship programs through the school curriculum, such as the Principle Account and Business subjects. The Ministry of Higher Education (MOHE) in the National Higher Education Transformation Strategic Plan has outlined the role of national higher education institutions in producing more innovative human capital, which is one of the important features of entrepreneurship. MOHE also has targeted 15% of graduates to venture into entrepreneurship while in higher learning institutions, with 5% having the interest and aspiration to become entrepreneurs upon graduation (The Star, 2017). The recent growth of entrepreneurship education and training in Malaysia demonstrates a critical nature in developing an entrepreneurship education environment in higher learning institutions that fosters an entrepreneurial culture not only among students but also among the citizens in general. The government has recently established The National Entrepreneurship Policy (NEP) 2030 as a long-term strategy for Malaysia to become an outstanding enterpreneurial nation by 2030. The NEP 2030 has outlined six strategic thrusts that address current economic growth globally and issues behind entrepreneurship achievements and challenges. The NEP 2030 also has outlined its target through mid-to-long term aspirations to achieve entrepreneurial nation status by 2030 (Table 2). It is worth to note that the target aspirations are achievable. Through this policy, an ecosystem conducive to an entrepreneurial environment will be established. As quoted by the NEP 2030, the country has allocated nearly RM14 billion for entrepreneurial capacity for 2018, involving more than 150 entrepreneurship development programs under the provision of 14 ministries and agencies, and benefiting almost 700,000 participants.

The policy has also outlined various assistance provided by the government through the commitment of various ministries and agencies in Malaysia. They strive to maximise performance and provide entrepreneurs with ways to grow and improve their businesses through market expansion, innovation and productivity growth. The programs offered can be classified into six focus areas, namely funding, research grants, training and capacity, infrastructure, technology, market access, social enterprise and internationalisation. Table 3 provides a summary of assistance and support for

Table 2. NEP 2030: policy targets

Year		2018	2025	2030
Malaysia's Position in Global Indices	Global Entrepreneurship Index	58/137	Top 35	Top 25
	Global Competitiveness Index	25/140	Top 20	Top 15
	World Bank Doing Business	15/190	Top 10	Top 10
	Global Innovation Index	35/126	Top 30	Top 20
SMEs Contribution to GDP		38.3%	45%	50%
SME-generated Job Opportunities		66.2%	72%	80%
SME Contribution to Export Value		17.5%	25%	30%
Contributions by Cooperative Yield		RM40.3 billion	RM60 billion	RM100 billion

Source: Ministry of Entrepreneur Development and Coorperatives (2019)

enterpreneurs in Malaysia as outlined in the NEP 2030 policy document. The focus for graduate is well mentioned especially under the training and capacity focus areas. Assistance is offered in terms of talent and skills development on entrepreneurship to help increase the business growth. However, another issue of concern is whether graduates is well informed on the types of assistance and programs available to them? Data from SWTS revealed that graduates were unaware of the importance of entrepreneurial skills as well as the support and incentives provided for entrepreneurs, especially micro, small and medium enterprises (MSME). In fact, very few (less than 10%) young entrepreneurs reported receiving any support assistance for their businesses (Khazanah Research Institute, 2018).

"Entrepreneurship is not just about organising and managing a business; it involves initiative and risk-taking and the skills finding, assessing feasibility, exploiting, and creating chances to develop new goods and services into a lucrative business enterprise, as well as fortitude in the face of adversity and failure" – SME Annual Report 2015–2016 (2016).

Issues and Challenges: Perception, Mindset, Education and Skills

Perception is vital in entrepreneurshipas it increases the likelihood of a person embarking an entrepreneurial venture if their entrepreneurship perception is favourable (Kobia & Sikalieh, 2010; Muñoz & Cohen, 2018). For instance, when

Table 3. Entrepreneurship development programs and support in Malaysia

Programs and support	Details
Funding	1. Entrepreneur development funds for B40 by Majlis Amanah Rakyat (MARA) and TEKUN Nasional 2. Financial support through bank guarantees by Credit Guarantee Corporation (CGC) 3. Soft loans by Malaysian Industrial Development Finance Berhad (MIDF) 4. Other initiatives such as tax exemptions for social enterprises, green technology sector, tax incentives for green technology sector, Green Investment Tax Allowance (GITA) and broader access to entrepreneurial financing from numerous non-banking networks and other funding platforms such as venture capital, investment account platform, crowdfunding and peer-to-peer loans.
Research grants	Commercialisation and Vendor Research Grant (GPPV) through production of high value-added products are encouraged for companies. Demand-driven Innovation Project through the establishment of Public - Private Research Network (PPRN) creates a knowledge-friendly ecosystem and technology-based assistance for businesses. PPRN has successfully enticed 549 enterprises with more than 300 successfully matched ventures.
Capacity building and training	1. Higher Learning Institutions (HLI) Entrepreneurship Policy and Strategic Plan by the Ministry of Education (MOE) Malaysia through the introduction and cultivation of entrepreneurial values for students, and attitude and mindset shift of HLI students from jobseeker to job creator 2. Human Resource Training and Intensification Programs • Establishment of Institut Koperasi Malaysia (IKM) that offers basic entrepreneurship programs aimed at developing comprehensive cooperative institutions • Establishment of Institut Keusahawanan Negara (INSKEN) that offers more comprehensive and targeted entrepreneurship programs such as INSKEN High Performing Programs, INSKEN Business Scale Up Program and INSKEN Start-Up Program 3. Up-skilling and Mentorship Programs through the establishment of Malaysian Global Innovation and Creativity Centre (MaGIC) via Global Accelerator Program (GAP) that provides support to potential start-ups to explore the Southeast Asian market 4. Entrepreneur Capacity Building Programs through the establishment of Professional Training and Education for Growing Entrepreneurs (PROTÉGÉ) to help encourage more young people to become entrepreneurs: i. Entrepreneurship training for students and graduate entrepreneurs ii. Marketability training for graduates to secure jobs
Infrastructure	1. Malaysia Palm Oil Board (MPOB) through Technology Transfer Seminar and Exhibition that introduces new inventions created through MPOB's main researches to industry players for adaptation and commercialisation 2. Establishment of Malaysia Automotive Robotics and IoT Institute (MARii) through the Dealer Entrepreneurship Enhancement Program (DEEP) that develops technical capability of automotive vendors and organises programs that emphasis on technology adaptation associated with Industry 4.0. It also establishes workshops on manufacturing of additives and augmented reality. 3. SIRIM Berhad provides services in Standard Conformity Assessment and infrastructure to calibrate and measure industrial equipment 4. MARA established Rural Premises Transformation Program that serves to enhance small business premises and infrastructure 5. Perbadanan Usahawan Nasional Berhad (PUNB) through PROSPER Property Program that assists entrepreneurs in finding strategic premise for their businesses
Technology	28 programs on technology and innovation adoption were carried out by the government and benefitted 32,683 local entrepreneurs. Other agencies and organisations involved which have conducted similar programs are SME Corp Malaysia, Malaysian Agricultural Research and Development Institute (MARDI), SIRIM Berhad, Technology Park Malaysia (TPM) and Malaysia Technology Development Corporation (MTDC)
Market access	1. Ministry of Tourism, Arts and Culture (MOTAC) through Tourism Malaysia and Kraftangan Malaysia helps promote and facilitate tourism industry to expand their market, product and services 2. Ministry of International Trade and Industry (MITI) links the value chain for entrepreneurial activities
Social enterprises	MEDAC created the Social Entrepreneurship Accreditation (SE.A) to validate the status of a social enterprise and enable it to access various support systems and opportunities for growth. Once accredited, the organisation will be classified as an Accredited Social Enterprise on SE.A MEDAC online platform, which enables customers and the general public to access information about a social enterprise more easily.
Internationalisation	1. Through eTrade, MATRADE provides support to local enterprises that are globally competitive in e-commerce through funding, training and professional advice 2. The Women Exporters Development Program (WEDP) provides assistance to women-owned businesses engaged in export activities 3. Youth Exporters Development Program (YEDP): an entrepreneurship training program for youth aged 20-40 years interested in exporting, offering training and specialised courses. Malaysia SME Corp (in association with MARA, MATRADE and Exim Bank) 4. Galakan Eksport Bumiputera (GEB): to increase the number of high-performing Bumiputera-owned SMEs and to strengthen their pre-export capabilities, while simultaneously developing a domestic supply chain of Bumiputera-owned SMEs.

Source: Ministry of Entrepreneur Development and Coorperatives (2019)

an individual believes they are capable of overcoming the difficulties inherent in entrepreneurship, a favourable attitude towards entrepreneurship is demonstrated. However, this favourable disposition can be disrupted by endogenous and exogenous factors. The term "endogenous factor" refers to factors over which an individual has control, such as personality and character. In contrast, exogenous factor is factors that are typically beyond one's control, such as government policies, taxes and the country's economy. In terms of how students perceive entrepreneurship as a possible career path, the literature has suggested that their social groups and academic environment are likely to have a significant impact on their perception of entrepreneurship as a career path (Bacq et al., 2017; Kickul et al., 2008; Lanero et al., 2016; Piperopoulos & Dimov, 2015; Turker & Selcuk, 2009). Additional factors that may influence their attitudes towards entrepreneurship are the availability of business opportunities, their ability to run a business, the level of risk involved, and their fear of failure when starting and running a business (Iwu et al., 2021). This implies that there are factors thatcan catalyse or impede a person's involvement in entrepreneurial endeavours in other than a person's perception of entrepreneurship,.

The NEP 2030 has also identified eight main issues and challenges that need to be addressed to ensure a condusive environment, support and ecosystem to assist Malaysian entrepreneurs (Table 4). The primary challenge in education and training is to balance supply and demand for people across industries. Employers are more circumspect when it comes to hiring graduates with simply paper credentials and no added value. At the same time, many graduates find themselves trapped in employment that are unrelated to their skills and education levels (education-job or skill mismatch). Highly skilled graduates should have the vision and creativity to explore new topics and transition from job seekers to job creator mindset. This is critical, particularly in today's cutthroat employment market, where the total number of graduate jobs creation is insufficient to match with the total number of graduates produced by the country (Abu Rahim et al., 2021). Based on its first strategy, the entrepreneurship culture should be fostered across all segments in Malaysia, including graduates. Here, a holistic approach must be taken to ensure graduates are well exposed and trained on entrepreneurial skills, mindset and interest as follows:

- To incorporate entrepreneurial culture throughout the education system starting from primary school and to university;
- To improve the quality of entrepreneurship education by providing certification and accrediting curriculum;
- To develop entrepreneurship apprentice programs as part of technical and vocational education (TVET);
- To provide entrepreneurship training and support to Bumiputera students and graduates; and

- To strengthen collaboration between industry/business and educational institutions/academic, particularly in the field of educator mentoring and training.

The NEP 2030 is a long-term strategic document that was drafted to set the direction for the country's entrepreneurship development by 2030. To fulfil this aspiration, a dynamic entrepreneurship ecosystem will be established to ensure all segments of the society can benefit from it and explore their potential in entrepreneurship – National Entrepreneurship Policy 2030 policy statement.

Recommendations

1. Entrepreneural mindset needs to be cultivated at an early age of life.

Fostering entrepreneurship requires a long-term commitment. Entrepreneurial mindset must be instilled early through education. The involvement of students at the elementary, secondary, and postsecondary levels, as well as the rest of society, will cultivate individuals with critical thinking abilities, entrepreneurial traits, and entrepreneurial mentality. This results in a greater number of entrepreneurs who are creative, innovative, risk-averse, and receptive to growth opportunities. It is critical for the country to develop a sufficient number of quality and highly trained entrepreneurs or communities to ensure that the entrepreneurial environment can be strengthened and improved. Business must be culturated holistically and ingrained in Malaysians so that they can grasp the benefits and advantages of entrepreneurship (Ministry of Entrepreneur Development and Coorperatives, 2019). In the future, the government can also consider entrepreneurship as a viable alternative career option for graduates encountering employment difficulties. Young people who are interested in pursuing that path should be encouraged to do so and supported by the government.

2. *Appraising and refining existing policies and program that benefit graduates to venture into entrepreneurship.*

Given that there are more than 40 institutions implementing entrepreneurship-related programs and initiatives in Malaysia, the issue of the effectiveness of program implementation and policies can be questioned. This is because there is no single body or institution responsible for overseeing the overall achievement of the programs. It is proposed that the Ministry of Entrepreneur Development and Cooperatives acts as

Table 4. Issues and challenges in entrepreneurship in Malaysia

Issues and challenges	Details
Culture and mindset	Entrepreneurs must cultivate a strong entrepreneurial spirit to survive and succeed. This is only possible if they can transition from a fixed to a growth attitude. Entrepreneurs must shift their mindset from a demand-driven business to an opportunity-driven business. Therefore, programs aiding entrepreneurs must be holistic and strategic in nature to prepare enterprises to be self-sufficient when the assistance ceases.
Changes in demographic and socioeconomic trends	Malaysia is on the right track to become an old aged nation by 2030. Over 7% of the Malaysian population is aged 65 and above. This figure is predicted to increaseto 14.5% by 2040. Local entrepreneurs must develop new ways of operating their firms through the use of technology. The inability of local entrepreneurs to adapt and use technology will limit their ability to compete in a dynamic market.
Planning, implementation, and performance monitoring	Concerns about policy overlap between government ministries and agencies are significant. It is necessary to construct key performance indicators and assessment tools for evaluating entrepreneurial success at all levels, including individual, group, agency and organisational achievements. Other performance metrics, such as the well-being index, should be included to indicate an inclusive economic model that incorporates the principle of "Shared Prosperity."
Procedure, policy and laws	Regulations and rules that are incompatible with the needs of entrepreneurs, technology, and social development are viewed as obstacles to the advancement of local entrepreneurs. A robust structure based on collaboration between ministries, agencies and regulatory organisations is required to enable the exploration of novel business models.
Access to funding	Some entrepreneurs are unsure how to obtain finance or which financing sources are most appropriate for their firms. Another challenge encountered by the firms is working capital. Nonetheless, many entrepreneurs continue to view investors, venture capital, and grants as a holy grail. Many entrepreneurs are discouraged to grab new opportunities in the field of entrepreneurship due to lack of incentives and desires. Similarlywith commercial banks, the role of Development Financial Institutions (DFIs) has made it more difficult for entrepreneurs to acquire financial support. This is because entrepreneurs must overcome significant risk to establish a new firm. As a result, holistic solutions must be developed to reduce these gaps and optimise funding sources for businesses.
Technology	The internet has democratised and flattened consumer spending, transforming the economic model of the retail sector. The 'shop' has evolved into a mobile phone or laptop, delivering new items to the buyer regardless of where he or she is. The growth of e-commerce shows no indications of abating, and Malaysian entrepreneurs must equalise. Retailers, 'mom-and-pop' enterprises and wholesalers see clients and consumers shopping online. Due to the lack of technology adoption and reliance on low-skilled labour, productivity scaling up has stalled. This makes it more difficult for local entrepreneurs to compete on a global scale, thus reducing their market share. If this trend continues, the country's strategy for fostering innovation-driven entrepreneurship will be jeopardised.
Capabilities, sustainability and scalability of micro, small and medium enterprises	Entrepreneurs who fail to view their enterprises through supply chain lens may struggle to maintain competitiveness and improve their firms. This can be exacerbated by supply chain monopolist through price control. To promote healthy market competition, inventive solutions must be sought. What worked previously may be obsolete in the digital age. Certain merchants are pleased with the current quo and have no desire to expand globally. The issue for organisational development is to identify high-potential entrepreneurs who can be assisted effectively without squandering resources.
Education and skills	The primary challenge in education and training is to balance the supply and demand of workers across industries. Numerous graduates are trapped in professions that are unrelated to their education. Graduates should have the vision and creativity necessary to expand their horizons and alter their perspectives from job seeker to job creator.

Source: Ministry of Entrepreneur Development and Coorperatives (2019)

the lead institution that regulates and oversees all programs and initiatives related to entrepreneurship in Malaysia to ensure efficiency, non-overlap and wider coverage of the target groups. Current and existing progress of programs and policies need to be updated and assessed consistently. This will shed light on the effectiveness of the programs and policies as benchmarks and thus provide guidance on how to move forward. The respective ministries or agencies can increase coverage and support to reach a larger number of participants or further improve the training structure to remain relevant to the current and future business landscape. For example, the government through MOHE, can provide an update and progress of Ministry of Higher Education Career Advancement Program (MOHE-CAP) initiative which has been introduced under the National Economic Reform Plan (PENJANA) as part of initiatives to spur interest in entrepreneurship among graduates (Megat Deraman, 2020). This initiative is critical as it aims to connect 20,000 graduates with career opportunities, placemenst, entrepreneurship and gig labour. MOHE-CAP is an exciting initiative from the MOHE; continuous involvement in its growth is critical. It is also critical that MOHE provides regular updates on the success of this program. If the program generates significant interest and involvement, MOHE may expand its coverage and assistance to reach more participants. According to the MOHE, about 116,000 graduate employments will be disrupted in 2021; therefore, the target of 20,000 graduates for the program's is too modest.

3. Encourage the establishment of initiatives to ensure the sustainability of entrepreneurship.

What can be gained from an entrepreneurship program is that training alone is insufficient; entrepreneurs need effective and consistent support network for long-term entrepreneurship, including access to capital, information, and markets, as well as ongoing mentoring support. In the national setting, organisations such as the Entrepreneurs' Organization of Malaysia, National Association of Women Entrepreneurs of Malaysia, Malaysian Association of ASEAN Young Entrepreneurs and Young Entrepreneur Organization of Malaysia can be exploited for networks, mentoring programs and awareness—to improve the ecosystem for young entrepreneurs, especially graduates.

4. The government may consider replicating various programs and initiatives for youth and graduates to become entrepreneurs:

a. The International Labour Organization's Know About Business program encourages prospects, assesses associated risks, drives networkin, and provides mentoring. By cultivating entrepreneurial mindsets and understanding what is needed at a young age, government can better prepare interested young people who may have previously intimidated or inhibited by lack of assistance. This can also be accomplished by restructuring MOHE-CAP into a platform with expanded objectives and services, ongoing policy support, and targeted communication and recruitment for graduates and young people (Abu Rahim & Filippi, 2021).

b. The Young Entrepreneurs Mentoring Partnership (YEMP)10 and Youth Business International (YBI) are two internationally renowned mentoring programs. The main objective of YEMP is to connect young entrepreneurs in underdeveloped countries with mentors who can assist them in navigating the difficult initial stages of business start-up. Mentors are experienced corporate and government leaders in the United States who recognise the value of mentoring the next generation of leaders and are willing to share their entrepreneurial expertise with college-aged ambitious young individuals around the world.

5. Strengthen the role of career guidance councellor.

There are a number of means in which government can assist young people to understand their employment and career alternatives, and to design curriculum that will assist their smooth transition from school to the employment world. Furthermore, career guidance for young people is crucial. According to SWTS, most students make educational decisions based on family influence (Khazanah Research Institute, 2018), which may not necessarily be based on reality with up-to-date information on job opportunities and employability. There was evidence that young people have excessive expectations about their future employment prospects as shown by the 2018 OECD Program for International Student Assessment (Kadir et al., 2020). Counselors with proper training and knowledge can assisst young people at crucial time in their lives when important decisions need to be made.

6. Enhancement of available labour market information.

Improved access to job search portals, career assistance and job search counselling are all important components of the present labour market information network. Some people may beunable to receive employment services as a result of digitization (OECD, 2015). As a result, remote areas such as Sabah and Sarawak, in particular, need to be adequately reached to access employment services. For example, the services can be conducted through collaboration with local stakeholders through a decentralised strategy to provide services in smaller distant vacinity.

7. Widely use of the Critical Occupations List (COL)

The COL (TalentCorp & ILMIA, 2020) is compiled anually to identify skills gaps and better coordination of Malaysin human resource development. This information should be widely disseminated. It is a fact-based list of the Malaysian most sought-after and difficult-to-fill jobs per industry, and it exposes the skills imbalance in the country's economy. The list is intended to serve as a starting point for businesses, educational institutions and government agencies to develop talent-development initiatives that recruit, retain, retrain and upskill workers. The list must be advertised and disseminated more effectively, and it must also be used practically. The workforce must be able to adapt to new technologies and shifting work demands, which necessitates a proactive approach to anticipating and matching skills requirements. While a solid foundation of early education is important, lifelong learning is critical to professional advancement and job retention.

8. *Universities should understand that the conviction to initiate a new venture different for each person and this is highly dependent on the personality and attitude of the graduates.*

Therefore, the identification of apropriate graduates based on their risk-taking behaviors and whether or not they internal locus of control appears to be a crucial first step. However, the initial perceived contextual behaviors of graduates can be transformed through university initiatives in promoting entrepreneurial education and culture. Certain measures should be included such as positive role models with entrepreneurial experience to lead the program, providing more practical lessons rather than theoretical ones, and providing entrepreneurial support networks. Universities should encourage students to use the technical skills they acquire during their studies to inspire innovation that can feed the market needs.

9. *Strengthen knowledge transfer, innovation and commercialisation incentives for business start-ups.* Malaysia is perceived as lagging far behind in terms of providing incentives for innovation, particularly among start-ups. Consider the Silicon Valley[11] initiative in the United States, which has effectively established a business environment that has proven highly conducive to the successful formation of start-up enterprises, revolutionary business models, and leadership in a wide range of high-tech domains. According to the report of World Bank (2020), there is a need for better implementation of incentives provided for technology transfer, innovation, and commercialization by recognising the quality of intellectual property (IP) rather than the quantity of IP, so that commercialization efforts receive greater rewards for researchers and business start-ups.

CONCLUSION

With graduate employability being the agenda in higher learning education policy, career aspirations play an important role in motivating students to attain their degree qualifications and in turn determine the types of opportunities available to them in the future (Humburg & van der Velden, 2015). As Covid-19 exacerbates the labour market landscape worldwide, including Malaysia, the government has taken a number of serious measures to address the issue of graduate employability – more measures to focus specifically on encouraging graduates to venture into self-employment. Despite various efforts and initiatives provided by the government to encourage entrepreneurship to students, another question that lingers is that whether it is practical to make entrepreneurship as career options for graduates, and whether it is desired by the graduates? This chapter attempts to address the question by first looking at the graduate and entrepreneurship labour market ladscape in Malaysia, and several relevent policy discourses. Ultimately, there are some recommendations to improve the entrepreneurship programs for graduates. Interest among graduates may not exhibit impressive outcome but future policy discourses focused on instilling entrepreneurial interest among graduates must be proactively reviewed and strengthened. Hence, graduates' aspirations towards entrepreneurship can also be further enhanced. Based on our previous analysis, it proved that youth at their later stage of life in the labour market recognized the importance of entrepreneurial skills; therefore, there is an opportunity to uplift their interest towards entrepreneurship at an early age. A brief overview of the National Entrepreneurship Policy (NEP 2030) also demonstrates the government's commitment to providing better business ecosystem for everyone, including young people and graduates.

REFERENCES

Abu Rahim, M. A. R. (2021, March 24). Graduan perlu sokongan tingkat kebolehpasaran ketika pandemik. *Berita Harian*. https://www.klik.com.my/item/story/18776198/graduan-perlu-sokongan-tingkat-kebolehpasaran-ketika-pandemik

Abu Rahim, M. A. R., & Filippi, D. (2021). Ensuring Youth and Graduate Employability in an Uncertain Labour Market. Academic Press.

Abu Rahim, M. A. R., Wahab, D. A., & Jani, R. (2021). Labour market challenges amidst the Covid-19 crisis: addressing youth vulnerability. In A. Wahab, J. S. Chowdhury, S. H. Abu Bakar Ah, & M. R. Mohd Saad (Eds.), *Handbook of Research on the Impact of COVID-19 on Marginalized Populations and Support for the Future*. IGI Global. doi:10.4018/978-1-7998-7480-5.ch014

Acs, Z. J., & Szerb, L. (2007). Entrepreneurship, Economic Growth and Public Policy. *Small Business Economics*, *28*(2-3), 109–122. doi:10.100711187-006-9012-3

Bacq, S., Ofstein, L. F., Kickul, J. R., & Gundry, L. K. (2017). Perceived entrepreneurial munificence and entrepreneurial intentions: A social cognitive perspective. *International Small Business Journal: Researching Entrepreneurship*, *35*(5), 639–659. doi:10.1177/0266242616658943

Blenker, P., Korsgaard, S., Neergaard, H., & Thrane, C. (2011). The Questions We Care About: Paradigms and Progression in Entrepreneurship Education. *Industry and Higher Education*, *25*(6), 417–427. doi:10.5367/ihe.2011.0065

Cheng, M. Y., Chan, W. S., & Mahmood, A. (2009). The effectiveness of entrepreneurship education in Malaysia. *Education + Training*, *51*(7), 555–566. doi:10.1108/00400910910992754

Chung, C. (2019, November 3). Gig economy a boost for women. *Sunday Star*. https://www.mef.org.my/MEFITN/Star191103a.pdf

Davey, T., Plewa, C., & Struwig, M. (2011). Entrepreneurship perceptions and career intentions of international students. *Education + Training*, *53*(5), 335–352. doi:10.1108/00400911111147677

Department of Statistics Malaysia. (2021a). *Graduate Statistics 2020*. Author.

Department of Statistics Malaysia. (2021b). *Labour Force Survey Report 2020*. Department of Statistics, Malaysia. https://www.statistics.gov.my/portal/download_Labour/files/labour_force/Labour_Force_Survey_Report_Malaysia_2013.pdf

Department of Statistics Malaysia. (2021c). Labour Market Review. In Economic & Labour Market Review (Vol. Q2). Author.

Department of Statistics Malaysia. (2021d). Labour Market Review. In First Quarter 2021. Author.

Department of Statistics Malaysia. (2021e). *Principal Statistics of Labour Force, 1982-2020*. Department of Statistics Malaysia. https://www.dosm.gov.my/v1/uploads/files/3_Time Series/LFS_1982-2018/01.TABLE_1.pdf

Flisi, S., Goglio, V., Meroni, E. C., Rodrigues, M., & Vera-Toscano, E. (2017). Measuring Occupational Mismatch: Overeducation and Overskill in Europe—Evidence from PIAAC. *Social Indicators Research*, *131*(3), 1211–1249. doi:10.100711205-016-1292-7

Humburg, M., & van der Velden, R. (2015). Skills and the graduate recruitment process: Evidence from two discrete choice experiments. *Economics of Education Review*, *49*, 24–41. doi:10.1016/j.econedurev.2015.07.001

Institute for Labour Market Information and Analysis. (n.d.). *Youth Unemployment*. Retrieved July 13, 2021, from https://www.ilmia.gov.my/index.php/en/dashboard-datamart/kilm/indicators/youth-unemployment

Iwu, C. G., Opute, P. A., Nchu, R., Eresia-Eke, C., Tengeh, R. K., Jaiyeoba, O., & Aliyu, O. A. (2021). Entrepreneurship education, curriculum and lecturer-competency as antecedents of student entrepreneurial intention. *International Journal of Management Education*, *19*(1), 100295. doi:10.1016/j.ijme.2019.03.007

Kamberidou, I. (2020). "Distinguished" women entrepreneurs in the digital economy and the multitasking whirlpool. *Journal of Innovation and Entrepreneurship*, *9*(3), 3. doi:10.118613731-020-0114-y

Khazanah Research Institute. (2018). The School-to-Work Transition of Young Malaysians. Khazanah Research Institute. doi:10.4337/9781845421694.00018

Khazanah Research Institute. (2020). *Work in an Evolving Malaysia. The State of Households 2020 Part II*. http://krinstitute.org/assets/contentMS/img/template/editor/KRI - Full report- Work in an Evolving Malaysia - 20201103.pdf

Kickul, J., Wilson, F., Marlino, D., & Barbosa, S. D. (2008). Are misalignments of perceptions and self-efficacy causing gender gaps in entrepreneurial intentions among our nation's teens? *Journal of Small Business and Enterprise Development*, *15*(2), 321–335. doi:10.1108/14626000810871709

Killingberg, N. M., Kubberød, E., & Blenker, P. (2020). Preparing for a future career through entrepreneurship education: Towards a research agenda. *Industry and Higher Education*.

Kobia, M., & Sikalieh, D. (2010). Towards a search for the meaning of entrepreneurship. *Journal of European Industrial Training*, *34*(2), 110–127. doi:10.1108/03090591011023970

Kushida, K. (2015). *A Strategic Overview of the Silicon Valley Ecosystem: Towards Effectively "Harnessing" Silicon Valley*. https://fsi-live.s3.us-west-1.amazonaws.com/s3fs-public/strategic_overview_of_sv_ecosystems.pdf

Lanero, A., Vázquez, J. L., & Aza, C. L. (2016). Social cognitive determinants of entrepreneurial career choice in university students. *International Small Business Journal: Researching Entrepreneurship, 34*(8), 1053–1075. doi:10.1177/0266242615612882

Malaysia Ministry of Education. (2015). *Malaysia Education Blueprint 2015-2025 (Higher Education).* Ministry of Education Malaysia. http://medcontent.metapress.com/index/A65RM03P4874243N.pdf

Matlay, H. (2008). The impact of entrepreneurship education on entrepreneurial outcomes. *Journal of Small Business and Enterprise Development, 15*(2), 382–396. doi:10.1108/14626000810871745

McGuinness, S., & Sloane, P. J. (2011). Labour market mismatch among UK graduates: An analysis using REFLEX data. *Economics of Education Review, 30*(1), 130–145. Advance online publication. doi:10.1016/j.econedurev.2010.07.006

Megat Deraman, N. S. (2020, November 27). KPT-CAP beri sinar baharu buat graduan, tingkatkan kebolehpasaran. *The Malaya Post.* https://www.themalayapost.my/kpt-cap-beri-sinar-baharu-buat-graduan-tingkatkan-kebolehpasaran/

Ministry of Entrepreneur Development and Coorperatives. (2019). *National Entrepreneurship Policy Malaysia: An Outstanding Entrepreneurial Nation 2030.* https://www.medac.gov.my/admin/files/med/image/portal/NEP2030-Final.pdf

Ministry of Higher Education Malaysia. (2013). Malaysia Education Blueprint 2013 - 2025 (Pre-school to Post-Secondary Education). Ministry of Education Malaysia. doi:10.1016/j.tate.2010.08.007

Ministry of Higher Education Malaysia. (n.d.). *Graduate Tracer Study.* http://graduan.moe.gov.my/v/Penerbitan/terbitan.aspx

Mohd Abdul Kadir, J., Naghavi, N., Subramaniam, G., & A'amilyn Abdul Halim, N. (2020). Unemployment among Graduates - Is there a Mismatch? *International Journal of Asian Social Science, 10*(10), 583–592. doi:10.18488/journal.1.2020.1010.583.592

Muñoz, P., & Cohen, B. (2018). Sustainable Entrepreneurship Research: Taking Stock and looking ahead. *Business Strategy and the Environment, 27*(3), 300–322. doi:10.1002/bse.2000

New Straits Times. (2021, March 12). *Higher Education Ministry: Malaysian graduates' employability down to 84.4pc in 2020.* https://www.malaymail.com/news/malaysia/2021/03/12/higher-education-ministry-malaysian-graduates-employability-down-to-84.4pc/1957347

OECD. (2015). *Strengthening public employment services*. https://www.oecd.org/employment/Strengthening-Public-Employment-Services.pdf

Oosterbeek, H., Van Praag, M., & Ijsselstein, A. (2010). The impact of entrepreneurship education on entrepreneurship skills and motivation. *European Economic Review*, *54*(3), 442–454. doi:10.1016/j.euroecorev.2009.08.002

Pastore, F. (2019). Why so slow? The school-to-work transition in Italy. *Studies in Higher Education*, *44*(8), 1358–1371. doi:10.1080/03075079.2018.1437722

Peng, T. N. (2020). The State of the Youth in Malaysia. In T. N. Peng, L. S. Li, & N. A. Ismail (Eds.), *Demographic Transition and Socio-Economic Development in Malaysia* (pp. 117–136). University of Malaya Press. doi:10.14425/9789674881368.117136

Piperopoulos, P., & Dimov, D. (2015). Burst Bubbles or Build Steam? Entrepreneurship Education, Entrepreneurial Self-Efficacy, and Entrepreneurial Intentions. *Journal of Small Business Management*, *53*(4), 970–985. doi:10.1111/jsbm.12116

Rae, D. (2010). Universities and enterprise education: Responding to the challenges of the new era. *Journal of Small Business and Enterprise Development*, *17*(4), 591–606. doi:10.1108/14626001011088741

Rahim, H. L., & Chik, R. (2014). Graduate entrepreneurs creation: A case of Universiti Technologi MARA, Malaysia. *Australian Journal of Basic and Applied Sciences*, *8*(23), 15–20.

Rahim, H. L., Kadir, M. A. B. A., Abidin, Z. Z., Junid, J., Kamaruddin, L. M., Lajin, N. F. M., ... Bakri, A. A. (2015). Entrepreneurship education in Malaysia: A critical review. *Journal of Technology Management and Business*, *2*(2).

SME Annual Report 2015–2016. (2016). SME Corp Malaysia. doi:10.5860/crln.77.11.9594

TalentCorp & ILMIA. (2020). *Critical Occupations List 2019/2020 Technical Report*. https://www.talentcorp.com.my/clients/TalentCorp_2016_7A6571AE-D9D0-4175-B35D-99EC514F2D24/contentms/img/TalentCorp_CriticalOccupationsList_TechReport_2019-2020_Final.pdf

The Star. (2017, May 7). More student entrepreneurs by 2020. *The Star News Paper*, 5–8. https://www.thestar.com.my/news/education/2017/05/07/more-student-entrepreneurs-by-2020

Turker, D., & Selcuk, S. S. (2009). Which factors affect entrepreneurial intention of university students? *Journal of European Industrial Training*, *33*(2), 142–159. doi:10.1108/03090590910939049

Von Graevenitz, G., Harhoff, D., & Weber, R. (2010). The effects of entrepreneurship education. *Journal of Economic Behavior & Organization*, *76*(1), 90–112. doi:10.1016/j.jebo.2010.02.015

Wennekers, S., Van Stel, A., Carree, M., & Thurik, R. (2010). The Relationship between Entrepreneurship and Economic Development : Is It U-Shaped? *Foundations and Trends in Entrepreneurship*, *6*(3), 167–237. doi:10.1561/0300000023

What we do - Youth Business International. (n.d.). Retrieved September 22, 2021, from https://www.youthbusiness.org/what-we-do

World Bank. (2020). *Assessing the research institutions effectiveness of public research institutions*. http://bit.ly/WB_blogsMY

World Bank. (2021). *Tertiary Education Overview*. https://www.worldbank.org/en/topic/tertiaryeducation

Xavier, S. R., Guelich, U., Kew, P., Nawangpalupi, C., & Velasco, A. (2014). *Asean Regional Entrepreneurship Report 2014/2015. Policy Opportunities for inclusiveness and sustainable entrepreneurial growth.* The Global Entrepreneurship Monitor 2014 Global Report. https://www.academia.edu/28192121/ASEAN_REGIONAL_ENTREPRENEURSHIP_REPORT_2014_15_Driving_Asean_Entrepreneurship_Policy_Opportunities_for_Inclusiveness_and_Sustainable_Entrepreneurial_Growth

Young Entrepreneurs Mentoring Partnership. (n.d.). Retrieved September 22, 2021, from https://world-mentors.org/

ENDNOTES

1. Author's calculation based on Graduate Tracer Study report 2002 to 2019 (Ministry of Higher Education Malaysia, n.d.) by using Compound Annual Growth Rate (CAGR) — a measure of growth over time, from its beginning year to its end year, assuming that the grow is at constant rate of each year of the timespan.
2. Reports are available here https://www.gemconsortium.org/report.
3. See MOE (2013)
4. Please note that the title/subtitles of this section should be content specific.

5 Type of occupation is classified based on Malaysia Standard Classification of Occupations (MASCO) 2013. The MASCO 2013 is developed by Department of Statistics Malaysia according to the International Standard Classification of Occupations (ISCO-08). The occupation classification are classified into eight categories, namely (1) managers, (2) professionals, (3) technicians and associate professionals, (4) clerical support workers, (5) services and sales workers, (6) skilled agricultural, forestry, livestock and fishery workers, (7) craft and related trades workers and (8) plant and machine operators and assemblers. The first three occupations are regarded as graduate-type of occupations (high-skilled) while the rest are non-graduate-type of occupations (medium to low-skilled).

6 The Graduate Tracer Study is a survey that collected new graduates' information on various aspects of their education institutions and their job status after completing their studies. The survey is conducted by the Ministry of Higher Education, through respective tertiary learning institutions in conjunction with their convocation ceremonies every year.

7 See for example (Flisi et al., 2017; McGuinness & Sloane, 2011; Pastore, 2019)

8 See Abu Rahim (2021)

9 Self-employment in this context defined as those employee, own account worker and unpaid family worker

10 See *What We Do - Youth Business International* (n.d) and *Young Entrepreneurs Mentoring Partnership* (n.d.)

11 See Kushida (2015) for Silicon Valley framework and information.

Section 3
The University Environment

Chapter 8
Role of University Entrepreneurial Ecosystem and Entrepreneurial Self-Efficacy in Shaping Entrepreneurial Intention:
A Study of Indian Students

Raj Karan Gupta
School of Business Studies, Sharda University, India

ABSTRACT

This chapter is an attempt to explore the role of the university ecosystem and entrepreneurial self-efficacy in shaping entrepreneurial intention of students of higher education institutions in India. The study is empirical in nature and is based on a survey conducted among the students of a private university in India. The causal research design approach was used to explore the causal relationship among dependent and independent variable. Data was collected through a structured questionnaire, and correlation and regression analysis were performed to explore the nature of relationship among the independent and dependent variables. The major finding of this study is that both the independent variables (university entrepreneurial ecosystem and entrepreneurial self-efficacy) have been found to significantly affect the dependent variable (entrepreneurial intention). Further, entrepreneurial self-efficacy has been to be a more influencing factor than the university entrepreneurial ecosystem.

DOI: 10.4018/978-1-7998-9581-7.ch008

INTRODUCTION

Today, unemployment has become a growing concern for every country in the world specially for developing and underdeveloped countries. Further, the Covid-19 pandemic has made this unemployment situation more challenging as it has been widely observed that unemployment has increased because of this pandemic. In this kind of situation, there is an urgent need to address this unemployment problem. Now the next question is that what to do to reduce the unemployment of a nation. Here, entrepreneurship can play an important role. As it is widely known fact that entrepreneurs are the job creators and hence, if any nation wants to address the unemployment problem, the nation will have to promote and develop entrepreneurship. Entrepreneurship can be understood as a process relating to the creation of a new venture through creativity, discovering opportunity, creating risk and also creating value along-with introducing goods and services for the purposes of satisfying the needs of customers' (Shane, 2012; Balan & Metcalfe, 2012).

There are studies where the relation of entrepreneurship and the unemployment reduction have been established. In a study (Audretsch D., 2007) mentioned that as per Schumpeter effect the entrepreneurship negatively relates with the unemployment. In another study (Babaginda & Semasinghe, 2013) concluded that there is an ambiguous relationship between entrepreneurship / self-employment and unemployment. (Babangida et al., 2013) also concluded that a country having high rate of entrepreneurial activity would have a low rate of unemployment. Studies (Arshad et al., 2019; Bakar et al., 2017; Molino et al., 2018; Bellò et al., 2018) also concluded an important role of entrepreneurship towards reducing unemployment rate, creating value, producing innovative products and services and also contributing towards income and wealth creation.

Further, needless to mention here that it is really a difficult task for a nation to provide jobs to all its job seekers and hence, a pool of job creators needs to be created. They will not only create jobs for themselves but also jobs for others. As higher education institutions / universities play an important role in shaping career of their students, these universities can be used for preparing their students for their entrepreneurial career. It can be done by not only providing entrepreneurial knowledge, skills, and attitudes through entrepreneurial education and training, but also developing students' entrepreneurial self-efficacy followed by an appropriate university entrepreneurial ecosystem as well. This study is about the students of India as India is a young country which has its own concerns of growing unemployment which needs to be addressed urgently.

With this background and realizing the need, this study was formulated. The aim of this study is to understand more about entrepreneurial intention of young Indian students and the role of university entrepreneurial ecosystem and entrepreneurial self-efficacy towards shaping their entrepreneurial intention. The other reason to conduct this study for India is that India is also a developing country and the studies like (Zamberi, 2011; Roundy, 2017; Akinwale et al., 2019; Bakar et al., 2017) already mentioned that most of the studies relating to entrepreneurial ecosystems have been done mainly for developed countries with a little focus on developing countries. And hence, it becomes relevant that studies should be conducted towards exploring the role of university entrepreneurial ecosystem and entrepreneurial self-efficacy on entrepreneurial intention specially in the context of students of higher education institutions in India.

LITERATURE REVIEW AND THEORETICAL BACKGROUND

The Entrepreneurial Ecosystem

Today, it has been observed that there is a growing interest towards ecosystems as an approach to understand more about the context of entrepreneurship specially at the macro level. The role of entrepreneurial ecosystem is very important as it has the capability to either enable or constrain entrepreneurial activity within a particular area / region / territory. Studies like (Stam. E, 2015; Spigel, 2017; Acs et al., 2017) and some of the practitioners (Feld, 2012; Isenberg, 2010) have used the concept of entrepreneurial ecosystem for understanding and exploring the context of entrepreneurship in a particular territory.

The idea of entrepreneurial ecosystems emerged in the 1980s and 1990s as a paradigm shift in the field of entrepreneurial studies away from individualistic personality-based approach to a broader community perspective approach which includes and considers the role of social, economic, cultural and other actors and factors relevant to the entrepreneurship process (Aldrich, 1990; Steyaert and Katz, 2004). Entrepreneurship ecosystem can be understood as a set of interdependent actors and also the factors which are governed and controlled in such a way that they can enable the productive entrepreneurship (Stam, 2015).

In a study (Isemberg, D. J., 2010) defined entrepreneurial ecosystem as a set of various individual elements which seems to be combined in a complex manner and also interdependent in nature. Further, an entrepreneurial ecosystem can vary based on the available technology, institutions, and actors and factors involved in that entrepreneurial ecosystem and the organizational variety as well (Hayter, C. S., Nelson, A. J., Zayed, S., & O'Connor, A. C., 2018). Studies (Phan, P., Siegel, D. S., & Wright, M., 2005; Kingma B., 2014; Rice, M.P., Fetters, M.L. & Greene, P.G., 2014; Miller, D. J. & Acs, Z. 2017; Breznitz, S. & Zhang Q., 2019) explained 'entrepreneurial ecosystem' as a mechanism consisting of various elements/actors such as science & technology parks, government, support organizations, incubators and also the universities as well.

University Entrepreneurial Ecosystem and its Role in Shaping Students' Entrepreneurial Intention

Universities have been widely considered as an important fundamental agent for the development of entrepreneurship (Muscio & Ramaciotti, 2019; Saeed, Yousafzai, Yani-De-Soriano, & Muffatto, 2015; Turker & Selcuk, 2009). Some studies (Ahmed, Chandran & Klobas, 2017; Fischer, B. B., Moraes, G. H. S. M. de, & Schaeffer, P. R., 2019; Moraes, Iizuka, & Pedro, 2018; Muscio & Ramaciotti, 2019) concluded in their work and found that university's mechanism towards developing and fostering entrepreneurship among the students is still a matter of further investigation. Few other studies (Fischer, Moraes, & Schaeffer, 2019; Moraes, Fischer, Campos, & Schaeffer, 2020) also concluded that still there is no widely consensus on the kind of policy or resources which are most effective towards fostering entrepreneurship among the students. This gap becomes more relevant for the developing countries which tend to emulate entrepreneurial ecosystem practices without much focus on their own particularities and needs. (Alves et al., 2019; Fischer et al., 2019; Moraes et al., 2018).

Several studies have conducted in the past to explain the role of university entrepreneurial ecosystem towards developing the entrepreneurial intention among the university students. Today, universities are seen as an important actor of an entrepreneurial ecosystem and the entrepreneurial ecosystem of a university contributes a lot in developing entrepreneurial spirit, capabilities and entrepreneurial competencies among the students. In a study (Stam, E., 2014), it has been found that university entrepreneurial ecosystem can be seen as a set of various interdependent actors which needs to be governed in such a manner that they can facilitate the entrepreneurial actions and activities. Studies (Saeed, S., Yousafzai, S. Y., Yani-De-Soriano, M., & Muffatto, M. 2015; Kraaijenbrink, J., Bos, G., & Groen, A. 2009) found that there is a close relationship between the university context, university entrepreneurial support system and the students' entrepreneurial intention. In another study (Lüthje, C., & Franke, N., 2003) examined and concluded a direct relationship between the environment of university and the students' entrepreneurial intention. Further, university environment was also found more influencing factor towards shaping students' entrepreneurial intention as compared to other factors like personality traits and socio-economic factors. (Turker, D., & Selcuk, S. S., 2009) also examined the relationship between the university supportive environment and the students' entrepreneurial intention in Turkey. Studies (Morris, M. H., Shirokova, G. and Tsukanova, T., 2017) also explained and established a relation of university entrepreneurial support system & programmes with the students' entrepreneurial intention. Studies (Saeed, S., Yousafzai, S. Y., Yani-De-Soriano, M., & Muffatto, M. 2015; Kraaijenbrink, J., Bos, G., & Groen, A., 2009; Morris, M. H., Shirokova, G. and Tsukanova, T., 2017). also found in their work that entrepreneurial support available at university increases the students' entrepreneurial intention to create a new venture.

H1: University entrepreneurial ecosystem has a positive effect on students' entrepreneurial intention.

Entrepreneurial Self-Efficacy and Entrepreneurial Intention

The entrepreneurial self-efficacy is also an important factor which plays an important role in shaping the entrepreneurial intention of an individual. A study (Tu and Wang, 2017) found that there is a positive relationship between the general self-efficacy and the entrepreneurial intention. In another study (Salami, 2019) examined and found entrepreneurial self-efficacy as a facilitating factor towards the development of entrepreneurial intention. (McGee and Peterson, 2019) also found self-efficacy as an important determinant of several entrepreneurial outcomes such as entrepreneurial behaviour, innovativeness and entrepreneurial performance as well. Studies like (Biraglia and Kadile, 2017; Chen et al., 1998; Kickul and D'Intino, 2005; Liñán et al., 2011) also established a relation between the entrepreneurial self-efficacy and entrepreneurial intention among individuals. Few other studies (Kolvereid, 1996; Miller et al., 2012; Martin et al., 2013) examined and found that entrepreneurial self-efficacy has a positive effect over the entrepreneurial intention of individuals.

H2: Entrepreneurial self-efficacy has also a positive effect on the entrepreneurial intention.

OBJECTIVES

The objectives of this study are to:

1. Understand and explore the relationship among the university entrepreneurial ecosystem, entrepreneurial self-efficacy and the entrepreneurial intention.
2. Develop more understanding about the nature and extent of relationship of factors like university entrepreneurial ecosystem and entrepreneurial self-efficacy towards affecting entrepreneurial intention.

Figure 1. Proposed framework

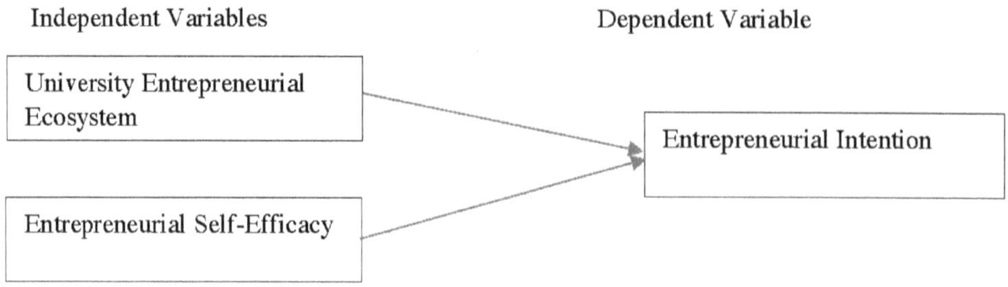

3. Providing suggestions and measures aiming to be helpful towards developing an effective policy framework for improving and strengthening the students' entrepreneurial intention.

RESEARCH QUESTIONS ADDRESSED

This study tries to address the following research questions:

1. How much the university entrepreneurial ecosystem affects the entrepreneurial intention of students of higher education institutions?
2. To what extent the entrepreneurial self-efficacy plays a role in shaping students' entrepreneurial intention?

METHODOLOGY

This study used the causal research design approach to explore the relationship among the independent variables (university entrepreneurial ecosystem and entrepreneurial self-efficacy) and the dependent variables (entrepreneurial intention).

Data Collection and Instruments

This study is empirical in nature and primary data were collected to understand and explore the relationship among the independent variables and the dependent variable used in this study. Data were collected with the help of a structured questionnaire which was developed after developing an understanding through the various literature available in this regard. The data were collected from the students of business and management discipline from a private university and between the age group of

Table 1. Reliability statistics

Reliability Statistics	
Cronbach's Alpha	**N of Items**
.831	16

(N=137). 80 Of these students were male and 57 were female. The questionnaire had two sections. Section-I contained the statements / items relating to the personal and demographic information of the respondents and the items relating to the variables / factors of this study were included in section-II of the questionnaire. In section-II, six items were used to gather data on university entrepreneurial ecosystem while five items were used to gather data on entrepreneurial self-efficacy and five items to collect data on entrepreneurial intention. The respondents were asked to rate their responses on a 5-point Liker scale ranging from 1 for strongly disagree to 5 for strongly agree. The reliability test was also done of the used instrument and the Cronbach's Alpha value was found .831 for the 16 items used in the questionnaire of this study. The details of the reliability test are provided in Table-1.

Data Analysis

The data of this study were analysed by using quantitative techniques / methods. The data were analysed by using the SPSS software and correlation and regression analysis were applied to explore the nature of relationship among the independent variables and the dependent variable.

RESULTS AND DISCUSSIONS OF THIS STUDY

The details of the analysed data are provided in the following tables.

The details of the correlation analysis are presented in Table-2. Table-2 clearly indicates that both the independent variables have a positive correlation (university entrepreneurial ecosystem +.302 and entrepreneurial self-efficacy +.526) with dependent variable (entrepreneurial intention).

However, it is also important to note here that the correlation of university entrepreneurial ecosystem with the dependent variable has been found low while a moderate correlation of entrepreneurial self-efficacy with the entrepreneurial intention.

Table 2. Correlation matrix

Correlations				
		EI	UEE	ESE
EI	Pearson Correlation	1	.302**	.526**
	Sig. (2-tailed)		.000	.000
	N	137	137	137
UEE	Pearson Correlation	.302**	1	.140
	Sig. (2-tailed)	.000		.103
	N	137	137	137
ESE	Pearson Correlation	.526**	.140	1
	Sig. (2-tailed)	.000	.103	
	N	137	137	137
**. Correlation is significant at the 0.01 level (2-tailed).				

Table 3. Model summary

Model Summary				
Model	**R**	**R Square**	**Adjusted R Square**	**Std. Error of the Estimate**
1	.574[a]	.330	.320	.46048
a. Predictors: (Constant), ESE, UEE				

The detail of the model summary is presented in Table-3 which indicates that 33% variation in the dependent variable is explained by the independent variables under this study.

Table-4 includes the coefficient details. The coefficient values (B) relating to independent variables (university entrepreneurial ecosystem (.215 with p value $< .05$) and entrepreneurial self-efficacy (.502 with p value $< .05$) consecutively were found which supported both hypotheses of this study. Hence, it can be concluded that both the independent variables (university entrepreneurial ecosystem and the entrepreneurial self-efficacy) have a significant positive effect on the dependent variable (entrepreneurial intention). In addition to that entrepreneurial self-efficacy has been found more influencing factor towards shaping the entrepreneurial intention.

Table 4. The coefficient output

Coefficients[a]						
Model		**Unstandardized Coefficients**		**Standardized Coefficients**	**t**	**Sig.**
		B	**Std. Error**	**Beta**		
1	(Constant)	1.264	.354		3.571	.000
	UEE	.215	.066	.233	3.264	.001
	ESE	.502	.073	.493	6.910	.000
a. Dependent Variable: EI						

FINDINGS AND SUGGESTIONS

This study found that the university entrepreneurial ecosystem and entrepreneurial self-efficacy both affect and play an important role in shaping entrepreneurial intention of the students. Thus, improving and strengthening the above said factors will improve the entrepreneurial intention as well that will further lead to creation of more entrepreneurs and creating more new jobs too. This will be further helpful towards addressing and reducing the unemployment. Now the question is how to strengthen the university entrepreneurial ecosystem and entrepreneurial self-efficacy of the students.

To strengthen the university entrepreneurial ecosystem, a systematic approach may be used and some mechanism like 'University Campus Entrepreneurship Policy' can be developed with a focus on an integrated approach to developing entrepreneurship at university level. In addition to that to encourage and motivate students, 'Student Entrepreneurship Award' may be introduced which can be offered based on the participation, engagement and performance of the students in various entrepreneurial activities / events within campus and also outside the campus. Development of Annual action plan along-with a close monitoring through a committee consisting of the members representing from various stakeholders' groups of the university entrepreneurial ecosystem would also be a valuable step in this regard.

In addition to providing formal entrepreneurship education / courses, specific need based customized training programmes should also be offered to those students having potential to become an entrepreneur or those who are willing to adopt an entrepreneurial career. To improve the self-confidence and strengthen students' entrepreneurial self-efficacy, more focus should be on teaching and training students with the 'Learning by doing' and or 'Action learning' pedagogy / approach. This kind of approach will not only improve their entrepreneurial skills, attitudes and competencies but also ultimately improve their beliefs towards their entrepreneurial behaviour / actions and performance.

CONCLUSION

The conclusion of this study is that university entrepreneurial ecosystem and entrepreneurial self-efficacy both are important towards strengthening the entrepreneurial intention of the students. Hence, adequate attention is required towards developing the entrepreneurial ecosystem at university level along-with the general and entrepreneurial capacity building of the students having potential to become an entrepreneur. If the efforts are done in this area, will improve the entrepreneurial intention of students and the students having an entrepreneurial mindset and competency will be able to create new ventures which will offer employment opportunities to others as well which will further contribute to reduction in unemployment of the country.

LIMITATION AND FUTURE DIRECTION OF WORK

This study has also its own limitations. The main limitation of this study is that it is based on not a very large sample size and is done by focusing only the students of a private university and hence, the findings of this study cannot be generalized to other institutions of higher education. However, this study gives a basis and understanding to conduct similar kind of work by incorporating a large sample size coming from different institutions of higher education and from a diverse group as well. Further studies can also be conducted to explore the entrepreneurial ecosystem at regional level / country level and the role of universities in the entrepreneurial ecosystem of a nation or region in which that university belongs to as one of the elements of that entrepreneurial ecosystem.

REFERENCES

Acs, Z. J., Stam, E., Audretsch, D. B., & O'Connor, A. (2017). The lineages of the entrepreneurial ecosystem approach. *Small Business Economics*, *49*(1), 1–10. doi:10.100711187-017-9864-8

Ahmed, T., Chandran, V. G. R., & Klobas, J. (2017). Specialized entrepreneurship education: Does it really matter? Fresh evidence from Pakistan. *International Journal of Entrepreneurial Behaviour & Research, 23*(1), 4–19. doi:10.1108/IJEBR-01-2016-0005

Akinwale, Y. O., Ababtain, A. K., & Alaraifi, A. A. (2019). Structural equation model analysis of factors influencing entrepreneurial interest among university students in Saudi Arabia. *Journal of Entrepreneurship Education, 22*(4), 1–14.

Aldrich, H. E. (1990). Using ecological perspective to study organizational founding rates. *Entrepreneurship Theory and Practice, 14*(3), 7–24. doi:10.1177/104225879001400303

Alves, A. C., Fischer, B., Schaeffer, P. R., & Queiroz, S. (2019). Determinants of student entrepreneurship: An assessment on higher education institutions in Brazil. *Innovation & Management Review, 16*(2), 96–117. doi:10.1108/INMR-02-2018-0002

Arshad, M., Farooq, O., & Farooq, M. (2019). The effect of intrinsic and extrinsic factors on entrepreneurial intentions: The moderating role of collectivist orientation. *Management Decision, 57*(3), 649–668. doi:10.1108/MD-04-2016-0248

Audretsch, D. B. (2007). Entrepreneurship capital and economic growth. *Oxford Review of Economic Policy, 23*(1), 63–78. doi:10.1093/oxrep/grm001

Babaginda, M. M., & Semasinghe, D. M. (2013). *Entrepreneurship and unemployment: A literature review*. https://www.academia.edu/5322204/Entrepreneurship_and_Unemployment_A_Litrature_Review

Bakar, A. R. A., Ahmad, S. Z., Wright, N. S., & Skoko, H. (2017). The propensity to business start-up: Evidence from global entrepreneurship monitor (GEM) data in Saudi Arabia. *Journal of Entrepreneurship in Emerging Economies, 9*(3), 263–285. doi:10.1108/JEEE-11-2016-0049

Balan, P., & Metcalfe, M. (2012). Identifying teaching methods that engage entrepreneurship students. *Education + Training, 54*(5), 368–384. doi:10.1108/00400911211244678

Bellò, B., Mattana, V., & Loi, M. (2018). The power of peers: A new look at the impact of creativity, social context and self-efficacy on entrepreneurial intentions. *International Journal of Entrepreneurial Behaviour & Research, 24*(1), 214–233. doi:10.1108/IJEBR-07-2016-0205

Biraglia, A., & Kadile, V. (2017). The role of entrepreneurial passion and creativity in developing entrepreneurial intentions: Insights from American homebrewers. *Journal of Small Business Management*, *55*(1), 170–188. doi:10.1111/jsbm.12242

Breznitz, S., & Zhang, Q. (2019). Fostering the growth of student start-ups from university accelerators: An entrepreneurial ecosystem perspective. *Industrial and Corporate Change*, *28*(4), 855–873. doi:10.1093/icc/dtz033

Chen, C. C., Greene, P. G., & Crick, A. (1998). Does entrepreneurial self-efficacy distinguish entrepreneurs from managers? *Journal of Business Venturing*, *13*(4), 295–316. doi:10.1016/S0883-9026(97)00029-3

de Moraes, G. H. S. M., Iizuka, E. S., & Pedro, M. (2018). Effects of Entrepreneurial Characteristics and University Environment on Entrepreneurial Intention. *Revista de Administração Contemporânea*, *22*(2), 226–248. doi:10.1590/1982-7849rac2018170133

Feld, B. (2012). *Startup communities: Building an entrepreneurial ecosystem in your city*. Wiley. doi:10.1002/9781119204459

Fischer, B. B., de Moraes, G. H. S. M., & Schaeffer, P. R. (2019). Universities' institutional settings and academic entrepreneurship: Notes from a developing country. *Technological Forecasting and Social Change*, *147*, 243–252. doi:10.1016/j.techfore.2019.07.009

Hayter, C. S., Nelson, A. J., Zayed, S., & O'Connor, A. C. (2018). Conceptualizing academic entrepreneurship ecosystems: A review, analysis and extension of the literature. *The Journal of Technology Transfer*, *43*(4), 1039–1082. doi:10.100710961-018-9657-5

Isenberg, D. J. (2010). How to start an entrepreneurial revolution. *Harvard Business Review*, *88*(6), 41–50.

Kickul, J., & D'Intino, R. S. (2005). Measure for measure: Modelling entrepreneurial self-efficacy onto instrumental tasks within the new venture creation process. *New England Journal of Entrepreneurship*, *8*(2), 39–47. doi:10.1108/NEJE-08-02-2005-B005

Kingma, B. (2014). Creating a dynamic campus–community entrepreneurial ecosystem: Key characteristics of success in academic entrepreneurship. *Emerald Group Publishing Limited*, *16*(August), 97–114.

Kolvereid, L. (1996). Prediction of employment status choice intentions. *Entrepreneurship Theory and Practice*, *21*(1), 47–57. doi:10.1177/104225879602100104

Kraaijenbrink, J., Bos, G., & Groen, A. (2009). What do students think of the entrepreneurial support given by heir universities? *International Journal of Entrepreneurship and Small Business*, *9*(1), 110–125. doi:10.1504/IJESB.2010.029512

Liñán, F., Rodríguez-Cohard, J. C., & Rueda-Cantuche, J. M. (2011). Factors affecting entrepreneurial intention levels: A role for education. *The International Entrepreneurship and Management Journal*, *7*(2), 195–218. doi:10.100711365-010-0154-z

Lüthje, C., & Franke, N. (2003). The "making" of an entrepreneur: Testing a model of entrepreneurial intent among engineering students at MIT. *R & D Management*, *33*(2), 135–147. doi:10.1111/1467-9310.00288

Martin, B. C., Mcnally, J. J., & Kay, M. J. (2013). Examining the formation of human capital in entrepreneurship: A meta-analysis of entrepreneurship education outcomes. *Journal of Business Venturing*, *28*(2), 211–224. doi:10.1016/j.jbusvent.2012.03.002

McGee, J. E., & Peterson, M. (2019). The long-term impact of entrepreneurial self-efficacy and entrepreneurial orientation on venture performance. *Journal of Small Business Management*, *57*(3), 720–737. doi:10.1111/jsbm.12324

Miller, D. J., & Acs, Z. (2017). The campus as entrepreneurial ecosystem: The University of Chicago. *Small Business Economics*, *49*(1), 75–95. doi:10.100711187-017-9868-4

Miller, T. L., Grimes, M. G., McMullen, J. S., & Vogus, T. J. (2012). Venturing for others with heart and head: How compassion encourages social entrepreneurship. *Academy of Management Review*, *37*(4), 616–640. doi:10.5465/amr.2010.0456

Molino, M., Dolce, V., Cortese, C. G., & Ghislieri, C. (2018). Personality and social support as determinants of entrepreneurial intention. gender differences in Italy. *PLoS One*, *13*(6), e0199924. doi:10.1371/journal.pone.0199924 PMID:29953517

Morris, M. H., Shirokova, G., & Tsukanova, T. (2017). Student entrepreneurship and the university ecosystem: A multi-country empirical exploration. *European Journal of International Management*, *11*(1), 65–85. doi:10.1504/EJIM.2017.081251

Muscio, A., & Ramaciotti, L. (2019). How does academia influence Ph.D. entrepreneurship? New insights on the entrepreneurial university. *Technovation*, *82–83*, 16–24. doi:10.1016/j.technovation.2019.02.003

Phan, P., Siegel, D. S., & Wright, M. (2005). Science parks and incubators: Observations, synthesis and future research. *Journal of Business Venturing*, *20*(2), 165–182. doi:10.1016/j.jbusvent.2003.12.001

Rice, M. P., Fetters, M. L., & Greene, P. G. (2014). University-based entrepreneurship ecosystems: A global study of six educational institutions. *International Journal of Entrepreneurship and Innovation Management*, *18*(5/6), 481–501. doi:10.1504/IJEIM.2014.064722

Roundy, P. T. (2017). Small town entrepreneurial ecosystems: Implications for developed and emerging economies. *Journal of Entrepreneurship in Emerging Economies*, *9*(3), 238–262. doi:10.1108/JEEE-09-2016-0040

Saeed, S., Yousafzai, S. Y., Yani-De-Soriano, M., & Muffatto, M. (2015). The role of perceived university support in the formation of students' entrepreneurial intention. *Journal of Small Business Management*, *53*(4), 1127–1145. doi:10.1111/jsbm.12090

Salami, S. O. (2019). Examining the emerging entrepreneurial mindset in adolescence: A study in Nigeria. *International Journal of Psychology*, *2*(1), 431. doi:10.1002/ijop.12431 PMID:28493413

Shane, S. (2012). Reflections on the 2010 AMR decade award: Delivering on the promise of entrepreneurship as a field of research. *Academy of Management Review*, *37*(1), 10–20. doi:10.5465/amr.2011.0078

Spigel, B. (2017). The relational organization of entrepreneurial ecosystems. *Entrepreneurship Theory and Practice*, *41*(1), 49–72. doi:10.1111/etap.12167

Stam, E. (2014). The Dutch entrepreneurial ecosystem. SSRN *Electronic Journal*. doi:10.2139/ssrn.2473475

Stam, E. (2015). Entrepreneurial ecosystems and regional policy: A sympathetic critique. *European Planning Studies*, *23*(9), 1759–1769. doi:10.1080/09654313.2015.1061484

Steyaert, C., & Katz, J. (2004). Reclaiming the space of entrepreneurship in society: Geographical, discursive and social dimensions. *Entrepreneurship and Regional Development*, *16*(3), 179–196. doi:10.1080/0898562042000197135

Tu, Y., & Wang, H. (2017). A study on the influence of college students' self-efficacy and creativity on entrepreneurial intention. *Journal of Higher Education (Columbus, Ohio)*, *3*, 95–100.

Turker, D., & Selcuk, S. S. (2009). Which factors affect entrepreneurial intention of university students? *Journal of European Industrial Training*, *33*(2), 142–159. doi:10.1108/03090590910939049

Zamberi Ahmad, S. (2011). Evidence of the characteristics of women entrepreneurs in the kingdom of Saudi Arabia: An empirical investigation. *International Journal of Gender and Entrepreneurship*, *3*(2), 123–143. doi:10.1108/17566261111140206

Chapter 9
The University Environment and Graduate Entrepreneurship:
A Study of Ranchi City

Bhavna Taneja
https://orcid.org/0000-0002-5447-7758
Amity University, Ranchi, India

ABSTRACT

Every individual wants to be self-sufficient and economically independent. Entrepreneurship is the activity of setting up a business, taking financial risks in the hope of earning profit. Entrepreneur education provides the students with the groundwork needed to start successful commercial or non-commercial businesses, create and endorse new products and processes, engage in social entrepreneurship, and serve as leaders in organizations. This study provides the basis for understanding the entrepreneurial intentions and role of education for a college student—of interest to both researchers and policymakers. The objectives of the study are to understand what graduate entrepreneurship is. The internal factors that encourage students to choose graduate entrepreneurship are entrepreneurial intentions, attitudes, and motivation of students. The external factors that motivate students to choose graduate entrepreneurship are the educational environment of colleges, interaction with existing entrepreneurs, and government policies.

DOI: 10.4018/978-1-7998-9581-7.ch009

INTRODUCTION

Every individual wants to be self-sufficient and economically independent. The individuals who become self-sufficient seems to be creative, innovative, and confident. They can take risks and initiatives in setting up their new business to raise income. These individuals may be termed as entrepreneurs and the phenomenon as entrepreneurship. The term entrepreneurship is business related phenomenon which explains the activities necessary to start and maintain ones' business, to raise ones' income, by enhancing opportunities of employment. Entrepreneurship consists of establishing a firm or a company, buying and selling things, public relations, understanding market dynamics, marketing etc. Based on recognition, evaluation and exploitation of opportunities, entrepreneurship is a process that stimulates economic growth, provides new products, boosts the incomes of houses-holds, and provides a solution to unemployment as it gives jobs to lots of people. In a world shifting towards sustainable development, entrepreneurship is of great importance.

The relevance of young people and students cannot be underestimated in any economy since they are the future of the economic sustainability of a country. A student's positive inclination towards entrepreneurial activity is of paramount importance in anticipating the entrepreneurship possibilities of a country. If the young generation realizes the significance of entrepreneurship and are ready to venture into business, the redundancy rate can be reduced, and a growth in the economy will be seen. It is evident that young graduates who are starting a new venture after completion of graduation represent a vital class on the national economic level.

Graduate Entrepreneurship education is associated with entrepreneurial self-efficacy to enhance entrepreneurial intentions among graduates. Entrepreneurship education builds and promotes entrepreneurial abilities and attitudes among graduates, so that they can take initiatives and start their business. Graduate entrepreneurship cultivates mindsets and aspirations among graduates to establish a new firm or a company. Entrepreneurship education promotes awareness among graduates about business planning and starting a new business. The graduates equipped with entrepreneurial knowledge and talents are more confident to start new business and become economically independent. They also facilitate others by extending employment prospects to them.

Graduate Entrepreneurship teaches business and non-business students the core aspects of entrepreneurship. It provides them the groundwork needed to start successful commercial or non-commercial businesses, create, and endorse new products and processes, engage in social entrepreneurship, and serve as leaders and thought generators in existing organizations. Studies confirm that entrepreneurship education can transfer the skills, ability, and knowledge necessary to identify business opportunities, in students in nations. According to Lombardi et al. (2017)

postgraduate studies may have an effective influence in students' decision to undertake entrepreneurship, based on the absorption of new knowledge, subjects focused on entrepreneurship and the university infrastructure. The importance of universities in supporting entrepreneurship has grown significantly in recent decades, leading to the emergence of new methods, cultures, and structures (Lombardi et al. 2017).

Graduate education can play a considerable role in the economic development of an individual, society, and the country. Many governments encourage their peoples to adopt entrepreneurship as a strategy to mitigate unemployment, particularly youth and graduate unemployment. A wide range of policies and initiatives across countries have apparently created momentum for the development of graduate entrepreneurship. Graduate entrepreneurship has become one of the top priorities in the policy agenda in many countries and world organizations over the past few years. There is now a consensus that new opportunities for students be created to develop entrepreneurial mindsets and behaviors.

Entrepreneurship seems to be the answer for the economic development in a developing country like India. Since the last decade India has made lots of efforts for economic growth. The GDP of the country has grown, because of the new investments and the growth of the services sector. The Indian Economy is going to be a leading power in the coming years. Other countries are looking up at India and China mainly because of low manufacturing cost. This will provide countless business opportunities. In the last few years, the Indian economy has reached new peaks, yet the country's economic development has not picked up proportionately to the amenities provided in higher education. The business education, as it occurs today in most of the Indian institutions, has little importance to the societal needs of the country. This has resulted in large scale unemployment amongst young graduates. This trend needs to be rectified at the earliest. India needs businesspersons in large numbers to take advantage of the new prospects and to create jobs for sustained development.

If India must bounce back, then start-ups need to be encouraged. Entrepreneurship is attracting the full attention of the Central and State Governments in India through its agencies like the Industrial Development Bank of India (IDBI), District Industries Centres, National Small Industries Corporation (NSIC) and National Institute for Entrepreneurship and Small Business Development etc. These organizations provide help with consultancy, marketing, exports etc. to the graduates trying to set up their own enterprises. In the last few years, the Government of India has taken many initiatives to drive the nation on the path of innovation and creating a conducive ecosystem because, innovation, economic growth and social development are intertwined. Prime Minister Shri Narendra Modi has said that a self-reliant India would be important in the post-COVID 19 world and would be based on five pillars - Economy, Infrastructure, System, Demography, and Demand. Some of the initiatives of the Government are - Start-up India, Accelerating Growth of New India's Innovations (AGNIi), ASPIRE scheme, Smart City Mission, Uchchatar Avishkaar Yojana, Make in India, Start-up India Initiative, Atal Incubation Centre (AIC), Atal Innovation Mission (AIM), AtmaNirbhar Bharat. The Indian Prime Minister has said "Atmanirbhar Bharat, is about being self-sustaining and self-generating" and pursuing "policies that promote efficiency, equity and resilience" *Outlook India* (2020).

The Central Government's New Education Policy 2020 is another initiative in this direction. This policy has provisions for some radical changes. Its pivotal focus is on optimizing use of resources, academic flexibility, critical thinking, experiential learning, interactive classrooms, integrated pedagogy, inter/transdisciplinary approach for proficiency, and outcome-based student-centric 21st century education. This is likely to spur applied learning, innovation, and an entrepreneurial culture in the Higher Education Institutions.

Objectives of the Study

This study provides the basis for understanding the entrepreneurial intentions and role of education for a college student– of interest to both researchers and policymakers. The objectives of the study are to understand-

- What is graduate entrepreneurship.
- Internal factors which encourage students to choose graduate entrepreneurship
- External factors which motivate students to choose graduate entrepreneurship

Research Methodology

The final year students of Commerce and Management, from selected institutions in the city of Ranchi, Jharkhand, were taken as the sample for this study. A well-structured questionnaire was filled by the postgraduates MBA (Master's in business administration) students and undergraduates BBA (Bachelor of Business Administration) and B.COM (Bachelor of Commerce) students at various universities in the city of Ranchi, Jharkhand.

For the study, the author applied random sampling method as it is less problematic and cost-effective. 222 responses were obtained from the selected colleges of Ranchi, Jharkhand.

BACKGROUND

A process of accomplishing something (being creative), being different (being inventive), and daring to take risks is how entrepreneurship is defined by Blesia et al. (2019). Holienka et al. (2017), refer to entrepreneurship as all students actively engaged in any innovative activities, i.e., acting on identified possibilities and created ideas, and changing them into value for others. Graduate entrepreneurship is a source of competitiveness; it has the power to drive the development of a knowledge-driven economy (Birch et al, 2017; Nabi & Holden, 2008); it can boost the start-ups within the economy. A risk-taker entrepreneur decides to promote an idea even if it has a chance of failing, whereas an innovative entrepreneur points out fresh ideas (Blesia et al. 2019). It is an important source of local revolution and economic growth (Matt & Schaeffer, 2018; Nabi & Linan, 2011).

Entrepreneurship is often seen as critical to economic growth, job creation, and technical advancement (Blesia et al. 2019; Nguyen 2020). Self-employment is becoming increasingly important because it leads to job creation and economic development (Baumol, 2010). In modern societies, our lives and careers are getting ever more unpredictable and unsure. As Savickas et al. (2009) highlight, "today occupational prospects seem far less definable and predictable, with job transition more frequent and difficult.

Mohd Abass Bhat and Arfat Ahmad (2020) discovered that young people in Kashmir see launching a business as a significant risk. Four composite aspects – economic, social, educational, and personal – were used to examine the evolution of this entrepreneurship threat. Personal characteristics were revealed to be much more influential in predicting the youth's attitude toward beginning their own business unit among the choose independent factors. R. Duraipandian, Rajib Kumar Roy (2021) proposed some factors related to entrepreneurial development that have a greater impact on business profitability than other factors, such as entrepreneurial competencies, competitive advantage of various offerings within organisations, entrepreneur's education, and supplier availability, among others.

Entrepreneurship can be discussed in a broader context by two terms i.e., entrepreneurship education and entrepreneurial intensions. Based on entrepreneurial self-efficacy theory of Bae, Qian, Chao Miao, and Fiet, (2014) a positive relationship exists between entrepreneurship intentions to entrepreneurial education. Bae, Qian, Chao Miao, and Fiet, (2014) distinguished between the two by describing that, entrepreneurial intentions are the desires and aspirations of the graduates [individuals] to start a business whereas entrepreneurship education refers to the education which is given for developing entrepreneurial attitudes and skills among graduates.

The educational organizations play a fundamental role in encouraging the attitudes and skills related with entrepreneurship. Education that promotes creativity, innovation, and self-employability, needs to be developed at all levels. Education systems foster the employability talents in the students (Teijeiro, Rungo, & Freire, 2013). Education systems should develop creative abilities in students, which allow them to develop complex cognitive processes: imagining, speculating, and inventing (Urban, 2006). These capabilities are essential to take vital decisions in a cool and prudent way (Santana, Feliciano, & Jimenez, 2012). Universities help the students by assisting them in developing inventive new possibilities, adopting strategic approaches, and designing organisational processes to experiment with and turn good ideas into reality (Dodgson and Gann 2020).

Entrepreneurship has been revolutionised by the rapid development of new technologies, which has resulted in knowledge or technology transfer (Barbini et al. 2021). The Internet can be viewed as a critical medium for the development of entrepreneurship and soft skills (Prameswari et al. 2020).

What is Entrepreneurial Intention

Intent can be defined as "a state of mind directing one's attention toward an explicit object or a direction to achieve something" (Vesalainen and Pihkala, 1999). Entrepreneurship is defined as the technique of organizational emergence. Intentions toward a behavior can lead to that behavior. Business intention is the main predictor of future entrepreneurial behavior (Krueger, 2000). Entrepreneurial intentions are the first in the series of actions to organizational start-ups. Therefore, investigating what factors determine the entrepreneurial intent may be crucial in entrepreneurship research. Due to limited research on entrepreneurial intentions, it is important to know what factors are more important for cultivating entrepreneurial intentions among students.

Education has an impact on entrepreneurial intent (Maresch et al. 2016; Trivedi 2016; Gelaidan and Abdullateef 2017), allowing students to learn organisational skills such as leadership development, time management, and interpersonal skills or two or more foreign languages to connect with as many people as possible (Sansone et al. 2021).

What is Entrepreneurship Education

To be beneficial in their working life and personal life education should foster creativity, innovation, and risk taking in the students so that they have the skills to plan, manage projects, ethically. Entrepreneurship education consists of university programs and courses, that are offered to potential entrepreneurs, under the supervision of an institute or department, through innovative pedagogical techniques and strategies.

These are skill-oriented programs and use methods and techniques like experiential learning etc. which suit the needs of the potential entrepreneurs in the finest way.

Imparting or offering entrepreneurship education usually heightens awareness among graduates about an alternative career to employment (Slavtchev, Laspita, and Patzelt, 2012). They think in a pragmatic way and choose business as profession. These graduates become aware of starting a business, maintaining it, and expanding it. According to Linan (2008) entrepreneurship education nurture the attitudes and aspirations of graduates to establish a new firm or a company. Linan (2008) says that entrepreneurship education offers courses about business planning and starting a new business. It creates jobs and risk-taking capacity among the graduates. Fayolle, Gailly, and Lassas-Clerc (2006) defined entrepreneurship education as "any pedagogical (program) or process of education to build entrepreneurial attitudes and skills". However, Johansen and Schanke (2012) put forward an elaborative concept of entrepreneurship education and believe that it is the promotion of different entrepreneurial skills, personal qualities, creativity, their attitude towards innovation, and ability to overcome risk.

Entrepreneurship education plays a catalyzing role in encouraging graduates to start some profit-based economic activity. Entrepreneurship education plays a very important role in cultivating entrepreneurship and innovation, and may help to shape a person's entrepreneurial skills, and competence (Kuratko, 2005), which are necessary for entrepreneurship (Unger et al., 2011).

Entrepreneurship education develops self-competence and social skills. The concept involves taking initiatives in opening a business or making innovation in the existing one. Entrepreneurship education prepares graduates by equipping them with necessary skills, abilities, and attitudes to become entrepreneurs. It also motivates them to own or start a business through conducive incubation training and internship. Entrepreneurship education also develops and sustains motivation among the graduates to become successful entrepreneurs. In real sense, the entrepreneurship education improves a human by helping graduates learn the skills and knowledge through investment on their education and on-the-job training (Davidsson and Honig, 2003; Unger, Rauch, Frese, and Rosenbusch, 2011).

Martin, McNally, and Kay (2013) found a relation between entrepreneurship education and human capital .They believed that knowledge and skills, lead to the intentions of recognizing entrepreneurship. According to Wilson, Kickul, and Marlino, (2007) association of entrepreneurship education with entrepreneurial self-efficacy appears to enhance entrepreneurial intentions which are necessary for successful entrepreneurs.

Higher education is adjusting to the dynamic local, national, and international context considering student entrepreneurship's contribution to the labour force (Blesia et al. 2019). The goal of Higher education has turned the university into a teaching, research, and economic development enterprise, with a focus on practical application and commercialization of research discoveries (Bauboniene et al. 2019).

The above discussion makes it understandable that entrepreneurship education enables graduates to set up new business by taking risk with firm intentions. Entrepreneurs who start their business and make it grows with time are called successful entrepreneurs and they become role models for others. It makes them employers rather than searching for a job. They play an active role in community development by empowering individuals through employment. They become independent, self- sufficient and self-reliant. Their lifestyles and living standards rise because of it.

Pedagogy for Imparting Entrepreneurship Education

Student entrepreneurship, according to Chiarello et al. (2021), is not limited to a single topic of study. Youndt, Subramaniam, and Snell (2004) viewed education as strengthening the skills of graduates regarding formulation of a business plan according to their entrepreneurial intentions. Accelerators, incubators, business plan competitions, and grants are all options (Wright et al. 2017). There are different techniques to impart entrepreneurship education including business planning (Kuratko, 2005). According to Honig, (2004) majority of the entrepreneur courses consist of business planning.

The students are involved in activities in the campus and during internship or incubation period. They get hands-on practice and training which leads them to becoming entrepreneurs. Brown, Collins, and Duguid (1989) emphasized hands-on practice and apprenticeship training to make young entrepreneurs independent initiators. It develops entrepreneurial skills like managing individual and others which are direly needed by entrepreneurs. Learning by doing and involving learners in learning process ensures effective learning. Hussain and Sultan (2010) asserted that learning by doing involves learners actively and suits best in developing skills among adults. Minniti and Bygrave (2001) endorsed it by describing that it enhances confidence of entrepreneurs in taking initiatives and important actions in critical situations. Learning by-doing enriches practical experience of the learners -the young entrepreneurs leading to venture creation as well.

Students discover and assess long-term potential in building their businesses, and they create project plans for developing their products and services, as well as undertaking market and competitive studies (Ilonen et al. 2018). Other significant advancements have been made through the introduction of business simulations, which are seen as a useful tool for the development and improvement of entrepreneurial abilities (Samaonok et al. 2020). Extra-curricular support activities like seminars, and training, are aimed at creating a supportive environment for entrepreneurship (Morris et al. 2017; Sendouwa et al. 2019).

In the current scenario, new technology development has been fostering technological entrepreneurship in universities through start-ups, university-industry partnerships, licencing, and patenting accelerated (Schimperna et al. 2020; Lombardi et al. 2021a). As a result, both alumni and current students support start-ups (Wright and Mustar 2019). According to Olawole A. Adetayo (2019), the forces of innovation, technology, and entrepreneurship promote business transformation synergies. Technology has played a critical part in the development of corporate growth, because of the evolution of the internet. If businesses can effectively employ technology, they will be able to flourish and make the world a smaller place for all consumers.

According to Olena Krylova and Kostiantyn Shaposhnykov (2020), to increase innovative entrepreneurship, several measures should be implemented. These measures include awareness of the national economy's ability to innovate, create markets for new products, and increase its competitiveness, ensuring diversification of sources of financing.

MAIN FOCUS OF THE CHAPTER

Factors Influencing the Decision to be an Entrepreneur

The literature on reasons that influence the decision to become an entrepreneur is extensive. Based on previous research, internal and external factors are incorporated in this study. Internal factors or Personal factors that are specific to that individual e.g., his intentions, attitude, perception. The personal factors include- gender, age, parents' profession, and their encouragement to become entrepreneurs. Nationality, type of school-(Private or Government), educational level, and performance are the other factors which influence the decision to become an entrepreneur.

Internal Factors

- Gender

Many research show that Gender influences the choice to work on a self-employed basis. The studies by Kourilsky and Walstad (1998), clearly show that men are more predisposed to starting an enterprise than women. When it comes to the age aspect, several studies show that men are more likely than women to start a business (Gupta et al. 2009). Some authors point out that: a) gender is a determining factor in the commitment of individuals to become entrepreneurs and b) women generally have less access to the resources and information necessary to be entrepreneur.

The analysis by Blanco-Gonzalez, Mercado-Idoeta and Prado-Roman (2012) in Spain, using data from the 2011 Global Entrepreneurship Monitor (GEM) report, shows low women presence in the business world. Women have more difficulty when they work for self . The results of Minniti and Nardone (2007) show that gender differences may exist in the risk appetite of perceptions and motivation for entrepreneurship, which are associated to self-esteem, fear of failure, and perception of opportunities.

Gonzalez-Morales (2004) did not find any gender differences in the desire to work for self in students in a non-compulsory secondary school and technical college. There is no difference between the genders regarding their predisposition to entrepreneurial initiative, at early ages. There is little, if any, gender disparities in entrepreneurship (Shirokova et al. 2016). These results may be influenced by the fact that, in recent years, educational authorities have included entrepreneurship education for all.

- Age

The decision to start an enterprise is conditioned by the different stages in a person's life. Some studies suggest that entrepreneurship spirit is greater in young folks and reduces with age (Blanchflower, 2004; Levesque & Minniti, 2006). The age factor has an impact on student entrepreneurship. Younger people, such as students, have different personality traits (they are more active, dynamic, passionate, and eager to achieve their goals, which makes it simpler to start a business (Shirokova et al. 2016).Young people perceive success or failure to a lesser extent and are less afraid to work for themselves. Honjo (2004) reports that young people have more learning ability and the ability to take on challenges. As people get older, they become less inclined to be entrepreneurs (Singh & Verma, 2001).

- Nationality

The nationality variable means the country of birth. According to Neupert and Baughn (2013) immigrants revitalize the economy because they have more ideas and start more businesses than local people. Cebrian, Bodega, & Martin, (2007) have analyzed the role of immigrants in the creation of firms. His work shows the link between economic and social growth and the employment integration of immigrants when they become self-employed. Immigrants must "fend for themselves" by setting up their own businesses says Santana, Feliciano & Jimenez, (2016). They are ready with ideas before they immigrate to other countries. A study on immigrant adolescent pupils, says that 65% of pupil thought that setting up their own business was a priority in their lives.

- State or private colleges.

The type (state or private) of college or the area (rural or urban) where it is located also affects the attitudes towards entrepreneurship. The advantages and disadvantages of state education versus private education is debatable (Ballou, 2001; Falck & Woessmann, 2013; Jimenez & Sawada,2001;). Some authors believe that private colleges charge a lot of fees, so they have good infrastructure and can give good input to the students, on the other hand in the government colleges fees is minimum and so are the facilities (except a few renounced colleges). Gunjan Kumar and Saundarjya Borbora (2019) led to a better understanding of why entrepreneurship's impact varies among states. They demonstrated that the local institutional environment has a distinct impact on entrepreneurial operations at a regional level in India.

- Educational level and academic performance

Educational level and academic performance have a decisive influence on the success of entrepreneurial ideas (Block, Hoogerheide & Thurik, 2013). A person's education conditions ascertain his attitude towards starting a new business. According to Hisrich (1990), it is not necessary to possess a high level of education to start a business, but it can be a plus point. People with minimum levels of education may see entrepreneurship to rise economically and to meet their employment needs. Cuadrado-Roura (2004) says that it is the people with little formal education or those with compulsory education who are more apt to work for themselves. Students who have low academic results are more predisposed to entrepreneurship because they know that they will not get good jobs. The companies while selecting candidates for jobs, look for toppers or students with higher IQ . For students who secured between 40 to 70 percentage marks, there are less chances of getting a job. These students then start their own ventures.

According to Krueger (1993), people with low levels of formal education may end up with a limited vision of business opportunities; whereas people with more formal education tend to have extra skills and competencies that lead to more opportunities for them. The current situation of a business requires managers with more training. Students who go in for Master's in Business Administration are more competent to face the day today challenges of a new business, than those students who do not go in for higher studies. Higher education allows the entrepreneur to deal better with the everyday problems of business activity (Dioneo-Adetayo, 2006).

- Voluntarily v/s Necessity entrepreneurs

Fossen and Buttner (2013) make a distinction between opportunity entrepreneurs, who happily start a business, and necessity entrepreneurs, who start a business because they have no other employment opportunity. Shane & Venkatarman, (2000) linked a business initiative to a process of detecting opportunities.

Bogenhold & Staber, (1991) related the hypothesis of necessity employment which says that self-employment is in response to counter cyclical patterns in the country's economy, since it becomes a necessity for the unemployed in recessionary times and its presence is less noted in times of growth. In the Covid pandemic when the companies have laid off a lot off employees, they have no other option but to start a small venture to survive. Also, this Covid has seen a lot of migrant labors going back to their villages and settling back there. Since they did not find employment at that time, they started their small ventures.

External Factors

The External factors which motivate students to choose graduate entrepreneurship are the educational environment of colleges, interaction with existing entrepreneurs, and government policies.

Education is critical in shaping an entrepreneurial personality (Ariyani et al. 2020), providing students with entrepreneurial skills, information, attitudes, and other human capital assets that are necessary for their personal development. The following two types of instructional practises have improved students' learning: (i) A pedagogical approach based on theory; (ii) A pedagogical approach based on practise. The first technique helps students gain a better understanding of entrepreneurship, while the second allows them to build entrepreneurial abilities.

Students' daily exposure to the university environment and its institutions might impact their entrepreneurial careers and behaviour, supporting the formation of new companies (Shirokova et al. 2016). A universities assistance for entrepreneurship might take several forms (Bazan et al. 2019). According to Saeed et al. (2015), educational support had the greatest impact on entrepreneurial self-efficacy, followed by concept creation support, business development support, and overall institutional support.

Universities differ in terms of competencies and resources, resulting in knowledge gaps and differences in entrepreneurial skills among students and graduates, which have an impact on venture creation (Beyhan and Findik 2018). Universities are confronted with new challenges in today's ultra-competitive environment. Recent corporate evolutions and innovations are pressuring universities to become more entrepreneurial and international to remain competitive (Minola et al. 2016), resulting in a significant increase in entrepreneurial courses in Europe and the United States

(Hoppe 2016). According to Bauboniene et al. (2019) even if there is a gap between knowledge gained during studies and the current situation in the economy Universities are trying to: (I) contribute to the spirit of entrepreneurship; (II) promote creativity and student aspirations to start a business; (III) provide adequate knowledge for the establishment and development of a business; and (IV) introduce new and innovative entrepreneurship curricula and programmes.

New techniques to encourage entrepreneurial talents include accelerators, incubators, company proposal competitions, and grants (Wright et al. 2017). Summer schools, exchanges, mentoring, internships, workshop programmes, games, contests, financial support, pre-incubators, business support programmes, student-led enterprise groups, and entrepreneurship societies and clubs should all be given special consideration (Siivonen et al. 2019). Students' knowledge, experience, interpersonal, and employability skills all benefit from these types of activities (Preedy and Jones 2017).

Environmental factors also encourage student entrepreneurship. Perceived financial and non-financial support, social support, the presence of an entrepreneurial environment (Nguyen 2020), and national culture are all factors that encourage student entrepreneurship (Laskovaia et al. 2017). Xiuzhai Zhao (2011) conducted 20 case studies and found some internal and external causes of Chinese graduate entrepreneurship dilemma: the internal one is that most graduates do not have the qualifications for entrepreneurship; the external one is that the present entrepreneurial climate in China is poor, resulting in the difficulty for Chinese graduates to start new ventures. Xiuzhai Zhao (2011) suggested that universities should develop and improve entrepreneurship education and training systems, and the government must refine policies and assist in creating entrepreneurial culture.

DISCUSSION/FINDINGS

During the study, it was found that the graduate and post graduate students of Ranchi City are not confident to start their enterprise and they would rather go in for jobs. The main reasons were lack of financial ability to invest and non-availability of a proper mentor. The internal and external factors are discussed at length below.

Internal Factors - Internal factors which encourage students to choose graduate entrepreneurship are-

- Gender and Course

The Gender and the Course of the students was analyzed, and the results are presented in Figure.1

Figure 1. Distribution of gender and course of students
Source: Primary & Computed Data

Course	%	Male%	Female%
MBA	30	80	20
Bba	30	60	40
B. Com	40	70.	30
Total	100	56.8	43.2

Source: Primary & Computed Data

Inference

From Table 1. it is apparent that in the Master of Business Administration Course 80% students were male and 20% were female. In the Bachelor of Business Administration Course 60% students were males and 40% females. In the Bachelor of Commerce course 70% enrolled students were males and only 30% were females. Out of 100%, 56.8% students enrolled in professional course are males, and 43.2% students are females. Males are in majority in the professional courses so there will be more male entrepreneurs than female entrepreneurs.

- Age

Younger students are more energetic, dynamic, enthusiastic, and eager to realize their ambitions, leading them to be more likely to be ready to start an entrepreneurial project. In this study, students were in the age group of 21-24 yrs. Significant differences in age were not found. Some students believed that this is the right time to commence business as they were ready to take risk rather than in later life. Other students believed that working for some other organization and gaining experience of 3-5 years was better before starting own business.

- Intention of Starting a business

Intention of Students to Start a business after graduation is shown in Figure. 2

Inference

The results show that only 24.2% student are interested in starting their enterprise. The reason for this low rate is-

Figure 2. Intention of starting a business
Source: Primary & Computed Data

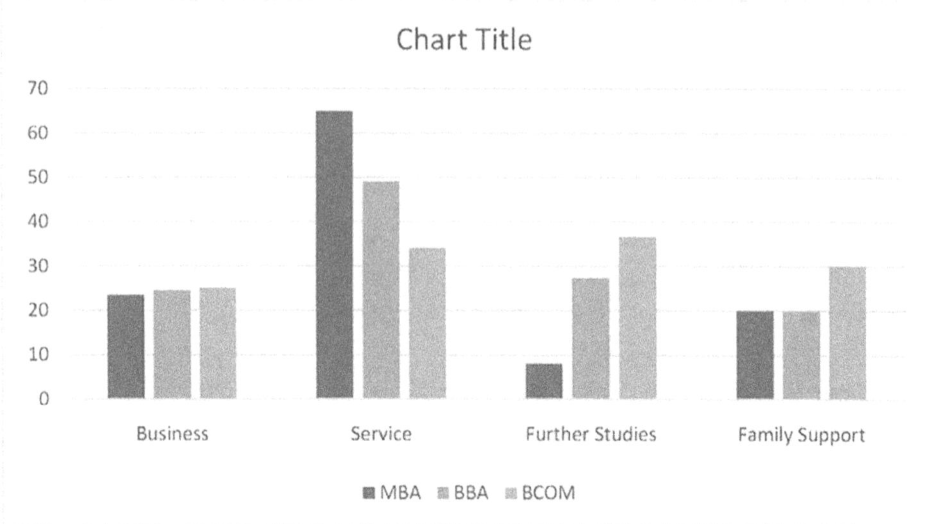

1. MBA is a postgraduate course in India. After completing it most of the students prefer to do a job. The reasons for the student's inclination towards service are-(i) Fixed working hours which would mean a better life. (ii) They believe that they have no practical guidance and mentor to start a business, therefore they would join the service sector.
2. BBA and B.Com are undergraduate course in India and due to high-level competition in the service market they are expected to get a post graduate degree if they want good pay cheques. Therefore, a lot of students in these two courses will pursue higher studies and not open their business.
3. Also, a lot of universities require two years of practical experience before giving admission in post graduate courses. This can be a reason for students wanting to do a job, then further studies.

The results show that in the professional MBA course 23.5% students want to start their business. Interestingly their parents are from business background therefore they all have family encouragement and support to start their business. 65% students would like to do service as they believe that the career options are better in the service sector. Only 8% would pursue higher studies.

The results show that in the BBA course, 24.2% students want to start their business. Another 49% students would like to do a job, as they believe that career prospects are better in the service sector. It is also possible that these students are

Figure 3. The internal factors influencing the choice of graduates to be an entrepreneur
Source: Primary & Computed Data

	% Yes	% No	% Maybe
Does your Family encourage you to become an entrepreneur	41.4	19.8	38.7
It is too costly to start own business.	51	43	6
I can identify Entrepreneurial Opportunities.	75.7	21.6	2.7
I have a lot of ideas for start-ups.	59	37	4

acquiring 2 years of service experience before taking admission in higher studies (M.B.A). 27.27% will go in for further studies.

The results show that in the B. Com course 25% students want to start their business. They enjoy the support of their parents. A majority of 34% students would like to do jobs, as they think that career prospects are superior in the service sector. It is also possible that these students acquire 2 years of service experience before taking admission for higher studies (M.B.A). 36.6% are going to go in for further studies.

- The other Internal Factors influencing the choice of Graduates to be an entrepreneur are shown in Figure 3.

Inference

- Parents' profession, and their encouragement to become entrepreneurs-

Having entrepreneurial parents represent a significant driver to stimulate the intention to start an entrepreneurial activity (Gubik and Farkas 2016; Holienka et al. 2017). Occupation of parents and relatives who are self-employed also encourages students to be an entrepreneur. In this survey 42% of parents were in the service- sector and 20% of them wanted their children to join the service-sector as they had no experience of starting and running a business. On the other hand, 58% of parents belonged to business- sector and 41% wanted their children to join their business. 39% parents were neutral about their children's careers.

Under the assumption that prior experience drives prosocial entrepreneurial behaviour, Hockerts (2017) divided prior entrepreneurial experiences into three categories: "prior family exposure," "prior employment experience," and "prior community service experience."

Despite growing recognition of the predictive ability of prior entrepreneurial experiences in entrepreneurial intentions models, additional research is needed to fully understand the impact of prior entrepreneurial experiences on graduate entrepreneurship development (Kollman, Stockmann, & Kensbock, 2019; Shepherd & Patzelt, 2018).

- Identify entrepreneurial opportunity-

75.7% students were able to identify entrepreneurial opportunities as they came along. The remaining 21% were at a loss of what to do as they could not identify opportunities. According to Rakib et al. (2020) self-efficacy theory people who have strong belief that they can start and run entrepreneurship tend to have strong intention to start and run the business.

- Ideas for business venture-

If a business must succeed it has to be unique. 59% students believed that they have good business ideas to start their entrepreneurship. Another 2.7% believed that existing ideas with enhancements could work for new ventures but 37% were unsure about what to do. Students' risk-taking capacity permits them to continue with their entrepreneurial ventures in the face of difficulties (Zollo et al. 2017; Ibidunni et al. 2020; Zhang et al. 2020).

- Finance-

When the students were asked about the main problem in starting a business, procuring finance was the primary concern for the majority of 43.2% of students. They believed that they do not have access to finance/capital which is required for starting a business.

- The other reasons were low confidence(19.8%), no guidance(18.9%) and lack of practical knowledge(18%).

Students said that they did not have the confidence to start a business themselves as they did not have practical experience. Almost 19.8% of them did not have mentors to guide them on the way of doing business. Their parents were in the service sector, so they do not have any guidance from them.18% of them didn't have the practical knowledge of starting their business.

- The key reason for students wanting to start their own firm-

    1. The main reason for 60% students to start their own firm was financial independence. They believed that they could take their businesses to greater heights and earn more than they could in a job.
    2. Not answerable to anyone was the reason for 25% students wanting to start their own firm. They wanted to be their own bosses and not being accountable for their actions to anybody.
    3. Flexible working hours was the reason for 15% students to become entrepreneur. A boss can afford to come late, take breaks, start early, or stay back till late. He does not have to follow a fixed routine.

External Factors

The External factors which motivate students to choose graduate entrepreneurship are the educational environment of colleges, interaction with existing entrepreneurs, government policies.

In this study it was found that the students are happy with the education provided in the colleges. Universities differ in terms of competencies and resources, resulting in knowledge gaps and differences in entrepreneurial skills among students and graduates, which have an impact on venture creation (Beyhan and Findik 2018). The students would like more interactions with the business sector and private entrepreneurs so that they get more practical tips. Most of the students were also aware of the government policies to help entrepreneurs. The above points are discussed in detail.

Inference

- The results show that 63.9% of the students are happy with their college curriculum and studies. Even though universities are attempting to innovate teaching methods and invest in developing entrepreneurship curricula to expand current knowledge, there is still little investment in practical programmes, and only a small percentage of entrepreneurship graduates choose to start businesses immediately after graduation (Nenzhelele et al. 2016).

Figure 4. How colleges have prepared the graduates for entrepreneurship
Source: Primary & Computed Data

	% Yes	% No	% Maybe
Has your college prepared you for entrepreneurship	63.9	11.8	24.3
Entrepreneurial or business-related examples are included in class studies.eg case studies, role playing	65	8	27
A start-up fund would encourage entrepreneurship	80	3	17
Do you have access to the assistance that you would need to start a business	69.5	30.5	-
Do you believe that More interaction with the business sector would encourage entrepreneurship	80	5	15
Private-sector assistance would result in more college-based business start-ups	91	9	-
Are you aware of the Government programmes that provides help to people to start businesses	73	27	-

- 65% students believe that they are being prepared for entrepreneurship by the training methods like case studies, role playing, Internship programs, seminars, trainings.
- 69.5% graduates have the assistance that they would need to start a new business.
- 80% want help with a start-up fund as availability of finance was a major reason of not starting a business. They believed that more interaction with the business- sector would encourage entrepreneurship.
- 91% young entrepreneur students believe that Private sector assistance would result in more university-based start-ups. Funding and guidance from the private sector would go a long way in encouraging these young entrepreneurs.
- 73% of the students were aware of Government programs and help for start-ups whereas 27% had no idea of the government incentives.

SOLUTIONS AND RECOMMENDATIONS

To encourage entrepreneurship among graduates, it is necessary to improve their perception of an entrepreneur and the self-employed person. Education affects entrepreneurial attitudes in the longer term. Training influences the attitudes and educates pupils by means of simulated activities or real practice for the planning, organization, and implementation of innovative business projects. College students should reinforce the study of professional knowledge, practical guidance, and related disciplines, such as computer, marketing, law, and Internet application to improve their knowledge. They should take the initiative to participate in various national and state level training programs to improve and enrich themselves. They should make efficient use of the various types of innovation and entrepreneurship platforms built by the government and universities for college students.

The following resolutions are suggested for strengthening graduate entrepreneurship:

- Enhancing entrepreneurship education,
- To improve the financing system and Industry interaction.
- To increase entrepreneurship opportunities by improvement at the Government level

The education system and industry should be synchronized. Strategies must be devised to offer young people a quality educational and vocational guidance service. Academic and career guidance helps students to reflect on the importance of entrepreneurship. Work needs to be done on entrepreneurial ability in the classroom, as it will help to change an individual's ideas into action. New technologies can help to incorporate innovative teaching resources. The Teachers and counsellors should be trained with new teaching skills as they are required to respond to the changing realities.

Mentoring becomes a major training tool of the professionals. Mentoring must be extended to the mothers and fathers of students since their influence is considerable at these ages. The family should consider other training options like professional training and occupational training, apart from university, to become self-employed. Attitudes, values, and habits are built cooperatively in the process of planning teaching activities and require a joint effort between the universities, teachers, students, and their families.

To improve college students' innovation and entrepreneurship education, colleges and universities must develop an innovation and entrepreneurship curriculum system that is tailored to their social and professional development, and their specific needs and career development. Colleges should provide an online and offline forum for college students to exercise innovation and entrepreneurship. Offline entity platform can provide students with a place for personal participation and experience. Colleges should allow online platform for students to provide real-time learning resources, interactive online guidance, and a variety of services. Colleges should, invite industry experts to give lectures on innovation and entrepreneurship, publicize the methods of innovation and entrepreneurship, identify the stars of innovation and entrepreneurship, and cultivate college students' awareness and ability of Internet innovation and entrepreneurship. Finally, schools and universities should build more infrastructure, create a network pioneer park, incubator park, and entrepreneurial base to provide a platform for enhancing the practical ability of innovation and entrepreneurship.

Entrepreneurs while raising capital face a few problems. Funding of business ventures usually poses a dilemma for entrepreneurs because many times entrepreneurs do not have funds to finance ventures and at times private banks are usually unwilling to lend money to a small and newly established firms. The studies on capital constraints provide evidence that an inability to obtain external financing limits many business ventures. Studies show that for smaller firms, capital constraints limit research-and-development expenditures. New and untried ideas are uncertain and therefore do not get funds from the usual financial sources like debt and equity. Uncertainty in the financial outcomes for a company can be due to uncertainty of whether the new product will succeed, what will be the response of rival firms. The Investors are concerned that entrepreneur may take measures that are in his self-interest. Fearing such actions from the entrepreneurs the financiers be reluctant to invest. Also, it is easier to raise funds when firms have tangible assets like land, machinery. But with intangible assets, it becomes relatively difficult to raise funds.

Han Mei (2019) believes that Colleges can ask Venture capitalist enterprises to provide start-up funds for innovative entrepreneurship programs. This will improve the public image of the enterprise and increases its economic benefits. It also solves the problem of funds for college students and achieves win-win situation for both sides. For enhancing the College student's success in entrepreneurship more Interaction with the industry experts can be done. Industry experts can also provide products, services, technology, management, and marketing support for college students.

Entrepreneurship education should be encouraged through incentives and continuous facilitation by the government. The government can create a good environment for innovation and promotion of entrepreneurship by improving the present policies and laws for university students' innovation and entrepreneurship. College students can be supported for innovative entrepreneurship projects in terms of financing, loans, and taxation, to reduce the expenses. Tax rebates may be given to the young and new entrepreneurs, particularly, to those who set their businesses in small and underdeveloped areas of the country. Mark-up free loaning schemes may also be useful to attract novice entrepreneurs. Government can simplify the examination and approval procedures to speed up paperwork and other processing.

FUTURE RESEARCH DIRECTIONS

More research can be done in the field of graduate entrepreneurship in developing countries as it may help to understand the issues of graduate entrepreneurial intentions and business start-up. This could be a powerful force to accelerate economic growth and development. This research has been conducted in the city of Ranchi, Jharkhand. It can be pursued in other cities. Further this study was done only with Management and Commerce students. Students of other courses like science and humanities can be included for further research.

CONCLUSION

Entrepreneurship has been encouraged because of the ambiguities in the world economy, and reduction in staff recruitments. Also, the dissatisfaction and disappointment in the corporate employment is attracting entrepreneurship amongst the youth. Entrepreneurship is being seen as a pioneering instrument, there-by creating development and advancement in the economy.

Education should encourage theoretical and practical knowledge, attitudes and qualities like responsibility, perseverance, creativity, flexibility, adaptability, complex problem solving, for the survival of the company in a highly competitive world. Guidance should be provided for student entrepreneurial practice by analyzing key factors such as business opportunities, resources, and entrepreneurial team. Practical activities, entrepreneurship environment, teacher training, team building, are some of the factors for successful entrepreneurship education.

Universities can execute the role they play in entrepreneurship in four primary ways: through entrepreneurship education, the development of entrepreneurial thinking and acting, supporting entrepreneurship activity and entrepreneurial leadership.

Academics and policy makers have been concentrating on the direct relationship of entrepreneurship and economic development over the past few years. Entrepreneurship is the vital instrument for global development. It is a capital maker for individuals and the economy. Policy makers must find ways to retain and generate entrepreneurship in countries (Sanyang & Huang, 2010).

ACKNOWLEDGMENT

This research received no specific grant from any funding agency in the public, commercial, or not-for-profit sectors.

REFERENCES

Adetaya. (2019). *IT Entrepreneurship Technology Entrepreneurship: Trend, opportunities, challenges*. Academic Press.

Ariyani, Dwi, Suyatno, and Zuhaery. (2020). Principal's entrepreneurial leadership in developing entrepreneurship at Magelang high school. *International Journal of Scientific and Technology Research, 9*, 1446–52.

Bae, T. J., Qian, S., Chao Miao, C., & Fiet, J. O. (2014). The relationship between entrepreneurship education and entrepreneurial intentions: A meta-analytic review. Baylor University.

Ballou, D. (2001). Pay for performance in public and private schools. *Economics of Education Review*, *20*(1), 51–61. doi:10.1016/S0272-7757(99)00060-6

Barbini, F. M., Corsino, M., & Giuri, P. (2021). How do universities shape founding teams? Social proximity and informal mechanisms of knowledge transfer in student entrepreneurship. *The Journal of Technology Transfer*, *46*(4), 1046–1082. doi:10.100710961-020-09799-1

Bauboniene, Kyong, Puksas, & Malinauskiene. (2019). Factors influencing student entrepreneurship ' intentions: The case of Lithuanian and South Korean universities. *Journal of Entrepreneurship and Sustainability Issues, 6*, 854–71.

Bazan, C., Shaikh, A., Frederick, S., Amjad, A., Yap, S., Finn, C., & Rayner, J. (2019). Effect of memorial university's environment & support system in shaping entrepreneurial intention of students. *Journal of Entrepreneurship Education*, *22*, 1–35.

Becker, G. S. (1975). *Human capital* (2nd ed.). University of Chicago Press.

Beyhan, B., & Findik, D. (2018). Student and graduate entrepreneurship: Ambidextrous universities create more nascent entrepreneurs. *The Journal of Technology Transfer*, *43*(5), 1346–1374. doi:10.100710961-017-9590-z

Birch, C., Lichy, J., Mulholland, G., & Kachour, M. (2017). An enquiry into potential graduate entrepreneurship: Is higher education turning off the pipeline of graduate entrepreneurs? *Journal of Management Development*, *36*(6), 743–760. doi:10.1108/JMD-03-2016-0036

Blanchflower, D. (2004). Self-employment: More May Not Be Better. *Swedish Economic Policy Review*, *11*(2), 15–74.

Blanco-Gonzalez, A., Mercado-Idoeta, C., & Prado-Roman, A. (2012). Perfil y motivacion de la juventud emprendedora espanola. *Revista de Estudios de Juventud, 99*, 23–34.

Blesia, J. U., Iek, M., Ratang, W., & Hutajulu, H. (2019). Developing an entrepreneurship model to increase students' entrepreneurial skills: An action research project in a higher education institution in Indonesia. *Systemic Practice and Action Research, 34*(1), 53–70. doi:10.100711213-019-09506-8

Block, J. H., Hoogerheide, L., & Thurik, R. (2013). Education and entrepreneurial choice: An instrumental variables analysis. *International Small Business Journal, 31*(1), 23–33. doi:10.1177/0266242611400470

Bogenhold, D., & Staber, U. (1991). The Decline and Rise of Self-Employment. *Work, Employment and Society, 5*(2), 223–239. doi:10.1177/0950017091005002005

Brown, J. S., Collins, A., & Duguid, P. (1989). Situated cognition and the culture of learning. *Educational Researcher, 18*(1), 32–42. doi:10.3102/0013189X018001032

Cebrian, J. A., Bodega, M. I., & Martin, M. A. (2007). Inmigracion y creacion de empresas. In R. Dominguez-Martin (Ed.), *Inmigracion: crecimiento economico e integracion social* (pp. 147–166). Parlamento de Cantabria, Universidad de Cantabria.

Chen, C. C., Greene, P. G., & Crick, A. (1998). Does entrepreneurial self-efficacy distinguish entrepreneurs from managers? *Journal of Business Venturing, 13*(4), 295–316. doi:10.1016/S0883-9026(97)00029-3

Chiarello, Fini, Ghiselli, Girotti, Meoli, & Sobrero. (2021). *Student and Graduate Entrepreneurship in Italy-Report 2020.* Academic Press.

Cuadrado-Roura, J. R. (Coord.). (2004). Empleo autonomo y empleo asalariado. Madrid: Subdireccion General de Publicaciones del Ministerio de Trabajo y Asuntos Sociales.

Davidsson, P., & Honig, B. (2003). The role of social and human capital among nascent entrepreneurs. *Journal of Business Venturing, 18*(3), 301–331. doi:10.1016/S0883-9026(02)00097-6

Delmar, F., & Holmquist, C. (2004). Women's entrepreneurship: issues and policies. 2nd Organization for Economic Cooperation and Development (OECD) Conference of Ministers Responsible for SMEs, Promoting Entrepreneurship, and Innovative SMEs in a Global Economy. doi:10.1080/02673843.2006.9747970

Dioneo-Adetayo, E. A. (2006). Factors influencing attitude of youth towards entrepreneurship. *International Journal of Adolescence and Youth, 13*(1-2), 127–145. doi:10.1080/02673843.2006.9747970

Dodgson & Gann. (2020). *Philanthropy, Innovation and Entrepreneurship*. Springer Books.

Duraipandian & Kumar. (2021). Entrepreneurship development factors which have impact on profit of IT entrepreneurship. *Psychology and Education Journal, 58*(1). doi:10.17762/pae.v58i1.2175

Fayolle, A., Gailly, B., & Lassas-Clerc, N. (2006b). Assessing the impact of entrepreneurship education programmes: A new methodology. *Journal of European Industrial Training, 30*(9), 701–720. doi:10.1108/03090590610715022

Fossen, F. M., & Buttner, T. J. (2013). The returns to education for opportunity entrepreneurs, necessity entrepreneurs, and paid employees. *Economics of Education Review, 37*, 66–84. doi:10.1016/j.econedurev.2013.08.005

Garavan, T. N., & O'Cinneide, B. (1994). Entrepreneurship education and training programmes: A review and evaluation-Part 1. *Journal of European Industrial Training, 18*(8), 3–12. doi:10.1108/03090599410068024

GEM. (2010). *Informe ejecutivo 2010 Espana*. GEM Espana.

Genesca-Garrigosa, E., & Veciana-Verges, J. M. (1984). Actitudes hacia la creacion de empresas. *Informacion Comercial Espanola, 611*, 147–155.

Gubik, A. S., & Farkas, S. (2016). Student Entrepreneurship in Hungary: Selected Results Based on GUESSS Survey. *Entrepreneurial Business and Economics Review, 4*(4), 123–139. doi:10.15678/EBER.2016.040408

Gupta, V. K., Turban, D. B., Wasti, S. A., & Sikdar, A. (2009). The role of gender stereotypes in perceptions of entrepreneurs and intentions to become an entrepreneur. *Entrepreneurship Theory and Practice, 33*(2), 397–417. doi:10.1111/j.1540-6520.2009.00296.x

Hockerts, K. (2017). Determinants of social entrepreneurial intentions. *Entrepreneurship Theory and Practice, 41*(1), 105–130. doi:10.1111/etap.12171

Holienka, M., Gál, P., & Kovačičová, Z. (2017). Drivers of student entrepreneurship in Visegrad four countries: Guesss evidence. *Central European Business Review, 6*(2), 54–63. doi:10.18267/j.cebr.180

Hoppe, M. (2016). Policy and entrepreneurship education. *Small Business Economics*, *46*(1), 13–29. doi:10.100711187-015-9676-7

Ibidunni, A. S., Mozie, D., & Adebanji Wlliam, A. A. A. (2020). Entrepreneurial characteristics amongst university students: Insights for understanding entrepreneurial intentions amongst youths in a developing economy. *Education + Training*, *63*(1), 71–84. doi:10.1108/ET-09-2019-0204

Ilonen, S., Heinonen, J., & Stenholm, P. (2018). Identifying and understanding entrepreneurial decision-making logics in entrepreneurship education. *International Journal of Entrepreneurial Behaviour & Research*, *24*(1), 59–80. doi:10.1108/IJEBR-05-2017-0163

Kollmann, T., Stöckmann, C., & Kensbock, J. M. (2019). I can't get no sleep—The differential impact of entrepreneurial stressors on work-home interference and insomnia among experienced versus novice entrepreneurs. *Journal of Business Venturing*, *34*(4), 692–708. doi:10.1016/j.jbusvent.2018.08.001

Krueger, N. F. Jr, Reilly, M. D., & Carsrud, A. L. (2000). Competing models of entrepreneurial intensions. *Journal of Business Venturing*, *15*(5-6), 411–432. doi:10.1016/S0883-9026(98)00033-0

Krylova, O., & Shaposhnykov, K. (2020). Activation Of Innovative Entrepreneurship Development. *Three Seas Economic Journal*, *1*(1), 66–72. doi:10.30525/2661-5150/2020-1-18

Kumar, G., & Borbora, S. (2019). Institutional environment differences and their application for entrepreneurship development in India. *Journal of Entrepreneurship in Emerging Economies*, *11*(2), 177–199. doi:10.1108/JEEE-11-2017-0081

Kuratko, D. F. (2005). The emergence of entrepreneurship education: Development, trends, and challenges. *Entrepreneurship Theory and Practice*, *29*(5), 577–598. doi:10.1111/j.1540-6520.2005.00099.x

Laskovaia, A., Shirokova, G., & Morris, M. H. (2017). National culture, effectuation, and new venture performance: Global evidence from student entrepreneurs. *Small Business Economics*, *49*(3), 687–709. doi:10.100711187-017-9852-z

Lee, S. M., Chang, D., & Lim, S.-B. (2005). Impact of entrepreneurship education: A comparative study of the U.S. and Korea. *The International Entrepreneurship and Management Journal*, *1*(1), 27–43. doi:10.100711365-005-6674-2

Levesque, M., & Minniti, M. (2006). The Effect of Aging on Entrepreneurial Behaviour. *Journal of Business Venturing*, *21*(2), 177–194. doi:10.1016/j.jbusvent.2005.04.003

Linan, F. (2004). Intention-based models of entrepreneurship education. *Piccola Impresa/Small Business, 3*, 11-35.

Linan, F. (2008). Skill and value perceptions: How do they affect entrepreneurial intentions? *The International Entrepreneurship and Management Journal, 4*(3), 257–272. doi:10.100711365-008-0093-0

Lombardi, R., Lardo, A., Cuozzo, B., & Trequattrini, R. (2017). Emerging trends in entrepreneurial universities within Mediterranean regions: An international comparison. *EuroMed Journal of Business, 12*(2), 130–145. doi:10.1108/EMJB-10-2015-0052

Lombardi, R., Schimperna, F., & Marcello, R. (2021a). Human capital and smart tourism's development: Primary evidence. *International Journal of Digital Culture and Electronic Tourism, 3*(3/4), 294–309. doi:10.1504/IJDCET.2021.116492

Maresch, D., Harms, R., Kailer, N., & Wimmer-Wurm, B. (2016). The impact of entrepreneurship education on the entrepreneurial intention of students in science and engineering versus business studies university programs. *Technological Forecasting and Social Change, 104*, 172–179. doi:10.1016/j.techfore.2015.11.006

Martin, B. C., McNally, J. J., & Kay, M. J. (2013). Examining the formation of human capital in entrepreneurship: A meta-analysis of entrepreneurship education outcomes. *Journal of Business Venturing, 28*(2), 211–224. doi:10.1016/j.jbusvent.2012.03.002

Matt, M., & Schaeffer, V. (2018). Building entrepreneurial ecosystems conducive to student entrepreneurship: New challenges for universities. *Journal of Innovation Economics Management*, (1), 9–32. doi:10.3917/jie.025.0009

Minniti, M., & Bygrave, W. (2001). A dynamic model of entrepreneurial learning. *Entrepreneurship Theory and Practice, 25*(3), 5–16. doi:10.1177/104225870102500301

Minniti, M., & Nardone, C. (2007). Being in Someone Else's Shoes: Gender and Nascent Entrepreneurship. *Small Business Economics Journal, 28*(2), 223–238. doi:10.100711187-006-9017-y

Minola, T., Donina, D., & Meoli, M. (2016). Students climbing the entrepreneurial ladder: Does university internationalization pay off? *Small Business Economics, 47*(3), 565–587. doi:10.100711187-016-9758-1

Morris, M. H., Shirokova, G., & Tsukanova, T. (2017). Student entrepreneurship and the university ecosystem: A multi-country empirical exploration. *European Journal of International Management, 11*(1), 65–85. doi:10.1504/EJIM.2017.081251

Nabi, G., & Holden, R. (2008). Graduate entrepreneurship: Intentions, education, and training. *Education + Training*, *50*(7), 545–551. doi:10.1108/00400910810909018

Nabi, G., & Linan, F. (2011). Graduate entrepreneurship in developing world: Intentions, education, and training. *Education + Training*, *53*(5), 325–334. doi:10.1108/00400911111147668

Nenzhelele, T. E., Moraka, N. V., & More, K. K. (2016). The impact of practical entrepreneurship project on future entrepreneurial intentions. *Problems and Perspectives in Management*, *14*(4), 67–75. doi:10.21511/ppm.14(4).2016.08

Neupert, K. E., & Baughn, C. C. (2013). Immigration, Education and Entrepreneurship in Developed Countries. *Journal of Enterprising Communities: People and Places in the Global Economy*, *7*(3), 293–310. doi:10.1108/JEC-12-2011-0033

Nguyen, T. T. (2020). Impact of entrepreneurship environmental support factors to university students' entrepreneurship self-efficacy. *Management Science Letters*, *10*, 1321–1328. doi:10.5267/j.msl.2019.11.026

Preedy, S., & Jones, P. (2017). Student-led enterprise groups and entrepreneurial learning: A UK perspective. *Industry and Higher Education*, *31*(2), 101–112. doi:10.1177/0950422216689349

Rakib, Tawe, Azis, Syam, & Sanusi. (2020). Determinants of entrepreneurial intention: Empirical study of student entrepreneurs. *Academy of Entrepreneurship Journal, 26*, 1–12.

Rangarajan, C. (1980). *Innovations in Banking. Domestic Financial Study 63*. World Bank.

Saeed, S., Yousafzai, S. Y., Yani-De-Soriano, M., & Muffatto, M. (2015). The role of perceived university support in the formation of students' entrepreneurial intention. *Journal of Small Business Management*, *53*(4), 1127–1145. doi:10.1111/jsbm.12090

Samašonok, K., Išoraitė, M., & Žirnelė, L. (2020). Education of entrepreneurship by participation in a business simulation ˙ enterprise activities: Conditions of effectiveness and opportunities for improvement. *Entrepreneurship and Sustainability Issues*, *7*(4), 3122–3144. doi:10.9770/jesi.2020.7.4(36)

Sansone, G., Ughetto, E., & Landoni, P. (2021). Entrepreneurial intention: An analysis of the role of Student-Led Entrepreneurial Organizations. *Journal of International Entrepreneurship*, *19*(3), 399–433. doi:10.100710843-021-00288-6

Santana, L. E., Feliciano, L., & Jimenez, A. B. (2016). Perceived family support and the life design of immigrant pupils in secondary education. *Review of Education, 372*, 35–62.

Savickas, M. L., Nota, L., Rossier, J., Dauwalder, J. P., Duarte, M. E., Guichard, J., Soresi, S., Van Esbroeck, R., & van Vianen, A. (2009). Life designing: A paradigm for career construction in the 21st century. *Journal of Vocational Behavior, 75*(3), 239–250. doi:10.1016/j.jvb.2009.04.004

Schimperna, F., Lombardi, R., & Belyaeva, Z. (2020). Technological transformation, culinary tourism and stakeholder engagement: Emerging trends from a systematic literature review. *Journal of Place Management and Development, 14*(1), 66–80. doi:10.1108/JPMD-03-2020-0028

Sendouwa, R. H. E., Lonto, A. L., & Saroinsong, S. J. R. (2019). Entrepreneurship development program in the higher education in Indonesia. *International Journal of Recent Technology and Engineering, 8*, 1006–1010.

Shane, S., & Venkatarman, S. (2000). The promise of entrepreneurship as a field of research. *Academy of Management Review, 25*(1), 217–226. doi:10.5465/amr.2000.2791611

Shepherd, D. A., & Patzelt, H. (2018). Motivation and entrepreneurial cognition. In *Entrepreneurial Cognition* (pp. 51–103). Palgrave Macmillan. doi:10.1007/978-3-319-71782-1_3

Shirokova, G., Osiyevskyy, O., & Bogatyreva, K. (2016). Exploring the intention–behavior link in student entrepreneurship: Moderating effects of individual and environmental characteristics. *European Management Journal, 34*(4), 386–399. doi:10.1016/j.emj.2015.12.007

Siivonen, P. T., Peura, K., Hytti, U., Kasanen, K., & Komulainen, K. (2019). The construction and regulation of collective entrepreneurial identity in student entrepreneurship societies. *International Journal of Entrepreneurial Behaviour & Research, 26*(3), 521–538. doi:10.1108/IJEBR-09-2018-0615

Singh, G., & Verma, A. (2001). Is there life after career employment? Labour market experience of early retirees. In V. Marshall, W. Heinz, H. Kruegar, & A. Verma (Eds.), *Restructuring Work and the Life Course* (pp. 288–302). University of Toronto Press. doi:10.3138/9781442679290-019

Slavtchev, V., Laspita, S., & Patzelt, H. (2012). Effects of entrepreneurship education at universities. *Jena Economic Research Papers, 25*, 1–33.

Smith, K., & Beasley, M. (2011). Graduate entrepreneurs: Intentions, barriers, and solutions. *Education + Training*, *53*(8/9), 722–740. doi:10.1108/00400911111185044

Taneja, B. (2021). The Digital Edge for M-Commerce to Replace E-Commerce. In *Emerging Challenges, Solutions and Best Practices for Digital Enterprises Transformation*. IGI Global.

Teijeiro, M., Rungo, P., & Freire, M. J. (2013). Graduate competencies and employability: The impact of matching firm's needs and personal attainments. *Economics of Education Review*, *34*, 286–295. doi:10.1016/j.econedurev.2013.01.003

Abass & Arfat. (2020). Threat perceptions towards entrepreneurship developments. *Pacific Business Review International*, *10*(October).

Trivedi, R. (2016). Does university play significant role in shaping entrepreneurial intention? A cross-country comparative analysis. *Journal of Small Business and Enterprise Development*, *23*(3), 790–811. doi:10.1108/JSBED-10-2015-0149

Unger, J. M., Rauch, A., Frese, M., & Rosenbusch, N. (2011). Human capital and entrepreneurial success: A meta-analytical review. *Journal of Business Venturing*, *26*(3), 341–358. doi:10.1016/j.jbusvent.2009.09.004

Vesalainen, J., & Pihkala, T. (1999). *Motivation structure and entrepreneurial intentions*. Academic Press.

Wilson, F., Kickul, J., & Marlino, D. (2007). Gender, entrepreneurial self-efficacy, and entrepreneurial career intentions: Implications for entrepreneurship education. *Entrepreneurship Theory and Practice*, *31*(3), 387–406. doi:10.1111/j.1540-6520.2007.00179.x

Wright, M., Siegel, D. S., & Mustar, P. (2017). An emerging ecosystem for student start-ups. *The Journal of Technology Transfer*, *42*(4), 909–922. doi:10.100710961-017-9558-z

Xu, Z., Lin, D., & Li, J. (2011). Graduate entrepreneurship in China. *Journal of Chinese Entrepreneurship*, *3*(3). Advance online publication. doi:10.1108/jce.2011.40503caa.001

Youndt, M. A., Subramaniam, M., & Snell, S. A. (2004). Intellectual capital profiles: An examination of investment and returns. *Journal of Management Studies*, *41*(2), 335–361. doi:10.1111/j.1467-6486.2004.00435.x

Zhang, S.-N., Li, Y.-Q., Liu, C.-H., & Ruan, W.-Q. (2020). Critical factors identification and prediction of tourism and hospitality students' entrepreneurial intention. *Journal of Hospitality, Leisure, Sport and Tourism Education*, *26*, 100234. doi:10.1016/j.jhlste.2019.100234

Zollo, L., Laudano, M. C., Ciappei, C., & Zampi, V. (2017). Factors affecting universities' ability to foster students' entrepreneurial behaviour: An empirical investigation. *Journal of Management Development*, *36*(2), 268–285. doi:10.1108/JMD-06-2016-0093

KEY TERMS AND DEFINITIONS

Entrepreneur Intention: The factors which determine the intention to start an enterprise.

Entrepreneurial Education: It can be defined as a training activities of university courses that fosters creativity, innovation, and risk taking in the students so that they have the skills to plan, manage projects, ethically. These courses are delivered through innovative pedagogical techniques and strategies.

Entrepreneurs: An entrepreneur is an individual who creates a new business, bearing its risks and rewards.

Graduate Entrepreneurship: Earning a degree in entrepreneurship qualifies graduates to work as experts in many business fields. Many individuals go on to lead a start-up and create a new business. Graduate may also work as consultants, offering advice and guidance to fledgling entrepreneurs.

Self-Employment: Self-employment means working for oneself rather than an employer. It entails earning income from a profession, a trade, or a business that they operate.

Chapter 10
Students' Hackathon, University Business Incubator, and Fourth Industrial Revolution (4IR) in South African Universities

Adetola Elizabeth Oyewo
University of KwaZulu-Natal, South Africa

Samuel Uwem Umoh
University of KwaZulu-Natal, South Africa

ABSTRACT

The chapter discusses how a public South African university, the University of KwaZulu-Natal (UKZN), teaches student entrepreneurship through hackathons, incubation programmes, and their impact on students' entrepreneurial journeys. Data was generated from various sources such as observation from student entrepreneurship week and a series of student elevator pitches. Interviews were conducted with 12 participants comprised of UKZN alumni, public relations manager, ENACTUS member, UKZN incubation centre managers, and students. Data also supplemented with secondary data sources such as UKZN magazine Indaba. Findings suggest that hackathons are utilized to identify students' start-ups for incubation. UKZN InQuabate has the capacity as a public research university by promoting innovation, commercialization, and entrepreneurship. Universities as business incubation also support student start-up business by bringing student entrepreneurs together in a common working space.

DOI: 10.4018/978-1-7998-9581-7.ch010

INTRODUCTION

Hackathon is increasingly used in universities to incubate students' business and develop entrepreneurship skills in the fourth industrial revolution era. Universities as business incubator are supporting student start-ups business by bringing student entrepreneurs together in a common working space to launch an actual company. A business incubator is a supplier of essential resources and capabilities to early start-up to become scalable and viable without substantial expenses (Prencipe 2016; Voisey, Jones & Thomas, 2013). Universities and college campuses contain about one-third of University Business Incubators [UBIs] (Robles (2017). Such UBIs are an effective technique of looking for collaboration and forming networks that bring value. Entrepreneurs, students, universities, and incubators benefit from UBIs–university cooperation (Roura, 2015).

Hackathon is a component of competitive ideas for student start-ups to present an idea, deliver it and produce a quick convincing prototype (Oleksii, Sklyar, Vladimir & Chris, 2015). Such hackathon is aimed at supporting activities in incubators by bringing student entrepreneurs together in a typical working space (Murage, 2018; Ninh Vu, 2016). Hackathon is also evolving to teach students the fundamentals of employment skills and explore innovative ideas (Prencipe, 2016).Globally more than 200 colleges and universities have launched business incubators in form innovation hubs as members of the Global Consortium of Entrepreneurship Centres in 2017 (Farman, 2018). Hassan (2020) stressed that although the entrepreneurial role for universities did not become widely accepted until the 1980s when governments in several countries, including the United States, the United Kingdom, Australia, Sweden, Germany, Italy, and Japan, provided policy measures to encourage entrepreneurial activities, which make universities engage in a "third mission."

Public universities in South Africa are not immune to the concept of student hackathons and business incubators. Universities in South Africa are embedding incubations and hackathon in their school programs aimed at addressing unemployment, developing business entrepreneurship amongst students in response to unemployment and preparation for the fourth industrial revolution (4IR) (Diphoko 2019; Murange 2018). South Africa's unemployment in 2020 was 28.48%, 28.18% in 2019, 26.92% in 2018, and 27.07% in 2017 (Statistics South Africa 2020). Statistics South Africa (2019) report indicates that youth between ages 15–24 years are the most vulnerable in the South African labor market because the unemployment rate among this age group was 55, 2% in 2019. The Statistics also indicate that graduate unemployment increased from 19.5% in the fourth quarter of 2018 to 31, 0%. Teaching entrepreneurship by hackathon alludes to universities also preparing their students for the 4IR skills and keeping up with the competitive job market shaped by automation. The fourth industrial revolution, also known as '4IR', is a term coined by Klaus Schwab, the World Economic Forum [WEF] chairman in 2015. A range of new technologies that characterize the 4IR are mobile supercomputing, intelligent robots, 3D printing, Internet of Things (IoT), and Artificial intelligence, which would radically change the prospects of jobs needed in the future (WEF, 2018; OECD, 2016). Skills that are needed in the 4IR are those that involve building complex relationships with people (Guardian, 2017). The rationale for establishment of university incubation alludes to initiatives such as Silicon Valley and lower survival of student businesses, unlike other experienced entrepreneurs. Murage (2018) attributes Silicon Valley's success to its association with universities such as Stanford University that provide a steady stream of innovations and subject-matter-experts in the form of university professors. Setting up university incubation also alludes to university students' innovation, and that companies worth trillions were established by students such as Mark Zuckerberg at Harvard and Sergey Brin and Larry Page, who founded Google at Stanford University (Diphoko, 2019).

Universities incubations produce more successful firms and spin-offs faster because of their capability to create innovation (Murage 2018; Prencipe 2016). At the institutional level, a few examples of South African universities' incubation hubs demonstrate how higher education institutions are becoming environments of entrepreneurial training for students. For instance, Stellenbosch University has incubator hub LaunchLab, the University of Cape Town has Solution Space, UKZN has 'ENSPIRE' and the Witwatersrand University, Tshimologong. These incubators mentioned above are start-up incubator that builds a thriving ecosystem for students entrepreneurs within the university. These incubators also provide office space, facilities, expert advice, mentorship, access to funding for students and the business community. Such student start-ups also compete at international hackathons for international exposure.

Given this context, the paper seeks unpack how a South African public university teaches students entrepreneurship through hackathon, incubation programmes and its impact on students' entrepreneurial journey. The paper discusses incubation programs and Hackathon programs for students using a public university in South Africa as a reference point, namely the University of KwaZulu-Natal [UKZN]. The paper also unpacks the impacts of incubation programs and hackathon programs on students' entrepreneurial and innovation skills. It also questions to what extent universities have the capacity as public research universities to perform incubator roles. It reveals the mechanisms that UKZN and its strategic partners use to promote innovation and identify new student start-ups. The next section unpacks key concepts such as Hackathon, Fourth Industrial Revolution [4IR] and universities as business incubators.

CONCEPT OF HACKATHON

Hackathon is a short-term event where students work in teams to create a working software prototype, application, or product addressing a specific project (Oxford Dictionary, 2018). Hackathon is also known as 'hack day','hackfest' or 'codefest' a design sprint-like event in which computer programmers, software development, graphic designers, interface designers, project managers and a host of others collaborate intensively on software projects (Walter, 2019; Lin 2018). Walter (2019) defines Hackathon as hack[ing mar] marathons where participants collaboratively and rapidly prototype new applications (apps) over a 24-48hour period. The potential of Hackathon as an informal strategy for stimulating interest in the Computer Science fields is well established (Alfonso, 2019; Alkema, Levitt, & Chen, 2017). A Hackathon aims to create usable software or hardware to create a viable prototype at the end of the event.

Detangling "Fourth Industrial Revolution" [4IR]

The World Economic Forum's chairman, Klaus Schwab, described society as experiencing a "Fourth Industrial Revolution" (4IR). The 4IR is different from the first industrial revolution, second Industrial Revolution, and Third Industrial Revolution. The First Industrial Revolution is characterized by mechanized production that used water and steam power. The second industrial revolution is characterized by mass production that used electric power. Lastly, the third industrial revolution is characterized by the digital revolution, which used electronics and information technology to automate production.

The fourth industrial revolution, often known as technological innovation, is defined by a fusion of technologies that distorts the physical, digital, and biological domains(Xu Min, Jeanne & Suk, 2018). The fourth industrial revolution is also characterized by automation which disrupts long-established business models and the status quo of opening up new possibilities for what people can do with their time (Schwab, 2016; Graham, 2017; Guardian, 2017; McKinsey Global Institute, 2013). Disruptive technologies in the 41R are characterized by the internet of things (IoT), Artificial intelligence, advanced robotics, and cloud technology. IoT implies the network of physical devices, vehicles, buildings, and other objects assembled with electronics, software, sensors, actuators, and network connectivity, allowing them to gather, analyze, and report data (McKinsey Global Institute, 2013). Artificial intelligence is exhibited by machines that work and react like humans capable of speech recognition, visual perception, decision-making, problem-solving, and learning (Guardian 2017; OECD, 2016). Equally, advanced robotics entails robots with enhanced dexterity and intelligence, which can take on tasks classified as too delicate to automate. The 4IR technologies will contribute to one-third of global GDP and economic impact between $14 trillion and $33 trillion a year in 2025. Automation will also lead to machines' substitution for a substantial part of routine jobs, irrespective of the skill level (OECD 2016).

The disadvantage of 4IR on jobs was highlighted in a report by Guardian in 2017. Jobs will not entirely disappear but will be redefined, and that individuals would be unemployed due to a lack of new skillsets required for new roles (Guardian, 2017). Guardian (2017) indicates that the death of human jobs has often been greatly exaggerated in the past, but rather technology has created a lot more jobs than it has wiped out. Guardian (2017) termed this ''Luddite Fallacy'', associated with a group of textile workers in the nineteenth century who shattered new weaving equipment that rendered their skills redundant.

Universities Business Incubators

Business incubator is a supplier of essential resources and capabilities to early start-up to become scalable and viable without substantial expenses (Hassan, 2020; Sanyal & Hisam, 2018; Prencipe 2016). Hassan echoed (2020) that the notion of University business incubators (UBIs) has been revolutionized. Hassan (2020) noted that UBIs was first identified in 1985 as facilities that provide various services to aid fresh start-ups in their early stages of development. In 1988, a new definition was added, indicating that the objective of UBIs is to link technology, capital, and expertise to talent to accelerate the growth of new businesses and the transfer of technology.

University business incubators offer tangible and intangible services to young business start-ups (Hassan, 2020). Business incubators provide an array of support services and infrastructure through a systematic process to start-ups. Such incubation could be specific to a particular industry or have a specific focus as a niche. For instance, the number of tech-focused incubation in Africa that started in 2012 totaled about 314 from 117 in 2015 (Dahir, 2016). Dahir (2016) observed that tech incubation hubs are spread across 93 cities in 42 countries across African continents. The top African countries with tech hubs are South Africa (54), Egypt (28), Kenya (27), Nigeria (23), Morocco (21), Ghana (16), Tunisia (15), Uganda (12), and Senegal (10). Business incubators offer varied support services and infrastructure through a systematic process to start-ups. Such incubation could be specific to a particular industry or have a particular focus as niche.

Hackathons are also utilized to identify students start-ups for incubation. Hackathon held nationally in South Africa occurs in the form of South Africa innovation summit and elevator pitches. Some of the popular Hackathon are Geekulcha Hackathon, Andza Entrepreneur, WineTech, Africa Cup, investors Garage, Seda pitch and perfect (ExpertHub Staff, 2019). The Geekulcha Hackathon is a yearly event organized for students that takes place for the Africa developer ecosystem. It is a 42 hours challenge that gathers different students under one roof to solve technology challenges (Geekulcha, 2020). Andza Entrepreneur innovation competition aims to find top investment-ready businesses to accelerate innovative ideas to greater heights and further develop the South African economy (ExpertHub Staff, 2019). Winetech finds innovators and disruptors that provide unique solutions and products which can be commercialized to wine producers and the agri-tech industries. The various hackathon aims to foster innovative ideas for student start-ups to compete for investment, showcase their products or services, gain market and media exposure and secure support in the stages of scaling and growth. Different Provinces in South Africa also have their Hackathon initiatives (Geekulcha, 2018). A few examples of universities incubation hubs in South Africa universities demonstrate how academic institutions are becoming innovation hubs for students. These include LaunchLab by Stellenbosch University, Solution Space by the University of Cape Town, University of KwaZulu-Natal ENSPIRE, and Tshimologong by Witwatersrand University.

Moving along this trend, South Africa Universities are also treading the part of setting up business incubators. There are twenty-six public universities in South Africa managed by the Department of Higher Education and Training (DHET). Universities as business incubation support student start-ups business by bringing student entrepreneurs together in a standard working space to launch an actual company. The University of Stellenbosch's LaunchLab is a start-up incubator that creates a vibrant ecosystem for businesses both inside and outside the university. LaunchLab provides office space, facilities, and incubation programs, as well as expert guidance, coaching, and funding to students (Diphoko 2018).

Similarly, Tshimologong at the University of Witwatersrand encourages tech innovation and collaboration between the university's researchers, students, private, public, and civil society sectors in Johannesburg. The space has flexible open-plan co-working areas with broadband connectivity for ICT start-ups, meetings, computer laboratories, training rooms, maker spaces, creative content development environments, administrative and infrastructure support offices. University incubators have human know-how and capital sources, fostering innovation and commercialization (Hassan, 2020; Murage, 2018; Prencipe, 2016). Farman (2018) argues that universities should meet the challenges of innovation ecosystems in a tech-driven economy while retaining their core mission of educating the next generation and cultivating new forms of knowledge.) Higher education institutions are a hotbed of significant innovations that should be harnessed to benefit society and create job (Diphoko, 2019). The benefits of universities as incubators include provision of training to students for preparation for technology-based entrepreneurship, promotion of research that creates opportunities for innovation and academic staff provision of consulting services to nascent firms (Diphoko, 2019; Murage, 2018). The rationale behind university incubators is also attributed to research commercialization for the optimal value of society. The benefit of university incubation provides adequate infrastructural support in the growing processes of university spin-offs, improvement of the entrepreneurial capabilities of university start-ups, in particular during the early phase of their existence (Hassan, 2020; OECD, 2016 Prencipe, 2016). The success of university incubators is linked to the physical closeness between entrepreneurs, academics, financers and executives, along with the sharing of the research laboratory, spaces, and facilities that accelerate the transfer of technology and knowledge (Murage, 2018; Prencipe 2016). However, studies suggest that incubation contributes minimally to incubated business survival, employment, and sales growth despite the time spent in incubation programs (Voisey, Jones & Thomas, 2013; Sehitoglu, & Ozdemir, 2013).

Hackathon is a top agenda in South Africa nationally, as reflected in South Africa's innovation policies enacted by the State Information Technology Agency (SITA). SITA was established in 1999 to manage the government's information technology resources to save costs, improve delivery capabilities, and improve interoperability. The importance of innovation is also underscored in the ten-Year Innovation Plan for South Africa (2008-2018) orchestrated by the Department of Science and Technology [DST]. These strategic frameworks have purposefully guided the government in increasing its funding for Hackathon and related student entrepreneurial activities. Human Research Science Council [HRSC] (2014) suggests that South Africa spent R23.871 billion on Research and Development (R & D) in 2012/2013 on five sectors: the government, Science Councils, higher educational institutions, business enterprises, and NGOs. Ramika (2016) argues that despite R& D funding, there is still a low rate of commercialization of innovations because of lack of support from university management, insufficient incentives for innovators, institutional bureaucratic regulations, limited access to funding opportunities, and inefficiency of intellectual property. The importance of the Hackathon is also indicated in the National Development Plan [NDP] 2030 Hackathon challenge, which SITA launched in 2018. This resulted in the '#NDP2030 Hackathon', which encourages students to create innovative and practical solutions to solve the socio-economic challenges that South Africa faces. SITA also introduced the National Development Plan (NDP) Hackathon as part of the agency's mission to leverage ICT to solve socio-economic issues.

RESEARCH METHODOLOGY

The study is a qualitative study. Data was generated from various sources such as observation and interviews. In addition to Student Entrepreneurship Week, series of student elevator pitches, the launch of UKZN ENSPIRE, Denim Friday and a series of Hackathon sessions held at UKZN in 2018/2019. Interviews was conducted with twelve participants [comprised of UKZN Alumni, Public Relations Manager, ENSPIRE Manager, Enactus member, UKZN incubation Centre managers, students]. Students who participated in the Hackathon elevation pitches were from different Departments compromised of postgraduate students and undergraduates. The twelve participants were assigned the pseudo names P1-P12 respectively. Data was also supplemented with secondary data sources such as UKZN magazine "indaba''.

FINDINGS

Findings suggests that Hackathon at UKZN is organized in partnership with organizations and industry representatives who mentors student start-ups. During such Hackathon, new student start-ups are scouted and sponsored after the end of the incubation program. Hackathons are also organized as boot camps to achieve different agendas such as experiential learning, incubate selection and pitching entrepreneurship ideas. Findings also show that the University incubation provided the platform for students to connect and learn from individuals who had walked the entrepreneurial path. Students also enter entrepreneurship competitions to stand a chance to pitch their business ideas. Finalists from pitching competitions showcase their business ideas rated by a panel of judges comprised of industry moguls and win business support packages and prizes. Hackathon is also incentivized with the monetary value ranging from R250 000 and R100 000 prize business support package.

Winners are also awarded business support based on their business models. Business support package ranges from aftercare program, business Mentorship, product development, business skills development programs, and patenting of inventions. Winners from the competition have developed a stove that combat shack fires, a major social problem amongst informal settlements in South Africa. Hackathon creates a culture that harnesses and grows innovation talent. Universities are rising to innovation hub learning because it teaches the fundamentals of employment skills, innovation, and explore new ideas.

Hackathon is also a platform where students are trained in one-minute pitching, software, coding, robotics, and IoT [P2].

P7 emphasized the role universities play in tackling South Africa's economic growth and unemployment by setting up incubators for students businesses.

It's not only about creating graduates, but it's also about producing graduates suitable for purpose and contribute meaningfully to society. Hackathons are about more than simply technology; they're also about training and problem-solving. [P7]

Findings indicate that through Hackathon and incubation programs, universities empower students to enhance student networking and funding. This is done by several initiatives as commercialization workshops, mentoring, and the development of entrepreneurs. Other themes that emerged from the findings are discussed below.

Theme 1: UKZN InQubate ENSPIRE

UKZN has an incubation called UKZN InQubate. UKZN InQubate promotes innovation, commercialization, and entrepreneurship. UKZN incubator sector involved with student entrepreneurship was formerly known as 'SHAPE', an acronym for Shifting Hope, Activating Potential Entrepreneurship. SHAPE started as an action research project within the UKZN College of Law and Management. However, SHAPE was renamed 'ENSPIRE' on 13 April 2018 at the UKZN Westville campus. UKZN InQubate section called the 'ENSPIRE' is an acronym for Entrepreneurship Skills Programme. ENSPIRE also offers student start-ups the opportunity to interact with successful entrepreneurs, self-confidence, and formal business friendship.

'ENSPIRE is derived from the Latin word 'inspirare', which means 'breathe or blow into', 'impart a concept for someone. The vibrant and dynamism linked with youth and entrepreneurship is represented in the ENSPIRE logo, derived from the UKZN colors[P5,Director of UKZN InQubate]. UKZN InQubate was established to equip university's students with entrepreneurial skills at a practical level. 'ENSPIRE' is launched based on the belief that students are business leaders of tomorrow. Therefore 'ENSPIRE' seeks to expose students to business, give them a head start and show them how to operate a business. Our researchers can assist the industry in finding solutions. As a result, we'd like to introduce our specialists to the business so they may perform their magic' [P4].

Theme 2: UKZN InQubate ENSPIRE

UKZN InQubate was established to stimulate entrepreneurship in the student body and develop solutions that can have a socio-economic impact. ENSPIRE program's goal is to turn students' burgeoning entrepreneurial spirit into viable, long-term businesses. The ENSPIRE model embraces entrepreneurial development holistically, utilizing effective mechanisms to transform student creativity and ideas into legally feasible business entities.

Findings also suggest that ENSPIRE has been designed as a fast-track model for assisting both new and experienced student entrepreneurs. The ENSPIRE model comprises a guided and coached process designed to help students realize their potential as individuals and entrepreneurs. ENSPIRE is designed on a two-stream programme that channels entrepreneurial energy into focused business goals. The first stream supports business ideas across all sectors of the economy. At the same time, the second stream supports the translation of student research and intellectual property into viable commercial businesses. P8 reiterated that many students come into the UKZN InQubate offices asking how to help them with their business ideas.

There are students university who manage their own enterprises. Since we began to engage in entrepreneurship, we have encountered an increasing number of these students. This helped us to realize that they are interested in starting a business[P8].

P9 explains further that most students aim to complete their degrees and find a job but are aware of the current economic condition and the possibility that they might not find a job when they graduate from university... Unfortunately, students did not appear to be connecting entrepreneurship to their academic studies at this time. We want engineering students to think about launching an engineering business that is related to their academics.

Similarly, students are currently pursuing entrepreneurship from a fundamental standpoint. They identify an opportunity such as a car wash because practically every scholar at the university owns a car. They also plan to open a tuck shop, a pop-corn stand, and other such businesses. P6 mentions that students are starting hi-tech businesses in advanced and first-world economies.

Many students come from rural areas and may not have been exposed to high-tech concepts. It's simply a matter of exposing students to more opportunities as they better grasp the world around them and the possibilities that exist. We'll start to see the levels of their ideas begin to rise(P6) .

While at a global level, the University of KwaZulu-Natal InQubate is embarking on an initiative with the WADHAANI Foundation to expose students to entrepreneurship. It also sought to take students to Silicon Valley to let them understand what was going on there.

Theme 3: UKZN InQubate 'ENSPIRE' Entrepreneurship Boot Camp

UKZN InQubate organize various Hackathons in the form of elevator Pitch campus challenge and student entrepreneurship program across UKZN five campus. ENSPIRE InQubate also organizes the pitching event 'Invest Den'. The Invest Den initiative was a partnered event between UKZN InQubate and the Technology Innovation Agency. A call for applications was announced to all UKZN students in September 2018, with 41 student business ideas submitted. The selected student cohort businesses were taken through an intensive entrepreneurial development programme using the Kawasaki Pitch Deck. The Kawasaki Pitch Deck is hinged on the 10/20/30 Rule of PowerPoint. This implies that a pitch should have ten slides, not more than twenty minutes, and thirty points font. The rule is applicable for any presentation to reach agreement. Thirty students entered the 'Invest Den' programme. The 'Invest Den' culminated in a weekend Entrepreneurship Boot Camp on 20th October 2018, with business pitch event which occurred on the 22nd October 2018, showcasing the top 10 candidates. Based on the commitment of the thirty students who entered the programme in their entrepreneurial development, they all received preliminary business support from UKZN InQubate.

ENSPIRE also has Business Club and Marketing platform. ENSPIRE performs an array of roles in business incubations. Students with business ideas and entrepreneurial skills contact the UKZN InQubate and students, who need a little, kick start getting off the mark. Such students are required to complete the Business Idea Disclosure. If such application is accepted, they are paired with experienced business mentors who guide them in developing a business plan. ENSPIRE also assists with developing an invention, Technology, and Transfer, such as management of intellectual property, negotiations, contractual agreements, licenses, and commercialization.

Also, ENSPIRE offers consultancy work to advance the knowledge economy and positively impact social and economic development in KwaZulu-Natal, South Africa, SADC, and the entire African continent. Thirdly, ENSPIRE provides consultancy where an expert service is provided for a fee or in-kind benefit and advice concerning problem-solving. Such consultancy comprises staff members of other institutions. It is professional services other than research, based on the client's articulated need, using UKZN space, equipment, services, facilities or staff time. Consultancy differs from research because it involves the application of existing knowledge and techniques. There is usually no academic output such as publications in an academic journal. It also recognizes that consultancy is a crucial aspect of an academic endeavor that can foster long-term relationships between industry, government, the public sector, and academia, which are critical in promoting innovation and information flow. UKZN

InQubate promotes consultancy through sourcing tenders and facilitating contract research with the industry.

Theme 4: UKZN Student Start-Ups Incubation Projects

Students pitched on different projects such as hydroponics, data mining and apps that took entrepreneurship to the next level. Students' businesses in ENSPIRE incubation projects are DataQuantify, APC Initiatives, Career Buddy app, and Anonaya Gardens hydroponic. DataQuantify is a 100% black youth-owned data science company founded by two UKZN students. DataQuantify seeks to create the first machine learning/ artificial intelligence hub in KwaZulu-Natal. . DataQuantify collects, organizes, processes, visualizes and interprets complex data to help clients make correct business decisions. DataQuantify provides smart analytics to its customers, leading to enhanced productivity and profitability.

APC Initiatives' Career Buddy app' seeks to improve education outcomes in South Africa. Using a scientific methodology, it is an online psychometric tool that matches the learners'" strengths and characteristics to career opportunities and ranks prioritized careers choice. The app gives feedback on the students' academic and extra curriculum performance. It also provides feedback on the students' conduct in school. In addition, using the primary information on the students' performance, the app conduct career assessment and career guidance service.

Anonaya Gardens is a hydroponic farm that produces high-quality vegetables in huge quantities in a short amount of time. Anonaya Gardens founders are passionate about producing high-quality products in a sustainable manner that does not damage the environment. Customers receive highly nutritious vegetables grown organically without the use of chemicals, non-exposure to microorganisms associated with the soil. Hydroponics is soil-less gardening – plants grown suspended directly in mineral solution.

Theme 5: UKZN Hackathon Format

ENSPIRE InQubate, the university incubator located at UKZN, has an established partnership with the Technology Innovation Agency and the KZN Department of Economic Development, Tourism and Environmental Affairs with annual calls for Innovation funding to assist technologies at Technology Readiness Level 3 and above to advance toward commercialization. Major participants at the tech Hackathon is SmartiPants, a group of Civil, Mechanical, Electronic, Computer Science Engineering students who offer professional engineering consulting and empower communities with fourth industrial revolutions skills. Tech Hackathon are organized in boot camp format and Camp Weekend to foster business ideas spearheaded by students from science backgrounds. SmartiPants also organize innovative mechatronics and robotics workshops to promote Science, Technology, Mathematics and Engineering for learners. Activities that occur here are UBER Innovation Master and master classes on drone technology for 120 learners.

The incubation is a stepping stone to achieve my dreams, and I am keen to undergo training and mentorship to set up my business.(P3)

The format of Hackathon is diverse depending on the agenda of the Hackathon. Hackathon starts with an introduction on the agenda of the Hackathon and presentations by university lecturers from the Department of Business & Leadership. Participants propose ideas and establish teams based on their abilities and interests. They are guided through this process by lecturers called mentors. Findings indicate that pitching competition aims to engage students in innovative thinking that can solve real problems and contribute to job creation. It does so by exposing students' start-ups to a relevant investor market. The panel of judges are made up of university lecturers, organizers and sponsors. During the start of the Hackathon, students receive information about start-up and pitching. The first day was spent networking, pitching ideas, and forming teams. At the event, 30 participants registered, while 17 students, mainly females, pitched their ideas. A total of nine ideas were chosen to advance to the next stage. On day two, participants validate their concepts and design business prototype models as they work on their business models. Teams were guided and assisted in the development of their concepts by experienced coaches and mentors. On the third day, eight teams presented five-minute presentations to a panel of experienced judges drawn from various sectors. These are Nedbank, SME Diagnostics and Technology and Innovation Agency (TIA). The judges were tasked with evaluating each team's presentations on their validation, execution, design and business models. A participant expressed that she has learned a lot from the start-up weekend to become a successful entrepreneur. She was also excited at investment prospects from GSWW sponsors Ithala Bank and SmartXchange [P7].

At Hackathon, students pitched on different ideas centered on agroponics, solar-powered electric transporter, an archery equipment for quadriplegic athletes, a bilingual university newspaper called Varsity Press, and beauty Apps. Findings suggest that participants do not necessarily have prior programming, data science, or IoT knowledge because they work in small groups with diverse talents. The participants stated that attending Hackathon is highly rewarding because of mentoring and that they were able to practice the skills gained. The winner's first Prize went to the team whose business idea was on Beauty Butler, aimed to maximize the convenience of consumers seeking beauty services and the capacity usage of beauty service providers. The winner also received a chance to compete in the Global Start-up Weekend Finals on March 7th, 2018, in Paris, France. While the Second, third and fourth runner-ups received cash prizes sponsored by UKZN InQubate and an opportunity to pitch directly for R500 000 worth of seed funding from SmartXchange.

UKZN InQuabate also works with a wide range of highly successful UKZN alumni across several fields and sponsors. Such as funding agencies like Ithala and Technology Innovation Agency (TIA). The Hackathon is co-sponsored by banks like Ithala, Technology Innovation Agency (TIA) and Innovate Durban. Seasoned business advisors support ENSPIRE with a wealth of industry experience, which provides advice from nurturing start-ups to providing high-level financial modelling and deal structuring to support patented technologies. Findings reveal that the five-minute elevator pitch is an avenue for student start-ups to market their business ideas to likely investors. Winners from Elevator pitches are mentored by industry experts on venture creation projects sourcing of fund, finance, support networks for entrepreneurial initiatives, entrepreneurship-driven support of students.

Teams were guided and assisted in the development of business concepts by experienced coaches and mentors. At the Hackathon, student entrepreneurs with excellent business ideas are assisted with inputs that see them through the various stages leading to a successful business enterprise. The key focus of the Hackathon competition is to drive innovation, specifically amongst students. Hackathon is also organized during Student Entrepreneurship Week. During the Student Entrepreneurship Week, campaigns are organized to raise awareness on entrepreneurship as a career. At the elevator pitch, Judges comprise a panel of experienced individuals from professionals and diverse fields tasked to evaluate the team's presentations on business models.

Many more young people needed to get involved in incubate programs to grow their entrepreneurial thinking and skills. Students need to be inspired by a space where they can identify who they are. Once they understand who they are and what they want out of life, they can go for their dreams. Incubation is also a response to one of the biggest problems in South Africa that individuals are trained at an early age to work to receive a monthly salary. Hackathon instills and exposes youth to think entrepreneurially, more than working or studying towards being somebody's employee [P10].

P11 describes that

We are one of the university in the country that does initiatives like this. Training in incubation provides you a better product that is more efficient. We, as universities, our initiatives must benefit and have an impact on the community. As a result, we are cognisant that we must serve the community in any way we can. As a result, we balance our initiatives with community awareness projects, research, design, and innovation projects, and pure mechanical tasks, such as vehicle mechanics. Some of the projects, particularly those for communities, have a commercial future that could be commercial and viable. Some projects are continuations of previous ones that have been constructed over time as technology improves, while others are for research purposes.

Theme 6: Other Forms of Student Entrepreneurship in UKZN

Other forms of Student Entrepreneurship in UKZN are Student Entrepreneurship Week (SEW), CAVE [Creative, Accelerator, Vibrant, and Entrepreneurial], Denim Friday and ENACTUS. Findings reveals that innovation is nurtured at South African universities through Student Entrepreneurship Week (SEW), aimed at instilling entrepreneurial spirit and developing a business mindset amongst university students. Finding suggests that Student Hackathon is conducted during the Student Entrepreneurship Week (SEW) across 27 South African universities. The Student Entrepreneurship Week (SEW) was piloted in 2017 and successfully executed in 2018 by public universities in South Africa. One of the objectives of student entrepreneurship week is to raise awareness for creating employment through Hackathon. The national launch of #SEW2019 is hosted across South African universities.

Through the SEW, students learn first-hand from Entrepreneurs about their businesses, meet incubators, and pursue entrepreneurship as a career. Student Entrepreneurship Week also features speakers and a design-thinking boot camp to showcase their ventures. Each higher education institution decides when to host the SEW. However, the SEW is usually held during the months of August because August is referred to as youth month in South Africa, whereby Youth Activities are organized nationally in South Africa.

The Student Entrepreneurship and Innovators Society also showcase the thriving culture of student entrepreneurship at UKZN and uncovers innovative ways of promoting student entrepreneurial activities within UKZN CAVE. A committee supports the society from the Discipline of Management and Entrepreneurship. Denim Friday allows budding entrepreneurs to sell their products, exhibit their abilities, and mingle with the UKZN network. The event enables UKZN students to take a proactive role in driving UKZN's social cohesion in line with the Strategic Plan 2017-2021. The Denim Friday provides the platform of creative students who love denim to meet and exchange fashion ideas, but it has grown to be much more than that. It is supported by the College of Law and Management Studies. Participants expressed that as a student entrepreneur, I have encountered many challenges, primarily because of insufficient knowledge when it comes to business. With all I have learned in my journey, I realized that an entrepreneurial ecosystem cultivated the culture of entrepreneurship and information sharing needed within UKZN and that's why I jumped at the opportunity to be part of this initiative.

The CAVE program is motivated by UKZN's desire to play a proactive role in developing entrepreneurial endeavors in South African society.

CAVE was established to help students by providing them with information, skills, and a practical understanding of entrepreneurship. The goal is a collaboration between students and lecturers. The result is that UKZN students graduating wh contribute to establishing new markets, hence growing the country's economy by igniting economic development through new products and services [P12].

Similarly, ENACTUS is also a platform university students develop entrepreneur skills. ENACTUS members also pitch at UKZN Hackathon. ENACTUS is formed from three words, 'Entrepreneurial, Action, and Us'. Entrepreneurial implies having the perspective to see an opportunity and the talent to create value from that opportunity. Action is the willingness to do something and the commitment to see it through even when the outcome is not guaranteed. 'Us' is the group of people who see themselves connected in some meaningful way because individuals are part of a greater whole. ENACTUS is a non-profit organization that assembles students, academic, and corporate leaders devoted leveraging on entrepreneurship to enhance the standard of living for the community ENACTUS UKZN was established in 2003 with only three members and two projects operating on one campus. Since its inception, the team has significantly increased and has about 100 UKZN students on four UKZN's campuses, namely Edgewood, Howard College, Pietermaritzburg, and Westville Campus. ENACTUS mobilizes students to apply classroom knowledge to address real-world business and economic concerns in their communities in collaboration with industry and higher education. ENACTUS students join groups on their university campuses to create outreach initiatives that teach entrepreneurship, business ethics, and environmental sustainability. Students get a practical understanding of how market economies work and establish a culture of ethical corporate conduct by empowering others. Faculty advisers and local business advisory boards serve as mentors.

CONCLUSION

University incubators play a critical role in developing student entrepreneurs and students wishing to experiment with entrepreneurship while studying. Such Hackathon also provides the means to accelerate innovation, scout new talent, and create new businesses and business opportunities.

REFERENCES

Alfonso, A. (2019). Learning by doing in business education: Using Hackathon to improve the teaching and learning of entrepreneurial skills. *Journal of Entrepreneurship Education*, *22*(1).

Alkema, P., Levitt, S., & Chen, J. (2017). *Agile and Hackathon: A case study of emergent practices at the FNB codefest.* . doi:10.1145/3129416.3129430

Dahir, A. (2016, August 17). *The number of tech hubs across Africa has more than doubled in less than a year.* https://qz.com/africa/759666/the-number-of-tech-hubs-across-africa-has-

Diphoko, W. (2018 June 20). *Why every university needs a start-up hub?* https://www.iol.co.za/business-report/opinion/opinion-why-every-university-needs-a-start-up-hub-15747518

Dludla, S. (2019). *At least 6.7 million South Africans jobless with unemployment rate at an 11-year high.* Academic Press.

ExpertHub Staff. (2019, May 14). *SA Startups Compete For R10m In The ANDZA Entrepreneur Competition.* https://www.experthub.info/news/experthub-today/introducing-the-andza-entrepreneur-competition/

Farnam, J. (2018). *4 ways universities are Driving Innovation.* https://www.weforum.org

Geekulcha. (2020). *Home of the Geeks.* https://www.geekulcha.dev/

Guardian. (2017). *What jobs will still be around in 20 years? Read this to prepare your future.* https://www.theguardian.com

Hassan, N. A. (2020). University business incubators as a tool for accelerating entrepreneurship: Theoretical perspective. *Review of Economics and Political Science*. doi:10.1108/REPS-10-2019-0142

HRSC. (2014). *R&D outlook in South Africa is improving, but not yet at the country's full potential.* http://www.hsrc.ac.za/en/media-briefs/cestii/research-and-development

McKinsey Global Institute. (2013). *Disruptive technologies: Advances that will transform life, business, and the global economy*, Academic Press.

Murage, G. (2018). *Effect of University Technology Business Incubator services on the performance of digital enterprises in Kenya* [Master's Thesis]. Strathmore University. Retrieved from https://su-plus.strathmore.edu/handle/11071/6016

OECD. (2016). *Getting Skills Right: Anticipating and Responding to Changing Skill Needs*. OECD Publishing. doi:10.1787/9789264252073-en

Oleksii, S., Kharchenko, V., Sklyar, V., & Chris, P. (2015). *Hacking the innovations with university-industry Hackathon*. Academic Press.

Prencipe, A. (2016). Do University Incubators Stimulate Innovation of University Spin-Offs? An Analysis of Italian Firms. *International Journal of Business and Social Science*, *7*(7).

Robles, N. (2017). *Development of university's business incubators in Panama* [Master Thesis]. Faculty of Engineering Economics and Management, Institute of Business, Riga Technical University.

Roura, J. C. (2015). Business incubation: Innovative services in an entrepreneurship ecosystem. *Service Industries Journal*, 1–18.

Sanyal, S., & Hisam, M. (2018). The role of business incubators in creating an entrepreneurial ecosystem: A study of the sultanate of Oman. *International Journal of Contemporary Research in Humanities and Social Sciences*, *7*(1), 60–77.

Schwab, K. (2016). The Fourth Industrial Revolution: what it means, how to respond. *WeForum.* Retrieved from https://www.weforum.org/agenda/2016/01/the-fourth-industrial-revolution-what-it-means-and-how-to-respond/

Sehitoglu, Y., & Ozdemir, O. C. (2013). The impact of business incubation on firm performance during post graduation period - Turkey. *British Journal of Arts and Social Sciences*, *12*(1), 171–190.

Stats, S. A. (2019). *Youth graduate unemployment rate increases in Q1: 2019*. www.statssa.gov.za

Voisey, P., Jones, P., & Thomas, B. (2013). The pre-incubator: A longitudinal study of 10 years of university pre-incubation in Wales. *Industry and Higher Education*, *27*(5), 349–363. doi:10.5367/ihe.2013.0168

Vu. (2016). *Analysis of the influencing factors for choosing an entrepreneurial career among students in Finland*. Academic Press.

Walter, U. (2019). *Hackathon as a Formal Teaching Approach in Information Systems Capstone Courses*. Academic Press.

Xu, M. J. M., & Kim, S. H. (2018). The Fourth Industrial Revolution: Opportunities and Challenges. *International Journal of Financial Research, 9*(2).

Section 4
Factors Influencing Career Choice

Chapter 11
An Expanded Framework of Factors Influencing Career Choice

Mohammad Izzuddin Mohammed Jamil
https://orcid.org/0000-0002-2967-7870
Universiti Brunei Darussalam, Brunei

ABSTRACT

Studies on career choice are crucial, and the earliest iteration of career choice framework is the three-dimensional framework that is composed to determine the underlying concepts of intrinsic, extrinsic, and interpersonal factors behind a career. However, most frameworks in literature does not consider the public and private sectors as a variable impacting career choice. Recent studies have shown that perceived work in the public sector or the private sector may alter factors influencing career choice. This is imperative as every economy is divided into two sectors. Private and public sector organisations have varying objectives, and a study is needed in order to study their effect on career choice. Therefore, the objective of this chapter is to propose a new, updated framework studying factors influencing career choice, whereby the two dimensions of public and private sector will be added as part of the framework of career choice. This chapter also specifies the items under intrinsic, extrinsic, and interpersonal factors.

INTRODUCTION

Career Choice is one of the most important dilemmas in life as it encompasses the lifetime aspects of personal, social and professional aspects. Without choosing the

DOI: 10.4018/978-1-7998-9581-7.ch011

right occupation, the likelihood of boredom from work routines will generate a sense of disillusion and frustration where self-actualisation and personal growth are not fulfilled, potentially leading to absenteeism and labour turnover due job dissatisfaction and demotivation. In fact, only about 15% of employees worldwide feel engaged, leaving the remaining 85% more likely to resign ("23+ Monumental Motivation Statistics for 2021 | TeamStage", 2021). Under employment, low quality production rates, and low employee satisfaction rates are just a few of the issues that many businesses are dealing with. These issues stemmed incorrect career pathways that lead to incorrect jobs, and incorrect occupations might result in low-quality goods or unemployment.

Career choice is an important issue in the development of youths since it has been linked to both good and negative psychological, physical, and socio-economic disparities that continue even after a person reaches adulthood (Auyeung & Sands, 1997). For most people, career choice and development are a lifetime process of interacting in the workforce by selecting from a variety of job possibilities. Many elements impact each person going through the process, including their living environment, personal aptitudes, and educational achievement (Van Der Heijden, Schalk & Van Veldhoven, 2008). The profession decision that people choose while in high school is a key turning point in their life. It is frequently seen by family and society as only a first step toward professional preparedness; nevertheless, this decision is critical in setting youngsters on a career path that both opens and closes doors.

PROBLEM STATEMENT

As a result, throughout the twenty-first century, job choice has been a phenomena that has impacted people all over the world. After completing their studies, whether in high school, college, or further education, young graduates will nearly always turn to the future to determine what type of employment best suits them. In fact, long before they finished their education, some of them would spend countless hours pondering the best employment they could find to support themselves. Should I either work in the public sector or the private sector? Will my parents approve of my new job? Will I be genuinely interested in the job? Will the pay be adequate enough to make a living? These are questions that often plague the minds of students everywhere and thus, they often face a dilemma in career choice. They often have to consider a lot of factors in mind such as parental influence, personal interests or financial incentives when deciding their jobs. Thus, studies on what led individuals to prefer and choose a particular occupation is important, and in literature, career choice studies are widespread yet varied among researchers in order to identify the factors influencing a career choice. The most popular and of the earliest frameworks that is used to measure career choice is the three-dimensional framework by Beynon, Toohey & Kishor (1998) and Carpenter & Foster (1977). The three-dimensional framework is composed to determine what are the underlying concepts of intrinsic, extrinsic and interpersonal factors behind a career. Because different person has different attitudes, some graduates may value financial rewards in their jobs above all (Abbasi and Sarwat, 2014), while others may prefer to work in a job that they enjoy (Aycan and Fikret-Pasa, 2003), regardless of the pay. In fact, some culture even places parents influence above all (Agarwala, 2008).

However, the simple nature of the three-dimensional framework means that it is too generalised and that it overlooks certain dimensions, namely the public and private sector. In today's economy, there are two sectors in which a young graduate may choose to work in; the public sector and the private sector (Boyne, 2002). The former refers to a part of an economy that is controlled by the government, whereas the latter refers to the other part of an economy that is run and controlled by private individuals, groups and firms. The public sector aims to provide goods and services in order to serve the general populace such as law and order, police force, national defense and infrastructure such as public roads, bridges, water and electricity. On the other hand, activities in the private sector are guided by the motive to earn money. Where there is market in the economy, the private sector would attempt to satisfy customer demand by supplying the relevant goods and services. Above all, the private sector dimension include start-ups and entrepreneurship, including those who are willing to start-up and become self-employed. There are those who are willing to take risks and set up their own ventures, and this would inevitably reduce unemployment rate as they are responsible for the creation of job opportunities.

The purpose of this paper is to analyse a range of factors that influences a career choice. The three factors in question are intrinsic, extrinsic and interpersonal variables. Another objective of this paper is to propose a new framework that takes into account the public and private sector. The two dimensions of public and private sector will be added as part of the variable of career choice. This paper will also specify the items under intrinsic, extrinsic and interpersonal factors. Above all, it is important to note that the career choice variable can be of any job occupation, such as human resource manager, accountant, digital marketing manager, salesman, clerk and etc. Thus, the new framework seeks to answer the question as to what are the underlying reasons behind individuals and people choosing a career choice of either the public sector or the private sector. This is extremely useful for managers, as identifying the reasons and motivations on why people choose a certain career choice is crucial in gaining competitive advantage and outperform competitors, especially in today's highly competitive business environment. The outbreak of the COVID-19 pandemic has affected every nation state, economic sector, and major demographic groups around the world. In this COVID-ridden era, global employment losses have risen by 81 million. In other words, according to International Labour Organisation (ILO), around 71% of of global employment losses are due to COVID-19. As a reference for a developed nation, in the United States for instance, unemployment rate has reached 14.8%, the highest it has ever been since 1948. Worse, that it is forecasted that this number will increase to 205 million people in 2022, hence the justification for this research is glaring.

By studying the factors underlying career choice, this paper can help readers better understand the labour markets and can help in identifying the root causes of unemployment. The New framework would be applicable for different regions, including identifying the factors influencing the career choice in other contexts or industries apart from education. Identifying the factors determining career choice can thus help reduce unemployment and help start-up managers better understand just what motivates individuals to work in a particular sector or organization, or become their own aspiring entrepreneurs. For managers, it is useful as it can in determining the right recruitment policy that can attract and retain fresh workers, eventually that can help transform small businesses into competent and growing enterprises, potentially increasing employment. In the context of this paper, the term 'manager' can be used to refer to all types of managers including managers in charge of start-up enterprises. An example of answering a general career choice question; should business managers find out that students from a remote college are motivated to work in the private sector by extrinsic factors such as financial incentives, then managers can see about increasing the wages and salaries in order to attract new employees away from competitors, as well as retain employees from ever leaving the organisation for competitors. An instance of answering a specific career choice question; should pure science students from a particular university be motivated to work in the public sector as laboratory assistants by intrinsic factors such as perceived job satisfaction due to job-related challenges, then the public sector manager can look to increase the difficulty of jobs as well as the number of jobs per person in a process known as job enrichment and job enlargement, respectively. Above all, should a particular student aspire to become an entrepreneur, the factors that led to them choosing that as a viable career choice is studied upon.

BACKGROUND

Definitions of Career Choice

Before delving into the details of Career choice, it is important to define the underlying concept behind career. The word 'career' is often related to a part of an individual's life that entails employment in order to make a living, whereas the inclusion of 'choice' on 'career' implies that it is made on one's own volatile freewill (Brown, 2002; Pavan, 2011).

Career choice from theory of work adjustment had stated that a career is something that matches an individual requirement in terms of skills (Dawis, 2005), while Holland's theory implies that career choice a holistic representation of an individual's personality traits (Holland,1997). Theory of trial and factor had also stated that career choice is the involvement of jobs to suit for skills and abilities (Parsons, Adler & Meece, 1984). A recent contribution of Gottfredson's theory of circumscription and compromise suggest that genetic and basic characteristics such as intelligence and values play an important role in career choice (Gottfredson, 2005).

Others have looked at career choice from a sociological perspective (Johnson & Mortimer, 2002) whereby career choice is ultimately determined by genetic endowments, environments factors, personal skills, and observing what others are doing (Krumboltz, Mitchell & Jones, 1976; Lent & Brown, 1996).

Others have explained that career choice is associated with culture of a country that is either collectivist or individualistic (Akosah-Twumasi et al, 2018, July) had stated that collectivist society often encompass various intrinsic, extrinsic and interpersonal values, while individualist society places parental intrusiveness as a main factor above all.

It is also important to note that career choice is often associated with career development. The fundamental difference between career choice and career development is that the latter involves complex long-term constructs that may involve longitudinal studies (McIlveen, Morgan & Bimrose, 2012).

Thus, a simplified holistic version on the definition of career choice by this paper; is that career choice is the culmination of a person's growth and activities throughout the course of their life, particularly those linked to their profession. The "path or progress of a person through life or a certain period of life. Parental advice, occupational guidance, identification with renowned individuals, trial or part-time employment, training options, personal interests, and ability tests, and many other determinants are all used to help people choose a career.

Conceptual Frameworks of Career Choice

Before reviewing the various career choice frameworks in literature, it is important to consider the Social Cognitive Career Theory (SCCT). The SCCT by Lent et al. is one of several theoretical models developed to describe the process of career career and development (1994). According to the SCCT, there are three social cognitive processes; the self-efficacy beliefs such as outcome expectations, career goals and intentions, interaction with ethnicity, culture, gender, socio-economic status, social support, and any perceived barriers to shape a person's educational and career trajectories to shape a person's educational and career trajectories (Lent et al., 2000). However, the SCCT is different in that it focuses more on long term career pathway rather than direct influencers or immediate determinants of career choice.

One of the first researchers to compose a framework of dimensions entailing short-term career choice is the three dimensional framework composed by Carpenter and Foster (1977) and Beynon et al. (1998). The three dimensional framework stresses the intricate interplay between a person inner goals and the environmental forces that impact their job choices and decision-making. Carpenter and Foster (1977) proposed that the early events and influences in which people are exposed to create the foundation on how they think about their professional goals (Carpenter and Foster, 1977). Furthermore, these authors' statement backs up the SCCT tenets, and they've created a three-dimensional framework to categorize the elements that affect career choice. All career-influencing elements, according to Carpenter and Foster, come from intrinsic, extrinsic, or interpersonal dimensions.

The intrinsic component of the three-dimensional framework was defined by them as a set of interests connected to a profession and its social role. Other researches have discovered that youngsters who are motivated by intrinsic variables are motivated by their personal interests in particular professions and jobs that are personally fulfilling (Gokuladas, 2010; Kunnen, 2013). Intrinsic elements, which include personality qualities, work satisfaction, professional growth, and learning experiences, are related to decisions made by the self, and the behaviors that follow are motivated by interest, enjoyment, curiosity, or pleasure (Kunnen, 2013; Nyamwange, 2016).

The need for social recognition and security is referred to as extrinsic, whereas the interpersonal dimension is linked to the influence of others such as family, friends, and instructors (Carpenter and Foster, 1977). External rules and the rewards associated with specific vocations are examples of extrinsic influences (Shoffner et al., 2015). Prestigious vocations, job availability, and well-paying positions have also been found to influence young people's career choices (Ryan and Deci, 2000). As a result, extrinsically driven adolescents may select a vocation based on the additional benefits that come with it, such as monetary compensation, job stability, work accessibility, and job pleasure (Ryan and Deci, 2000). The actions of agents of socialization in one's life are referred to as interpersonal factors, and they include the impact of family members, teachers or educators, peers, and societal duties (Gokuladas, 2010)

According to Beynon et al., students in Canada's primary motivation in choosing a job was to bring respect to the family (Beynon et al., 1998). Students who are influenced by interpersonal variables place a great importance on the opinions of family members and significant others; as a result, they consult and rely on these others, and they are ready to put their personal interests aside to do so.

There is some evidence that social, economic, and political developments influence young people's job choices. According to Bai (1998), the market economy shifted the ideals of university students, who prioritized self-interest over society concerns. Money and power were ranked as the most important motivators for finding work. The The proportional effect of several influences on students' job choices has been discovered to be Ozbilgin et al. (2005) found that cultural differences exist. A research is conducted in one of the leading universities in Southeast Asia Jamil, M. I. M. (2019, November)., which is considered collectivist nature had revealed that intrinsic factors such as relevant skills and personal job satisfaction are the main influence for undergraduate students to decide their career choice, although extrinsic factors comes a close second. Interpersonal factors however play a small role in influencing career choice. However, this study contradicts the statement that had stated that collectivist society often encompass various intrinsic, extrinsic and interpersonal values, while individualist society places parental intrusiveness as a main factor above all (Akosah-Twumasi et al, 2018, July).

Public Sector and Private Sector

The ownership of the organisations between the private and public sectors is the most fundamental distinction between them (Ross, 1988). The government owns and controls organizations in the public sector. Organizations in the private sector, on the other hand, are owned and managed by people or private businesses. This paper explains the fundamental differences between public and private sector, including accountability, risk preference and job security, work motivation, strategies involved, and Human resource Management conducts and practices. Because of the different natures of public and private sectors, it is important to take note of their potential influences on career choice, especially from the perspectives of these differences.

However, most framework does not consider the public and private sectors as a variable impacting career choice. Some recent studies had shown that perceived work in the public sector or the private sector may alter factors influencing career choice (Kjeldsen & Hansen, 2018; Gabris & Simo, 1995). This is imperative as every economy is divided into two sectors; namely public and private sector. Above all, private and public sector managers and organisations have varying objectives (Zeffane & Bani Melhem, 2017), and a study is needed in order to identify relevant factors in order to apply in today's context. Therefore, the objective of this paper is to propose a new framework that takes into account the public and private sector. The two dimensions of public and private sector will be added as part of the variable of career choice. This paper will also specify the items under intrinsic, extrinsic and interpersonal factors.

Employees and managers in the private sector place a higher importance on economic incentives than those in the public sector (Buelens & Van den Broeck, 2007; Blank, 1985). Employees in the public sector have less direct economic benefits than those in the private sector. Pay is a much greater motivator for private sector employees, supervisors (Buelens & Van den Broeck, 2007), and managers (Blank, 1985) than it is for their public sector counterparts. Unlike private sector managers, public sector managers are not strongly motivated by pay expectancy. The three-dimensional framework had classified pay or economic rewards as extrinsic rewards, thus the question must be asked if preference for public or private sector will moderate the effect on career choice.

However, because the government is not under any profit pressures, people who are concerned about their job security will look for work in the public sector (Clark & Postel-Vinay, 2009). There are just a few articles that specifically discuss concerns to illustrate that managed risk is a sectoral decision; there is a considerable increase in worker aversion towards the private sector (Bellante & Link, 1981). Those who are in bad health or who are more risk averse should be more inclined to seek help as they perceived themselves less economically well off. Thus, the less economically stressed a person is, the more likely he or she is to be creative (Bellante & Link, 1981; Clark & Postel-Vinay, 2009). People who are risk averse may look for jobs towards public sector rather than the private sector. The government sector may experience lower employee turnover, as the government sector is perceived as safe (Munnell & Fraenkel, 2013).

Because of the high level of unionization in the public sector, it is discovered that management places a premium on Human Resource Management domains that deal with employee selection and grievance processes (Harel & Tzafrir, 2001). Private-sector management, on the other hand, places a premium on employee development and compensation for performance. Nonetheless, indications that the public sector is "getting" closer to the private sector model by adopting "high performance work methods" to deal with the volatile environment (Absar & Mahmood 2011), and public demand may ultimately change risk-aversion. It is this difference in human management practice that may influence the career choice.

On the other hand, strategy in the public sector is slowly adopting the corporate planning models in single public sector companies. Private sector on the other hand could choose from a variety of models but places emphasis on consulting stakeholders before making a strategic decision (Alford & Greve, 2017). Now, strategy is a larger and more widely spread activity that involves multiple managers and organizations. For public managers, the way forward is to focus less on the content of strategy and more on achieving the appropriate performance and optimized outcome. Instead, public managers must focus more on creating and shaping public value propositions, as well as collaborating with other stakeholders and citizens (Stewart,

2004). Politicians, stakeholders, and people all have a role in achieving a strategy's objectives in the public sector. Thus, should the private sector failed to maximise profit due to non-adherence to stakeholders, or worst-case scenario, the company will be forced to liquidate, affecting its entire employees.

When comparing big private firms' general accountability to that of government agencies, the most obvious parallel is with a company's shareholders' rights (Mulgan, 2000). In the same way that a government belongs to its citizens, a corporation may be considered to belong to its shareholders. Commercial secrecy claims in the private sector, on the other hand, typically go farther than executive privilege and cabinet confidentiality claims in the public sector (Shaoul, Stafford & Stapleton, 2012). Certain material provided to the annual general meeting, such as annual accounts, is available to shareholders. Accountabiltiy may influence certain individuals to avoid the public sector due to perceived burden of responsibility.

MAIN FOCUS OF THE CHAPTER

Intrinsic

Personal values are what are referred to be intrinsic elements in a person (Price, 2007). It comprises of their own interests and values in their profession, which may be defined by their education and training abilities and competencies (Carpenter & Foster, 1977; Beynon et al., 1998). Employment-related contents, such as a personally rewarding job owing to favorable working circumstances, are also intrinsic elements (Aycan & Fikret-Pasa, 2003). When a person is driven by intrinsic reasons, he or she is more likely to work for a job that he or she finds fascinating, or even one that is linked to their studies, as well as a work environment that is acceptable to a degree, or at least up to standard.

Interests

Morgan, Isaac & Sansone (2001) has found that interests as one of the most crucial factors in determining career choice among male college students compared to female counterparts. While conventional wisdom claims that a person's interest is often crucial in determining their career choice, other factors may have stronger correlation (Sultana & Mahmud, 2020). The research concluded that students should be given the freedom to express their interests, that they should discuss their interests with students in a pleasant manner, that they should not be put under any pressure, that they should not underestimate students' judgments, and so on. This is further supported by (Smith, Sansone & White, 2007) that stated that when under threat or pressure, interests and motivations tend to change dramatically, affecting. The change could be affected by interpersonal factors such as family expectations whereby interpersonal factor will supersede intrinsic factors.

Job Satisfaction

Another intrinsic factor involves job satisfaction. Findings have shown that perceived job satisfaction was positively influenced by perceived employability, whereas job satisfaction was negatively influenced by expectation gaps in working circumstances (Jeong & Choi, 2017). Second, work satisfaction was linked to a lower likelihood of starting a business. Furthermore, work happiness and entrepreneurial ambition were influenced by self-efficacy and result expectancies (Jeong & Choi, 2017; Blaese, Noemi & Brigitte, 2021). Finally, work satisfaction influenced overconfidence and had a favorable impact on self-efficacy. In conclusion, academic scholars used the concepts of work satisfaction and Social Cognitive Career Theory to better understand the process of entrepreneurial career decisions.

Job Condition

Perceived Job Condition is also a potential factor influencing career choice. The debate on job conditions emphasizes the necessity of creating supportive work environments by organisations (Teo & Poon, 1994). This is especially important throughout the employee's formally induction year in order to socialize them into a collaborative and participative work ethic that will keep them committed (Teo & Poon, 1994; Weiss, 1999). Thus, in the workplace, there should be a sense of security and comfort in order to keep up the perception of healthy job condition. Studies have shown that work-life balance, which includes lifestyle, flexibility, and working hours and circumstances, is the most significant element in deciding whether or not to pursue a speciality (Teo & Poon, 1994; Weiss, 1999; Douglas et al., 2018). Sibson (2011) had found that the most important factors were good working environment and pay.

Job Security

Job Security is usually referred to protection from job loss; the absence of concern about being laid off or fired. Extrinsic factors such as acknowledgment of achievement, fair performance appraisal, and job security were placed first and are the most significant components of job satisfaction, whereas intrinsic factors such as appropriate daily working hours and kind of work were near the bottom of the list (Alansari, 2011). Because non-education majors place a high value on job stability, efforts to recruit future African American teachers should include efforts to modify attitudes about the security of a teaching career. Given current circumstances, job stability is likely to become a more appealing component of a teaching profession. Massive white-collar layoffs in a number of private-sector businesses have indicated a rising lack of security throughout the private sector over the last decade (Shipp, 1999). In addition, it is revealed that extrinsic variables such as development opportunities and job stability, as well as firsthand knowledge sources such as work experiences and personal experiences were the most significant when deciding on a future career (Kim, McCleary & Kaufman, 2010).

Extrinsic

Extrinsic factors consider the external environment, which includes sub-variables such as employment availability, well-paying vocations, and high pay structures (Carpenter & Foster, 1977; Beynon et al., 1998). Extrinsic factors assume that current labor market conditions may have an impact on a person's job decision (Ng, Burke & Fiksenbaum, 2008). A company's brand image and employment stability are two more sub-variables (Edvardsson Stiwne, 2005). External benefits, such as financial incentives, may be a person's major drive to labor. A study shows that "a decent income" is becoming more important in graduate employment selection (Bai, 1998), which reflects a set of new notions that are clashing with official ideology. Because of the abolition of old values and the lack of new ethical norms of conduct, "money talks" has become a norm governing social behavior and personal relationships, and has aided in the formation of a force to counteract the strength of political moral education (Wong, Wan & Gao, 2017). They also provide the most fundamental demand of most informants, which is financial security. For these young individuals, monetary reward is a critical issue, and one of the main reasons for advancement is to earn more money. Indeed, the data show that those who view employment as labor are the least committed to their jobs and employers. They would just change jobs if another firm offered a higher salary plan. As a result, these personnel are focused on monetary compensation.

Financial Incentives

Job satisfaction, earnings potential, job availability, and aptitude for the topic were the variables that most substantially affected the decision to pursue accountancy as a field (Myburgh, 2005). Financial remuneration, job availability, employment stability, and development possibilities have all been identified as key variables in career choice (Felton, Buhr & Northey, 1994). Because of the patient care, employment availability, variety in work content, and high levels of teamwork, physiotherapy was viewed as an appealing career choice (Park, Coombs, Wilkinson, Loan-Clarke, Arnold & Preston, 2003). These good characteristics, however, were countered by high levels of stress and strain, personnel shortages, and inadequate equipment.

Non-Financial Incentives

On the other side of the coin, there are non-financial incentives such as fringe benefits, holiday packages, workers' compensation and health insurance. The top reason for selecting a profession in law enforcement is the existence of good income and fringe benefits (Tarng, Hsieh & Deng, 2001).. To put it another way, police officials should pay well for police work, make promotions more appealing to parents in order to urge their children to join the force, and use various recruitment tactics for males and females to help entice individuals to join the force. The most commonly utilized and easily available measures of extrinsic professional success are fringe perks and promotions (Wong & Liu, 2010). These extrinsic measurements can have a number of advantages, including being easily available from existing records, being standardized among businesses, as well as being simple to gather.

Opportunity

Discovering satisfaction in one's job, receiving financial benefits, finding possibilities, and completing work obligations appeared as a common theme from participants' tales (Fouad, Kantamneni, Smothers, Chen, Fitzpatrick & Terry, 2008). When an individual senses a unique opportunity, they are motivated to pursue a career. An example include opportunity-driven entrepreneurship that are often present in developed economies (Williams, 2008). Another example includes a desire to attain the ''American Dream" (Fouad, Kantamneni, Smothers, Chen, Fitzpatrick & Terry, 2008), where five people said that their job decisions were affected by their impressions of prospects and a desire to fulfill the "American Dream." These participants saw America as a land of opportunity, which influenced the sorts of jobs they thought were possible.

Interpersonal

Parents, significant others, family, relatives, friends, and coworkers are all examples of interpersonal variables. For example, a person may have selected a professional path based on his or her father's expectations or a friend's suggestion that he or she pursue a particular position (Carpenter & Foster, 1977; Beynon et al., 1998). Morgan, Isaac & Sansone (2001) had stated that peer groups and teachers are two more sub-variables of interpersonal influence that can have a significant impact on a person's job decision. To put it another way, interpersonal variables consider the effects of early exposure to various vocations and professions (Marinas, Igret, Marinas & Prioteasa, 2016).

Parents

Perceived parental support, perceived parental career worries about welfare and status, and perceived parental impediments to career choice are the three main criteria (Wong, & Liu 2010). Three of the six parental influencing variables generated from 22 characteristics were shown to be the most important indicators of students' decision to pursue a profession. Research has shown that mothers and fathers may influence their children's career aspirations in different ways (Jungen, 2008). Otto (2000) reported that young adults most often look to their mothers for career guidance. Kumar (2016) found that fathers have a more significant impact on children's career choices, while Jacobs, Chhin & Bleeker (2006) concluded that children respond differently to maternal and paternal expectation depending on the gender of the child. Clutter (2010) came to the conclusion that the most significant element was a child's relationship to their parent. According to the study's findings, 48.36% of respondents believed that their parents influenced their job choice (Olaosebikan & Olusakin, 2014), where the goal of this study was to look at the impacts of parental influence on secondary school pupils in Lagos State's Badagry Local Government Area's profession choices.

Friends

The majority of medical students believed their parents had a significant effect on their decision to pursue medicine as a vocation (Ausman et al., 2013). Friends had a weak effect on their profession choice among non-familial social variables. While more medical students picked their job with the help of their parents, the majority of non-medical students made their decision on their own. As a result, school counselors' influence in non-Asian foreign students' career choices may be overshadowed by the role of family and friends. It's worth noting that Asian overseas students scored the highest on the impact of friends scale (Singaravelu, White & Bringaze, 2005). This study suggests that Asian international students, more than the other groups examined, rely on their friends, who may be studying or have studied abroad, for advise on their major or career decision.

Teachers

It is shown that the influence of most of the accounting career-choice determinants studied differed in degrees of influence between cultures (Auyeung & Sands, 1997). Hong Kong and Taiwanese students were more impacted by parental influence, instructors' influence, peers' influence, and affiliation with others in the field than Australian students, but Australian students were more influenced by aptitude for subject matter. The importance of teachers' effect on accountants' job choices highlights the necessity for motivated, capable, dedicated teachers, and accounting tutors that are extremely driven (Paolillo & Estes, 1982).

Peers

The students' perceptions of their peers' effect on their job choice were used to measure peer influence (Alika, 2012). Students' job choices were affected by their classmates, according to the findings of a study (Kimiti & Maria, 2012). From one school to the next, the amount of peer impact differed. Male students were more affected by their classmates in picking a job than their female counterparts. Teaching, nursing, engineering, and law were among the professions selected by these students. This means that the influence of peers on secondary students' job choices should not be overlooked, since it may lead to pupils making poor decisions.

SOLUTIONS AND RECOMMENDATIONS

To enable the hypothesis testing to be derived from the expanded framework in order to be applied to any career choice, the Three Dimensional Framework (Beynon, Toohey, & Kishor, 1998; Carpenter & Foster, 1977) was used in this study, which includes the first three independent variables of Intrinsic, Extrinsic, and Interpersonal Factors, as well as the subsequent dependent variable of Career Choice. Thus, by gathering and synthesizing the aforementioned intrinsic, extrinsic and interpersonal factors that is derived from academic literature, this paper is able to compose a new conceptual framework. In addition to the normal dependent and independent variables, a new variable is added to the framework to showcase a moderating variable showing the influence and effect of public and private sector. As shown as Figure 1, this study developed a new and distinct framework that is a variant of the Three Dimensional Framework.

Table 1 shows the intrinsic factors, extrinsic and interpersonal factors are thus broken down into specific items. These items are some of the most used items in

Figure 1. Proposed expanded framework of factors influencing career choice with the moderating effect of economic sector

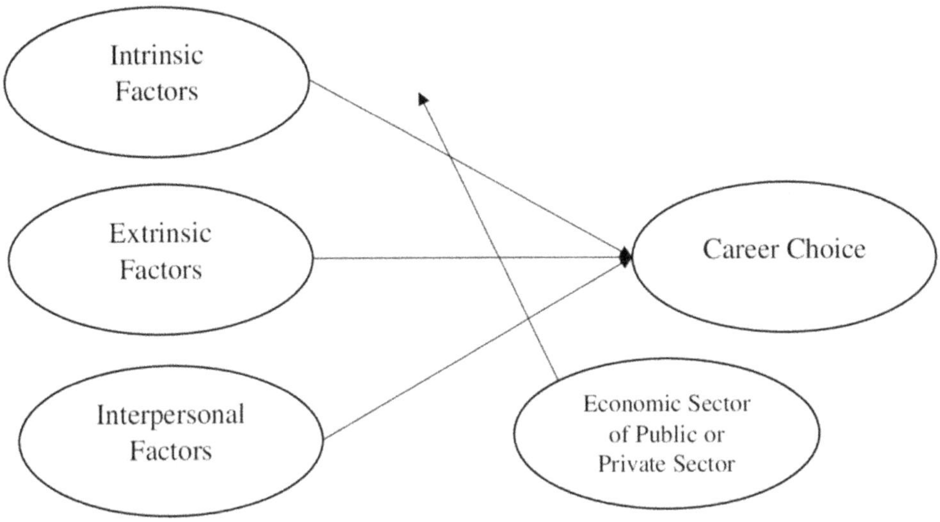

academic literature by researchers looking to study factors influencing career choice towards a particular occupation.

Table 1. Summary of intrinsic, extrinsic and interpersonal factors

Intrinsic	Extrinsic	Interpersonal
Job Interest	Monetary Rewards including salaries and wages (financial)	Parental influence: Father
Perceived Job Satisfaction	Extra Benefits; Fringe Benefits (non-financial)	Teacher/Lecturers/Educators
Perceived Job Condition	Opportunities for Career Development	Friends
Perceived Job Security	-	Peers

The fundamental difference is because this framework enables the study of the moderating effect of public and private sector on the intrinsic, extrinsic and interpersonal factors towards career choice. These two variables might be thought of as alternative consequences of the variable of career choice. Thus, on a technical term, the independent variables consist of intrinsic, extrinsic and interpersonal factors, while depedent variable consists of career choice.

By perusing this framework, not only will researchers able to identify the correlation as well as the cause and effect of the three variables on career choice, but also study the effect of economic sector of public and private sector. For instance, should an individual value his personal interests towards deciding a career choice, will the effect of working in a public or private sector change their opinion or otherwise? As mentioned above public and private sector have varying characteristics, and while public sector is slowly adopting the model being used in the private sector, ultimately objectives are still different. The benefit or perusing this framework is that it not only that it included the three-dimensional framework, but also items derived are also some of most used and applied items in empirical researches.

CONTRIBUTIONS AND IMPLICATIONS

The countless factors influencing career choice in literature have further led to confusion and ambiguity over which factor is the most crucial. Inconsistent findings and lack of updated coherent theories have inspired this chapter. Furthermore, this chapter enhances the work of Beynon, Toohey & Kishor (1998) as well as Carpenter & Foster (1977).

There is a glaring research gap whereby there is a dearth of studies of career choice, especially public and private sector as moderating variable. Private and public sector managers and organisations have varying objectives (Zeffane & Bani Melhem, 2017), and a study is needed in order to identify relevant factors in order to apply in today's context. Employees and managers in the private sector place a higher importance on economic incentives than those in the public sector (Buelens & Van den Broeck, 2007).

The managerial implication is that the framework identifies the factors influencing career choices in terms of intrinsic, extrinsic and interpersonal point of view. Practising managers looking to enhance their manpower will find that the framework's intrinsic factors are within their control and is the key to attracting employees. Furthermore, by adding a moderating variable of public and private sector, this framework can be applied in contemporary context whereby both small businesses and large corporations in either private and public can understand which specific factors that are relevant for them.

Understanding the underlying motivation of employees in choosing their careers can serve as a guideline on how to grow their enterprises in order to survive in nowadays' uncertain, competitive and dynamic business environment. Thus, another managerial implication is that the framework offers an opportunity for start-up entrepreneurs, owners and managers to study the factors influencing offered job occupation, which can help them identify how and what motivates their employees.

Worldwide job markets and business environments are becoming increasingly competitive more so than ever, and it is easy for unhappy employees to leave for another organisation. Thus, in addition to motivation, the expanded framework can also help entrepreneurs determine how to retain their employees. Analysing career choices could serve as a pathway to determining the underlying reasons for unemployment in an industry.

The policy implication here is that by identifying the extrinsic factors that influences career choice, orgnisation-friendly policies can be implemented by governments in order to foster an atmosphere that can promote job hunting and increase employment. This means that policies focusing on extrinsic factors are key to enhancing the growth of organisations, which in turn mean more income for the government, resulting in economic growth.

FUTURE RESEARCH DIRECTIONS

The focus of this paper is to illuminate the importance of identifying factors underlying career choice. With the composition of the expanded framework by this paper, the paper hopes to provide a clearer outlook into the minds of individuals on why they chose a career in the first place. This paper is conceptual in nature, thus the expanded framework can be used by researchers in order to empirically identify the factors influencing career choice of any job occupation. This expanded framework is suitable in contemporary context and it considers a new variable; the economic sector of public or private sector which studies its potential effect on career choice. This newer and updated framework can be applied in any industry or context such as schools, universities, workplace, managerial positions, entrepreneurship and others. Furthermore, the paper has only scratched the surface on the items of intrinsic, extrinsic and interpersonal factors. Researchers can find other relevant variables from literature and synthesise with the expanded in order to take into account even more items to represent factors influencing career choice.

CONCLUSION

In conclusion, career choice is one of the most important aspect of life as it encompass all individuals looking to make a living. However, it is more than just selecting what they will do for a living. Many individuals don't put enough thought into their career choices, or they choose them for the wrong reasons. As a result, in contemporary context, the overall number of instances of work-related stress and depression have skyrocketed dramatically, and this is especially prevalent among employees. Thus, this paper has composed an expanded framework to determine and analyse the reasons for selecting a job.

Thus, investigations on what caused people to favor and pick a specific employment are essential, and career choice studies are common in the literature but vary across researchers in order to discover the variables that influence a career choice. The expanded framework is composed to provide a newer and latest version of the framework representing factors influencing career choice. Intrinsic factors include four items; interests, job satisfaction, job condition, and job security, extrinsic factors include three items; financial incentives, non-financial incentives, opportunity, and interpersonal factors include four items; parents, friends, teachers, peers. In addition, this paper also fills in the research gap of career choice frameworks in literature not taking into account the economic sector of public and private sectors. Most frameworks ignore the public and private sectors as a factor influencing job choice and the expanded framework has included the moderating effect of economic sector of public and private sector.

This study contributes to management studies by focusing on identifying which factors are the most crucial (Aycan & Fikret-Pasa, 2003; Price, 2007). Thus, this study contributes and extends the career choice theory by researching on including whether public and private sector as possible aspects of career choice theories (Zeffane & Bani Melhem, 2017).

REFERENCES

Abbasi, M. N., & Sarwat, N. (2014). Factors Inducing Career Choice: Comparative Study of Five Leading Professions in Pakistan. *Pakistan Journal of Commerce & Social Sciences*, *8*(3).

Absar, M. M. N., & Mahmood, M. (2011). New HRM practices in the public and private sector industrial enterprises of Bangladesh: A comparative assessment. *International Review of Business Research Papers*, *7*(2), 118–136.

Agarwala, T. (2008). Factors influencing career choice of management students in India. *Career Development International*, *13*(4), 362–376. doi:10.1108/13620430810880844

Akosah-Twumasi, P., Emeto, T. I., Lindsay, D., Tsey, K., & Malau-Aduli, B. S. (2018, July). A systematic review of factors that influence youths career choices—The role of culture. *Frontiers in Education*, *3*, 58. doi:10.3389/feduc.2018.00058

Alansari, H. A. (2011). Career choice, satisfaction, and perceptions about their professional image: A study of Kuwaiti librarians. *Library Review*, *60*(7), 575–587. doi:10.1108/00242531111153597

Alford, J., & Greve, C. (2017). Strategy in the public and private sectors: Similarities, differences and changes. *Administrative Sciences*, *7*(4), 35. doi:10.3390/admsci7040035

Alika, H. (2012). Career choice in engineering: The influence of peers and parents implication for counselling. *College Student Journal*, *46*(3), 537–542.

Ausman, J., Javed, A., Ahmed, S., Samad, M. A., Pour, A. S., Mathew, E., ... Sreedharan, J. (2013). Social factors influencing career choice in a medical school in the United Arab Emirates. *Education in Medicine Journal, 5*(1).

Auyeung, P., & Sands, J. (1997). Factors influencing accounting students' career choice: A cross-cultural validation study. *Accounting Education*, *6*(1), 13–23. doi:10.1080/096392897331596

Aycan, Z., & Fikret-Pasa, S. (2003). Career choices, job selection criteria, and leadership preferences in a transitional nation: The case of Turkey. *Journal of Career Development*, *30*(2), 129–144. doi:10.1177/089484530303000203

Bai, L. (1998). Monetary reward versus the national ideological agenda: Career choice among Chinese university students. *Journal of Moral Education*, *27*(4), 525–540. doi:10.1080/0305724980270406

Bellante, D., & Link, A. N. (1981). Are public sector workers more risk averse than private sector workers? *Industrial & Labor Relations Review*, *34*(3), 408–412. doi:10.1177/001979398103400307

Beynon, J., Toohey, K., & Kishor, N. (1998). Do visible minority students of Chinese and South Asian ancestry want teaching as a career?: Perceptions of some secondary school students in Vancouver, BC. *Canadian Ethnic Studies Journal*, *30*(2), 50–75.

Blaese, R., Noemi, S., & Brigitte, L. (2021). Should I Stay, or Should I Go? Job satisfaction as a moderating factor between outcome expectations and entrepreneurial intention among academics. *The International Entrepreneurship and Management Journal*, *17*(3), 1–30. doi:10.100711365-021-00744-8

Blank, R. M. (1985). An analysis of workers' choice between employment in the public and private sectors. *Industrial & Labor Relations Review*, *38*(2), 211–224. doi:10.1177/001979398503800204

Blustein, D. L., Phillips, S. D., Jobin-Davis, K., Finkelberg, S. L., & Roarke, A. E. (1997). A theory-building investigation of the school-to-work transition. *The Counseling Psychologist*, *25*(3), 364–402. doi:10.1177/0011000097253002

Boyne, G. A. (2002). Public and private management: What's the difference? *Journal of Management Studies*, *39*(1), 97–122. doi:10.1111/1467-6486.00284

Brown, D. (Ed.). (2002). *Career choice and development*. John Wiley & Sons.

Buelens, M., & Van den Broeck, H. (2007). An analysis of differences in work motivation between public and private sector organizations. *Public Administration Review*, *67*(1), 65–74. doi:10.1111/j.1540-6210.2006.00697.x

Carpenter, P., & Foster, B. (1977). The career decisions of student teachers. *Education Research and Perspectives*, *4*(1), 23–33.

Cerny, P. G. (2010). The competition state today: From raison d'État to raison du Monde. *Policy Studies*, *31*(1), 5–21. doi:10.1080/01442870903052801

Clark, A., & Postel-Vinay, F. (2009). Job security and job protection. *Oxford Economic Papers*, *61*(2), 207–239. doi:10.1093/oep/gpn017

Clutter, C. (2010). *The effects of parental influence on their children's career choices*. Academic Press.

Dawis, R. V. (2005). *The Minnesota Theory of Work Adjustment*. Academic Press.

Douglas, P. S., Rzeszut, A. K., Merz, C. N. B., Duvernoy, C. S., Lewis, S. J., Walsh, M. N., & Gillam, L. (2018). Career preferences and perceptions of cardiology among US internal medicine trainees: Factors influencing cardiology career choice. *JAMA Cardiology*, *3*(8), 682–691. doi:10.1001/jamacardio.2018.1279 PMID:29847674

Edvardsson Stiwne, E. (2005). *The first year as Engineering Students-the experiences of four cohorts of engineering students in Applied Physics and Electrical Engineering in Linkoping University*. Academic Press.

Felton, S., Buhr, N., & Northey, M. (1994). Factors influencing the business student's choice of a career in chartered accountancy. *Issues in Accounting Education*, *9*(1), 131.

Ferry, N. M. (2006). Factors influencing career choices of adolescents and young adults in rural Pennsylvania. *Journal of Extension*, *44*(3), 1–6.

Fouad, N. A., Kantamneni, N., Smothers, M. K., Chen, Y. L., Fitzpatrick, M., & Terry, S. (2008). Asian American career development: A qualitative analysis. *Journal of Vocational Behavior*, *72*(1), 43–59. doi:10.1016/j.jvb.2007.10.002

Gabris, G. T., & Simo, G. (1995). Public sector motivation as an independent variable affecting career decisions. *Public Personnel Management, 24*(1), 33–51. doi:10.1177/009102609502400103

Gati, I., & Saka, N. (2001). High school students' career-related decision-making difficulties. *Journal of Counseling and Development, 79*(3), 331–340. doi:10.1002/j.1556-6676.2001.tb01978.x

Gokuladas, V. K. (2010). Factors that influence first-career choice of undergraduate engineers in software services companies: A south Indian experience. *Career Development International, 15*(2), 144–165. doi:10.1108/13620431011040941

Gottfredson, L. S. (2005). Using Gottfredson's theory of circumscription and compromise in career guidance and counseling. *Career development and counseling: Putting theory and research to work*, 71-100.

Harel, G. H., & Tzafrir, S. S. (2001). HRM practices in the public and private sectors: Differences and similarities. *Public Administration Quarterly*, 316–355.

Holland, J. L. (1997). *Making vocational choices: A theory of vocational personalities and work environments*. Psychological Assessment Resources.

Hood, K. M., Robles, M., & Hopkins, C. D. (2014). Personal branding and social media for students in today's competitive job market. *The Journal of Research in Business Education, 56*(2), 33.

International Labour Organisation. (2021). *ILO: Uncertain and uneven recovery expected following unprecedented labour market crisis*. Retrieved from: https://www.google.com/url?sa=t&rct=j&q=&esrc=s&source=web&cd=&cad=rja&uact=8&ved=2ahUKEwi4ye-ll_vyAhXMBd4KHesIB8EQFnoECAMQAQ&url=https%3A%2F%2Fwww.ilo.org%2Fglobal%2Fabout-the-ilo%2Fnewsroom%2Fnews%2FWCMS_766949%2Flang--en%2Findex.htm&usg=AOvVaw3ZVMIEv6xCHRQHC8i8wSjg

Jacobs, J. E., Chhin, C. S., & Bleeker, M. M. (2006). Enduring links: Parents' expectations and their young adult children's gender-typed occupational choices. *Educational Research and Evaluation, 12*(4), 395–407. doi:10.1080/13803610600765851

Jamil, M. I. M. (2019, November). The Factors influencing the Career Choice of University Students: A Descriptive Analysis of Pure Science and Social Science Students in Universiti Brunei Darussalam. In *Proceedings of the 1st International Conference on Business, Management and Information Systems 2019 (ICBMIS 2019)* (Vol. 1, pp. 566-588). Academic Press.

Jeong, J., & Choi, M. (2017). The expected job satisfaction affecting entrepreneurial intention as career choice in the cultural and artistic industry. *Sustainability*, *9*(10), 1689. doi:10.3390u9101689

Johnson, M. K., & Mortimer, J. T. (2002). Career choice and development from a sociological perspective. *Career Choice and Development, 4*, 37-81.

Jungen, K. A. (2008). *Parental influence and career choice: How parents affect the career aspirations of their children*. Academic Press.

Kim, B. P., McCleary, K. W., & Kaufman, T. (2010). The new generation in the industry: Hospitality/Tourism students' career preferences, sources of influence and career choice factors. *Journal of Hospitality & Tourism Education*, *22*(3), 5–11. doi:10.1080/10963758.2010.10696979

Kimiti, R. P., & Maria, M. M. (2012). *The dilemma of career choice: A case study of Kenyan secondary school students.* Academic Press.

Kjeldsen, A. M., & Hansen, J. R. (2018). Sector differences in the public service motivation–job satisfaction relationship: Exploring the role of organizational characteristics. *Review of Public Personnel Administration*, *38*(1), 24–48. doi:10.1177/0734371X16631605

Krumboltz, J. D., Mitchell, A. M., & Jones, G. B. (1976). A social learning theory of career selection. *The Counseling Psychologist*, *6*(1), 71–81. doi:10.1177/001100007600600117

Kumar, S. (2016). Parental influence on career choice traditionalism among college students in selected cities in Ethiopia. *International Journal of Psychology and Educational Studies*, *3*(3), 23–30. doi:10.17220/ijpes.2016.03.003

Kunnen, E. S. (2013). The effects of career choice guidance on identity development. *Education Research International*, *2013*, 2013. doi:10.1155/2013/901718

Lent, R. W., & Brown, S. D. (1996). Applying social cognitive theory to career counseling: An introduction. *The Career Development Quarterly*, *44*(4), 307–309. doi:10.1002/j.2161-0045.1996.tb00447.x

Marinas, L. E., Igret, R. S., Marinas, C. V., & Prioteasa, E. (2016). Factors influencing career choice: The Romanian business and administration students' experience. *European Journal of Sustainable Development*, *5*(3), 267–278.

McIlveen, P., Morgan, T., & Bimrose, J. (2012). A longitudinal study of the experience of a career development program for rural school students. *Australian Journal of Career Development*, *21*(1), 22–30. doi:10.1177/103841621202100104

Monumental Motivation Statistics for 2021. (2021). *TeamStage*. Retrieved 13 September 2021, from https://teamstage.io/motivation-statistics/

Morgan, C., Isaac, J. D., & Sansone, C. (2001). The role of interest in understanding the career choices of female and male college students. *Sex Roles*, *44*(5), 295–320. doi:10.1023/A:1010929600004

Mulgan, R. (2000). Comparing accountability in the public and private sectors. *Australian Journal of Public Administration*, *59*(1), 87–97. doi:10.1111/1467-8500.00142

Munnell, A. H., & Fraenkel, R. C. (2013). Public sector workers and job security. *State and Local Pension Plans Issue in Brief, 31*.

Myburgh, J. E. (2005). An empirical analysis of career choice factors that influence first-year Accounting students at the University of Pretoria: A cross-racial study. *Meditari: Research Journal of the School of Accounting Sciences*, *13*(2), 35–48. doi:10.1108/10222529200500011

Ng, E. S., Burke, R. J., & Fiksenbaum, L. (2008). Career choice in management: Findings from US MBA students. *Career Development International*, *13*(4), 346–361. doi:10.1108/13620430810880835

Nyamwange, J. (2016). Influence of Student's Interest on Career Choice among First Year University Students in Public and Private Universities in Kisii County, Kenya. *Journal of Education and Practice*, *7*(4), 96–102.

Olaosebikan, O. I., & Olusakin, A. M. (2014). Effects of Parental Influence on Adolescents' Career Choice in Badagry Local Government Area of Lagos State, Nigeria. Academic Press.

Otto, L. B. (2000). Youth perspectives on parental career influence. *Journal of Career Development*, *27*(2), 111–118. doi:10.1177/089484530002700205

Özbilgin, M., Küskü, F., & Erdoğmuş, N. (2005). Explaining influences on career 'choice': The case of MBA students in comparative perspective. *International Journal of Human Resource Management*, *16*(11), 2000–2028. doi:10.1080/09585190500314797

Paolillo, J. G., & Estes, R. W. (1982). An empirical analysis of career choice factors among accountants, attorneys, engineers, and physicians. *The Accounting Review*, 785–793.

Park, J. R., Coombs, C., Wilkinson, A. J., Loan-Clarke, J., Arnold, J., & Preston, D. (2003). Attractiveness of physiotherapy in the National Health Service as a career choice: Qualitative study. *Physiotherapy*, *89*(10), 575–583. doi:10.1016/S0031-9406(05)60056-9

Parsons, J. E., Adler, T., & Meece, J. L. (1984). Sex differences in achievement: A test of alternate theories. *Journal of Personality and Social Psychology*, *46*(1), 26–43. doi:10.1037/0022-3514.46.1.26

Pavan, R. (2011). Career choice and wage growth. *Journal of Labor Economics*, *29*(3), 549–587. doi:10.1086/659346

Price, A. (2007). *Human resource management in a business context*. Cengage Learning EMEA.

Ross, B. H. (1988). Public and Private Sectors—The Underlying Differences. *Management Review*, *77*(5), 28.

Ryan, R. M., & Deci, E. L. (2000). Intrinsic and extrinsic motivations: Classic definitions and new directions. *Contemporary Educational Psychology*, *25*(1), 54–67. doi:10.1006/ceps.1999.1020 PMID:10620381

Shaoul, J., Stafford, A., & Stapleton, P. (2012). Accountability and corporate governance of public private partnerships. *Critical Perspectives on Accounting*, *23*(3), 213–229. doi:10.1016/j.cpa.2011.12.006

Shipp, V. H. (1999). Factors influencing the career choices of African American collegians: Implications for minority teacher recruitment. *The Journal of Negro Education*, *68*(3), 343–351. doi:10.2307/2668106

Shoffner, M. F., Newsome, D., Barrio Minton, C. A., & Wachter Morris, C. A. (2015). A qualitative exploration of the STEM career-related outcome expectations of young adolescents. *Journal of Career Development*, *42*(2), 102–116. doi:10.1177/0894845314544033

Sibson, R. D. (2011). *Career choice perceptions of undergraduate event, sport and recreation management students: An Australian case study*. Academic Press.

Singaravelu, H. D., White, L. J., & Bringaze, T. B. (2005). Factors influencing international students' career choice: A comparative study. *Journal of Career Development*, *32*(1), 46–59. doi:10.1177/0894845305277043

Smith, J. L., Sansone, C., & White, P. H. (2007). The stereotyped task engagement process: The role of interest and achievement motivation. *Journal of Educational Psychology*, *99*(1), 99–114. doi:10.1037/0022-0663.99.1.99

Stewart, J. (2004). The meaning of strategy in the public sector. *Australian Journal of Public Administration*, *63*(4), 16–21. doi:10.1111/j.1467-8500.2004.00409.x

Sultana, T., & Mahmud, M. K. (2020). Exploring the influential stimulators of career choice: An empirical assessment by exploratory factor analysis. *Asian Journal of Empirical Research*, *10*(5), 137–149. doi:10.18488/journal.1007/2020.10.5/1007.5.137.149

Tarng, M. Y., Hsieh, C. H., & Deng, T. J. (2001). Personal background and reasons for choosing a career in policing: An empirical study of police students in Taiwan. *Journal of Criminal Justice*, *29*(1), 45–56. doi:10.1016/S0047-2352(00)00075-1

Teo, H. A., & Poon, J. T. F. (1994). Career choice of undergraduates and SMEs in Singapore. *International Journal of Career Management.*

Van Der Heijden, B. I., Schalk, R., & Van Veldhoven, M. J. (2008). Ageing and careers: European research on long-term career development and early retirement. *Career Development International*, *13*(2), 85–94. doi:10.1108/13620430810860512

Weiss, E. M. (1999). Perceived workplace conditions and first-year teachers' morale, career choice commitment, and planned retention: A secondary analysis. *Teaching and Teacher Education*, *15*(8), 861–879. doi:10.1016/S0742-051X(99)00040-2

Williams, C. C. (2008). Beyond necessity-driven versus opportunity-driven entrepreneurship: A study of informal entrepreneurs in England, Russia and Ukraine. *International Journal of Entrepreneurship and Innovation*, *9*(3), 157–165. doi:10.5367/000000008785096647

Wong, I. A., Wan, Y. K. P., & Gao, J. H. (2017). How to attract and retain Generation Y employees? An exploration of career choice and the meaning of work. *Tourism Management Perspectives*, *23*, 140–150. doi:10.1016/j.tmp.2017.06.003

Wong, S. C. K., & Liu, G. J. (2010). Will parental influences affect career choice? Evidence from hospitality and tourism management students in China. *International Journal of Contemporary Hospitality Management.*

Zeffane, R., & Bani Melhem, S. J. (2017). Trust, job satisfaction, perceived organizational performance and turnover intention: A public-private sector comparison in the United Arab Emirates. *Employee Relations*, *39*(7), 1148–1167. doi:10.1108/ER-06-2017-0135

ADDITIONAL READING

Malach-Pines, A., & Kaspi-Baruch, O. (2008). The role of culture and gender in the choice of a career in management. *Career Development International*, *13*(4), 306–319. doi:10.1108/13620430810880808

Stead, G. B. (2004). Culture and career psychology: A social constructionist perspective. *Journal of Vocational Behavior*, *64*(3), 389–406. doi:10.1016/j.jvb.2003.12.006

KEY TERMS AND DEFINITIONS

Career Choice: The culmination of a person's development and actions throughout the course of their life, especially those related to their career "A person's route or development through life or a certain time of existence." Parental counsel, vocational guidance, identification with well-known persons, trial or part-time employment, training choices, personal interests, and ability tests, among many other factors, are all utilized to assist people in making career decisions.

Extrinsic Factors: Takes into account the external environment, which includes sub-variables such job availability, well-paying jobs, and high pay structures (Carpenter & Foster, 1977; Beynon et al., 1998). Extrinsic variables imply that current labor market conditions may influence a person's employment decision. Two other sub-variables are a company's brand image and job stability (Edvardsson Stiwne, 2005). Financial incentives, for example, may be a person's primary motivation to work.

Interpersonal Factors: Includes parents, significant others, family, relatives, friends, and coworkers. For instance, a person may have chosen a career path based on his or her father's expectations or a friend's recommendation that he or she pursue a specific position (Carpenter & Foster, 1977; Beynon et al., 1998). Peer groups and teachers, according to Morgan, Isaac, and Sansone (2001), are two more sub-variables of interpersonal influence that can have a substantial impact on a person's employment selection. Interpersonal factors, to put it another way, take into account the impact of early exposure to diverse occupations and professions.

Intrinsic Factors: Personal values are what are referred to as a person's inherent elements. It is made up of their own professional interests and values, which are determined by their educational and training abilities and competences (Carpenter & Foster, 1977; Beynon et al., 1998). Employment-related information, such as a personally satisfying job due to excellent working conditions, is likewise an essential component (Aycan & Fikret-Pasa, 2003). When a person is motivated by intrinsic motivations, he or she is more likely to work for a job that is intriguing to them, or even one that is related to their studies, as well as a work environment that is acceptable to a degree, or at the very least up to par.

Private Sector: The private sector is the component of the economy that is operated for profit by individuals and businesses rather than by the government. As a result, all for-profit enterprises that are not owned or run by the government are included.

Public Sector: Governments, as well as other publicly owned or sponsored organizations, companies, and other entities that offer public programs, commodities, or services, are considered part of the public sector.

Chapter 12
Entrepreneurship: Scope of Addressing Educated Unemployment in India

Badal Chandra Das
https://orcid.org/0000-0003-2445-4210
Vidyasagar University, India

Sebak Kumar Jana
https://orcid.org/0000-0002-3532-4350
Vidyasagar University, India

ABSTRACT

In the social science research understanding the link between entrepreneurship and unemployment has become an interesting issue of investigation. In the context of unemployment, it is the entrepreneurship, which is not just a mixture of innovation, ideas, attitudes for success, but also depends on the country specific laws and the infrastructure facilities. The countries with better entrepreneurial infrastructure are definitely more open to competition and entrepreneurial activities than others. The international economic crisis has further accelerated the flow of restructuring the entrepreneurship intervention in order to address continuous rise of unemployment. It is, therefore, necessary for each country to adopt measures to encourage people with self-employment and entrepreneurship for generating gainful income and livelihood promotion. This chapter has made an attempt to highlight the role of entrepreneurship development to combat the problem of unemployment among educated youths in India.

DOI: 10.4018/978-1-7998-9581-7.ch012

INTRODUCTION

In this section a brief description is given about entrepreneurship and educated unemployment in Indian perspective.

Definition of Entrepreneurship

Schumpeter is one of the foremost economists and the father of entrepreneurship research who defined entrepreneurship as 'The function of the entrepreneur is to reform or revolutionize the pattern of production by exploiting an invention or, more generally, an untried technological method of producing a new commodity or producing an old one in a new way, opening a new source of supply of materials or a new outlet for products, by organizing a new industry' (Schumpeter, 1952).

Anandakrishnan (2020) has pointed that the word 'entrepreneur' comes from the French verb entreprendre, meaning, 'to undertake'. Entrepreneurship is the process of designing, launching and running a new business. It is the capacity and willingness to develop, organise and manage a business venture along with any of its risks to make a profit. Definitions of entrepreneurship typically focus on the launching and running of businesses with innovative ideas. Entrepreneurs provide a good opportunity to employ people, generate direct as well as indirect employment to the unemployed persons by setting more units at micro, small and medium scale of investment. Indian enterprises create lot of employment opportunities for different sections of the society in order to alleviate the unemployment crisis. There are evidences in Indian entrepreneurship that have engaged workers as shown in the Table-1.

Definition of Educated Unemployment

The situation wherein a number of youth having standard of education with matriculation, graduation and post-graduation degree are not able to find suitable jobs for them may be described as educated unemployment. There is unemployment among technically educated persons because their technical knowledge and skills are not up to industry standard. It is the perception of most of the Indian that education benefits both individuals and the nation in material terms so that a majority of Indian willing to even borrow money for the education of their children. According to a report (Gupta, M., and Pushkar, 2020) of Centre for Sustainable Employment at Azim Premji University, unemployment among well-educated is thrice the national average. There are approximately 55 million people in the Indian labour market with at least a graduate degree out of which nine million are estimated to be unemployed. The increasing trend of educated unemployment in India can be had of from the following table-2.

Table 1. Percentage distribution of enterprises by range of number of workers in India

Sl. No	Range of workers employed	% As per EC	% As per BR	% As per MCA
1	1=>10	11.8	38.9	26.6
2	11=>20	22.4	25.1	16.7
3	21=>40	26	17.2	13
4	41=>60	12.9	5.7	6.7
5	61=>80	7.4	3	4.9
6	81=>100	4.9	1.4	3.3
7	101=>200	9.2	2.2	9.3
8	201=>500	3.8	1.1	9

Range of workers excluding those having below 1% of enterprise.

(Selection of enterprises was made for NSS 74th round from three frames. EC-Economic Census frame, BR-Business Register frame, MCA- Ministry of Corporate Affairs frame

Source: Technical Report on Services Sector Enterprises in India 2016-17, NSSO, MOSPI

Table 2. Educated unemployment rates (figures in %) in India across different level of education

<table>
<tr><th>Sl No.</th><th>Level of Education</th><th>2011-12</th><th>2017-18</th><th>2021*</th></tr>
<tr><td>1</td><td>Diploma/Vocational Course</td><td>18.5</td><td>33</td><td>-</td></tr>
<tr><td>2</td><td>Secondary</td><td>5.9</td><td>14.4</td><td rowspan="2">10.3</td></tr>
<tr><td>3</td><td>Higher Secondary</td><td>10.8</td><td>23.8</td></tr>
<tr><td>4</td><td>Graduate</td><td>19.2</td><td>35.8</td><td rowspan="2">19.4</td></tr>
<tr><td>5</td><td>Post Graduate and above</td><td>21.3</td><td>37.3</td></tr>
<tr><td></td><td>Technical Degree</td><td>18.8</td><td>37.3</td><td>-</td></tr>
</table>

Source: Adapted from Mehrotra, S., and Parida, K. J. (2019) and Basuroy. (2022).

The Scope of the Entrepreneurship and Educated Unemployment

Indian educated youths are witnessing serious issues like unemployment and underemployment. Most important reasons are shortage of jobs, non-availability of suitable job matching to their education and family burden (Dixit et al. 2011).The struggle for survival and the motive to earn money after completion of education are encouraging youths to choose a self-employed profession like entering into entrepreneurship. There is good relationship between entrepreneurship and unemployment that has been shrouded with ambiguity. As a result of that empirical evidence found that unemployment is associated with greater entrepreneurial activities. Some other scholars (Evans and Leighton 1990) found that unemployment is positively associated with a great propensity to start a firm. Large populated country like India has been gradually accelerating the start-up initiatives with certain entry-point support from the government like subsidised bank loan, online registration, e-marketing of the products of entrepreneurs as well as organising fairs and rural business hubs (marketing points) which are creating increasing scope for learning and doing business by educated unemployed across the globe.

REVIEW OF LITERATURE ON ENTREPRENEURSHIP AND EDUCATED UNEMPLOYMENT

Unemployment refers to people who would like to work but do not have a job. It is generally specified as a percentage and calculated by diving among the unemployed people by the total workforce. There are increasing trend among educated unemployed mainly the youths with graduate and above level of education entering into various self-employment avenues after obtaining required skills and entrepreneurship education. Scholar (Sharone 2007) has emphasized that job searching itself has become a type of profession which involves work like creating resume, networking, motivating youths and such other forms of work participation that leverage economic value in future(Jana and Das 2019). Different argues have been made by scholars (Deuchar and Dyson 2019) that the young men creatively engage with notions of enterpriseto make an income and acquire a measure of respect. The theoretical debates advanced by them about enterprise cultures and neoliberal subjectivity in India.

There are various opinions about the educated unemployment in India. About 2 million graduates and half a million post-graduates are unemployed in India. Report indicates (Dixit, et al. 2011) that the level of unemployment increases with the increasing level of education. At the 'primary' level, unemployment is 3.6%, which increases to 5.2% at matriculation. It rises to 8% at graduation and further to 9.3% at the post-graduate level. The vast majority of the unemployed are from the Arts and Science streams. The percentage of unemployment among arts degree holders increases with the level of qualification but declines in the case of science degree holders. 39% of arts graduates are unemployed, the percentage rises to 49% among the professional degree holders of the arts stream. There is more unemployment among engineering post-graduates than among ordinary graduates and the reverse is the case with commerce graduates.

In reference to Table-2, it is to state that the rate of educated unemployment mainly graduates is quite alarming inIndia. Scholars (Jana et al. 2019) have pointed out on the possible reasons that though highly educated people are in a better position in urban areas in order to find a job than the rural people. The unemployment rate among graduates and above is higher than those with secondary and above level of education both in rural and urban areas (Bairagya 2015).

Chaudhury (2020) has made a comparative study of unemployment in India and USA. The study indicates that educated unemployment mainly the graduate+ educated unemployment in India was 12.1% during September-December of 2017 which has been increased to 13.2% during September-December 2018 in India. The report (CMIE), represents that the unemployment rate in India rises to 7.2% in 2019 which is the worst in 28 months. The total no. of employed person in India in 2019 is estimated at 400 million as compared to 406 million in 2018 and 407.5 million in 2017. On the other hand, the total number of employed persons in USA is estimated at 156.95 million in 2019 as compared to 155.21 million in 2018 and 153.34 million in 2017. The Labour Force Participation Rate in India fell from 43.2% in Jan.2019 to 42.7% in Feb.2019. The comparative analysis shows that employment rate in India is gradually decreasing from year after another.

OBJECTIVES

The major objectives of the present study are to assess the following:

1. Magnitude of Graduate Unemployment in India,
2. Government programmes available for graduates for entrepreneurship development
3. Participation of graduates in entrepreneurship in India
4. Problems in taking entrepreneurship as occupation
5. Scope of entrepreneurship for graduates in India
6. Policy implications

METHODOLOGY

Attempt has been made to locate the context within which the study took place and outlined methodology. The result and discussions have been made on the basis of reviewing the work of other scholars who have demonstrated how educated unemployed youths emphasizing to reconfigure unemployment into an entrepreneurial initiative. All relevant data have been collected from secondary sources like all India Report on 6th Economic Census 2016, Annual Report of Ministry of MSME, Govt of India (2016-17) and reports of international agencies.

RESULT AND DISCUSSION

The result and discussion of literature review and data captured from secondary sources have been made as follows

Government Programmes Available for Educated Unemployed in India

One of the identified measures to combat educated unemployment in India is Enhanced focus on entrepreneurial, communication, and inter-personnel skill (Dixit et al 2011). Also, there are government schemes related to entrepreneurial development in India (Kaviarasu et al. 2019), some of which are mentioned below.

- Sabla, Rajib Gandhi Scheme for empowerment of Adolescent Girls launched in 2011 for empowering girls of 11-18 years through skill development and vocational training.
- National Urban Livelihood Mission launched in 2013 with an aim to reduce poverty of urban poor households specially, street vendors who constitute an important segment of urban poor by enabling them access skilled wage employment opportunities.
- National Rural Livelihood Mission launched in 2013 to organise rural poor women into Self Help Group and make them capable for self-employment.
- Deen Dayal Upadhyaya Grameen Kaushalya Yojana launched in 2015 to provide rural youth specially, Below the Poverty Line (BPL)and Scheduled Caste/Scheduled Tribes (SC/ST)segment of population, with gainful employment by training them.
- Pradhan Mantri Kaushal Vikas Yojana launched in 2015 to encourage youth for development of employable skills by giving monetary rewards by recognition of prior learning or skill development.
- Digital India Programme launched in 2015 with main objective is to ensure that government services are available to citizens electronically and people get benefited from all the latest technology.

Former Union Minister of India Mr Arun Jaitley asserted “If the economy is growing at 12% nominal growth for the last five years, it would be an economic absurdity to say that such a large economic growth, the highest in the world, doesn’t lead to the creation of jobs...if no job creation takes place, then there is social unrest. This has been a peace period where no major social agitation has been witnessed in the last five years.”

National Institution for Transforming India (NITI) Ayog, Government of India has prepared a strategy paper to 'Rebrand India as Study Destination' in order to transform the current education system in the country. The strategy aims at improving the quality of tertiary education in India to create nationally and internationally competitive education by enhancing the capacity of higher education institutions, promoting industry-relevant education, and leveraging the strengths of traditional knowledge systems. In reference to the report of Ministry of Education, Government of India, the paper has shown that while in 2018–19, India was home to 47,427 foreign students, during the same time in reference to the report of Ministry of External Affairs, Government of India, more than 7,50,000 Indian students went abroad for higher education. It has shown that career opportunities, safe and clean environment, better labour laws, quality of education, etc., continue to be the major driving factors behind this movement. The countries having top destinations to Indian students, are Canada (1,07,650), USA (42,694), Australia (34,334), UK (19,505) and New Zealand (7883), as of 2018.

Participation of Graduates in Entrepreneurship in India

Krishna(2020) has pointed out that employment is all about getting a job or searching for a job. Employability refers to a person's capability of gaining initial employment. This capability is about having an effective mix of knowledge, skills and personal attitudes in order to be employed initially and function successfully in the required roles. A graduate's employability therefore depends on:

- Knowledge -what she/he knows
- Skills - what she/he does with what he knows
- Attitudes - how he/she approaches things

Report (GEM 2021) shows that the relationship between educational attainment and the propensity to start a new business is complex, not least because of thepositive association between education andlifetime income, and any link between education and the ability to spot opportunities. The report presents the level of total early-stage entrepreneurial activity (TEA) for graduates and for non-graduates in central and East Asian countries. There are nearly 20% graduates in Kazakhstan who enter into total early-stage entrepreneurial activity and comparatively Indian graduates constitute one third (nearly 6%) to them to enter. It suggests that those with a degree are more likely to be starting a new business.Certainly, increasing the supply of graduates could be an important step towards higher levels of early-stage entrepreneurial activity.

Small and micro enterprises are the backbone to the economy of every country. Policies that encourage the growth of medium, small and micro businesses and the role of entrepreneurship in the market are considered to be healthy for the economic growth to a larger extent. It has been observed that, unemployment is negatively related to new-firm start up, that is, as new businesses are established employment of resources is stimulated and unemployment reducessubstantially. In reference to research (Monsen, et al. 2010) based on National Data Survey on Savings Patterns of Indians(NDSSP2005) of Planning Commission of India, it has been presented that 14.46% of the graduates and 6.63% of the post graduates have been transitioned from employment to self-employment in India.

Scope of Entrepreneurship for Graduates in India

It has pointed out that there is very close relation between entrepreneurship and industrialization, and have a mutual coordination which is dependent on natural resources of a nation(Manjunatha, 2017). Development of entrepreneurship is fundamental to economic growth of a country and numbers of small-scale units have increased from 8.74 lakhs to 32.25 lakhs in 2000 comparing to 1981. Meanwhile 60% of employment opportunities are given in India and many organizations are continuously making an effort for training people to make them potential entrepreneur. These organizations start up their work with fundamental element of finding a true entrepreneur among the educated youths. Economic development provides with a high standard of economy, investment scenario both domestic and foreign. The stock market sentiment becomes positive creating boom in the market for new investments and innovation which are few determinants of entrepreneurship development. This has cyclic effect with development in one develops other which benefits the earlier.

Reports (GEM 2021)on the attitudes and perception of Indian entrepreneurs have pointed out that 82.5% of adults agreed on good opportunities to start business in their local areas. In terms of capacity, it shows that 81.7% have personal skills and knowledge. Besides, 61.9% of them know someone who started a new business. The study (GEM 2021) has also pointed out on the entrepreneurship impact i.e., 0.9% have job expectation to employ six or more people in five years' time which is quite remarkable in the context of creation of employment opportunities for other youths. There are 87.3% of the entrepreneurs who think to earn a living is an important motivational factor. Entrepreneurship makes a difference is perceived by 80.7% of the entrepreneurs and continue to family tradition is factor to 76.8% of the entrepreneurs. In the context of COVID 19, it shows that 85.8% of the entrepreneurs agree on the fact that pandemic has led to decrease household income and 65.2% have opined on pursuance of new opportunities due to pandemic.

One of the biggest problems that India facing towards addressing its unemployment is the inter-temporal issue of making a living versus learning a skill. The traditional

12+4 pattern schooling needs to be modified to be different stream where skills are imparted to those who need to earn a living.

Policy Implication

India needs to frame need-based education policy to upgrade gainful and employable skills among educated youths for addressing the problem of unemployment. We are in a position to change our vision from working only at clerical level to work and serve the country by physical and mental skills. Dixit et al. (2011) have suggested some remedial measures which can be adopted for addressing the problem of educated unemployment. Some of the policy measures are as follows:

- Rapid industrial growth and economic development which will generate more jobs.
- The need of skills and capacities, improvement in the education system and training provided to youth can be made with greater focus on the vocational skills and self-employment.
- Government support to sick and struggling industries is necessary to save and creation of jobs.
- Enhancing thrust on entrepreneurial, communication and inter-personal skill development.
- Women's education, entrepreneurship development and empowerment should be given more focused.
- Initiatives should be taken for integrated counselling, evaluation, career guidance and psychological support to unemployed youths.

In addition to the above, some more initiatives need to be taken up to address educated unemployment through entrepreneurship development, such as-

- Integrated policy framework for land, electricity, water supply, raw materials and marketing facilities should be arranged jointly by government and private sector undertakings.
- Entrepreneurship environment with improved social networking and business communication with infrastructural support may be created.
- Entrepreneurial training programme and short-term refresher courses may be organized from time to time to train and skill building on problem solving, conflict management and retail outlet operations.
- Legal literacy and financial literacy campaign should be arranged to encourage entrepreneurs better understanding about legal provisions and financial rules for establishment and control of small business by themselves.

- For better publicity of the entrepreneurship and its success, there should have literature on entrepreneurship with stories of successful entrepreneurs, publicity on products, goods and services availability and other functional activities of the enterprises.

It is very relevant to state that India is strongly emerging in different sectors more demanding of which are arresting educated unemployed from low-income groups towards small and micro-enterprise development and creating gainful self-employment opportunities.

CONCLUSION

In the conclusion, it is to admit that unemployment is a growing problem in India due to its rapid population growth and very lower rate of employment creation. Educated unemployment is one of the issues which drawing attention of the national think-tankers. The gradually increasing rates of educated unemployment need appropriate attention by the policy makers not only to create a gainful self-employment opportunity in order to mitigate the frustrations faced by the new entrants into the workforce but also to give the nation a fruitful contribution in its economic growth and development by expanding the scope of entrepreneurship development among youths. The international commission oneducation, UNESCO report says, education must be organized around four pillars of knowledge i.e., learning to know, learning to do, earning to live together and learning to be. The efforts made by the Indian states and policy-makers in this perspective need to be reviewed from time to time but the extent of these efforts is inadequate to its demand. There are considerable variations in the participation of educated unemployed to start a business/enterprise in their area who see it as a start-up initiatives as opportunities towards their self-employment. This is why the Govt. of India has launched Start-up India to promote and support new start-ups, and also others like the Make in India initiative to attract foreign companies and their FDI into the Indian economy. All these in turn create lot of job opportunities, and is helping in augmenting our standards to a global level. Policies that encourage the growth of small businesses and the role of entrepreneurship in the market are considered to be healthy for both employing unemployed youths as well as for the economy of the country at large.

REFERENCES

Anandakrishnan, M. (2020). Employability and Entrepreneurship: Critical Twin Factors for India Higher Education. In Reimagining Indian Universities. AIU.

Bairagya, I. (2015). *Socio-Economic Determinants of Educated Unemployment in India*. Institute for Social and Economic Change.

Basuroy. (2022). *Rate of Unemployment in India 2021 by Highest Education Level*. https://www.statista.com/statistics/1001039/india-unemployment-rate-by-education-level/

Chaudhury, N. (2020). A Comparative Study of Unemployment in India and USA. International Journal of Scientific and Research Publications, 10(12).

Deuchar, A., & Dyson, J. (2019). Between unemployment and enterprise in neoliberal India: educated youth creating work in the private education sector. *Transactions of the Institute of British Geographers*. wileyonlinelibrary.com/journal/tran

Dixit, J. K., Tiwari, P., Gupta, S. K., Singh, P., & Gupta, H. (2011). Educated Unemployment: A Challenge before Sustainable Education, Sustainable Manufacturing. In *Proc. of the International Conference on Sustainable Manufacturing: Issues, Trends and Practices (ICSM – 2011)*. BITS.

Evans, D. S., & Leighton, L. (1990). Small Business Formation by Unemployed and Employed Workers. *Small Business Economics*, *2*(4), 319–330. doi:10.1007/BF00401628

GEM. (2020). *Global Report 2020-2021*. Global Entrepreneurship Research Association, London Business School.

Government of India. (2020-2021). *Annual Report*. NITI Ayog. https://www.niti.gov.in/sites/ default/files/2021-02/Annual-Report2020-2021-English_0.pdf

Gupta, M., & Pushkar. (2020). *Why India should Worry about its Educated but Unemployed Youth*. Global Development Commons. https://gdc.unicef.org/resource/why-india-should-worry-about-its-educated-unemployed-youth

Jana, S., Das, B. C., Manna, S. S., Payra, T., Maiti, A., & Paul, P. K. (2019). Women Entrepreneurship in Backward Region: A Study in Jhargram district of WB. *Asian Journal of Multidimensional Research, 8*(3). http://www.tarj.in

Jana, S. K., & Das, B. C. (2019). Women entrepreneurs in transitioning Indian economy. In Approaches to Sustainable Development. Renu Publishers.

Kaviarasu, S. J., Ruban, A. H., & Dinesh, J. J. (2019). *Entrepreneurship as the better solution for unemployment of the people in India*. JETIR. www.jetir.org

Krishna, K. S. R. (2020). Employability and entrepreneurship: issues and challenges for Indian Universities. In Reimagining Indian Universities. AIU.

Manjunatha, K. (2017). Entrepreneurship: A Scope for Employment in India. *Journal of Business Management*, *3*(12).

Mehrotra, S., & Parida, K. J. (2019). *India's Employment Crisis: Rising Education Levels and Falling Non-Agriculture Job Growth.* CSE Working Paper, Azim Premji University. cse.azimpremjiuniversity.edu.in

Monsen, E., Mahagaonkar, P., & Dienes, C. (2010). *Entrepreneurship in India: The Question of occupational Transition. Schumpeter Discussion Papers, No. 2010-007.* Schumpeter School of Business and Economics, University of Wuppertal.

Schumpeter, J. A. (1942). *Capitalism, socialism and democracy* (3rd ed.). George Allen and Unwin. Retrieved from www.eet.pixel-online.org

Sharone, O. (2007). Constructing unemployed job seekers as professional workers: The depoliticizing work – game of job searching. *Qualitative Sociology*, *30*(4), 403–416. doi:10.100711133-007-9071-z

UNICEF. (2019). *Why India Should Worry About its Educated but Unemployed Youth*. https://gdc.unicef.org/resource/why-india-should-worry-about-its-educated-unemployed-youth

KEY TERMS AND DEFINITIONS

Deen Dayal Upadhyaya Grameen Kaushalya Yojana (DDU-GKY): Deen Dayal Upadhyaya Grameen Kaushalya Yojana (DDU-GKY) launched in 2015 in India aims to skill rural youth who are poor and provide them with jobs having regular monthly wages or above the minimum wages. It is one of the cluster of initiatives of the Ministry of Rural Development, Government of India that seeks to promote rural livelihoods.

Educated Unemployment: When an educated people with formal education do not find jobs it is called educated unemployment.

Entrepreneur: An entrepreneur is an individual who takes the risk to start their own business based on an idea they have or a product they have created while assuming most of the risks and reaping most of the rewards of the business.

NITI Aayog: National Institution for Transforming India, better known as NITI Aayog, was formed via a resolution of the Union Cabinet on 1 January 2015. NITI Aayog is the premier policy think tank of the Government of India, providing directional and policy inputs.

SABLA: It is a government scheme for the empowerment of teenage and young girls in India.

SC and ST: The Scheduled Castes (SCs) and Scheduled Tribes (STs) are officially designated groups of people and among the most disadvantaged socio-economic groups in India. The terms are recognized in the Constitution of India and the groups are designated in one or other of the categories.

Self-Help Group (SHG): Self-help groups in India are referred to self-governed, peer-controlled, and informal group of people with similar socio-economic backgrounds and having a desire for common good. In a self help group, people come voluntarily together to save whatever amount they can save in a convenient manner out of their earnings, to mutually agree for the contribution to a common fund and lend to the members for meeting their dynamic and emergent needs.

Chapter 13
Graduate Employability in an African Country:
A Study of the Potential Roles of Psychological Capital, Social Capital, and Career Identity

Peter Dithan Ntale
https://orcid.org/0000-0002-6378-7184
Business School, Makerere University, Kampala, Uganda

ABSTRACT

Employability is a positive and competitive state arising out of psychological capital, career identity, and social capital. Three studies were administered as censuses, (N=205), (N=214), (N=232), from graduates undertaking a skills training programme from Uganda Skills Development Programme (USDP). Quantitative analysis shows that psycap contributed greatly to employability, and social capital contributed less to employability of the unemployed but more to the employed in 2019 and 2020. Career identity showed a negative but significant relationship to employability in 2018 and 2019 while positive and significant relationship with employability in 2020. Social capital partially mediated the relationship between psycap and employability while the same fully mediated the relationship between career identity and employability. These results emphasize the importance of social capital and psycap in enhancing the various graduates' capabilities for positive employability outcomes. The negative career identity results reflect a boundaryless career mindset which is characterized by high physical and psychological mobility.

DOI: 10.4018/978-1-7998-9581-7.ch013

INTRODUCTION

Employability of graduates has been on the agenda of political and policy debates for the past three decades with scholars, psychologists, policy analysts and politicians taking multidimensional interests in the subject (Van 2020; Tentama, 2020; Monteiro, S., & Almeida, 2021). However, Sub-Saharan Africa and Uganda in particular presents an interesting phenomenon because of the increasing number of graduates and the seemingly disconnected reality between governments, graduates and the labor market realities (Kabay, 2021). An early reference to the subject warned that the emerging East African regional economy would be presenting a different economy altogether and young people must be ready to change their current views of what a career is because these views tend to distort the labor market (Baluku and Onderi, 2021). Another direct reference to the subject appeared in Ampaire (2021) with respect to career choices of secondary school students in Uganda. She observed that a properly developed career identity accounts for a significant variance of advanced level graduates who remain and succeed in the various professions. An indirect reference to the subject is found in Andersen (2021) who sought to improve the adaptability (employability) of public service managers to changing job demands through a process of reflecting on their actions.

Earlier studies spanning a period from the 1950s to the 1970s were mainly concerned with inclusion of sections of society into the labour force and tended to utilize motivational, vocational behavior, and discrimination theories (Munene, 1983). The current debate seems to be motivated by national rather than individual competitiveness coming with a shift from a manufacturing to a knowledge economy (Christopherson & Clark, 2020). The declining capacity of nations to generate employment may be one of the explanations for this interest while a major practical consequence of this trend is that individuals come to the labour market where opportunities continue to decline (Ntale et al., 2020). A related consequence is that job seekers tend to give up after a time, cease to look for employment and sink into despair with the consequence of committing suicide, robbery, drug abuse and other anti-social behavior. According to the African Economic Outlook Report (2017), Africa has a total of 200 million unemployed youth. Out of these, 53 (fifty-three) million are in unstable employment, 80 (million) are totally out of work, 30 (millions) are the only ones looking for jobs while 37 million (thirty-seven) have totally given up. (Refer to figure 1- Africa's level of graduate employment vulnerability)

Uganda, the site of this study is one of the most vulnerable in Africa because it has the youngest population, which constitutes 78 per cent of 45 million Ugandans and, at 3.5 per cent, the third highest population growth rate in the World (World Bank, 2017). Youth unemployment in Uganda stands at 32% as against 4.8% of Ugandan adults. More significantly that of the graduates stands at 36% (UBOS,

Figure 1. Africa's level of youth unemployment

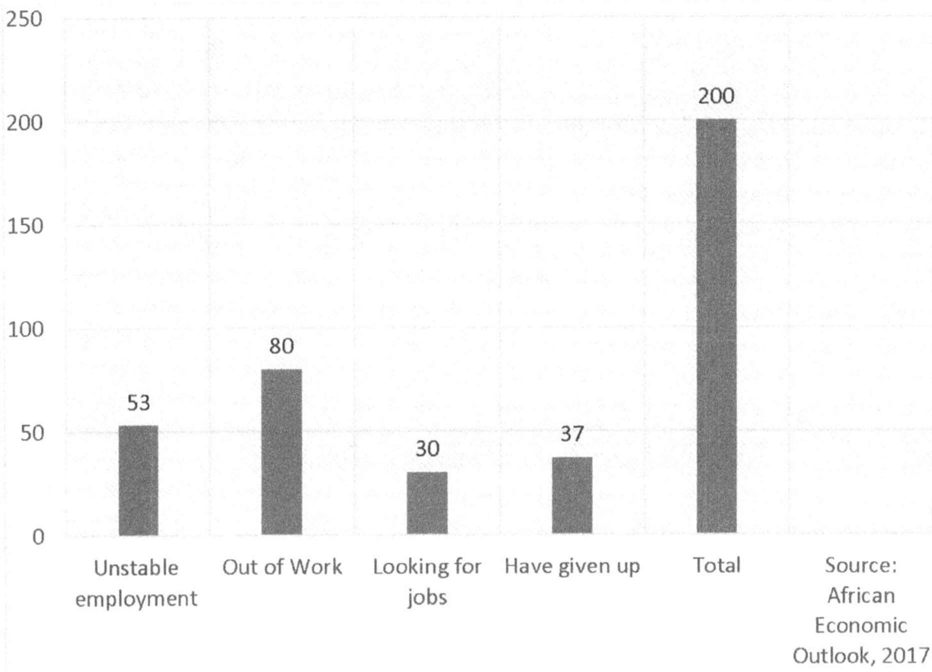

2012). Estimates indicate that out of the 400,000 graduates from various institutions of higher learning, only a fraction of graduates with some form of qualification get absorbed in the limited job market. Further reports from Uganda Investment Authority indicate that 150,000 jobs are created annually leaving an estimated 300,000 potentially jobless. However, official reports from civil society organizations corroborated with empirical research findings indicate that only 10,000 jobs are created from the Ugandan job market against the 400,000 graduates that are churned out by different institutions of higher learning (Bagonza et al., 2021). The World Bank Report on Youth Forum (2014) suggests that if half of those that are churned out of institutions of higher learning are well prepared for labor markets in Uganda and Africa in general there would be more than double increase in the production of goods and services which would consequently propel African economies to middle class. This however is unlikely to happen unless African countries including Uganda, pay particular attention to the employability of its young population and what makes an individual employable.

This report attempts to address the employability question using current understanding of the phenomenon and considers employability as a positive state that can be learned and retained for a time (Kinicki, Fugate, 2017; Caballero et al., 2020,

Hogan, Chamorro-Premuzic & Kaiser, 2013). In the study we consider employability as a state like behavior (Luthans, Youssef, & Avolio, 2015) that may remain stable during and outside employment (Cooper & McArdle, 2017). It keeps employees progressing in their careers while ensuring that a first job will be accessed or a new or a better job is gained after a job loss (Fugate, et al, 2004). The report continues with a brief view of the literature on employability by examining strengths-oriented states and processes that collectively address what we are, what we know, who we know and what we want to be (Luthans, 2002; Youssef & Luthans, 2012). It then proceeds to the methodology utilized in the study, analysis, discussion and tentative conclusions follow in this order.

EMPLOYABILITY AS A POSITIVE STATE: A SELECTED REVIEW OF THE LITERATURE

Positive approaches to productive behavior focus on life giving events while keeping in mind life draining ones. They seek to make prominent those episodes when people and societies are at their best (Peterson, 2006). As mentioned in the introduction, African nations can leverage on their young people and convert the population into human capital to provide services, goods or export labour directly. They may however, consider the population a problem and spend resources to control it. Thus, positivity and negativity see the same events but different realities as the recommendation from the World Bank regarding the youthful population of African nations imply. One way of looking at employability as a positive state is to consider employable people as protean workers. These are people who are self-directed and intrinsically driven (Rodrigues et al, 2019). Here employability is an attitude with knowledge, evaluative and behavioral components defined in terms of self-directed and value conception of what we want to be what and who we should know. Employability is however partly an attribution from an external agent (Hogan and Sherman, 2019). For this reason, an internally oriented conception of employability may not suffice the complexity of employability as a state or a practice of being employable. For this reason, researchers have tended to consider the protean concept along with the boundaryless view of careers which suggests that employability is being able to move across physical, social, and psychological boundaries (Kundi et al., 2021). The latter is more outward looking conceiving of an individual who is capable, ready and willing to open whichever job boundaries will motivate the external attribution of employability. In our practice we have encountered professionals such as engineers and medical doctors looking forward to expanding their career opportunities by embarking on managerial careers. These professionals become ideal managers of fellow surgeons or engineers. We have also encountered the other class of professionals who feel that they should stick to their original professions no matter what opportunities emerge in their own environments. They for instance find it difficult to accept and perform managerial responsibilities even when that would be the best option for their organizations and sometimes their careers. A three-component model of rewarding, ability, and willingness (RAW) provides additional evidence of employability as a potential positivity-oriented state (Hogan et al, 2019). According to the model an employer determines that an employee is employable if his or her presence adds perceived value, he or she is perceived to perform according to expectation, and is perceived as willing to deliver. For this to happen the individual should be able to attribute to herself as well as demonstrate to the employer the potential to relate qualitatively with others (quality interaction), to deliver the product or service required of her, and the energy to want to do more.

The brief review of some of the current debate on employability is in tandem with the earlier debate on the subject (Munene, 1983), which concluded that employability is an interactive outcome of what the employer wants and what the employee is, and is able to offer (see for instance, Hogan et al, 2013 and Rothwell and Arnold, 2007). It also suggests strongly that employability is a combination of soft and technical skills with the soft skills apparently accounting for a larger variance (Succi & Canovi, 2020). With regards to the first observation, Super (1953,1990) suggested that an individual learns what she or he is through a compromising process between her/his capabilities, values and opportunities. The same individual at the same time becomes what the employer wants by developing a work personality reflecting states that are appropriate in a specific work environment (Savickas, 2019). It is also reasonable to argue that the work personality may be a significant component of the soft skills that accounts for the variance observed. The rest of this section examines potential models that may be used to explain both observations and pave way for promoting employability as a positive state.

CAREER IDENTITY AND EMPLOYABILITY

At the center of an individual's component of employability seems to be the concept of career identity (Jackson 2018). Career identity enables an individual to focus on a trajectory in order to become a resource person or a competitive worker in some area. This view is exemplified by the current developments in studies of the protean and boundaryless career. The former has a crystallized rather monolithic but self-directed and value-based identity (Brisco and Hall, 2006) very similar to a crystallized occupational self-concept (Super, 1953; 1990). The latter has a more flexible and a more elastic occupational self-concept both physically and psychologically. Moreover, its drivers may originate as much from within as from without (Jain & Sullivan, 2019). Recent studies on identity indicate that individuals develop their identities in one or more of three ways (Berzonsky (1990): In the first place individuals build up their identities by actively seeking information to define or redefine themselves. This is referred to as information driven identity. In the second instance individuals find their identities through following rules, expectations of significant others or tradition. This is described as norm directed identity. The third is where individuals find their identities primarily through reflecting on their experiences. This is referred to as self-reflection driven identity.

In a traditional labor market, career identity is considered an important component of employability (Super, 1953; 1990). In a dynamic labour market on the other hand, where a protean and especially, a boundaryless worker are more likely to operate, and where employability is measured by mobility rather than stability (Lyons et al., 2015), there may be weak or no direct relationship between career identity and employability (Brown et al, 2003). A boundaryless worker, and to a certain extent a protein one, may require multiple identities. This will in turn depend on opportunities to change jobs both vertically and horizontally, which may be difficult for fresh graduates with little opportunity for work experience or because of rigging dynamics prevalent in the labour market (Brown et al 2003). Moreover, with the current levels of unemployment in Africa and in the World as observed before, this may also be difficult for even those already in employment. In essence, becoming a protean or boundaryless worker is not as easy in the current environment as the theories suggest. This is because individuals are not always in control of the contingencies that must be in place for the opportunities to materialize (Fishbein, 1976, Brown, 2003).

Hypothesis One: *Null Hypothesis*: *There is no relationship between career identity and employability among graduate employees.*

Psychological Capital and Employability

A main assumption of this study is that employability is a way of looking at work related behavior or career from the point of view of the strengths of an individual on which the employable individual leverages. For instance, it would be reasonable to argue that a protean worker leverages on the view of her career as a calling whereas the boundaryless individuals capitalizes on "psychophysical" or a combination of physical and psychological agility and mobility (see for instance Briscoe and Hall, 2006 and Surges et al, 2008). One of the general models that attempts to explain what it takes for individuals to take charge of their work-related lives, capitalize on and flourish in them is Psychological Capital (Luthans, et al 2007a; Luthans 2007b, Kim et al., 2017).

Psychological Capital (Psycap) subscribes to the emerging orientation of emphasizing healthy and successful behaviors, traits, and states in order to promote self-actualization, make health people healthier and successful people more successful (Seligman, 1998; Peterson, 2006; Cameroon, Dutton & Quinn, 2003; Luthans et al 2007a). This is in line with van der Heijde et al's (2014) view of employability where one of the components is a proactive individual characteristic referred to as personal adaptability. It is comprised of "optimism, propensity to learn, openness, internal locus of control, and generalized self-efficacy" (p 22). It is also the pertinent way of approaching the subject in view of the observation that a naive individual focus ignores the reality of structured labor markets, which may sometimes be rigged in favor of some sections of society and not others (Brown et al, 2003). The Psychological Capital model attempts to convert employees into competitive or employable workers by equipping them with relatively stable characteristics that enable them to build on their strengths and deal with obstacles to their dreams (Luthans et al, 2007a). We address the model by first outlining its context and follow this up by sketching out each of the characteristics that the model might use to explain or promote employability or employee competitiveness. These are Psycap self-efficacy, Psycap hope, Psycap optimism and Psycap resilience.

One of the contexts of Psychological Capital is appropriately the employment market, which is increasingly characterized by a serious search for talented employees or those who can make a difference to their employer. The talented employee however is increasingly more difficult not only to find but also to retain. This has come as a result of organizations no longer being able to offer lifetime employment (Rousseau, 1995) dictating that a normal person's work life span may be characterized by no less than a dozen job changes whether voluntary or involuntary (Fugate et al 2004). Employees are reacting by asking for a more lucrative employee value proposition (Lawler III, 2008) and in turn creating a situation where to succeed organizations require employees who are able to "own their work space" (Luthans et al 2007; p 5) and able to quickly graduate from role taking to role making (Uhl-Bien, Graen, & Scndura, 2000) or to psychological ownership (Parker, Wall and Jackson, 1997). This is a challenging shift, which will nevertheless make a worker competitive or employable while steadily dismantling traditional labour market opportunity structures and generating novel opportunities to be exploited by those who are capable of making the transition. We argue in this paper that making this transition successfully, simultaneously addresses the external and internal components of employability addressed earlier. We now address the components of Psycap beginning with Psycap Self-Efficacy.

When we think of self-efficacy, we bring to mind the feeling that we can accomplish the task before us even if it is novel, and more challenging than the ones we had accomplished before (Bandura, 1977; 1997). This confidence is possible because we feel that we can summon the motivation to start on the task, we can envisage the technical resources required, the social support we need, who to rely on and so on. In other words, it is about feeling that we are still in control. Based on Bandura's theory of Social Cognitive Learning, the image of potential success that drives self-efficacious people emerges from prior direct learning through simulated or real experience, observational learning, by just watching others perform successfully similar or related tasks, or from imagined role modeling (Bandura, 1977). In order to translate learning into performance, the theory recommends that the learner needs to experience a certain amount of positive reinforcement. Consequently, self-efficacy will be operative when we reinforce the learner in ways that will indicate that the achieved learning is indeed important. Positive reinforcement can come in terms of psychological, social or economic rewards. Rewards that have worked include recognition, ensuing work life balance and empowerment (Luthans et al 2007a, b).

Psycap hope is based on Luthans et al' (2015) concept of hope, which is a positive and active state that all individuals possess. According to the theory, human beings engage in goal thinking, in order to know what to do; pathways thinking, so as to know which strategies to use to reach the goals, and agency thinking or how to sustain the will to continue with the strategies. The theory suggests that although people engage in goal thinking or imagining, not everyone is efficient in progressing to agency and pathways. As implied immediately above, agency is the action an individual performs whereas pathways are the different approaches to perform the action. Consequently, employees may need to be assisted in how to execute these two components of hope in order to ensure that they don't confuse active hope with wishful thinking. With reference to goals, individuals need to learn to set high but achievable goals, which would assist agentic thinking and pathways thinking while providing more opportunities for additional learning as well as indirectly building self-efficacy. Finally, goals are operationalized in manageable steps. This is referred to as goal stepping and or goal framing. The process of operationalization makes it possible to visualize pathways. In practice this is also achieved through commitment planning (Schein, 1993) or the more conventional action planning at an individual or organizational level.

Psycap Optimism is about looking for what has gone well in any situation and finding one's role in the successful action. This is referred to as "positive attribution" (p. 17). It is based on Schneider's (2001) model of positivity, which advocates for looking at the past more leniently especially since it cannot be changed, appreciating what we have in the present, and planning for the future. According to Prayag et al., (2020), The general understanding of an optimist is one who attributes success to own competences and attributes and failure to temporally, identifiable individual causes and external issues. The pessimist attributes success to external events or to temporally individual opportunities. Luthans et al (2019) caution that the optimism they are advocating is realistic especially at the work place where accountability and responsibility is expected. However, even here, to be able to move on, the individual worker needs to learn to identify where he or she has done well even when the total result may not be as good as expected. Holding on to what has gone well provides more energy to continue building on one's strengths.

Unlike the other three components, resilience leans more towards survival rather than flourishing (Vera et al., 2020) strategies. Under normal adverse conditions, a resilient person will be able to navigate his or her way through and "bounce back" to level ground where the other three Psycap components can now take over. You build resiliency by accumulating personal and organizational resources. These could be physical, financial, psychological or social. You can also build resilience by hedging against anticipated risks. This may be by avoiding taking careless risks while limiting yourself to only calculated ones. The third way of building resiliency is through process. Process resilience is a proactive coping strategy that emerges from refining procedures of identifying risks and assets that one needs to either hedge against or work with (Bajwa et al., 2019).

No literature has come to our attention during the work reported here relating Psycap directly with employability. However, there is increasing evidence that Psycap can empirically explain potential positive and negative correlates of employability. A recent study showed that an internalized motivation to search for reemployment correlated with employability and job search intensity (Koen, Klehe, and van Vianen, 2014); another conducted in south Africa showed a positive relationship between work engagement and Psycap and negative relationship with stress (Görgens-Ekermans, & Herbert, 2013). A study conducted by Avey, Luthans & Youssef (2010) sought to show that a positive relationship exists between Psycap and organizational citizenship behavior and negative relationship between counterproductive behavior, cynicism and turnover. The study controlled for a number of competing constructs such as conscientiousness, extraversion, person job fit, personal organization fit and Core Self-evaluations which is an interactive outcome of self-definition that determines a number of behaviors especially evaluations of others, the world in general, and other people (Judge and Bono, 2001). Psycap was able to explain unique variance for all dependent variables. As hypothesized, it accounted for a unique negative variance for cynicism, turnover intentions, and unique positive variance for OCBs. Among a number of observations made regarding the findings, the authors noted the negative correlation between cynicism and Psycap is that the latter could be instrumental in promoting innovations since many of them fail because of former (cynicism) that is generally responsible for counter measures against innovations. In the context of the study reported here, where we noted that in practice a viable equivalent of employability is competitiveness in securing, retaining, and flourishing in one's job, then an employee who is able to overcome cynicism and innovates or adopts an innovation, can be considered employable and also competitive. This is especially so, as observed earlier, in a work environment that of necessity is demanding more role making than role taking from employees (Uhl-Bien et al, 2000). In an earlier study (Luthans et al, 2008) conducted three separate studies to test the mediation effect of Psycap on supportive climate as an independent variable and performance. The first study was composed of management students, the second study sample was drawn from a service organization, while the sample for the third study took place in a high technology manufacturing firm. The results indicated that a supportive climate correlated with Psycap, which in turn correlated with performance. Further analysis confirmed that Psycap plays a full mediation role between supportive climate and performance. From these studies we consider it reasonable to infer a relationship between Psycap and employability.

Hypothesis Two: *There is a positive relationship between Psycap and employability*

SOCIAL CAPITAL AND EMPLOYABILITY

The discussion on the Psycap and employability was premised on the understanding that a crystallized career identity such as a protean or boundaryless identity is a necessary but not sufficient condition for employability (Kostal & Wiernik, 2017) even if the crystallized career identity meets Super's (1963) definition of a compromise between an individual's capabilities, values and opportunities. For one to become employable or competitive, one requires additional capabilities such as those promoted by Psycap and briefly outlined above. However, a problem still exists when we consider that both career identity and Psycap would fundamentally fit in a group of resources referred to as human capital resources Van Der Heijde, & Van Der Heijden, 2006; Ntale et al. 2020); leaving out other important categories such as cultural and social capital (Brown et al, 2003). Consequently, we proposed a relationship between social capital and employability or competitiveness.

Since the pioneering work of Coleman (1988) which proposed the relevance of social capital in building human capital and Putnam's (1993) study demonstrating the application of social capital to economic development, the study of social capital has continued unabated being used to explain networks (Granovetter, 1985; Burt, 1997) behaviors in organizations (Leana, and Van Buren, 1999), as well as individuals and groups (Adler, and Seok-Woo, 2002). A summary review indicated that social capital research could be categorized under community associations, networks, an outcome of formal institutions, and synergy arising from complementarity of institutions (Woolcock and Narayan, 2000). Efforts directed to employability have utilized networks, which are assumed to open doors to the labour market

(Fugate et al, 2004). The doors are about information, influence and goodwill. Two characteristics of networks have been studied in relation to employability namely network size and network strength (Granovetter, 1985; Higgins & Kram, 2001). Size indicates the amount of information that one can possess on the job market and is relevant to his/her career expectations (Seibert, Kraimer & Crant, 2001). The larger the network, the more formal and informal opportunities an individual enjoys in accessing information about potential vacancies. Strength relates to influence in terms reciprocity and solidarity and refers to how much one feels obligated to return a favor (Adler and Kwon, 2002). Network strength and network size are a result of the relatively little studied mechanisms of social capital referred to as bonding and bridging (Putnam, 1993; Narayan, 1997). Bridging is the process and mechanism through which individuals connect with one another in order to access resources such as information or support (Temkin and Rohe, 1998). Bonding on the other hand is volunteerism involving premeditated willingness to help another or a community (Munene, 2009; Munene, Schwartz, and Kibanja, 2005). In our view, studying the mechanisms of social capital rather than the output of these mechanisms such as networks, may have an advantage as it could indicate who may not only be able to access and maintain network connections, but may indeed be able to form and support sustainable networks.

Hypothesis Three: *Bridging and bonding social capital are positively related with employability*

Building social bridges (bridging social capital) and sustaining them (bonding social capital) are in our view effortful exercises, and there is no guarantee that such efforts are always rewarded. It is consequently reasonable to explore the possibility that social capital, as measured in this study, mediates the relationship between Psycap and employability. Similarly, social capital is expected to mediate the relationship between career identity and employability in the sense that a crystallized career identity will sustain the bridging and bonding efforts, which in turn will relate positively to employability.

Hypothesis Four: *Social capital mediates the relationship between Psycap and employability.*

Hypothesis Five: *Social capital mediates the relationship between career identity and employability.*

METHODOLOGY

The Study Context: Uganda Skills Development Project (USDP)

The Uganda Skills Development Project (USDP) is a youth skills enhancement project under the Ministry of Education and Sports. With the main objective of enhancing Higher Education institutions' capacity to deliver high-quality, demand-driven training programs in targeted sectors, the USDP establishes the Sector Skills Councils (SSC) for proper institutional skills management, aligns and strengthens the skills development standards, assessment and certifications, skills quality improvement, funding, communication and marketing of the available technical skills to the potential employers. Most importantly, at the end of every academic year, the USDP conducts a skills training, awareness, evaluation, a go to labor market readiness assessment of the graduates. The annual youth graduate camp assesses the graduates physco-social capabilities, leadership and management competencies, creativity, analytical and practical skills, computing, data managements and social media fluency as well as local and international knowledge of the economy and the geo-politics. These, together with the content obtained during the three years of university training determine the graduates' readiness and success in the labor market. The interest of this study was to establish the career identities as well as psycho-social capabilities of the graduates in readiness to employability. Therefore, conducting surveys at the end of the skills and leadership trainings would provide real experience from both the employed and unemployed graduates and this would help to understand the potential roles the variables under study play in the employability of graduates from an African context like Uganda.

RESEARCH DESIGN

The study utilized a simple cross sectional study design where the effort was to track down graduates who had passed through the Skills Training and Leadership Development Programme for years 2018, 2019 and 2020. Each of the studies were conducted at the end of the year when different components of the training were covered. Both employed and unemployed were interviewed, data collected, analyzed and interpreted. Government requires that all graduates from various institutions of higher learning attend such skills development program to enhance their employability skills. However, the program is not mandatory and participation in the annual skills training camp is optional.

Table 1. Sampling design

Year	Population	Sample	Employed (N)	%	Unemployed	%
2018	480	204	120	25%	84	50%
2019	430	205	155	33%	50	30%
2020	313	232	199	42%	33	20%
Totals	1,223	641	474	100%	167	100%

Sampling Design

The three studies reported here intended to conduct a census among all graduates who had undergone the Skills Training and Leadership Development Programme from 2018, 2019 and 2020. We conveniently selected graduates who attended these trainings from which some of them were employed while others were unemployed. A total of 1,223 graduates had undertaken the training for a period of three years from which (641) graduates usefully responded to our questionnaires, accounting for 52 percent response rate. Of these, (474), approximately 75 percent were recorded as having secured and retained their employment status for a period of five years and above while 24 percent said that they had not secured any employment since their completion of studies. Refer to Table 1 – sampling design.

Respondents' Characteristics

The respondents who participated in all the three studies, majority 53 percent were females and only 47 percent were males. In terms of age, 11 percent were between 21-25 years, 67 percent were between 26-30 years, 12 percent were between 31-35 years, 6 percent were between 36-40 and finally 3% were 40 years and above. The skills development training was done for people who had completed graduate level education for which higher diplomas, bachelors' and masters' degree are the main qualifications. Therefore, 20 percent had completed diploma level, 75 percent Bachelors' degrees, while only 5 percent had completed their masters' degree programs. In terms of employment status; majority of the respondents (74 percent) were employed while 26 percent were not employed. In terms of marital status; majority 75 percent were singles while 25 percent were married. (Refer to Table 2 - characteristics of the respondents)

Table 2. Respondents Characteristics

		Frequency	Percent
Gender	Female	338	53
	Males	303	47
Age	21-25	70	11
	26-30	430	67
	31-35	75	12
	36-40	41	6
	40 and above	25	3
Education	Diploma	128	20
	Bachelors	481	75
	Masters	32	5
Employment	Employed	474	74
	Unemployed	167	26
Marital Status	Married	160	25
	Singles	481	75

Means and Standard Deviation of Both the Employed and Unemployed

In comparison to the mean, the standard deviations range from 0.53 to 0.72. These small standard deviations relative to the mean values indicate that the data points are close to the means which is an indication that the mean represents the data observed. The outstanding contribution of psychological capital to employability of both the employed and unemployed (Mean = 4.63, SD = 0.72; 4.65, SD=.62) followed by social capital (Mean=4.51, SD=0.60;4.57, SD = .62) is clearly evident. Career identity (Mean = 4.28, SD = 0.64; 4.19 = .60) came last with less contribution to employability. Refer to Table 3 which shows the means and standard deviation of both the employed and unemployed.

RELIABILITY AND VALIDITY OF THE INSTRUMENTS

Research reliability refers to the degree to which research method produces stable and consistent results. A specific measure is considered to be reliable if its application on the same object of measurement number of times produces the same results. The internal consistency is traditionally checked using Cronbach's alpha and only

Table 3. Means and standard deviation of both the employed and unemployed

	Employed		Unemployed	
	Mean	**SD**	**Mean**	**SD**
Employability	4.63	.72	4.65	.69
Career Identity	4.28	.64	4.19	.60
Psychological Capital	4.67	.53	4.60	.55
Social Capital	4.51	.60	4.57	.62

those items that provided a Cronbach Alpha co-efficient of 0.7 and above were retained as guided by (George and Malley, 2003). Validity refers to the extent to which the instrument measures what it was designed to measure in consistence with theoretically based concepts (Carmines and Zeller 1979). We obtained expert judgement from psychologists of Makerere University School of Psychology as well as employment experts from both the youth and the Gender ministry to confirm whether our instruments validly measured the exact content that we were looking for. The higher the content validity index the more the instrument is valid for research. The results of both reliability and validity indices are shown in table four below. (Refer to Table 4 for reliability and validity measurements).

Table 4. Shows reliability and validity measurements

Variable	Reliability (Cronbach's Alpha)	Validity (CVI)
Employability	.899	.901
Social Capital	.789	.899
Psychological Capital	.786	.923
Career Identity	.776	.921

Measurement of Variables

Employability: To measure employability, we utilized a self-evaluation questionnaire of employability scale created and validated by Rothwell & Arnold (2007). This questionnaire had eight items all anchored on a six-point scale ranging from strongly agree (6) to strongly disagree Some of the questions included are; "I have skills in discovering, collecting, and analyzing information", "I have skills in calculating, examining, and interpreting data and financial records" and "I am skilled at working on my own, build, grow, and produce results".

Career identity: This variable had two parts; The Vocational Identity Scale (VIS) and the Work Salience Scale (Holland, Daiger & Power, 1980) which both taps into the possession of a clear and stable picture of one's goals, interests, talents and career path. The questions included; "I am confused about the whole problem of deciding on a career", "Making up my mind about a career has been long and difficult", "I intend to pursue the job of my choice even if cuts deeply into the time I have for my family" which were anchored on a six-point scale ranging from strongly agree (6) to strongly disagree (1).

Psychological Capital: Psycap was measured using the psychological Capital scale by Luthans et al (2007) which consisted of 24 items. Some of these items included; "I always manage to solve difficult problems if I try hard enough", "I am confident that I could deal efficiently with unexpected events" and "I would rather depend on myself rather than others". All the 24 items were anchored on a six-point scale ranging from strongly agree (6) to strongly disagree (1).

Social Capital: The study utilized a local measure based on value based social capital (Munene, Schwartz, and Kibanja, 2005). The instrument examines two roles played by members of networks namely bonding and bridging - see also (Westaby, Pfaff, and Redding 2014) for additional roles). It is a six-point comparison scale ranging from "Very like him/her (6) to very unlike him/her).

ANALYSIS

We performed correlation analysis for each of the three datasets corresponding to 2018, 2019 and 2020. The aim was to establish the strength and direction of the linear relationship between variables. The strength and direction are shown by the correlation coefficient with the higher coefficient denoting strong relationship and the lowest indicating weak relationship between the variables. (Refer to Table 5 for hypothesis testing and coefficients).

Findings

Hypothesis 1: There was a negative relationship between career identity and perceived employability (r = -022, P-value is < 0.05; r = -131; p-value is <.05) for both 2018 and 2019 while a weak though positive and significant relationship (r=012; p<.05) for the study in year 2020. The 2018 and 2019 negative correlations as well as the 2020 weak though positive and significant results indicate that a unit change in graduate career identities makes little and or no significant change in

Table 5. showing hypothesis and coefficients

Hypothesis	Status of hypothesis after analysis and evidence with summary coefficient			Brief explanation
	2018 N = 205	2019 N = 214	2020 N = 232	
Hypothesis 1: There is a negative relationship between career identity and graduate employability for both employed and the unemployed.	Negative but significant (r = -022, P<0.05)	Negative but Significant (r = -131; p<.05),	Positive but weak (r=012; p<.05),	The insignificant values of career identity may explain the boundarylessness of careers
Hypothesis 2: There is a positive relationship between Psycap and perceived employability	Significant r = .464**, P-value is < 0.05	Significant R = .180**, P< 0.05	Significant R=.535, p<0.05).	The positive and significant values explain the greater importance of psycap in enhancing employability
Hypothesis 3: Social capital is positively related with perceived employability	Positive and Significant r = -041, P-value is < 0.05	Positively Significant R=0.341**, P< 0.05	Positive significant r=0.422, p<0.05	The big number of the unemployed in 2018 didn't find social capital useful in employability
Hypothesis 4: Social capital mediates the relationship between Psycap and perceived employability.	No mediation	Partial mediation	Partial mediation	2018 had higher unemployed people whose social capital and psycap didn't help them gain employment
Hypothesis 5: Social capital mediates the relationship between career identity and perceived employability.	Full mediation	Full mediation	Full mediation	Greater career orientation with greater social capital greatly enhances employability

graduate employability. This negative correlation of career identity and employability can be explained by the fact that the skills, work values, interpersonal, and multi-tasking skills, which are currently valued by the labor market and define the labor market environment are lacking from the graduates. Bourn (2018) proposes that in situations where organizations are becoming flatter, jobs becoming less formal, structured and non-routine, psycho-social abilities of a graduate and not his or her career identity will determine employability in the long run. This is because the labor market currently demands high critical thinkers, highly analytical and creative personnel who can independently interpret the social environment where they live and make appropriate decisions (Shmatko et al. 2018). This shifts demand from being able to perform a particular collection of tasks and having well defined careers to being able to work cooperatively. Although this conflicts Nazar (2012) who said that career identity is the key to employability and without it, even the most intelligent person will miss out on the job opportunity because he or she cannot be considered under the preliminary requirements of that selection and recruitment, the truth is that labor market has become too competitive and volatile that graduates need to have skills that are beyond their careers if they are to easily maneuver the world of employment. This maneuverability calls for graduates and the training institutions to consider combinations of other pyscho-social skills and abilities such as extraversion (tendency to be outgoing, assertive and energetic), psychological capital (hope, optimism, resiliency), agreeableness and emotional stability, other than straight pursuance of careers. When we introduced the psycho-social training in the management of graduates' careers in 2018 and 2019 respectively, we saw the relationship between career identity and employability becoming positive and significant in 2020, further confirming Praskova's (2015) assertion that when psychosocial skills are introduced in any training program, there is a likelihood of positive and significant improvement in the psychosocial abilities of the trainees.

Hypothesis 2: There is a positive relationship between psychological capital and perceived employability. Statistical analysis reveals that there is a positive significant relationship between psychological capital and employability for the employed ($r = .464^{**}$, P-value is < 0.05; $r = .180^{**}$, P-value is < 0.05; $R=.535$, $p<0.01$) for all the years. This implies that when psychological capital (improves) there is an improvement in the level of employability for both employed and non-employed. This is consistent with Seligman, 1998; Peterson, 2006; Cameroon, Dutton & Quinn, 2003; Luthans et al 2007a) who found out that psychological capital and its major constructs of hope, efficacy, resilience and optimism emphasizes healthy and successful behaviors, traits, and states in order to promote self-actualization, make health people healthier and successful people more successful. Therefore, employed people make use of psychological resources like hope, efficacy, resilience and optimism to excel at work and maintain their employability agenda (Jessie Koen, 2010, Luthans et al., 2007). The non-employed graduates use psychological resources such has hope which keeps a positive motivational state of the unemployed through agency (goal directed energy) and pathways creation (planning to meet goals) which improves their success in search of opportunities (Snyder, 2000). They also use psychological resources like resilience. Whenever the individuals are faced with adversaries, they are able to come back even stronger that before (Luthans, 2007).

Hypothesis 3: Analysis for 2018 data shows that there was no significant relationship between social capital and employability ($r = -041$, P-value is < 0.05). The possible explanation for this is that there was a high number of unemployed people in 2018 whose social interactions with others didn't help them in securing employment opportunities possibly because they didn't invest useful time and resources in initiating and maintaining quality social capital. The time and other resources they would use to invest in initiating and maintaining these relationships is diverted on job hunting, job-related information synthesis and career enhancement (Neary, 2015). However, analysis for 2019 and 2020 found positive and significant relationship between social capital and employability ($R=0.341^{**}$, $P<0.05$; $r=0.422$, $p<0.01$) respectively. A unit change in social capital of the employed graduates caused significant changes in employability, the inference being that people who have reliable and active networks are able to boost their access to significant amount of information and resources regarding employment opportunities (Batistic, 2017). One may wonder why in 2018, the unemployed were many as compared to 2019 and 2020, thus reflecting more significant values for 2019 and 2020. The possible explanation is that one of the core leadership training programs is the emphasis to invest time and other resources in the creation of valuable networks. It is possible that the graduates that we interviewed in 2019 and 2020 had experienced and embraced the importance of investment in valuable networks hence the positive and significant values.

Hypothesis 4: Social capital did not mediate the relationship between psychological capital and perceived employability for 2018 possibly due to higher number of the unemployed graduates who may have evaluated negatively the role of social capital in aiding employability. Social capital mediated the relationship between psychological capital and perceived employability for 2019 and 2020 confirming Luthans et al., (2005) findings where he noted that people who possessed social capital characteristics had high hopes, optimism and resilience which enabled their achievement levels. Without social capital, individuals are unable to invest in quality social networks which would help in providing the right connections, networks and job-related information thus endangering peoples' psychological abilities which compromises peoples' achievement levels (Batistic, 2017).

The benefits of social capital and its influence on employability are seen in the job search behaviors of individuals. People with well-developed social capital often utilize informal job search networks (e.g., ''friend of a friend''), in addition to more formal networks (e.g., company sponsored placement services). In fact, Boxman, de Graaf, and Flap (1991) found that top managers more often found jobs through informal networks. Therefore, social networks extend an individuals' ability to

Figure 2. Social capital partially mediates the relationship between Psycap and perceived employability

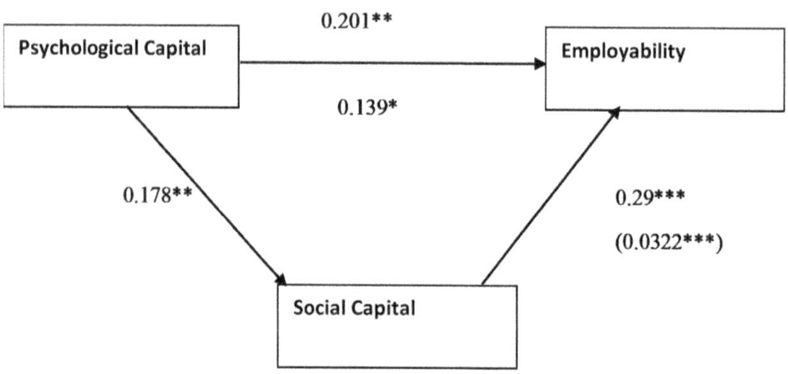

Type of mediation = Partial

Sobel-Z Value = 2.265297 Significance 0.023494

Standardized co-efficient of psychological capital on employability

Direct = 0.139

Indirect = 0.062

identify and realize opportunities between organizations, across industries, and over entire careers (Dess & Shaw, 2001; Higgins & Kram, 2001). Therefore, much as psychological capital is needed to define employability of unemployed graduates, this relationship is defined partially by the intervention of social capital of the unemployed graduates (figure 2 shows the mediation results).

Hypothesis 5: Social capital mediates fully the relationship between career identity and perceived employability for both the employed and unemployed graduates. According to Cheng et al., (2020), job searching requires someone to keep key and useful network of people for employment to take place as well as regular communication between the person searching and the individuals of the network is very crucial. Higher levels of social capital enhance more efficient use of information related to labor market conditions, reduces the search and transaction costs on both sides of the market, promotes higher quality of applicants, helps in the efficient placement of individual workers, and minimizes the misunderstandings between insiders and outsiders (Subramony et al., 2018). Therefore, the role of social capital in defining the relationship between graduate careers identities and perceived employability can be observed from Figure 1 where the coefficient for career identity on employability dropped significantly from 0.161 to 0.102 when social

Figure 3. Social capital fully mediates the relationship between career identity and perceived employability

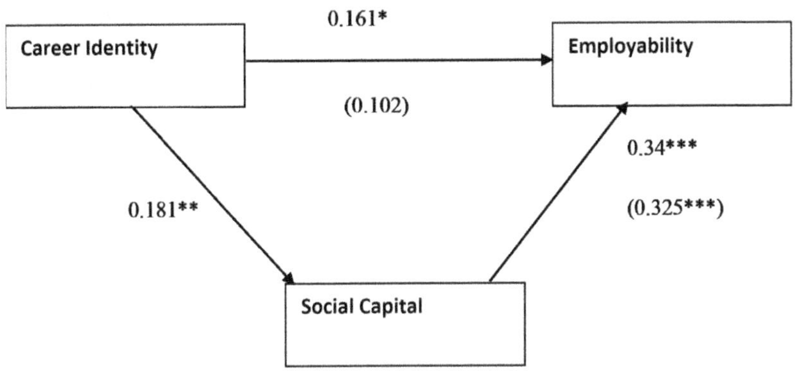

Type of mediation : Full

Sobel-Z Value = 2.360917; Significance 0.01823

Standardized co-efficient of psychological capital on employability

Direct = 0.102

Indirect = 0.069

capital is introduced as a mediator, suggesting that social capital may be exerting a full mediating effect. The (Sobel Z-Value .52.360917; sig.50.01823) as obtained from the mediational analysis is a confirmation that social capital fully mediates the relationship between career identity and employability. Our study is in agreement with Markus (2011) who found out that in situations where graduates are limited by information search of opportunities and where the employability landscape is not well levelled, social capital stands out as a good mediator of graduates' careers and employability. Hällsten et al (2017) in his research on the 19-year-old Iranians, Swedish and Yugoslavian undergraduate youths prove our hypothesis. They found out that occupational contact networks reduce unemployment risks for all groups of careers. Therefore, the careerists, the unemployed and employed should place much emphasis in the identification, building, maintaining and engaging a network of useful and reliable people if their respective careers are to yield positive returns on graduate employment (Refer to figure 3 shows the mediation results).

HIERARCHICAL REGRESSION ANALYSIS

In order to determine the effect of the study variables on graduate employability for all the three years, we combined the three datasets to make one dataset from which we made further statistical tests. A hierarchical regression is one of those tests that help in ascertaining if variables of our interest (career identity, social capital and psychological capital) explain a statistically significant amount of variance in our Dependent Variable (graduate employability) after accounting for all other variables. To achieve this, we created three models whereby the predictor variables were regressed against the dependent variable. This was done in order to explain the variation in graduate employability.

Model One involved the introduction of career identity. Results indicate that career identity was

not a significant predictor of graduate employability (P>0.05, F52.180). The F-value was also not significant. Model two was added into the analysis which turned out to be a significant predictor of graduate employability with R^2 increasing from 0% to 20.5 per cent. Thus, social capital accounts for 20.5 per cent increase in the variation in graduate employability. Model 2 is statistically significant (sig.50.000, P<0.01, F51.232). This finding gives further support for hypothesis 3. It is important to note that when we introduced social capital into the model, career identity which was originally non-significant became a significant predictor as previously shown in the mediation tests. Finally, Model three involved psychological capital which turned out to be a significant predictor of graduate employability. The R^2 in model 3 increased to 37.6 per cent,

implying that psychological capital accounts for 17.1 per cent increase in the variation in graduate employability. Model 3 is also significant (sig.50.001, P<0.05, F34.014). Thus overall, the three constructs (career identity, psychological capital and social capital) explain about 38 per cent of the variation in graduate employability. Social capital indicated to be the most significant predictor of graduate employability (beta51.232) followed by psychological capital (beta34.014). Career identity becomes a significant predictor of graduate employability in model 2 only when social capital is introduced confirming the existence of mediation as seen earlier. (Refer to Table 6 for hierarchical regression results).

DISCUSSION

The subject of career identity invokes a discussion on two important career aspects. These are; protean and boundaryless careers. The protean careers present flexibility and dynamism as individuals use internal and external measures to sail through different

Table 6. Hierarchical Regression Results

	Model 1 *Beta Sig.*	*Model 2* *Beta Sig.*	*Model 3* *Beta Sig.*
Career Identity	0.100 .088	.045 .000	.128 .000
Social Capital		.0201 .000	.328 .000
Psychological capital			.213 .000
F	2.180	51.232	34.014
Sig. F	0.144	0.000	0.000
R	0%	38.8%	49.2%
R^2	0%	20.5%	37.6%
R^2 change	0%	20.5%	17.1%
Adjusted R^2	0%	14.9%	16.2%

careers and organizations. Protean careers are characterized by frequent change and self-invention, autonomy and self- management, guided by individual needs instead of organizational needs (Hall, 2002). However, as technology advances, organizations flattening, competition setting in and job security decreasing, individuals find it difficult to keep within the same career and organization thereby finding safety in navigating the changing work landscape by enacting careers which are characterized by different levels of physical and psychological movement commonly known by Sullivan and Arthur (2006) as boundaryless careers. Boundaryless careers are composed of organizational mobility and boundaryless career mindset. Organizational mobility is the preference by individuals to pursue and switch in between different careers and also conduct an actual movement between different organizations. In contrast, a boundaryless mindset deals with the mental abilities of individuals to work on projects across different careers and organizations. Individuals with boundaryless mindset are inspired and motivated by the new knowledge and experiences learnt from engagements with the various external stakeholders.

Seen from above, whether protean or boundaryless, careers may not stand on their own if they are to promote employment opportunities for the graduates. Careers are hugely influenced by the historical, cultural and the social environment where they are natured and developed, making them highly dynamic and evolving phenomena (Zhang et al., 2021). The 19th century careers did not demand as much as the 20th and the 21st centuries because of the changing dynamics. Therefore, to achieve the careers' desired effects, there is need to enhance them as they evolve based on the existing level of demands. All types of careers demand high level creativity, analytical and practical skills to maneuver through the competitive world of work whether static or boundaryless (Sternberg, 2020) which the findings of our study found lacking among the graduates, consequently making it hard for their employability. The implication of this finding is that pursuance of careers alone does not predict graduate employability and that the long-term pursuance of straight careers is likely to create societies that are highly knowledgeable in their professions but highly detached from the environment and social reality where they live because the current environmental demands are more than what careers can offer. The current labor market demands people who are highly creative, analytical and practical, attributes that are gained through embracing a series of psycho-social support. The psychosocial approach looks at individuals in the context of psychological factors and surrounding social environment have on their physical and mental wellness in naturing graduates to adopt relational abilities, information processing skills and positivity orientedness to help them improve their chances of employability (Xia et al., 2021). Different scholars such as Ntale (2020) have attributed the lack of these key employability resources among graduates to largely a colonial education system whose major aim was to train and educate a few colonial administrators in dispensing colonial administration. This kind of education system has outlived its usefulness because of its failure to respond to the existing social, psychological and environmental realities that determine the existing labor context (Oyugi, 2021). As a number of graduates are churned out, there is glaring evidence to show that there are no bonding and bridging arrangements between the systems/institutions that churn out employees and the employers, pointing at a total societal disconnect. This gap makes it difficult for graduates to easily connect to employers for career enrichment and possible employment opportunities. According to Ngoma and Ntale (2016), this lack of social disconnect between the graduates and employers is to a larger extent caused by inadequate psychological aptitude in terms less or no hope of their future, lack of optimism and resilience to bounce back once faced with challenges. Lack of these psychological ingredients will limit the amount of social networks/bonds through which useful career related information, guidance, connections and support that is available to an individual for employability purposes.

Different scholars such as (Kabay, 2021; Jjuuko et al, 2021 and Kim 2021) have long attributed this lack of psycho-social prowess to the colonial education system which, despite gaining independence in 1962, has continuously been bent on the colonial systems and structures of the time with the objective of training colonial administrators and collaborators to aid colonial administration. However, different governments have since realized that the colonial education system cannot serve the current social and economic challenges and thus a few amendments have been proposed to cope up with the existing national, regional and global challenges. Despite this, the education system has largely remained theoretical thus providing little innovative, creativity, analytical, practical and vocational skills to equip the graduates with knowledge and skills to maneuver through the complicated work environment of the 21st century.

To solve the employability challenges, there is need to redesign the education system so that it responds to the current labor market challenges where so many graduates lack the requisite social and psychological competencies that would provide them with abilities to be innovative, creative, practical and analytical in what they do, ingredients that would enable them get jobs, sustain them and maneuver from one job/organization to another. Training modules in the science of hope, optimism, efficacy and resilience as components of psychological strength should be proposed at different career levels with the consequence that these psychological ingredients will 1) predict adaptive outcomes; (2) buffer the effects of adversity; and (3) they can be influenced and sustained. The positive psychology modules should present "hands-on" tools to assess the components of psychological capital (hope, resilience, efficacy and optimism) and develop strategies to nurture them. As we saw, career identity with no social capital cannot guarantee graduate employability. This calls for training in leadership training program with the aim of providing a forum for social capital creation through the establishment and maintenance of networks and through discussion and problem solving by participants. Such leadership programs will emphasize the critical role of formal and informal training in establishing bonding, bridging and linking social capital.

SUGGESTIONS FOR FURTHER STUDIES

This study collected data from well educated people who had completed their graduate and undergraduate programs. There are other people who have not gone beyond high school education and have not gone through this kind of career progression. These may include; Senior Secondary, Primary level drop outs and those who never went to school at all. Future studies should be carried out to let scholars and policy makers know whether the psychological and social capital highly required for employability of graduates have significant implications on non-graduates.

REFERENCES

Ampaire, A., Kajumba, M. M., & Muwagga, A. (2021). Do Students' Career Aspirations Predict their Career Choices? A Qualitative Survey of Advanced Level Secondary School Students in Uganda. *African Journal of Education. Science and Technology*, *6*(3), 344–351.

Andersen, L. B., Jensen, U. T., & Kjeldsen, A. M. (2021). Public service motivation and its implications for public service. The Palgrave Handbook of the Public Servant, 241-258.

Bagonza, G., Kaahwa, M. G., & Mbabazi, E. G. (2021). Graduates Employability: Has the Expansion of the University Sector in Uganda improved Employment Prospects for Graduates? Employers and Lecturers Perspective. *International Journal of Educational Administration and Policy Studies, 13*(1), 66–71. doi:10.5897/IJEAPS2021.0699

Baluku, M. M., Onderi, P., & Otto, K. (2021). Predicting self-employment intentions and entry in Germany and East Africa: An investigation of the impact of mentoring, entrepreneurial attitudes, and psychological capital. *Journal of Small Business and Entrepreneurship, 33*(3), 289–322. doi:10.1080/08276331.2019.1666337

Bourn, D. (2018). *Understanding global skills for 21st century professions*. Springer. doi:10.1007/978-3-319-97655-6

Caballero, G., Álvarez-González, P., & López-Miguens, M. J. (2020). How to promote the employability capital of university students? Developing and validating scales. *Studies in Higher Education, 45*(12), 2634–2652. doi:10.1080/03075079.2020.1807494

Cheng, G. H. L., Chan, D. K. S., & Au, W. T. (2020). Profiles of employability and their career and psychological implications among unemployed youth. *Applied Research in Quality of Life*, 1–15.

Christopherson, S., & Clark, J. (2020). *Remaking regional economies: Power, labor, and firm strategies in the knowledge economy*. Routledge.

Cooper, S. L., & McArdle, S. (2017). *Preparing to Moot: A step-by-step guide to mooting*. Routledge. doi:10.4324/9781315713342

Fugate, M., Kinicki, A. J., & Ashforth, B. E. (2004). Employability: A psycho-social construct, its dimensions, and applications. *Journal of Vocational Behavior, 65*(1), 14–38. doi:10.1016/j.jvb.2003.10.005

Hogan, R., Chamorro-Premuzic, T., & Kaiser, R. B. (2013). Employability and career success: Bridging the gap between theory and reality. *Industrial and Organizational Psychology: Perspectives on Science and Practice, 6*(1), 3–16. doi:10.1111/iops.12001

Hogan, R., & Sherman, R. A. (2019). New (ish) directions for vocational interests research. In *Vocational Interests in the Workplace* (pp. 189–204). Routledge. doi:10.4324/9781315678924-10

Jackson, D. (2018). Developing graduate career readiness in Australia: Shifting from extra-curricular internships to work-integrated learning. *International Journal of Work-Integrated Learning, 19*(1), 23–35.

Jain, A. K., & Sullivan, S. (2019). An examination of the relationship between careerism and organizational commitment, satisfaction, and performance. *Personnel Review, 49*(8), 1553–1571. doi:10.1108/PR-05-2019-0280

Jjuuko, R., Tukundane, C., & Zeelen, J. (2021). Reclaiming the educative power of vocational placements: Experiences from agriculture education practice in Uganda. *International Journal of Training and Development, 25*(2), 144–159. doi:10.1111/ijtd.12212

Kabay, S. (2021). *Access, Quality, and the Global Learning Crisis: Insights from Ugandan Primary Education*. Oxford University Press. doi:10.1093/oso/9780192896865.001.0001

Kim, M., Perrewé, P. L., Kim, Y. K., & Kim, A. C. H. (2017). Psychological capital in sport organizations: Hope, Efficacy, Resilience, and Optimism among Employees in Sport (HEROES). *European Sport Management Quarterly, 17*(5), 659–680. doi:10.1080/16184742.2017.1344284

Kinicki, A., & Fugate, M. (2017). *Loose Leaf for Organizational Behavior: A Practical, Problem-Solving Approach*. McGraw-Hill Education.

Kostal, J. W., & Wiernik, B. M. (2017). A meta-analytic investigation of demographic differences in protean, boundaryless, and proactive career orientations. *Career Development International, 22*(5), 520–545. doi:10.1108/CDI-08-2017-0139

Kundi, Y. M., Hollet-Haudebert, S., & Peterson, J. (2021). Linking protean and boundaryless career attitudes to subjective career success: A serial mediation model. *Journal of Career Assessment, 29*(2), 263–282. doi:10.1177/1069072720959782

Luthans, F. (2002). The need for and meaning of positive organizational behavior. *Journal of Organizational Behavior: The International Journal of Industrial. Occupational and Organizational Psychology and Behavior, 23*(6), 695–706. doi:10.1002/job.165

Luthans, F., Youssef, C. M., & Avolio, B. J. (2015). *Psychological capital and beyond*. Oxford University Press.

Luthans, K. W., Luthans, B. C., & Chaffin, T. D. (2019). Refining grit in academic performance: The mediational role of psychological capital. *Journal of Management Education, 43*(1), 35–61. doi:10.1177/1052562918804282

Lyons, S. T., Schweitzer, L., & Ng, E. S. (2015). How have careers changed? An investigation of changing career patterns across four generations. *Journal of Managerial Psychology*, *30*(1), 8–21. doi:10.1108/JMP-07-2014-0210

Monteiro, S., & Almeida, L. S. (2021). Employability of higher education graduates: Reflections and pedagogical implications. *Revista Lusófona de Educação*, *51*(51).

Ntale, P. D., Ssempebwa, J., Musisi, B., Musoke, G. G., Joseph, K., Mugimu, C. B., Muhammed, N., & Ntayi, J. (2020). Gaps in the structuring of organizations in the graduate employment context in Uganda. *Journal of Organization Design*, *9*(1), 1–10. doi:10.118641469-020-0066-5

Ntale, P. D., Ssempebwa, J., Musisi, B., & Pope, H. C. (2019). Inter-agency collaboration for graduate employment opportunities in Uganda: A case for investigating the structure, social capital, and agency of organizations. *Journal of African American Studies*, *23*(1), 111–130. doi:10.100712111-019-09419-9

Oyugi, J. L. (2021). From Ivory Tower to Entrepreneurial University: Agenda for Sustainable Job Creation among University Graduates in Uganda. *Journal of Education and Learning*, *15*(1), 127–134. doi:10.11591/edulearn.v15i1.15982

Peterson, C. (2006). *A primer in positive psychology*. Oxford university press.

Praskova, A., Creed, P. A., & Hood, M. (2015). Career identity and the complex mediating relationships between career preparatory actions and career progress markers. *Journal of Vocational Behavior*, *87*, 145–153. doi:10.1016/j.jvb.2015.01.001

Prayag, G., Ozanne, L. K., & de Vries, H. (2020). Psychological capital, coping mechanisms and organizational resilience: Insights from the 2016 Kaikoura earthquake, New Zealand. *Tourism Management Perspectives*, *34*, 100637. doi:10.1016/j.tmp.2020.100637

Rodrigues, R., Butler, C. L., & Guest, D. (2019). Antecedents of protean and boundaryless career orientations: The role of core self-evaluations, perceived employability and social capital. *Journal of Vocational Behavior*, *110*, 1–11. doi:10.1016/j.jvb.2018.11.003

Savickas, M. (2019). *Career counseling*. American Psychological Association. doi:10.1037/0000105-000

Shmatko, N. M., Pantelieiev, M. S., & Kurchenko, A. A. (2018). Creative Intelligence And Ideas Generation In The Context Of Strategic Management By Personnel. *Adaptive Management: Theory and Practice. Series Economics*, *5*(10).

Sternberg, R. J. (2020). Creativity from start to finish: A "straight-A" model of creative process and its relation to intelligence. *The Journal of Creative Behavior*, *54*(2), 229–241. doi:10.1002/jocb.223

Subramony, M., Segers, J., Chadwick, C., & Shyamsunder, A. (2018). Leadership development practice bundles and organizational performance: The mediating role of human capital and social capital. *Journal of Business Research*, *83*, 120–129. doi:10.1016/j.jbusres.2017.09.044

Succi, C., & Canovi, M. (2020). Soft skills to enhance graduate employability: Comparing students and employers' perceptions. *Studies in Higher Education*, *45*(9), 1834–1847. doi:10.1080/03075079.2019.1585420

Tentama, F., & Yusantri, S. (2020). The Role of Entrepreneurial Intention in Predicting Vocational High School Students' Employability. *International Journal of Evaluation and Research in Education*, *9*(3), 558–563. doi:10.11591/ijere.v9i3.20580

van der Heijde, C. M. (2014). Employability and self-regulation in contemporary careers. In *Psycho-social career meta-capacities* (pp. 7–17). Springer. doi:10.1007/978-3-319-00645-1_1

van Harten, J., De Cuyper, N., Guest, D., Fugate, M., Knies, E., & Forrier, A. (2020). Introduction to special issue on HRM and employability: mutual gains or conflicting outcomes? Vera, D., Samba, C., Kong, D. T., & Maldonado, T. (2020). Resilience as thriving: The role of positive leadership practices. *Organizational Dynamics*.

World Bank. (2017). *Uganda Economic Update, December 2017: Accelerating Uganda's Development, Ending Child Marriage, Educating Girls*. World Bank.

Xia, T., Gu, H., Huang, Y., Zhu, Q., & Cheng, Y. (2020). The relationship between career social support and employability of college students: A moderated mediation model. *Frontiers in Psychology*, *11*, 28. doi:10.3389/fpsyg.2020.00028 PMID:32047461

Youssef, C. M., & Luthans, F. (2012). Positive global leadership. *Journal of World Business*, *47*(4), 539–547. doi:10.1016/j.jwb.2012.01.007

Zhang, M., Wang, F., Weng, H., Zhu, T., & Liu, H. (2021). Transformational leadership and perceived overqualification: A career development perspective. *Frontiers in Psychology*, *12*, 12. doi:10.3389/fpsyg.2021.597821 PMID:33643130

Chapter 14
Graduate Un/Employment in Turkey:
A Holistic Entrepreneurship Strategy to Increase Employment and Reduce Unemployment

İrfan Kalaycı
İnönü University, Turkey

ABSTRACT

The subject and aim of this study are to examine the problem of globalizing graduate employment/unemployment and the holistic entrepreneurship strategy against this problem in the axis of Turkey. Two types of methods were followed here: First, as a method of thought, the "deductive" path was followed, since the focus was on specific graduate unemployment instead of the general unemployment problem and the solution based solely on graduate entrepreneurship instead of general employment entrepreneurship. Secondly, as a research method, with the help of official statistical data and literature, the problem and solution (i.e., diagnosis and treatment) were described and parsed-synthesized. One of the expected results from this study is to introduce the Turkish dimension of the graduate labor market and entrepreneurship problem to the world; the other is to emphasize global cooperation to tackle the problem of graduate unemployment.

INTRODUCTION

General and graduate unemployment is one of the chronic socio-economic problems

DOI: 10.4018/978-1-7998-9581-7.ch014

of not only Turkey but the entire contemporary capitalist world. Youth unemployment is a national and global crisis that cannot be considered temporary, that is, it seems to be permanent. Like many countries, Turkey also updates and implements various population, education and employment policies to combat this problem that threatens human capital and wastes public resources.

It is very difficult to distinguish between graduate unemployment and youth unemployment, because after the compulsory education period in Turkey was increased to 12 years, these two derivative unemployment categories began to intertwine. Therefore, the young unemployed are now largely counted as graduate unemployed. In this study, unless otherwise stated, it should not be considered a big mistake if the unemployed graduates are mentioned as young unemployed as a reflection of a common point of view.

According to the general definition of the Organization for Economic Co-operation and Development (OECD), the youth unemployment rate is the number of unemployed people aged 15-24 as a percentage of the youth workforce. The unemployed are people who report being unemployed, available for work, and taking active steps to find a job in the past four weeks. According to June 2021 data, while the G-7 average in youth unemployment is 10.5% and the OECD average is 12.9%, this rate is 24% in Turkey. The average of the European Union (EU), which Turkey is trying to become a full member of but has not yet become, is 17%. However, Turkey has fewer youth unemployed than Spain and Greece. (Among OECD countries, Japan has the lowest with 4.5% and Costa Rica the highest with 39.9%.) (See OECD Data, 2021.)

Of course, the world is not just OECD, so unemployment is rather the most burning socio-economic problem of underdeveloped and developing countries. According to estimates, there is a youth unemployed population of around 700 million in the world. The United Nations (UN) and the International Labour Organization (ILO) warn governments by stating that youth unemployment has once again raised the alarm all over the world with the effect of the Covid-19 pandemic. The ILO develops serious policies and programs to prepare young people for employment in conflict and fragile environments. Considering that youth is an indispensable age group for both violence and peace, it is known that permanent and sustainable peace and stability can be achieved with the least possible unemployment and maximum employment. This assumption is also valid for Turkey as an Afro-Eurasian economy, which is an important player in preventing regional conflicts and establishing peace.

Four important reminders can be made here:

First, the unemployed graduates may be in the young or older age groups: Today, almost every young person is a graduate one, but not every graduate may be young. Therefore, the fact that every graduate is young or old does not reduce the quality and importance of the graduate unemployment problem. It is very difficult to always see the graduate-young distinction in statistics, so this study makes use of the obligatory inference that there is a transitivity between these two concepts.

Secondly, the problem of graduate unemployment is not only a structural problem of underdeveloped and developing countries, but also continues to be a cyclical problem of developed countries. Therefore, this dramatic mass problem cannot be reduced to a single geography of the world on the denominator of development and has already become globalized. The "global village", in which Turkey is located, has graduate unemployees from the east, west, north and south, and as long as they remain unemployed, they begin to lose hope against the governers of that village. At this point, in order to revive hopes, employment packages that are generally broad in developed countries but narrow in underdeveloped/developing countries are updated and activated. Although the problem is global but the struggle against the problem seems local, labor migration movements that gained momentum with globalization have drawn this perspective to the "glocalization" line.

Thirdly, while governments implement local employment policies open to the support of international financial organizations against the global graduate unemployment problem, they do not want to make the distinction between graduates and young people. For example, in Turkey, especially if the populist electoral economy process has been entered, new employment areas with the contribution of foreign loans are created for graduates-young voters who have high voting potential. Thus, the unemployment gas stuck in the labor market is removed and the trust of these voters and their families in the economy is renewed.

Fourth, this particular observation aside, it is a reality that many developed states, from Western Europe to Scandinavia and Canada, are successful in their prestigious and sustainable graduate employment policies against this chronic global problem, and they also affect developing states such as Turkey. Graduate unemployed seek high-standard welfare budgets that include attractive internships, social security-health benefits, job guarantees, and unemployment benefits. For this, the reconciliation of the government-union-employer trio is essential.

METHODOLOGY

In this study, the following two types of methods were preferred: First, a method of thinking called deductive was followed, since the focus was on graduate unemployment instead of general unemployment in the problematization stage, and on only graduate employment entrepreneurship instead of general employment entrepreneurship in the solution stage. This will already be visible in the text flow. Secondly, as a research method, the problem and its solution (ie diagnosis and treatment) were explained and decomposed-synthesized with the help of global and national official statistical data and literature.

BACKGROUND

There are many researchers who look at the graduate unemployment problem and employment solution of the huge global village from different countries and from different perspectives. The opinions of some of them are compiled below.

Zhang (2018) examined the causes and consequences of global graduate unemployment in the context of China. Extremely high student enrollment rates are cited as one reason for mass educated unemployment in this rapidly growing market economy. In order to alleviate graduate unemployment, the transition from a fully state-controlled school system to a university system that is held accountable for more flexible labor market conditions has been achieved.

Harari (2018) examines the issue of work and unemployment as the 2nd lesson in his famous book 21 Lessons in the 21st Century: according to him, automation, artificial intelligence and robot technology are a revolution; this revolution creates a prosperous mass as well as a victim mass. It is predicted that this revolution will make serious changes in the labor market towards 2050, causing more employment loss in adult people, eliminating some jobs and creating new ones based on expertise. He says that the algorithm specifically pointed out by the author will enter the labor market as a servant of capitalism and will throw unnecessary and unqualified labor force out of this market. It can be inferred as follows: Against the danger of mass-global unemployment, the transition of authority from people to digital dictatorships and algorithms should be prevented.

Bell and Blanchflower (2010) refer to youth unemployment as "déjà vu" for the USA and Europe: because with the 2007-2008 global financial crisis, unemployment is increasing rapidly, especially among women, blacks and immigrants, while the labor force participation rate and employment-population are falling. According to them, European and American labor markets do not tend to view the institutions that orthodox economists care about as a cause of unemployment. Apart from the known harmful effects of unemployment, especially long-term unemployment causes permanent scars when you are young, the youth labor market is highly cyclically sensitive and this market is struggling in a recession. The authors reiterate that low interest rate monetary policy should be used to realize Keynesian ideal of full employment and statist fiscal policy for high investment should be used.

According to a report by the African Development Bank (AfDB) (2016), Africa's share of the world's youth population is projected to increase from 1/5 in 2012 to 1/3 by 2050: young people in West, Central and East African countries Employment is primarily a demand-side problem. Decreases in fertility rates and the development of related skills could get Africa as good a spot as Asia. African economies are heterogeneous, with varying demographic paths, economic structures and youth development policies. The report argues that advanced public policies in the youth context are needed for positive and sustainable youth employment rates.

Olowe (2010) investigated graduate unemployment as a reflection of good governance and development in Africa, taking Nigeria as a reference, and its impact on the country's economy. The author states that the graduate unemployed are presented with options for full, under- and over-employment in the form of self-employment and white-collar workers, on the path to human capacity building and nation-building for developing countries.

Shi et al (2018) focused on the unemployment duration of graduates: graduates will be able to shorten their unemployment period to the extent that they fit their job application profile to the job profile and complete the necessary training process for this. The longer the unemployment period, the greater the risk of human capital falling. A controversial finding by the authors from a survey of Switzerland, one of the favorite economies of unemployed youth, is that the worse the match between the applicant's profile and the job profile, the smaller the detrimental effects of unemployment. Their findings suggest that the impacts of unemployment need to be examined in relation to country-specific institutional settings, applicants' previous educational and employment experiences, and job characteristics.

Eichhorst and Tobsch (2015) draw attention to the dual structure in the labor market: the business world likes a flexible labor market because this flexibility will allow employers to create jobs in the quality and conditions they want. For example, in Germany, the largest stronghold of capitalism in Europe, the labor market has transformed into a dual structure since the mid-1990s. According to their theoretical and empirical work, non-standard contracts are liberalized, contributing to the growth of jobs and employment in Germany. It is emphasized that atypical contracts do not necessarily undermine the dominance of standard employment relations and quality of work, but rather form an integral part of employment in sectors and occupations that rely on more flexible and perhaps cheaper forms of labor.

Verd and colleagues (2019) discuss whether there is a polarization between the employed and the unemployed in the orbits of young people: according to a multi-orbital survey of youth labor markets in recessionary Spain and Italy, stable and unpaid employment trajectories have very low unemployment levels. while the precarious trajectory offers much higher levels of unemployment and instability. Those with a temporary employment trajectory faced primarily short-term unemployment, while those with an unstable trajectory faced long-term unemployment and more discontinuity and unstable employment. The following is also true for Turkey, which is located in the Mediterranean economies belt with these two countries:

Low-educated and unskilled youth display a vulnerable social profile and even lead to the establishment of a "de facto" derivative labor market based on low wages and poor working conditions.

Felgueroso and Jansen (2015) discussed the "Youth Guarantee" (YG) as a new plan to combat youth unemployment in EU countries: in their view, although such a plan could improve the school-to-work transition of young workers, the expected gains in the periphery, at least in the short term, are rather small. High youth unemployment in crisis-stricken southern countries is the result of structural problems and weak links between education and the labor market. Therefore, it will take time to fix these structural problems and the available resources are insufficient to provide the necessary support to young people. The governments of southern countries should agree with those in the north on an agenda that will promote economic growth.

Salas-Velasco (2021) has mapped the education – job (mis)match in the labor market for university graduates: in his study, he considered the amount of resources that both individuals and society allocate to the production of highly skilled workers. It examines the horizontal mismatch that occurs when university graduates work at formal qualification levels but in jobs not related to their field of study.

Finally, Han and Hart (2021) examined the relationship between precarious employment and the probability of income or job loss during the Covid-19 pandemic, with a US specific and multivariate regression: the findings confirm a strong positive association between precarious employment and job or income loss. Specifically, working part-time in the service sector and feeling powerless in the workplace, receiving low financial rewards, few benefits, and facing barriers to the exercise of rights significantly doubled the likelihood of losing income or employment.

This study, on the other hand, can be included among other Turkey-based studies, examples of which are not given here, but have been entered in the literature.

THE PROBLEM OF GLOBALIZATION OF GRADUATE EMPLOYMENT AND UNEMPLOYMENT

Since graduate and / or youth unemployment types and rates have increased relatively all over the world, it has turned into a global and/or international problem. For this reason, there is a need for public programs to bring unemployed graduates into the labor market more than ever before. Only the sustainable and stable ones among these programs have deemed successful. Optimistically, thanks to the globalization and / or internationalization of graduate unemployment, each government can contribute to solution-oriented sustainable employment programs through its own financial resources and economic policies.

According to data from ILO (2020) (see Figure 1), there are arround 1.3 billion young people aged 15 to 24 worldwide. Of the approximately 497 million global youth population, roughly 41% are in the labor market, of which 429 million are employed, while approximately 68 million are looking for work and are available for work (ie unemployed). More than 50% of young people – about 776 million – are outside the market, meaning they are not in employment, unsuitable and not looking for work. Besides their education, young people can be employed by seeking a (part-time) job and thus being considered unemployed or avoiding participation in the labor market. Thus, a broad measure of youth workforce underutilisation is the number of young people *not in employment, education or training* (NEET), of 267 million – a high statistic reflecting how many young people are currently not working worldwide. On the other hand, approximately 126 million young people, or 30% of working youth, live in extreme or moderate poverty, i.e. "precariat" (working poor class), despite having a job. In addition, more than 75% of young workers are employed informally. Globally, around 46% of young workers are self-employed or contributing family workers, while around 54% are wage and salaried workers, although often in non-standard arrangements.

The subregional distribution of global youth unemployment rates can also be scrutinized (see Table 1): According to the data of ILO (2020), which found that unemployment affects 67.6 million young men and women or 13.6% of the youth workforce, the highest youth unemployment rate is in Northern Africa and in the Arab States, at around 2.2 and 1.7 times the global rate, respectively. In these two subregions, youth unemployment rates have been much higher than in the rest of the world since 1991 due to structural labor market barriers. Despite having the lowest unemployment probability of all sub-regions, youth in Sub-Saharan Africa and North America faced an unemployment rate of around 9% in 2019. The global youth unemployment rate is expected to increase by 0.1 percentage point in 2021.

Every young who job seeker in the contemporary global world has graduated from any school (primary, secondary, high school, university, even graduate level). Therefore, graduate unemployment also includes youth unemployment. Giving high priority to youth employment, the ILO has been developing and recommending policies for governments within the framework of the *"Decent Work Agenda"* for a while. Based on the example of the Asia-Pacific region, it has established a *"Youth Employment Network (YEN)"* specific to each global region. This network is based on the four pillars of employability, entrepreneurship, equal opportunity and job creation. As the ILO strongly emphasizes, there is no "one-size-fits-all" paradigm regarding the causes and solutions of youth unemployment and underemployment in a region of considerable diversity in the Asia-Pacific. Because, as Morris (2006) reminds, in line with the systematic ILO employment policy, youth employment is a global issue, including globalization, structural reforms, aggregate demand, demographic trends, employment intensity of economic growth, the regulatory environment for business development, education and training, among others. It is linked to many factors affecting employment.

Morris (2006) has identified the following employment policy steps while promoting *"paths to decent work"*: i- Investment in vocational education and lifelong learning that increases youth employability and access to universal, free, quality public primary and secondary education. ii- Targeted initiatives and incentive schemes to increase labor demand for youth, particularly disadvantaged youth, without reducing the quantity and quality of work for others. iii- Entrepreneurship and productive and sustainable self-employment as career options and sources of decent employment for young people. iv- Employment services, guidance and labor market information and career counselling, as well as more intensive financial assistance to young people who are long-term unemployed. v- Wage policies that ensure that young people earn a fair and sufficient income for productive work, policies that promote freedom of association, collective bargaining, safe and secure working conditions and decent working hours. vi- Strengthening existing networks of young entrepreneurs and young trade unionists worldwide.

TURKEY'S MACROECONOMIC AND GRADUATE LABOUR MARKET OUTLOOK

In this section, first the general macroeconomic structure of Turkey is summarized, and then the graduate labor market phenomenon is detailed.

General Macroeconomic Structure of Turkey

Turkey, the 18th most populous country in the world with a population reaching 84 million with the last wave of migrants, is a consumer market the size of Germany and the only Afro-Eurasian country. Although it has a relatively dynamic and young structure, it is turning into a society like Westerners but gradually aging. It is in the "BRICS-T" (Brazil, Russia, India, China, South Africa, Turkey) or "MIST" (Mexico, Indonesia, South Korea, Turkey) group of emerging markets.

Although Turkey, which is a candidate country of the EU and a G-20 country, is rich in terms of natural and human resources, she has an official youth unemployment rate of more than 24%. With more than 200 universities and 8 million students, it is home to an increasing potential unemployed. The country's graduate unemployed can be involved in almost any type of unemployment (structural, cyclical, frictional, hidden, etc.) in the globalized labor market.

Figure 1. Overview of the global labour market for youth, 2019
Source: ILO, 2020.

Table 1. Youth unemployment rates, global and by subregion and sex, 2019–21

Region	Subregion	Youth total (%)			Youth male (%)			Youth female (%)		
		2019	2020	2021	2019	2020	2021	2019	2020	2021
World		13.6	13.7	13.8	14.0	14.0	14.1	13.0	13.1	13.2
Africa	Northern Africa	30.2	29.8	29.6	26.4	25.7	25.3	39.6	39.8	40.3
	Sub-Saharan Africa	8.7	8.7	8.7	8.2	8.3	8.3	9.2	9.2	9.1
Americas	Latin America and the Caribbean	17.9	18.0	18.1	15.2	15.2	15.4	22.0	22.1	22.2
	Northern America	8.8	9.1	9.4	9.9	10.1	10.4	7.6	8.1	8.4
Arab States	Arab States	22.9	23.0	22.9	19.7	19.8	19.6	42.2	42.1	42.5
Asia and the Pacific	Eastern Asia	9.8	10.0	10.2	10.8	11.0	11.1	8.7	8.9	9.0
	South-Eastern Asia and the Pacific	10.5	10.9	11.0	10.3	10.6	10.7	10.8	11.2	11.5
	Southern Asia	18.7	18.8	18.9	18.7	18.9	19.0	18.4	18.5	18.6
Europe and Central Asia	Northern, Southern and Western Europe	14.8	14.8	15.1	15.8	15.6	15.9	13.8	13.9	14.2
	Eastern Europe	14.9	14.4	14.2	14.6	14.1	13.9	15.3	14.8	14.5
	Central and Western Asia	17.8	17.5	17.7	16.6	16.6	17.0	19.7	19.0	18.9

Source: ILO, 2020.

The latest policy interest rate in Turkey (as of June-August 2021) is about 19%: this means expensive loans that are unpleasant for real sector investors and almost zero or even negative real interest rates, which means equal to or below the inflation rate, for depositors. Due to the uncertainties created by the Covid-19 epidemic, this high interest rate may partially attract foreign capital. But more importantly, this interest rate, which cannot be lowered for now, shows that the value of the Turkish Lira (TL) is low and inflation is high. There is always the risk of making the national economy fragile and throwing it into a crisis, with the increasing current account deficit (approximately $ 30 billion) and external debt stock (approximately $ 450 billion). High exchange rates (for example: on average 1 $ = 8.5 TL; 1 € = 10 TL, in July 2021) continue to make imports more expensive despite increasing exports. (For this and other data, see Central Bank of the Republic of Turkey, TCMB, 2021.)

In Turkey, where state capitalism is dominant under the guise of a mixed economy as an economic order, both the subsistence index is low and the total age dependency ratio is high: The monthly subsistence limit for a family of four has already exceeded 9 thousand TL, or $ 1000, due to high consumer inflation (official 20%, informal at least twice) and high cost of living. Also, an employee in a family has to support several people because of unemployment. According to the data of the Turkish Statistical Institute (TUIK), the "total age dependency ratio", which means the number of people aged 0-14 and 65 and over, per 100 people of working age in the 15-64 age group, was 47.7% in 2020. .

According to the results of the research of the Turkish Confederation of Trade Unions (Türk-İş), which is in alliance with the government, in July 2021; i- the monthly food expenditure (hunger limit) required by a family of four for a healthy, balanced and adequate diet is 2,903 TL, that is, $ 341 (approximately at the minimum wage level); ii- together with food expenditure, the total amount of other mandatory monthly expenditures for clothing, housing (rent, electricity, water, fuel), transportation, education, health and similar needs increased to 9,457 TL or $ 1117, which is the poverty line; iii- the cost of living for a single employee is 3,546 TL, or $ 417 per month.

Figure 2 can be consulted for Turkey's general complementary macroeconomic indicators and its ranking in the world according to these indicators.

Qalitative and Quantitative Outlook of Graduate Uneployment and Employment in Turkey

The changing structural and numerical view of the labor market in Turkey is largely under the influence of the intermittent macroeconomic stability or crisis. First of all, it is necessary to know that there are many causes and consequences of graduate unemployment – partly global and partly Turkey-specific (see Table 2).

The developments in unemployment and employment of graduates, which are tried to fit into some items below, should be evaluated according to this fact.

Figure 2. Turkey according to selected macroeconomic indicators: comparison with the world
Source: CIA, 2021. (Author's scheme)

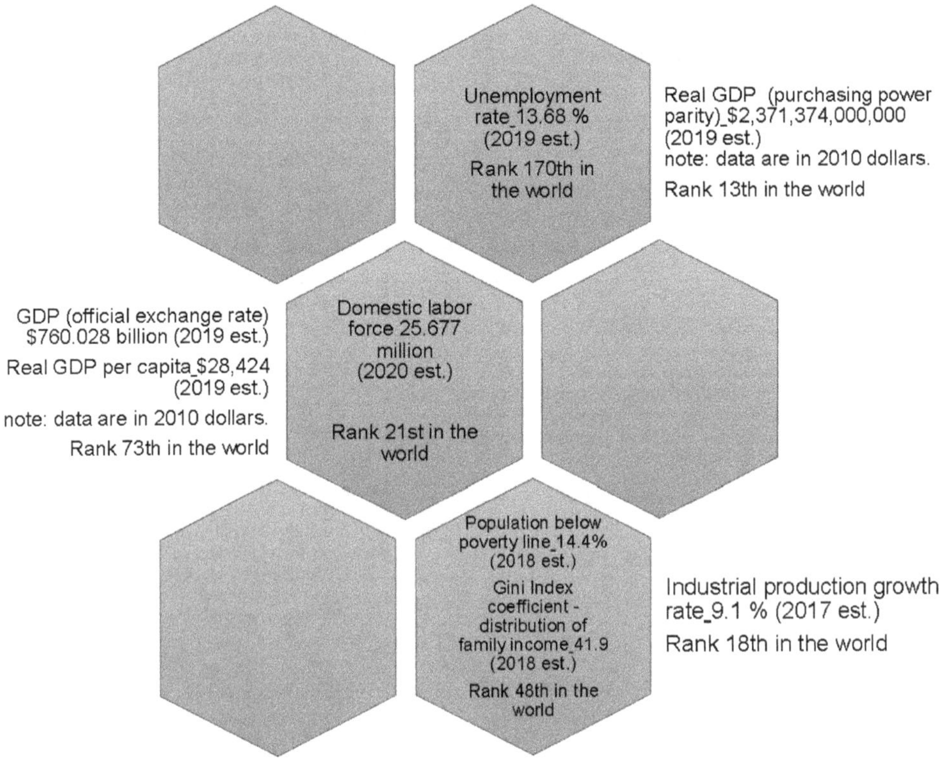

i-The employment of graduates in Turkey is concentrated in certain professions. Medicine, dentistry, psychology-guidance, civil engineering, etc. When everyone wants to enter such job-guaranteed departments, the quotas are inflated with political concerns rather than economic ones, and with the effect of inadequate infrastructure, backlog and poor quality graduates increase.

ii- The number of graduates/young unemployed is increasing day by day and the society is getting used to this bad situation. According to TUIK's August 2021 data, youth unemployment rate is 22.7% and employment rate is 32.6%. (For aggregated and detailed data, see Figure 3.) These gray (not so bright) ratios undermine confidence and hope in the country's macroeconomic governance.

iii- Until a few years ago, law school graduates were popular like medical graduates and could find a job very easily. However, now lawyers are not able to get jobs right away and they are at risk of unemployment. Those who are not among the favorite engineerings have difficulty in finding a job, they are called as

Table 2. Causes and consequences of graduate unemployment in Turkey

	Causes	Consequences
Micro Economic	-Failure to provide sufficient and productive vocational knowledge, education and skills to young people; - Bankruptcy of companies or inability to establish a new company due to cyclical fluctuations; -Companies working at low capacity; -Due to the information asymmetry in the labor market, the labor supply (youth side) and labor demand (employers' side) parties do not have the same and sufficient information about employment needs; - Precarious and low-paid employment conditions; -Long and tedious job search time; -The incompatibility of the desires and education level of young people ready to work and the structure of institutions and companies ready to employ.	-Not being able to find a job, losing the job found (open unemployment) - Changing of jobs and sectors (short-medium-term frictional unemployment) -When the diplomas of the youth and the expectations of the workplaces do not match, mutual dissatisfaction arises; - When the job search period is prolonged, young people get into bad psychology and may give up on looking for a job.
Macro Economic	- Increasing the youth population more than employment areas; -The absence of effective central planning for the triple balance of population-education-employment; - Insufficient public budget for necessary production facilities (factory, facility, school, etc.) to create youth employment; - The inability of private sector entrepreneurship to support state entrepreneurship; - Contraction of aggregate demand, negative growth; -Transition from labor-intensive technology to capital-intensive and knowledge-intensive technology; -Inclusion of young people who do not want to work in the unemployment fund according to the advanced welfare state model (not valid for Turkey for now) -Macroeconomic and political instabilities feeding each other	-Decrease in total production and income (structural unemployment) -Decrease in real income, slowdown in income-expenditure flow, inflation in stagnation (stagflation) - Reduction in the need for live labor due to intensive mechanization (technological unemployment) -As a marginal group, those who agree to low unemployment benefits and heirs who give up looking for a job (voluntary unemployment) -Inequalities and injustices in income distribution -The growing socio-economic class in terms of the working poor and/or precarious workers. [British economist G. Standing (2011) calls this new dangerous class ***"precariat"***. It is a combination of the words precarious and proletariat.]
Global Economic	- Contagious effect of financial crises that erupted in major economies due to globalization - Uneven distribution of the workforce - Increase in migration movements due to terrorism, war and political refugees -Economic embargoes imposed by states against each other -High tariffs and non-tariff barriers such as quotas, that restrict free trade -Erosion, flood, fire, etc. arising due to global warming or climate change. destruction of soil, water and forest resources as a result of natural disasters -Because of the Covid-19 pandemic, closures, disruption of the income-expenditure flow and breaking the supply chain -Countries that are dependent on foreign oil and gas products, such as Turkey, are faced with high current account deficits and potential energy crises. When it becomes easier to turn the economy with the current account deficit (ie foreign savings), the export sector shrinks and employment cannot be increased accordingly.	- The labor surplus in the countries of immigration and the labor shortage in the countries of emigration as a result of the increase in the migration movements in the labor force; -The country that loses its qualified / educated / skilled workforce becomes impoverished in the context of human capital; the country that gains this workforce through immigration becomes richer; thereby creating of imbalance in the global labor market; -If the labor supply (Ls) increases while the labor demand (Ld) is constant, that is, if there is an excess of Ls, unemployment (underemployment) and low equilibrium wage (poverty) will occur; -Change in the demographic composition of countries -When the climate crisis is combined with bad resource management, first of all, the increase in input costs in the agriculture and industry sectors and therefore the increase in cost inflation - Factories and firms that cannot turn the wheels of production against cost inflation cannot employ new graduates, and they start to lay off existing workers, starting from young and single ones.

Source: Author

"pavement engineers" in the sense of unemployed. New engineers who can find a job usually are starting with minimum wage.

iv-Faculty graduates as well as vocational school graduates cannot find a job for a long time, especially in industry and service sectors, although they are practitioners or trainees in a particular profession. More of them are willing to work for low wages and without insurance.

v- In Turkey, the need for teachers and the number of unemployed teacher graduates are increasing due to the increase in population. According to the 2021 estimates of the education unions, while the teacher shortage is around 150 thousand, the number of teachers waiting to be appointed or unemployed has reached 4-5 times (for now 700 thousand) that (cited from Eğitim-Sen; Nazlıer, 2022). Ironically, this corresponds to the population of many small countries in the world or medium-sized cities in Turkey. This dramatic contradiction has led to the creation of an artificial and temporary profession, such as paid teaching, which is not permanent. The government is planning to solve this problem by preparing the long-awaited "Teacher Profession Law".

vi-Despite the current minimum wage laws, many companies and employers employ uninsured workers below the minimum wage. In this unfavorable situation, Syrians and other immigrants, who make up the cheap and poor quality labor stock in Turkey, have a serious impact.

vii- In Turkey, families send their children to universities so that they can have a job. Primary and secondary school graduates can't even be garbage collectors anymore. Thousands of high school graduates apply to be appointed to the staff of five or ten municipal workers or civil servants. If the exam conditions are relaxed, even unemployed university graduates will be able to apply for high school graduate positions.

viii-Turkey is also becoming capitalist in the new world economic order, she has established a "screening system" that will select and employ cheap and high-quality graduates for the labor market. The private sector ruthlessly sifts the unemployed graduates according to their economic interests, not humanitarian concerns. Even though the young mass graduates, underemployment arises when it is caught in the sieve because they are generally considered to be under-educated.

ix- The retirement age has been kept high so that the budget of the Social Security Institution (SGK in Turkish) does not cause excessive deficit. This situation is considered as an obstacle for employment with new diplomas. Implicitly, the "working system to the grave" is in effect. Some of the retirees are also looking for a job because their pensions are usually very low. Young graduates have less chance of finding a job as retirees get jobs.

Figure 3. Basic statistics of unemployment, employment and labour force in Turkey: June 2021
Source: TUIK, August 10, 2021. (Author's scheme)

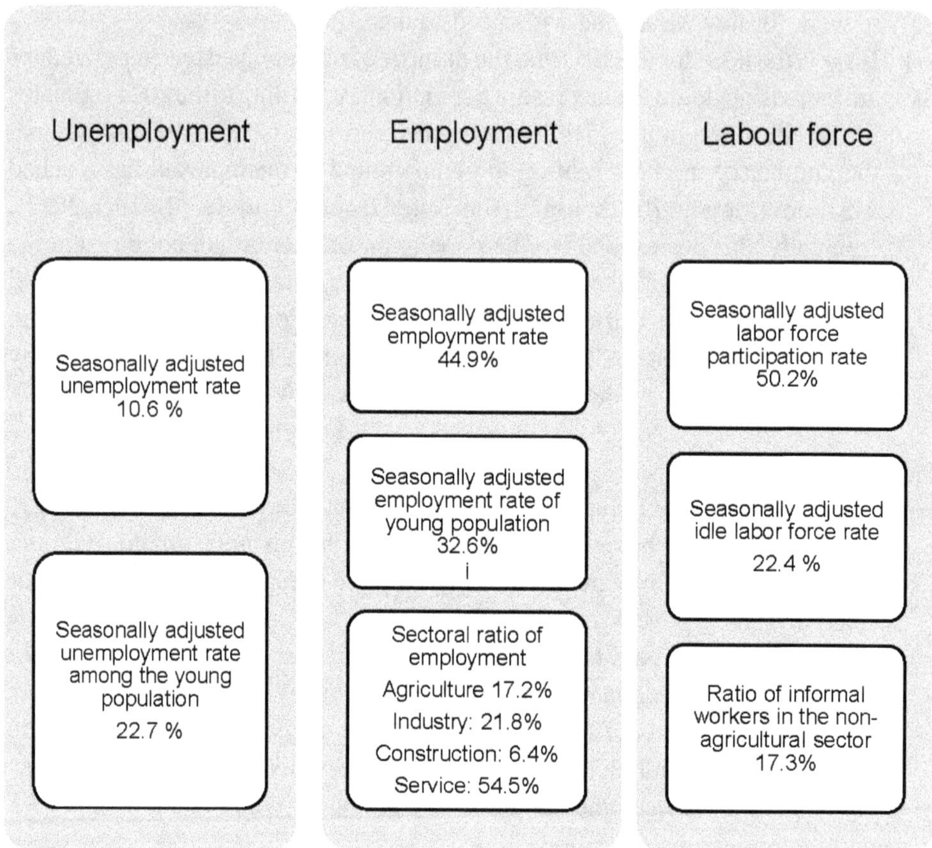

x. The public and private sectors do not distinguish between university name and university graduate on paper when posting jobs. However, institutions and companies make this distinction in written and interview exams and prefer graduates of prestigious universities (if there is no favoritism). This creates a kind of "negative selection" situation.

xi. Some company executives hire engineers to replace them because they can't find lab technicians to work the shift. In technical areas where there is a shortage of qualified personnel, the "engineer / technician ratio" has begun to reverse. While 7-8 technicians work alongside an engineer in a similar organization in Europe, it is observed that 3-5 engineers work together with a technician in Turkey (Çiftçi, 2021). This is a distorted situation that could set a bad example for other industries as well.

xii. Turkey is a constitutionally democratic state of law, but in practice, graduates are employed, especially in the public sector, with a favoritism mechanism. This mechanism, which is against democracy and justice, evokes a kind of kleptocracy and crony capitalism established between the politician-bureaucrat-boss.

A HOLISTIC ENTREPRENEURSHIP STRATEGY TO REDUCE GRADUATE UNEMPLOYMENT AND INCREASE EMPLOYMENT IN TURKEY

This strategy can be based on a four-plate foot. Government, private sector, graduate workforce and global organizations. These components interact with each other. Their common goal is the same: to contribute to lower unemployment and higher employment. Of course, the methods they will apply for the same goal may be different. These different methods will create a unity by completing each other's deficiencies.

What Can the State Do?

1. The Turkish state, like every contemporary state, can determine the quota of students who will graduate according to population projections and potential employment areas, or rather the need-resource ratio. If quotas are unnecessarily inflated, the bloated graduates are added to the stock of the unemployed. Realistic medium and long-term development programs and plans can be made against this problem.
2. Government can implement correct and adequate economic policies in a way that sticks to these population-employment plans. "Fiscal policy" consisting of public expenditures and taxes, "monetary policy" consisting of money supply and interest, "control policy" regarding production and prices, as well as modern changes in the structure of political and bureaucratic institutions can be put into action with a holistic approach for "sustainable graduate employment".
3. The public sector, which is identified with the state, is preferred more than the private sector in Turkey. Because the concept of "father state" is strong in society. The state, like the father of the family, can implement an employment policy based on the principles of merit-justice, without discriminating between their children, that is, their citizens. Otherwise, he will not be considered a reliable and guarantor father.
4. The official employment agency (İş-Kur in Turkey) and private employment offices can be made more functional with the regulation and supervision of the

state. These institutions and offices can be given points and financial-monetary support according to the employment opportunities they provide.

5. With legal regulations, student loan and scholarship debts of graduates who cannot find a job can be deleted or postponed to a later date until a job is found.
6. Moreover, according to the current welfare state model, the unemployment insurance fund (ISF) can be expanded and strengthened to include unemployed graduates. ISF can be used not for company owners for profit reinforcement, but for graduates who urgently need a vital income.

What Can Business (Employers) Do?

1. In Turkey, private companies should not exploit the state (that is, the tax resources of the society) by immorality in public tenders, should not be tempted to bid by partisanship, and can create humane employment conditions as well as economic.
2. Cooperation platforms between university and economic sectors (agriculture, industry, services), technoparks and modern employment fairs can always keep their doors open to university students and graduates.
3. Appropriate loan programs can be opened to increase youth employment through cooperation between private sector and banks. It is known that micro-credits have important macroeconomic consequences. Here, an important responsibility falls on employment-friendly public banks. Almost all young graduates, regardless of region and gender, should be included in the micro-credit programs implemented only for women who want to start their business in the Southeastern Anatolia region in the recent past. In addition, the amount of micro-credit can be increased by taking into account inflation and other developing conditions.
4. The private sector should be prohibited from firing employees arbitrarily; unionized workforce should be respected, international labor law and ethics should be followed. In this context, the private sector can enter into employment competition with the state.

What Can Graduates Themselves Do?

1. Graduated youth in Turkey should never lose hope of getting a job; they can update their job applications and job successes without forgetting that they constitute the greatest potential dynamism of the national production economy and the strongest link in the supply chain.

2. Graduates can strengthen their school diplomas with various certificates (computer programming, foreign language courses, etc.). In this way, it will be easier for them to apply for and get a job at home or abroad.
3. If graduates cannot find a job in the public or private sector, which they idealize, they can start their own companies thanks to their special skills. Even through a one-man company, they can provide goods and services to both the public and private sectors.
4. Graduates can go to Anglo-Saxon and European countries by raising the target bar against the possibility of not being able to find a job in their own country or working in a job that is not suitable for their education and expectations. If this brain drain, of which there are examples, can be managed correctly, it can return to the country of origin as abundant worker remittances and high knowledge, manners and experience, which will create significant added value after a while.

What Can İnternational Organizations Do?

Since the causes and consequences of unemployment and graduate unemployment also have a global dimension, international organizations related to the solution of this problem have duties and responsibilities.

1. The relevant institutions (UN, EU, ILO, WB, IMF, etc.) of the superstructure can update the human rights regarding employment and contribute to the financing of the fight against unemployment in Turkey and similar developing countries. Especially, the World Bank (WB) can apply medium and long-term low interest loan programs to young entrepreneurs in countries that want to create jobs and employment. WB (2021) finances youth employment transformation projects in various countries around the world. It aims to improve employment services and labor market outcomes, especially for young people.
2. ILO can offer provocative incentives to and even pressure goverments that to find jobs for young people and improve working conditions for them. Namely: Employment-intensive public investment approaches to create instant employment; Skills development for better employability; Enabling environments for self-employment and micro, small and medium business and cooperative development; Employment services that bridge the gap between labor demand and supply; Interventions to rebuild trust in institutions, support social cohesion and protect work and human rights, etc. For this, the ILO's bundle of interventions, the Employment Services Convention and the Private Employment Agencies Convention are functional (Selva et al., 2021).

3. The European Union (EU) can encourage the candidate country of Turkey to adopt the modern norms of labour market and graduate youth who will be the first to enter and later enter the market, in the direction of job and employment reforms. The European Commission (EC, 2020) supports EU's member states in reducing youth unemployment and inactivity. The aim is to help young people develop their potential to shape the future of the EU and move the digital and green transitions forward. The EC urges member states to increase support for youth employment using the substantial funding available under the next generation EU and the future EU budget. For example, the EU can help fund: start-up grants and loans for young entrepreneurs, mentoring programs and business development centres, bonuses to small and medium-sized enterprises (SMEs) employing apprentices, training to acquire new skills needed in the labor market seminars, capacity building of public employment services, career management training in formal education, investments in digital learning infrastructure and technology, etc. Also, the new active and passive policies within the scope of the Lisbon strategy (EU-2020), which was started to be implemented by EC in 2010, can be taken as a guide. Turkey also partially implements these policies in the fight against unemployment.
4. A "Global Unemployed Fund" (GUF) and/or "Global Employment Bank" (GEB) can be established within the ILO for the unemployed all over the world, in which Turkey can be a stakeholder. The International Monetary Fund (IMF) and the WB may transfer a monetary share to such organizations according to the dues of the member states. A part of seigniorage revenues of central banks, revenues of international sports organizations and advertising revenues of media organizations can be allocated to this GUF / GEB. More importantly, progressive savings in high armament expenditures of developed and developing states can be a good and sustainable source of finance.

CONCLUSION

Remarkably, graduate unemployment in the world is growing with an uncontrolled and almost automatic trend. Employers chasing cheap wages may enjoy a surplus supply of graduates, but an unhappy majority remains. The world, which has become globalized with mainstream liberal capitalism, may revolve for a long time with deregulation-flexibilization practices in the labor market. It also revolves around the Sun, but it will always appear with its dark side to the graduates it left unemployed. Changing the mainstream regime may not come to mind for now, but all decision-making components of that regime should stop overinflating the graduate unemployment bubble. If the bubble of graduates waiting for jobs and food for a decent life bursts, the world may see the greater of the 1929 economic crisis. The thesis that technology is pushing people out of the labor market doesn't seem very convincing, which can only be an excuse to cover up mismanagement, because there are now employment-friendly technologies. If every stage of education and the distribution of resources and income are planned correctly and fairly, graduates can be included in that market despite the same technology according to their abilities and diplomas.

Starting from the fact that the unemployed graduates is a global problem, this study emphasized that Turkey's youth labor market is experiencing various problems, fluctuations and vulnerabilities. Youth unemployment rate is high in Turkey; it is known that this bad result is not independent of lack of planning or wrong central planning, but also fed by other macro-economic problems.

If Turkey wants to fight youth unemployment realistically and resolutely, she should not stray from her goal of production economy that offers wide opportunities and sufficient income for graduate employment. Once the unemployed graduates are employed in the production economy, they should not be allowed to become a part of the precariat class, thanks to effective economic policies and strong institutions.

This productive understanding will not contradict Turkey's evolution towards a consumer society identified with the Western welfare bar. Attention should be paid to the fact that factories, which have an important share in the production economy, produce with renewable energy and without polluting the nature. Otherwise, it will not be able to contribute much to the global climate change and sustainable development goals.

REFERENCES

African Development Bank. (2016). Chapter 5: Africa's youth in the labour market. In African Development Report 2015: Growth, Poverty and Inequality Nexus: Overcoming Barriers to Sustainable Development. Author.

Bell, D. N. F., & Blanchflower, D. G. (2010). *Youth Unemployment: Déjà Vu?* IZA Discussion Paper No. 4705.

CIA. (2021). *The World Factbook: Turkey*. Retrieved August 25, 2021, from https://www.cia.gov/the-world-factbook/ countries/turkey/ # economy

Çiftçi, T. (2021). Ya meslek lisesi ya da diplomalı işsizlik. *T24, 25.*

Eichhorst, W., & Tobsch, V. (2015). Not so standard anymore? Employment duality in Germany. *Journal for Labour Market Research, 48*(2), 81–95. doi:10.100712651-015-0176-7

European Commission. (2020). *Press release Commission launches Youth Employment Support: a bridge to jobs for the next generation.* Retrieved December 10, 20021, from https://ec.europa.eu/commission/presscorner/ detail/en/IP_20_1193

Felgueroso, F., & Jansen, M. (2015). The Youth Guarantee: Theory or reality? In J. J. Dolado (Ed.), *No Country for Young People? Youth Labour Market Problems in Europe* (pp. 129–137). CEPR Press.

Han, W., & Hart, J. (2021). Job Precarity and Economic Prospects During the COVID-19 Public Health Crisis. *Social Science Quarterly*, 1–18. doi:10.1111/ ssqu.13031

Harari, Y. N. (2018). *21 Lessons for the 21st Century*. Spiegel & Grau.

ILO. (2020). *Global Employment Trends for Youth 2020: Technology and the future of jobs*. International Labour Office. Retrieved December 10, 2021, from https:// www.ilo.org/wcmsp5/groups/ public/---dgreports/---dcomm/---publ/documents/ publication/ wcms_737648.pdf

Morris, E. (2006). *Globalization and its effects on youth employment trends in Asia.* Paper presented to the Regional Expert Group Meeting on Development challenges for young people, Bangkok, Thailand. Retrieved December 1, 2021, from https://www. un.org/esa/socdev/unyin/workshops/regm_ asia_ilo_elizabeth_morris_paper .pdf

Nazlıer, E. (2022). Eğitim sistemi… *Evrensel Gazetesi*. Retrieved February 2, 2022, from https://www.evrensel.net/ haber/453888/egitim-sisteminin-son

OECD. (2021). *Data: Unemployment rate by age group*. Retrieved August 31, 2021, from https://data.oecd.org/unemp/ unemployment-rate-by-age-group.htm#indicator-chart

OloweO. (2010). Graduate Unemployment and its Resultant Effects on Developing Economies. SSRN. doi:10.2139/ssrn.1457041

Salas-Velasco, M. (2021). Mapping the (mis)match of university degrees in the graduate labor market. *Journal for Labour Market Research, 55*(1), 14. doi:10.118612651-021-00297-x

Selva, E., & Negro, F. (2021). *Youth employment in conflict and fragile settings*. ILO.

Shi, L. P., Imdorf, C., Samuel, R., & Sacchi, S. (2018). How unemployment scarring affects skilled young workers: Evidence from a factorial survey of Swiss recruiters. *Journal for Labour Market Research, 52*(1), 7. doi:10.118612651-018-0239-7 PMID:30046769

Standing, G. (2011). *The Precariat: The New Dangerous Class*. Bloomsbury Academic.

TCMB. (2021). *İstatistikler*. Retrieved December 21, 2021, from https://www.tcmb.gov.tr/

The World Bank. (2021). *Youth Employment Transformation Initiative Project*. https://projects.world bank.org/en/projects-operations/project-detail/P160696

TÜİK. (2021). *İşgücü İstatistikleri*. Haziran, No: 37482.

Türk-İş. (2021). *Açlık ve Yoksulluk Sınırı*. Temmuz. Retrieved November 3, 2021, from http://www.turkis.org.tr/TEMMUZ-2021-ACLIK-VE-YOKSULLUK-SINIRI-d542757#sthash.nmRDQCzT.dpuf

Verd, J. M., Barranco, O., & Bolíbar, M. (2019). Youth unemployment and employment trajectories in Spain during the Great Recession: What are the determinants? *Journal for Labour Market Research*, *53*(1), 4. doi:10.118612651-019-0254-3

Zhang, L. (2018). What are the Causes and Consequences of Graduate Unemployment in China? *2nd International Conference on Modern Education and Information Technology (MEIT 2018)*.

KEY TERMS AND DEFINITIONS

Cost of Living: Means that purchasing power decreases in the face of inflation or that the wages of the fixed income class cannot catch up with the inflation rate.

Crony Capitalism: An artificial system in which the success of an economic enterprise in the guise of a liberal economy depends on the close relations between corporations and government.

Kleptocracy: Systematic robbing of a country's natural, human and financial resources by a family or political party or religious group that has seized power in a country, that is, planned and widespread corruption, in short, the thieves' regime.

Policy Interest Rate: The central bank's control of the money supply and short-term interest rates through official interest rates; the interest rate applied to one-week repo or monthly/annual bills and bonds.

APPENDIX

Basic Un/Employment Concepts:

1. *Total Labor Force population (L):* Employed (E) + Unemployed (U) population
2. *Employment level (E):* difference between L and U
3. *Unemployment level (U):* difference between L and E
4. *Labor force participation rate:* Percentage of L to non-institutional population (NICP).
5. *NICP:* except for the population aged 15+ who live in compulsory places such as hospitals, prisons, barracks, student and orphanages and are not involved in working life.
6. *Employment rate (e, %):* Percentage of L to NICP.
7. *Unemployment rate (u, %):* Percentage of U to NICP.
8. *Inactive workforce:* time-related underemployment + potential workforce + unemployed.
9. *Full employment:* full and complete use of L in the narrow sense and other factors of production (capital, natural resources, entrepreneurship, knowledge) in the broad sense.

Compilation of References

Monumental Motivation Statistics for 2021. (2021). *TeamStage*. Retrieved 13 September 2021, from https://teamstage.io/motivation-statistics/

Abass & Arfat. (2020). Threat perceptions towards entrepreneurship developments. *Pacific Business Review International*, *10*(October).

Abbasi, M. N., & Sarwat, N. (2014). Factors Inducing Career Choice: Comparative Study of Five Leading Professions in Pakistan. *Pakistan Journal of Commerce & Social Sciences*, *8*(3).

Absar, M. M. N., & Mahmood, M. (2011). New HRM practices in the public and private sector industrial enterprises of Bangladesh: A comparative assessment. *International Review of Business Research Papers*, *7*(2), 118–136.

Abu Rahim, M. A. R. (2021, March 24). Graduan perlu sokongan tingkat kebolehpasaran ketika pandemik. *Berita Harian*. https://www.klik.com.my/item/story/18776198/graduan-perlu-sokongan-tingkat-kebolehpasaran-ketika-pandemik

Abu Rahim, M. A. R., & Filippi, D. (2021). Ensuring Youth and Graduate Employability in an Uncertain Labour Market. Academic Press.

Abu Rahim, M. A. R., Wahab, D. A., & Jani, R. (2021). Labour market challenges amidst the Covid-19 crisis: addressing youth vulnerability. In A. Wahab, J. S. Chowdhury, S. H. Abu Bakar Ah, & M. R. Mohd Saad (Eds.), *Handbook of Research on the Impact of COVID-19 on Marginalized Populations and Support for the Future*. IGI Global. doi:10.4018/978-1-7998-7480-5.ch014

Acs, Z. J., Stam, E., Audretsch, D. B., & O'Connor, A. (2017). The lineages of the entrepreneurial ecosystem approach. *Small Business Economics*, *49*(1), 1–10. doi:10.100711187-017-9864-8

Acs, Z. J., & Szerb, L. (2007). Entrepreneurship, Economic Growth and Public Policy. *Small Business Economics*, *28*(2-3), 109–122. doi:10.100711187-006-9012-3

Adeeko, J. D. (2017). *Role of Entrepreneurship Education in the Ability of Students to Set up*. Academic Press.

Adetaya. (2019). *IT Entrepreneurship Technology Entrepreneurship: Trend, opportunities, challenges*. Academic Press.

Adeyemo, S. A. (2017). *Understanding and Acquisition of Entrepreneurial Skills: A Pedagogical Re-Orientation for Classroom Teacher.* University of Lagos.

African Development Bank. (2016). Chapter 5: Africa's youth in the labour market. In African Development Report 2015: Growth, Poverty and Inequality Nexus: Overcoming Barriers to Sustainable Development. Author.

Agarwala, T. (2008). Factors influencing career choice of management students in India. *Career Development International, 13*(4), 362–376. doi:10.1108/13620430810880844

Ahlstrom, D., Chang, A. Y., & Cheung, J. S. (2019). Encouraging entrepreneurship and economic growth. *Journal of Risk and Financial Management, 12*(4), 178. doi:10.3390/jrfm12040178

Ahmed, T., Chandran, V. G. R., & Klobas, J. (2017). Specialized entrepreneurship education: Does it really matter? Fresh evidence from Pakistan. *International Journal of Entrepreneurial Behaviour & Research, 23*(1), 4–19. doi:10.1108/IJEBR-01-2016-0005

Akinwale, Y. O., Ababtain, A. K., & Alaraifi, A. A. (2019). Structural equation model analysis of factors influencing entrepreneurial interest among university students in Saudi Arabia. *Journal of Entrepreneurship Education, 22*(4), 1–14.

Akosah-Twumasi, P., Emeto, T. I., Lindsay, D., Tsey, K., & Malau-Aduli, B. S. (2018, July). A systematic review of factors that influence youths career choices—The role of culture. *Frontiers in Education, 3*, 58. doi:10.3389/feduc.2018.00058

Alansari, H. A. (2011). Career choice, satisfaction, and perceptions about their professional image: A study of Kuwaiti librarians. *Library Review, 60*(7), 575–587. doi:10.1108/00242531111153597

Aldrich, H. E. (1990). Using ecological perspective to study organizational founding rates. *Entrepreneurship Theory and Practice, 14*(3), 7–24. doi:10.1177/104225879001400303

Alexandre, F., Bação, P., Carreira, C., Cerejeira, J., Loureiro, G., Martins, A., & Portela, M. (2017). *Investimento empresarial e o crescimento da economia portuguesa.* Fundação Calouste Gulbenkian.

Alfonso, A. (2019). Learning by doing in business education: Using Hackathon to improve the teaching and learning of entrepreneurial skills. *Journal of Entrepreneurship Education, 22*(1).

Alford, J., & Greve, C. (2017). Strategy in the public and private sectors: Similarities, differences and changes. *Administrative Sciences, 7*(4), 35. doi:10.3390/admsci7040035

Alika, H. (2012). Career choice in engineering: The influence of peers and parents implication for counselling. *College Student Journal, 46*(3), 537–542.

Alkema, P., Levitt, S., & Chen, J. (2017). *Agile and Hackathon: A case study of emergent practices at the FNB codefest.* . doi:10.1145/3129416.3129430

Altinay, L., Madanoglu, M., Daniele, R., & Lashley, C. (2012). The influence of family tradition and psychological traits on entrepreneurial intention. *International Journal of Hospitality Management, 31*(2), 489–499.

Altman, M., Mokomane, Z., & Wright, G. (2014). Social security for young people amidst high poverty and unemployment: Some policy options for South Africa. *Development Southern Africa, 31*(2), 347–362. doi:10.1080/0376835X.2013.873346

Alvarez-Galvan, J. (2015). *Organization for Economic Co-operation and Development review of vocational education and training: Skills beyond school review of Egypt. OECD. Accessed from* https://read.oecd-ilibrary.org/education/a-skills-beyond-school-review-ofegypt_9789264209626-en#page1

Alves, A. C., Fischer, B., Schaeffer, P. R., & Queiroz, S. (2019). Determinants of student entrepreneurship: An assessment on higher education institutions in Brazil. *Innovation & Management Review, 16*(2), 96–117. doi:10.1108/INMR-02-2018-0002

Alves, R. (2017). Portugal: A paradox in productivity. International Productivity Monitor. *Centre for the Study of Living Standards, 32*, 137–160.

Ampaire, A., Kajumba, M. M., & Muwagga, A. (2021). Do Students' Career Aspirations Predict their Career Choices? A Qualitative Survey of Advanced Level Secondary School Students in Uganda. *African Journal of Education. Science and Technology, 6*(3), 344–351.

Anandakrishnan, M. (2020). Employability and Entrepreneurship: Critical Twin Factors for India Higher Education. In Reimagining Indian Universities. AIU.

Andersen, L. B., Jensen, U. T., & Kjeldsen, A. M. (2021). Public service motivation and its implications for public service. The Palgrave Handbook of the Public Servant, 241-258.

Apple, M. W. (2014). *Official knowledge: Democratic education in a conservative age*. Routledge. doi:10.4324/9780203814383

Araújo, S. (2017). *Raising skills in Portugal*. OECD Economics Department Working Papers, No. 1405. OECD Publishing.

Ariyani, Dwi, Suyatno, and Zuhaery. (2020). Principal's entrepreneurial leadership in developing entrepreneurship at Magelang high school. *International Journal of Scientific and Technology Research, 9*, 1446–52.

Arshad, M., Farooq, O., & Farooq, M. (2019). The effect of intrinsic and extrinsic factors on entrepreneurial intentions: The moderating role of collectivist orientation. *Management Decision, 57*(3), 649–668. doi:10.1108/MD-04-2016-0248

Aslam, S., & Hasnu, S. A. F. (2016). Issues and constraints perceived by young entrepreneurs of Pakistan. *World Journal of Entrepreneurship, Management and Sustainable Development, 12*(1), 50–65. doi:10.1108/WJEMSD-03-2015-0015

Aubert-Taby, C., Escobar, O. R., & Rayna, T. (2018). *The impact of technological change on employment: The case of press digitalisation. Technological Forecasting and Social Change. Elsevier. Accessed from* www.sciencedirect.com/science//article/abs/pii/S0040162

Audretsch, D. B. (2004). Sustaining innovation and growth: Public policy support for entrepreneurship. *Industry and Innovation*, *11*(3), 167–191. doi:10.1080/1366271042000265366

Audretsch, D. B. (2007). Entrepreneurship capital and economic growth. *Oxford Review of Economic Policy*, *23*(1), 63–78. doi:10.1093/oxrep/grm001

Ausman, J., Javed, A., Ahmed, S., Samad, M. A., Pour, A. S., Mathew, E., ... Sreedharan, J. (2013). Social factors influencing career choice in a medical school in the United Arab Emirates. *Education in Medicine Journal*, *5*(1).

Auyeung, P., & Sands, J. (1997). Factors influencing accounting students' career choice: A cross-cultural validation study. *Accounting Education*, *6*(1), 13–23. doi:10.1080/096392897331596

Aycan, Z., & Fikret-Pasa, S. (2003). Career choices, job selection criteria, and leadership preferences in a transitional nation: The case of Turkey. *Journal of Career Development*, *30*(2), 129–144. doi:10.1177/089484530303000203

Ayyagari, M., Demirguc-Kunt, A., & Maksimovic, V. (2014). Who creates jobs in developing countries? *Small Business Economics*, *43*(1), 75–99. doi:10.100711187-014-9549-5

Azevedo, J. (2014). *Ensino profissional em Portugal, 1989-2014: os primeiros vinte e cinco anos de uma viagem que trouxe o ensino profissional da periferia para o centro das políticas educativas*. Mimeo.

Babaginda, M. M., & Semasinghe, D. M. (2013). *Entrepreneurship and unemployment: A literature review*. https://www.academia.edu/5322204/Entrepreneurship_and_Unemployment_A_Litrature_Review

Bacq, S., Ofstein, L. F., Kickul, J. R., & Gundry, L. K. (2017). Perceived entrepreneurial munificence and entrepreneurial intentions: A social cognitive perspective. *International Small Business Journal: Researching Entrepreneurship*, *35*(5), 639–659. doi:10.1177/0266242616658943

Bae, T. J., Qian, S., Chao Miao, C., & Fiet, J. O. (2014). The relationship between entrepreneurship education and entrepreneurial intentions: A meta-analytic review. Baylor University.

Bagonza, G., Kaahwa, M. G., & Mbabazi, E. G. (2021). Graduates Employability: Has the Expansion of the University Sector in Uganda improved Employment Prospects for Graduates? Employers and Lecturers Perspective. *International Journal of Educational Administration and Policy Studies*, *13*(1), 66–71. doi:10.5897/IJEAPS2021.0699

Bahareh, A. N., & Hossein, J. (2017). *Effective Approach toward Entrepreneurship*. Research paper in Senges's Learning Organization. Payame Noor University Iran.

Bai, L. (1998). Monetary reward versus the national ideological agenda: Career choice among Chinese university students. *Journal of Moral Education*, *27*(4), 525–540. doi:10.1080/0305724980270406

Bairagya, I. (2015). *Socio-Economic Determinants of Educated Unemployment in India*. Institute for Social and Economic Change.

Bakar, A. R. A., Ahmad, S. Z., Wright, N. S., & Skoko, H. (2017). The propensity to business start-up: Evidence from global entrepreneurship monitor (GEM) data in Saudi Arabia. *Journal of Entrepreneurship in Emerging Economies*, *9*(3), 263–285. doi:10.1108/JEEE-11-2016-0049

Balan, P., & Metcalfe, M. (2012). Identifying teaching methods that engage entrepreneurship students. *Education + Training*, *54*(5), 368–384. doi:10.1108/00400911211244678

Ballou, D. (2001). Pay for performance in public and private schools. *Economics of Education Review*, *20*(1), 51–61. doi:10.1016/S0272-7757(99)00060-6

Baluku, M. M., Onderi, P., & Otto, K. (2021). Predicting self-employment intentions and entry in Germany and East Africa: An investigation of the impact of mentoring, entrepreneurial attitudes, and psychological capital. *Journal of Small Business and Entrepreneurship*, *33*(3), 289–322. doi:10.1080/08276331.2019.1666337

Barbini, F. M., Corsino, M., & Giuri, P. (2021). How do universities shape founding teams? Social proximity and informal mechanisms of knowledge transfer in student entrepreneurship. *The Journal of Technology Transfer*, *46*(4), 1046–1082. doi:10.100710961-020-09799-1

Barnes, S. A., Bimrose, J., & Brown, A. (2006). *Older workers' careers: upskilling, reskilling and transitions*. Academic Press.

Barreneche, G. I. (2011). Language learners as teachers: Integrating service-learning and the advanced language course. *Hispania*, 103–120.

Basuroy. (2022). *Rate of Unemployment in India 2021 by Highest Education Level*. https://www.statista.com/statistics/1001039/india-unemployment-rate-by-education-level/

Bauboniene, Kyong, Puksas, & Malinauskiene. (2019). Factors influencing student entrepreneurship intentions: The case of Lithuanian and South Korean universities. *Journal of Entrepreneurship and Sustainability Issues*, *6*, 854–71.

Bazan, C., Shaikh, A., Frederick, S., Amjad, A., Yap, S., Finn, C., & Rayner, J. (2019). Effect of memorial university's environment & support system in shaping entrepreneurial intention of students. *Journal of Entrepreneurship Education*, *22*, 1–35.

Becker, G. S. (1975). *Human capital* (2nd ed.). University of Chicago Press.

Bell, D. N. F., & Blanchflower, D. G. (2010). *Youth Unemployment: Déjà Vu?* IZA Discussion Paper No. 4705.

Bellante, D., & Link, A. N. (1981). Are public sector workers more risk averse than private sector workers? *Industrial & Labor Relations Review*, *34*(3), 408–412. doi:10.1177/001979398103400307

Bellò, B., Mattana, V., & Loi, M. (2018). The power of peers: A new look at the impact of creativity, social context and self-efficacy on entrepreneurial intentions. *International Journal of Entrepreneurial Behaviour & Research*, *24*(1), 214–233. doi:10.1108/IJEBR-07-2016-0205

Bergami, R., Schüller, A., & Cheok, J. (2009). Building bridges through industry placements: Perceptions from Malaysian academics. *Journal of the Worldwide Forum on Education and Culture*, *1*(1), 50–61.

Beyhan, B., & Findik, D. (2018). Student and graduate entrepreneurship: Ambidextrous universities create more nascent entrepreneurs. *The Journal of Technology Transfer*, *43*(5), 1346–1374. doi:10.100710961-017-9590-z

Beynon, J., Toohey, K., & Kishor, N. (1998). Do visible minority students of Chinese and South Asian ancestry want teaching as a career?: Perceptions of some secondary school students in Vancouver, BC. *Canadian Ethnic Studies Journal*, *30*(2), 50–75.

Bhorat, H., & Kanbur, S. R. (Eds.). (2006). *Poverty and policy in post-apartheid South Africa*. HSRC press.

Biraglia, A., & Kadile, V. (2017). The role of entrepreneurial passion and creativity in developing entrepreneurial intentions: Insights from American homebrewers. *Journal of Small Business Management*, *55*(1), 170–188. doi:10.1111/jsbm.12242

Birch, C., Lichy, J., Mulholland, G., & Kachour, M. (2017). An enquiry into potential graduate entrepreneurship: Is higher education turning off the pipeline of graduate entrepreneurs? *Journal of Management Development*, *36*(6), 743–760. doi:10.1108/JMD-03-2016-0036

Bischoff, K. M., Gielnik, M. M., & Frese, M. (2020). When capital does not matter: How entrepreneurship training buffers the negative effect of capital constraints on business creation. *Strategic Entrepreneurship Journal*, *14*(3), 369–395. doi:10.1002ej.1364

Blaese, R., Noemi, S., & Brigitte, L. (2021). Should I Stay, or Should I Go? Job satisfaction as a moderating factor between outcome expectations and entrepreneurial intention among academics. *The International Entrepreneurship and Management Journal*, *17*(3), 1–30. doi:10.100711365-021-00744-8

Blakely-Gary, R. (2017). *Addressing the skills shortage in the construction sector.* https://probuildermag.co.uk/features/addressing-skills-shortage-construction-sector

Blanchflower, D. (2004). Self-employment: More May Not Be Better. *Swedish Economic Policy Review*, *11*(2), 15–74.

Blanco-Gonzalez, A., Mercado-Idoeta, C., & Prado-Roman, A. (2012). Perfil y motivacion de la juventud emprendedora espanola. *Revista de Estudios de Juventud*, *99*, 23–34.

Blank, R. M. (1985). An analysis of workers' choice between employment in the public and private sectors. *Industrial & Labor Relations Review*, *38*(2), 211–224. doi:10.1177/001979398503800204

Blenker, P., Korsgaard, S., Neergaard, H., & Thrane, C. (2011). The Questions We Care About: Paradigms and Progression in Entrepreneurship Education. *Industry and Higher Education, 25*(6), 417–427. doi:10.5367/ihe.2011.0065

Blesia, J. U., Iek, M., Ratang, W., & Hutajulu, H. (2019). Developing an entrepreneurship model to increase students' entrepreneurial skills: An action research project in a higher education institution in Indonesia. *Systemic Practice and Action Research, 34*(1), 53–70. doi:10.100711213-019-09506-8

Block, J. H., Hoogerheide, L., & Thurik, R. (2013). Education and entrepreneurial choice: An instrumental variables analysis. *International Small Business Journal, 31*(1), 23–33. doi:10.1177/0266242611400470

Bloom, D., Canning, D., & Sevilla, J. (2003). *The demographic dividend: A new perspective on the economic consequences of population change.* Rand Corporation. doi:10.7249/MR1274

Blume, B. D., Ford, J. K., Baldwin, T. T., & Huang, J. L. (2010). Transfer of training: A meta-analytic review. *Journal of Management, 36*(4), 1065–1105. doi:10.1177/0149206309352880

Blustein, D. L., Phillips, S. D., Jobin-Davis, K., Finkelberg, S. L., & Roarke, A. E. (1997). A theory-building investigation of the school-to-work transition. *The Counseling Psychologist, 25*(3), 364–402. doi:10.1177/0011000097253002

Bogenhold, D., & Staber, U. (1991). The Decline and Rise of Self-Employment. *Work, Employment and Society, 5*(2), 223–239. doi:10.1177/0950017091005002005

Booysen, L. (2017). Leadership Excellence across Cultural settings. In Leadership Excellence: Perspectives from the Front Line (pp. 31-51). KR Publishing.

Bourn, D. (2018). *Understanding global skills for 21st century professions.* Springer. doi:10.1007/978-3-319-97655-6

Bouzid, B. N. (2016). Dynamic relationship between corruption and youth unemployment: empirical evidences from a system GMM approach. *World Bank Policy Research Working Paper*, (7842). https://openknowledge.worldbank.org/handle/10986/25158

Boyne, G. A. (2002). Public and private management: What's the difference? *Journal of Management Studies, 39*(1), 97–122. doi:10.1111/1467-6486.00284

Breznitz, S., & Zhang, Q. (2019). Fostering the growth of student start-ups from university accelerators: An entrepreneurial ecosystem perspective. *Industrial and Corporate Change, 28*(4), 855–873. doi:10.1093/icc/dtz033

Bringle, R. G., & Hatcher, J. A. (1995). *A service-learning curriculum for faculty.* Academic Press.

Brown, D. (Ed.). (2002). *Career choice and development.* John Wiley & Sons.

Brown, J. S., Collins, A., & Duguid, P. (1989). Situated cognition and the culture of learning. *Educational Researcher, 18*(1), 32–42. doi:10.3102/0013189X018001032

Buckley, S. (2017). *Conceptualisations of Youth and Implications for Policy: A Study of Four Cases in Aotearoa/New Zealand*. Te Herenga Waka – Victoria University of Wellington.

Buelens, M., & Van den Broeck, H. (2007). An analysis of differences in work motivation between public and private sector organizations. *Public Administration Review*, *67*(1), 65–74. doi:10.1111/j.1540-6210.2006.00697.x

Burger, P. (2018). *Getting It Right: A New Economy for South Africa*. Review Publishing Company Ltd.

Busetto, L., Wick, W., & Gumbinger, C. (2020). How to use and assess qualitative research methods. *Neurol. Res. Pract.*, *2*, 14.

Business Tech. (2021). *Youth still find it difficult to secure jobs in South Africa.* http://www.statssa.gov.za/?p=14415

Butin, D. (2010). *Service-learning in theory and practice: The future of community engagement in higher education.* Springer. doi:10.1057/9780230106154

Caballero, G., Álvarez-González, P., & López-Miguens, M. J. (2020). How to promote the employability capital of university students? Developing and validating scales. *Studies in Higher Education*, *45*(12), 2634–2652. doi:10.1080/03075079.2020.1807494

Campos, F., Frese, M., Goldstein, M., Iacovone, L., Johnson, H. C., McKenzie, D., & Mensmann, M. (2017). Teaching personal initiative beats traditional training in boosting small business in West Africa. *Science*, *357*(6357), 1287–1290. doi:10.1126cience.aan5329 PMID:28935805

Cardon, M. S., Wincent, J., Singh, J., & Drnovsek, M. (2009). The nature and experience of entrepreneurial passion. *Academy of Management Review*, *34*(3), 511–532. doi:10.5465/amr.2009.40633190

Carpenter, P., & Foster, B. (1977). The career decisions of student teachers. *Education Research and Perspectives*, *4*(1), 23–33.

Cebekhulu, A. (2018). *Umhlaba Uyahlaba! The World is Thorny*. Reach Publishers.

Cebekhulu, A. (2018). *Umhlaba Uyahlaba! The World is Thorny. Wandabeck*. Reach publishers.

Cebrian, J. A., Bodega, M. I., & Martin, M. A. (2007). Inmigracion y creacion de empresas. In R. Dominguez-Martin (Ed.), *Inmigracion: crecimiento economico e integracion social* (pp. 147–166). Parlamento de Cantabria, Universidad de Cantabria.

Cerny, P. G. (2010). The competition state today: From raison d'État to raison du Monde. *Policy Studies*, *31*(1), 5–21. doi:10.1080/01442870903052801

CES. (2018). *Parecer do CES sobre o Programa Nacional de Reformas 2018 (PNR 2018)*. Conselho Económico e Social.

Chandler, G. N., & Hanks, S. H. (1998). An examination of the substitutability of founders human and financial capital in emerging business ventures. *Journal of Business Venturing, 13*(5), 353–369. doi:10.1016/S0883-9026(97)00034-7

Chankseliani, M., Keep, E., & Wilde, S. (2017). *People and Policy: A comprehensive study of apprenticeship across eight national contexts (Study)*. University of Oxford.

Chaudhury, N. (2020). A Comparative Study of Unemployment in India and USA. International Journal of Scientific and Research Publications, 10(12).

Chell, E. (2018). Review of Skill and the Entrepreneurial Process. *International Journal of Entrepreneurial Behaviour & Research, 19*(1), 6–31. doi:10.1108/13552551311299233

Chen, C. C., Greene, P. G., & Crick, A. (1998). Does entrepreneurial self-efficacy distinguish entrepreneurs from managers? *Journal of Business Venturing, 13*(4), 295–316. doi:10.1016/S0883-9026(97)00029-3

Cheng, G. H. L., Chan, D. K. S., & Au, W. T. (2020). Profiles of employability and their career and psychological implications among unemployed youth. *Applied Research in Quality of Life*, 1–15.

Cheng, M. Y., Chan, W. S., & Mahmood, A. (2009). The effectiveness of entrepreneurship education in Malaysia. *Education + Training, 51*(7), 555–566. doi:10.1108/00400910910992754

Chiarello, Fini, Ghiselli, Girotti, Meoli, & Sobrero. (2021). *Student and Graduate Entrepreneurship in Italy-Report 2020*. Academic Press.

Chimucheka, T. (2014). Entrepreneurship Education in South Africa. *Mediterranean Journal of Social Sciences, 5*(2), 403–416.

Chliova, M., Brinckmann, J., & Rosenbusch, N. (2015). Is microcredit a blessing for the poor? A meta-analysis examining development outcomes and contextual considerations. *Journal of Business Venturing, 30*(3), 467–487. doi:10.1016/j.jbusvent.2014.10.003

Cho, Y., Margolis, D. N., Newhouse, D., & Robalino, D. A. (2012). *Labor Markets in Low and Middle-Income Countries: Trends and Implications for Social Protection and Labor Policies.* https://openknowledge.worldbank.org/bitstream/handle/10986/13550/676130NWP012070Box367885B00PUBLIC0.pdf;sequence=1

Christopherson, S., & Clark, J. (2020). *Remaking regional economies: Power, labor, and firm strategies in the knowledge economy*. Routledge.

Chung, C. (2019, November 3). Gig economy a boost for women. *Sunday Star*. https://www.mef.org.my/MEFITN/Star191103a.pdf

CIA. (2021). *The World Factbook: Turkey*. Retrieved August 25, 2021, from https://www.cia.gov/the-world-factbook/ countries/turkey/ # economy

Çiftçi, T. (2021). Ya meslek lisesi ya da diplomalı işsizlik. *T24, 25*.

Clark, A., & Postel-Vinay, F. (2009). Job security and job protection. *Oxford Economic Papers*, *61*(2), 207–239. doi:10.1093/oep/gpn017

Clayton, P. H., Bringle, R. G., & Hatcher, J. A. (2013). *Research on service learning: Conceptual frameworks and assessment, Vol. 2B: Communities, institutions, and partnerships. Stylus.*

Clayton, P. H., Bringle, R. G., Senor, B., Huq, J., & Morrison, M. (2010). Differentiating and assessing relationships in service-learning and civic engagement: Exploitative, transactional, or transformational. *Michigan Journal of Community Service Learning*, *16*(2), 5–21.

Cloete, A. (2015). Youth unemployment in South Africa-a theological reflection through the lens of human dignity. *Missionalia: Southern African Journal of Mission Studies*, *43*(3), 513–525. doi:10.7832/43-3-133

Clutter, C. (2010). *The effects of parental influence on their children's career choices*. Academic Press.

Construction Education and Training Authority. (2019). https://static.pmg.org.za/CETA_APP_2019_2020.pdf

Cooper, S. L., & McArdle, S. (2017). *Preparing to Moot: A step-by-step guide to mooting*. Routledge. doi:10.4324/9781315713342

Cornyn, P., & Brewer, L. (2018). *Does workplace learning facilitate transitions to decent work?* ILO, Employment Working Paper (242). Accessed from: https://www.ilo.org/employment/Whatwedo/Publications/workingpapers/WCMS_635797/lang--en/index.htm.

Coursera. (2020). *Global Skills Index 2020*. www.coursera.org/gsi

Cross, C., & Ngandu, S. (2014). Youth unemployment dynamics in the labour market of the periphery. In State of the Nation (2014). South Africa 1994-2014: A twenty-year review (pp. 198-222). Cape Town: HSRC Press.

Cruz-González, J., López-Sáez, P., Navas-López, J. E., & Delgado-Verde, M. (2014). Directions of external knowledge search: Investigating their different impact on firm performance in high-technology industries. *Journal of Knowledge Management*, *18*(5), 847–866. doi:10.1108/JKM-06-2014-0243

Cuadrado-Roura, J. R. (Coord.). (2004). Empleo autonomo y empleo asalariado. Madrid: Subdireccion General de Publicaciones del Ministerio de Trabajo y Asuntos Sociales.

Dahir, A. (2016, August 17). *The number of tech hubs across Africa has more than doubled in less than a year*. https://qz.com/africa/759666/the-number-of-tech-hubs-across-africa-has-

Dahlstedt, M., & Hertzberg, F. (2012). Schooling entrepreneurs: Entrepreneurship, governmentality and education policy in Sweden at the turn of the millennium. *Journal of Pedagogy*, *3*(2), 242–262. doi:10.2478/v10159-012-0012-x

Davey, T., Plewa, C., & Struwig, M. (2011). Entrepreneurship perceptions and career intentions of international students. *Education + Training*, *53*(5), 335–352. doi:10.1108/00400911111147677

Davidsson, P., & Honig, B. (2003). The role of social and human capital among nascent entrepreneurs. *Journal of Business Venturing*, *18*(3), 301–331. doi:10.1016/S0883-9026(02)00097-6

Dawis, R. V. (2005). *The Minnesota Theory of Work Adjustment*. Academic Press.

De Beer, J., Armstrong, C., Ellis, M., & Kraemer-Mbula, E. (2017). *A scan of South Africa's maker movement*. Open African Innovation Research Working Paper.

De Kok, M. B. (2019). *Remedying unemployment through affirmative development: The validation of the prediction model and qualitative assessment of an employment accelerator programme* (Doctoral dissertation). Stellenbosch University.

De Mel, S., McKenzie, D. J., & Woodruff, C. (2009). Measuring microenterprise profits: Must we ask how the sausage is made? *Journal of Development Economics*, *88*(1), 19–31. doi:10.1016/j.jdeveco.2008.01.007

De Mel, S., McKenzie, D., & Woodruff, C. (2008). Returns to capital in microenterprises: Evidence from a field experiment. *The Quarterly Journal of Economics*, *123*(4), 1329–1372. doi:10.1162/qjec.2008.123.4.1329

de Moraes, G. H. S. M., Iizuka, E. S., & Pedro, M. (2018). Effects of Entrepreneurial Characteristics and University Environment on Entrepreneurial Intention. *Revista de Administração Contemporânea*, *22*(2), 226–248. doi:10.1590/1982-7849rac2018170133

Delmar, F., & Holmquist, C. (2004). Women's entrepreneurship: issues and policies. 2nd Organization for Economic Cooperation and Development (OECD) Conference of Ministers Responsible for SMEs, Promoting Entrepreneurship, and Innovative SMEs in a Global Economy. doi:10.1080/02673843.2006.9747970

Deloitte & Aspen Institute. (2018). *A Guide to Upskilling America's Frontline Workers*. https://assets.aspeninstitute.org/content/uploads/2018/03/Upskilling_Employer_Handbook_042015.pdf

Department of Economic Development. (2019/20). *Estimates of Provincial Revenue and Expenditure*. Gauteng Provincial Treasury.

Department of Higher Education and Training. (2020). *Apprenticeship of the 21st Century A1. Department of Higher Education and Training*. Government Printers.

Department of Public Works. (2017). *Capacity Building Programme*. http://www.publicworks.gov.za/prof-services-new.html

Department of Public Works. (2020). *Public Works welcomes Cuban Technical Advisors*. http://www.publicworks.gov.za/prof-services-new.html

Department of Statistics Malaysia. (2021a). *Graduate Statistics 2020*. Author.

Department of Statistics Malaysia. (2021b). *Labour Force Survey Report 2020*. Department of Statistics, Malaysia. https://www.statistics.gov.my/portal/download_Labour/files/labour_force/Labour_Force_Survey_Report_Malaysia_2013.pdf

Department of Statistics Malaysia. (2021c). Labour Market Review. In Economic & Labour Market Review (Vol. Q2). Author.

Department of Statistics Malaysia. (2021d). Labour Market Review. In First Quarter 2021. Author.

Department of Statistics Malaysia. (2021e). *Principal Statistics of Labour Force, 1982-2020*. Department of Statistics Malaysia. https://www.dosm.gov.my/v1/uploads/files/3_Time Series/LFS_1982-2018/01.TABLE_1.pdf

Deuchar, A., & Dyson, J. (2019). Between unemployment and enterprise in neoliberal India: educated youth creating work in the private education sector. *Transactions of the Institute of British Geographers*. wileyonlinelibrary.com/journal/tran

DGERT. (2016). *Vocational education and training in Europe: Portugal*. CEDEFOP Refernet VET in Europe reports.

Dhiliwayyo, S., & Vuuren, V. (2019). Evolution View of Entrepreneurial Mindset Theory. *International Journal of Business and Social Science*, *10*(6). Advance online publication. doi:10.30845/ijbss.v10n6p13

Diphoko, W. (2018 June 20). *Why every university needs a start-up hub?* https://www.iol.co.za/business-report/opinion/opinion-why-every-university-needs-a-start-up-hub-15747518

Dixit, J. K., Tiwari, P., Gupta, S. K., Singh, P., & Gupta, H. (2011). Educated Unemployment: A Challenge before Sustainable Education, Sustainable Manufacturing. In *Proc. of the International Conference on Sustainable Manufacturing: Issues, Trends and Practices (ICSM – 2011)*. BITS.

Dlamini, S., & Bimha, H. (2017). The effectiveness of youth entrepreneurship programmes in enhancing an entrepreneurial culture in Swaziland. *IOSR Journal of Research & Method in Education*, *7*(3), 73–82.

Dludla, S. (2019). *At least 6.7 million South Africans jobless with unemployment rate at an 11-year high*. Academic Press.

Dodgson & Gann. (2020). *Philanthropy, Innovation and Entrepreneurship*. Springer Books.

Dörner, N., Morhart, F., Gassmann, O., & Tomczak, T. (2011). Inter-institutional collaboration for new integrative teaching programs. *On the Horizon*, *19*(3), 217–225. doi:10.1108/10748121111163922

Douglas, P. S., Rzeszut, A. K., Merz, C. N. B., Duvernoy, C. S., Lewis, S. J., Walsh, M. N., & Gillam, L. (2018). Career preferences and perceptions of cardiology among US internal medicine trainees: Factors influencing cardiology career choice. *JAMA Cardiology*, *3*(8), 682–691. doi:10.1001/jamacardio.2018.1279 PMID:29847674

Drummond, M. P., Thakoor, V., & Yu, S. (2014). *Africa rising: harnessing the demographic dividend*. International Monetary Fund.

Dufour, M., & Jacq, L. (2017). *Engagement of young graduates in Entrepreneurship: Entrepreneurship*. Strategy and Business Development.

Duraipandian & Kumar. (2021). Entrepreneurship development factors which have impact on profit of IT entrepreneurship. *Psychology and Education Journal, 58*(1). doi:10.17762/pae.v58i1.2175

Dweck, C. (2017). *Mindset: The New Psychology of Success, Self-theory, Mindset: Key Takeaways*. Stanford University.

Edvardsson Stiwne, E. (2005). *The first year as Engineering Students-the experiences of four cohorts of engineering students in Applied Physics and Electrical Engineering in Linkoping University*. Academic Press.

Eichhorst, W., & Tobsch, V. (2015). Not so standard anymore? Employment duality in Germany. *Journal for Labour Market Research, 48*(2), 81–95. doi:10.100712651-015-0176-7

Eliasson, K., & Westlund, H. (2013). Attributes influencing self-employment propensity in urban and rural Sweden. *The Annals of Regional Science, 50*(2), 479–514. doi:10.100700168-012-0501-9

Eller, F. J., Gielnik, M. M., Yeves, J., Alvarado, Y. C., & Guerrero, O. A. (in press). Adjusting the Sails: Investigating the Feedback Loop of the Opportunity Development Process in Entrepreneurship Training. *Academy of Management Learning & Education*. doi:10.5465/amle.2020.0041

Emmanuel, O. O., & Daniya, A. A. (2017). Development of small and Medium Scale Enterprises. *Arabian Journal of Business and Management Review., 1*(7), 2.

Emuze, F., van Eeden, L., & Geminiani, F. (2015). Causes and effects of building collapse: A case study in South Africa. *Proceedings CIB W099 Belfast 2015*, 408.

Er, B., Şahin, Y. E., & Mutlu, M. (2015). Alternative Sources of Financing for Entrepreneurs. *Present Situation and Recommendations, 1*(1), 31–54.

Eurobarometer. (2012). *Entrepreneurship Survey of the EU*. Flash EB Series 354.

Eurofound. (2017). *Sixth European Working Conditions Survey – Update*. Eurofound.

European Commission. (2013). *Entrepreneurship Education: A Guide for Educators*. Author.

European Commission. (2020). *Press release Commission launches Youth Employment Support: a bridge to jobs for the next generation*. Retrieved December 10, 20021, from https://ec.europa.eu/commission/presscorner/ detail/en/IP_20_1193

Evans, D. S., & Leighton, L. (1990). Small Business Formation by Unemployed and Employed Workers. *Small Business Economics, 2*(4), 319–330. doi:10.1007/BF00401628

Evans, D., & Leighton, L. (1989). Some empirical aspects of entrepreneurship. *The American Economic Review, 79*, 519–535.

ExpertHub Staff. (2019, May 14). *SA Startups Compete For R10m In The ANDZA Entrepreneur Competition*. https://www.experthub.info/news/experthub-today/introducing-the-andza-entrepreneur-competition/

Eyler, J., Giles, D. E., Jr., Stenson, C. M., & Gray, C. J. (2001). At a glance: What we know about the effects of service-learning on college students, faculty, institutions and communities. *Higher Education*. 139. https://digitalcommons.unomaha.edu/slcehighered/139

Farnam, J. (2018). *4 ways universities are Driving Innovation*. https://www.weforum.org

Farstad, H. (2002). *Integrated entrepreneurship education in Botswana, Uganda and Kenya. World Bank*. National Institute of Technology.

Fatoki, O., & Chindoga, L. (2011). An investigation into the obstacles to youth entrepreneurship in South Africa. *International Business Research*, *4*(2), 161–169. doi:10.5539/ibr.v4n2p161

Fayolle, A., Klandt, H. (2006). Issues and newness in the field of entrepreneurship education: new lenses for new practical and academic questions. *International Entrepreneurship Education*, 1-17.

Fayolle, A., Gailly, B., & Lassas-Clerc, N. (2006b). Assessing the impact of entrepreneurship education programmes: A new methodology. *Journal of European Industrial Training*, *30*(9), 701–720. doi:10.1108/03090590610715022

Federation of Kenya Employers. (2018a). *Skills Mismatch Survey*. Retrieved from: https://www.fke-kenya.org/

Fejes, A., Nylund, M., & Wallin, J. (2018). How do Teachers Interpret and Transform Entrepreneurship Education? *Journal of Curriculum Studies*, *51*(4), 554–566. doi:10.1080/00220272.2018.1488998

Feld, B. (2012). *Startup communities: Building an entrepreneurial ecosystem in your city*. Wiley. doi:10.1002/9781119204459

Felgueroso, F., & Jansen, M. (2015). The Youth Guarantee: Theory or reality? In J. J. Dolado (Ed.), *No Country for Young People? Youth Labour Market Problems in Europe* (pp. 129–137). CEPR Press.

Felton, S., Buhr, N., & Northey, M. (1994). Factors influencing the business student's choice of a career in chartered accountancy. *Issues in Accounting Education*, *9*(1), 131.

Fernández-Esquinas, M., Merchán-Hernández, C., & Valmaseda-Andía, O. (2016). How effective are interface organizations in the promotion of university-industry links? Evidence from a regional innovation system. *European Journal of Innovation Management*, *19*(3), 424–442. doi:10.1108/EJIM-07-2013-0068

Ferry, N. M. (2006). Factors influencing career choices of adolescents and young adults in rural Pennsylvania. *Journal of Extension*, *44*(3), 1–6.

Filser, M., Tiberius, V., Kraus, S., Zeitlhofer, T., Kailer, N., & Müller, A. (2020). Opportunity Recognition: Conversational Foundations and Pathways Ahead. *Entrepreneurship Research Journal*, *0*(0), 20200124. Advance online publication. doi:10.1515/erj-2020-0124

Fischer, B. B., de Moraes, G. H. S. M., & Schaeffer, P. R. (2019). Universities' institutional settings and academic entrepreneurship: Notes from a developing country. *Technological Forecasting and Social Change*, *147*, 243–252. doi:10.1016/j.techfore.2019.07.009

Flecky, K., & Gitlow, L. (2009). *Service-Learning in Occupational Therapy Education: Philosophy & Practice*. Jones & Bartlett Publishers.

Flisi, S., Goglio, V., Meroni, E. C., Rodrigues, M., & Vera-Toscano, E. (2017). Measuring Occupational Mismatch: Overeducation and Overskill in Europe—Evidence from PIAAC. *Social Indicators Research*, *131*(3), 1211–1249. doi:10.100711205-016-1292-7

Forrest, C., & Jali, P. (2012). *LED is a young person's game: youth employment and local economic development*. http://www.durban.gov.za/City_Services/Economic_Development/PSIR/Documents/Skills@ Work%20FINAL%20Vol5.pdf

Fossen, F. M., & Buttner, T. J. (2013). The returns to education for opportunity entrepreneurs, necessity entrepreneurs, and paid employees. *Economics of Education Review*, *37*, 66–84. doi:10.1016/j.econedurev.2013.08.005

Fouad, N. A., Kantamneni, N., Smothers, M. K., Chen, Y. L., Fitzpatrick, M., & Terry, S. (2008). Asian American career development: A qualitative analysis. *Journal of Vocational Behavior*, *72*(1), 43–59. doi:10.1016/j.jvb.2007.10.002

Fourie, F. (2011). *The South African unemployment debate: Three worlds, three discourses?* Academic Press.

Frese, M., & Zapf, D. (1994). Action as the core of work psychology: A German approach. Handbook of Industrial and Organizational Psychology, 4(2), 271-340.

Frese, M. (2009). *Toward a psychology of entrepreneurship: An action theory perspective*. Now Publishers Inc.

Frese, M., Gielnik, M. M., & Mensmann, M. (2016). Psychological training for entrepreneurs to take action: Contributing to poverty reduction in developing countries. *Current Directions in Psychological Science*, *25*(3), 196–202. doi:10.1177/0963721416636957

Frese, M., Kring, W., Soose, A., & Zempel, J. (1996). Personal initiative at work: Differences between East and West Germany. *Academy of Management Journal*, *39*(1), 37–63.

Fugate, M., Kinicki, A. J., & Ashforth, B. E. (2004). Employability: A psycho-social construct, its dimensions, and applications. *Journal of Vocational Behavior*, *65*(1), 14–38. doi:10.1016/j.jvb.2003.10.005

Funken, R., Gielnik, M. M., & Foo, M. D. (2020). How can problems be turned into something good? The role of entrepreneurial learning and error mastery orientation. *Entrepreneurship Theory and Practice*, *44*(2), 315–338. doi:10.1177/1042258718801600

Gabris, G. T., & Simo, G. (1995). Public sector motivation as an independent variable affecting career decisions. *Public Personnel Management*, *24*(1), 33–51. doi:10.1177/009102609502400103

Gammarano, R. (2020, August 18). Education pays off, but you have to be patient. *ILO STAT spotlight on work statistics*. https://ilostat.ilo.org/education-pays-off-but-you-have-to-be-patient/

Garavan, T. N., & O'Cinneide, B. (1994). Entrepreneurship education and training programmes: A review and evaluation-Part 1. *Journal of European Industrial Training*, *18*(8), 3–12. doi:10.1108/03090599410068024

Gati, I., & Saka, N. (2001). High school students' career-related decision-making difficulties. *Journal of Counseling and Development*, *79*(3), 331–340. doi:10.1002/j.1556-6676.2001.tb01978.x

Geekulcha. (2020). *Home of the Geeks*. https://www.geekulcha.dev/

GEM. (2010). *Informe ejecutivo 2010 Espana*. GEM Espana.

GEM. (2020). *Global Entrepreneurship Monitor 2019-2020*. London: Global Entrepreneurship Research Association.

GEM. (2020). *Global Report 2020-2021*. Global Entrepreneurship Research Association, London Business School.

Genesca-Garrigosa, E., & Veciana-Verges, J. M. (1984). Actitudes hacia la creacion de empresas. *Informacion Comercial Espanola*, *611*, 147–155.

George, C. (2015). Retaining professional workers: What makes them stay? *Employee Relations*, *37*, 102–121. doi:10.1108/ER-10- 2013-0151

Gheorghe, N., & Georgeta, N. L. (2013). The Entrepreneurship, an Actual Challenge for the Young Graduates of Higher Education Institutions. *Ovidius University Annals, Series Economic Sciences*, *13*(1).

Giaccone, S. C., & Longo, M. C. (2016). Insights on the innovation hub's design and management. *International Journal of Technology Marketing*, *11*(1), 97. doi:10.1504/IJTMKT.2016.073318

Gielnik, M. M., Bledow, R., & Stark, M. S. (2020). A dynamic account of self-efficacy in entrepreneurship. *The Journal of Applied Psychology*, *105*(5), 487–505. doi:10.1037/apl0000451 PMID:31535872

Gielnik, M. M., & Frese, M. (2013). Entrepreneurship and poverty reduction: Applying IO psychology to microbusiness and entrepreneurship in developing countries. In J. Olson-Buchanan, L. Koppes Bryan, & L. Foster Thompson (Eds.), *Using I-O Psychology for the Greater Good: Helping those who Help Others* (pp. 394–438). Routledge, Taylor and Francis.

Gielnik, M. M., Frese, M., Bischoff, K. M., Muhangi, G., & Omoo, F. (2016). Positive impact of entrepreneurship training on entrepreneurial behavior in a vocational training setting. *Africa Journal of Management*, *2*(3), 330–348. doi:10.1080/23322373.2016.1206804

Gielnik, M. M., Frese, M., Kahara-Kawuki, A., Wasswa Katono, I., Kyejjusa, S., Ngoma, M., Munene, J., Namatovu-Dawa, R., Nansubuga, F., Orobia, L., Oyugi, J., Sejjaaka, S., Sserwanga, A., Walter, T., Bischoff, K. M., & Dlugosch, T. J. (2015). Action and action-regulation in entrepreneurship: Evaluating a student training for promoting entrepreneurship. *Academy of Management Learning & Education*, *14*(1), 69–94. doi:10.5465/amle.2012.0107

Gielnik, M. M., Uy, M. A., Funken, R., & Bischoff, K. M. (2017). Boosting and sustaining passion: A long-term perspective on the effects of entrepreneurship training. *Journal of Business Venturing*, *32*(3), 334–353. doi:10.1016/j.jbusvent.2017.02.003

Glaub, M. E., Frese, M., Fischer, S., & Hoppe, M. (2014). Increasing personal initiative in small business managers or owners leads to entrepreneurial success: A theory-based controlled randomized field intervention for evidence-based management. *Academy of Management Learning & Education*, *13*(3), 354–379. doi:10.5465/amle.2013.0234

Gokuladas, V. K. (2010). Factors that influence first-career choice of undergraduate engineers in software services companies: A south Indian experience. *Career Development International*, *15*(2), 144–165. doi:10.1108/13620431011040941

Goppers, K., & Cuong, M. T. (2007). *Business training for entrepreneurs in Vietnam: An evaluation of the Sida-supported Start and Improve Your Business (SIYB) project*. Sida. https://www.ilo.org/wcmsp5/groups/public/---ed_emp/---emp_ent/---ifp_seed/documents/publication/wcms_143285.pdf

Gorman, G., & King, W. (2017). *Research Perspectives on Entrepreneurship Education, Enterprise Education and Education for Small Business Management*: A ten year literature review. *International Small Business Journal*, *15*(3), 56–77. doi:10.1177/0266242697153004

Gottfredson, L. S. (2005). Using Gottfredson's theory of circumscription and compromise in career guidance and counseling. *Career development and counseling: Putting theory and research to work*, 71-100.

Gouveia & Fernandes. (2017). *Structural reforms and long-term growth – a model based analysis*. Article GPEARI 05/2017.

Gouveia, A., Santos, S., & Gonçalves, I. (2017). *The impact of structural reforms on productivity: the role of the distance to the technological frontier*. OECD Productivity Working Papers, 2017-08. Paris: OECD Publishing.

Government of India. (2020-2021). *Annual Report*. NITI Ayog. https://www.niti.gov.in/sites/default/files/2021-02/Annual-Report2020-2021-English_0.pdf

Graham, L., & Mlatsheni, C. (2015). Youth unemployment in South Africa: Understanding the challenge and working on solutions. *South African Child Gauge, 2*, 51-59.

Guardian. (2017). *What jobs will still be around in 20 years? Read this to prepare your future.* https://www.theguardian.com

Gubik, A. S., & Farkas, S. (2016). Student Entrepreneurship in Hungary: Selected Results Based on GUESSS Survey. *Entrepreneurial Business and Economics Review*, *4*(4), 123–139. doi:10.15678/EBER.2016.040408

Gundling, E., Caldwell, C., & Cvitkovich, K. (2016). Global talent: Beyond outsourcing. In Advances in global leadership (pp. 353–374). http: //doi. org/ doi:10.1108/S1535-120320160000009025

Gupta, M., & Pushkar. (2020). *Why India should Worry about its Educated but Unemployed Youth.* Global Development Commons. https://gdc.unicef.org/resource/why-india-should-worry-about-its-educated-unemployed-youth

Gupta, V. K., Turban, D. B., Wasti, S. A., & Sikdar, A. (2009). The role of gender stereotypes in perceptions of entrepreneurs and intentions to become an entrepreneur. *Entrepreneurship Theory and Practice*, *33*(2), 397–417. doi:10.1111/j.1540-6520.2009.00296.x

Gwija, S. A., Eresia-Eke, C., & Iwu, C. G.Chux Gervase Iwu. (2014). Challenges and Prospects of Youth Entrepreneurship Development in a Designated Community in the Western Cape, South Africa. *Journal of Economics and Behavioral Studies*, *6*(1), 10–20. doi:10.22610/jebs.v6i1.465

Hall, S. (2017). *Youth employment in Kenya.* British Council. Retrieved from: https://www.britishcouncil.co.ke/

Han, W., & Hart, J. (2021). Job Precarity and Economic Prospects During the COVID-19 Public Health Crisis. *Social Science Quarterly*, 1–18. doi:10.1111/ssqu.13031

Handley, A. (2016). Cui Bono? A Political-Economy Assessment of 20 Years of South African Freedom. In T. Kepe, M. Levin, & B. von Lieres (Eds.), *Domain of Freedom: Justice, Citizenship and Social Change in South Africa* (pp. 61–83). UCT Press.

Harambee. (n.d.). https://harambee.co.za/harambee/

Harari, Y. N. (2018). *21 Lessons for the 21st Century*. Spiegel & Grau.

Harel, G. H., & Tzafrir, S. S. (2001). HRM practices in the public and private sectors: Differences and similarities. *Public Administration Quarterly*, 316–355.

Hassan, N. A. (2020). University business incubators as a tool for accelerating entrepreneurship: Theoretical perspective. *Review of Economics and Political Science*. doi:10.1108/REPS-10-2019-0142

Hayter, C. S., Nelson, A. J., Zayed, S., & O'Connor, A. C. (2018). Conceptualizing academic entrepreneurship ecosystems: A review, analysis and extension of the literature. *The Journal of Technology Transfer*, *43*(4), 1039–1082. doi:10.100710961-018-9657-5

Hegarty, C., & Porter, S. (2018). Rediscovering Enterprise: Developing appropriate University Entrepreneurship Education. *Education + Training*, *5*.

Henry, C., Hill, F., & Leitch, C. (2019). Entrepreneurship Education and Training: Can Entrepreneurship be Taught? Part 1. *Education + Training*, *47*(2), 98–111. doi:10.1108/00400910510586524

Hermanto, B., & Suryanto, S. E. (2017). Entrepreneurship ecosystem policy in Indonesia. *Mediterranean Journal of Social Sciences*, *8*(1), 110–110. doi:10.5901/mjss.2017.v8n1p110

Hicks, J., & Buccus, I. (2016). Public participation in South Africa: Strengthening state accountability in a dominant system. In State, governance and Development in Africa (pp. 100-120). Lansdown: UCT Press.

Hinga, J. (2021, May 10). *Service-based learning: Going beyond academics*. Strathmore University Business School. Retrieved February 1, 2022, from https://sbs.strathmore.edu/service-based-learning-going-beyond-academics/

Hockerts, K. (2017). Determinants of social entrepreneurial intentions. *Entrepreneurship Theory and Practice*, *41*(1), 105–130. doi:10.1111/etap.12171

Hofstede, G. (1980). Culture's Consequences: International Differences in Work-Related Values. Academic Press.

Hogan, R., Chamorro-Premuzic, T., & Kaiser, R. B. (2013). Employability and career success: Bridging the gap between theory and reality. *Industrial and Organizational Psychology: Perspectives on Science and Practice*, *6*(1), 3–16. doi:10.1111/iops.12001

Hogan, R., & Sherman, R. A. (2019). New (ish) directions for vocational interests research. In *Vocational Interests in the Workplace* (pp. 189–204). Routledge. doi:10.4324/9781315678924-10

Holienka, M., Gál, P., & Kovačičová, Z. (2017). Drivers of student entrepreneurship in Visegrad four countries: Guesss evidence. *Central European Business Review*, *6*(2), 54–63. doi:10.18267/j.cebr.180

Holland, J. L. (1997). *Making vocational choices: A theory of vocational personalities and work environments*. Psychological Assessment Resources.

Honwana, A. (2013). *The Time of Youth; Works, social Change and Politics in Africa*. Kumarian Press.

Honwana, A. (2013). *Youth and revolution in Tunisia*. Zed Books Ltd.

Hood, K. M., Robles, M., & Hopkins, C. D. (2014). Personal branding and social media for students in today's competitive job market. *The Journal of Research in Business Education, 56*(2), 33.

Hoppe, M. (2016). Policy and entrepreneurship education. *Small Business Economics*, *46*(1), 13–29. doi:10.100711187-015-9676-7

Hossain, A., Zaman, K. N. A., & Nuseibeh, R. (2009). Factors influencing women business development in the developing countries. *The International Journal of Organizational Analysis*, *17*(3), 202–224. doi:10.1108/19348830910974923

Howard, J. (2001). *Michigan journal of community service learning. In Service-learning Course Design Workbook*. OCSL Press.

HRSC. (2014). *R&D outlook in South Africa is improving, but not yet at the country's full potential.* http://www.hsrc.ac.za/en/media-briefs/cestii/research-and-development

Huber, L. R., Sloof, R., & Van Praag, M. (2014). The effect of early entrepreneurship education: Evidence from a field experiment. *European Economic Review, 72*, 76–97. doi:10.1016/j.euroecorev.2014.09.002

Humburg, M., & van der Velden, R. (2015). Skills and the graduate recruitment process: Evidence from two discrete choice experiments. *Economics of Education Review, 49*, 24–41. doi:10.1016/j.econedurev.2015.07.001

Ibidunni, A. S., Mozie, D., & Adebanji Wlliam, A. A. A. (2020). Entrepreneurial characteristics amongst university students: Insights for understanding entrepreneurial intentions amongst youths in a developing economy. *Education + Training, 63*(1), 71–84. doi:10.1108/ET-09-2019-0204

ILO. (2019). *Skills and jobs mismatches in low- and middle-income countries.* https://www.ilo.org/

ILO. (2020). *Global Employment Trends for Youth 2020: Technology and the future of jobs.* International Labour Office. Retrieved December 10, 2021, from https://www.ilo.org/wcmsp5/groups/ public/---dgreports/---dcomm/---publ/documents/publication/ wcms_737648.pdf

Ilonen, S., Heinonen, J., & Stenholm, P. (2018). Identifying and understanding entrepreneurial decision-making logics in entrepreneurship education. *International Journal of Entrepreneurial Behaviour & Research, 24*(1), 59–80. doi:10.1108/IJEBR-05-2017-0163

Institute for Labour Market Information and Analysis. (n.d.). *Youth Unemployment.* Retrieved July 13, 2021, from https://www.ilmia.gov.my/index.php/en/dashboard-datamart/kilm/indicators/youth-unemployment

International Labour Office. (2020). *Global Employment Trends for Youth 2020: Technology and the future of jobs.* International Labour Office. https://www.ilo.org/wcmsp5/groups/public/---dgreports/---dcomm/---publ/documents/publication/wcms_737648.pdf

International Labour Office. (2021). *World Employment and Social Outlook: Trends 2021.* International Labour Office. https://www.ilo.org/wcmsp5/groups/public/---dgreports/---dcomm/---publ/documents/publication/wcms_795453.pdf

International Labour Organisation. (2021). *ILO: Uncertain and uneven recovery expected following unprecedented labour market crisis.* Retrieved from: https://www.google.com/url?sa=t&rct=j&q=&esrc=s&source=web&cd=&cad=rja&uact=8&ved=2ahUKEwi4ye-ll_vyAhXMBd4KHesIB8EQFnoECAMQAQ&url=https%3A%2F%2Fwww.ilo.org%2Fglobal%2Fabout-the-ilo%2Fnewsroom%2Fnews%2FWCMS_766949%2Flang--en%2Findex.htm&usg=AOvVaw3ZVMIEv6xCHRQHC8i8wSjg

Isenberg, D. J. (2010). How to start an entrepreneurial revolution. *Harvard Business Review, 88*(6), 41–50.

Iwu, C. G., Opute, P. A., Nchu, R., Eresia-Eke, C., Tengeh, R. K., Jaiyeoba, O., & Aliyu, O. A. (2021). Entrepreneurship education, curriculum and lecturer-competency as antecedents of student entrepreneurial intention. *International Journal of Management Education, 19*(1), 100295. doi:10.1016/j.ijme.2019.03.007

Jackson, D. (2018). Developing graduate career readiness in Australia: Shifting from extra-curricular internships to work-integrated learning. *International Journal of Work-Integrated Learning, 19*(1), 23–35.

Jacobs, J. E., Chhin, C. S., & Bleeker, M. M. (2006). Enduring links: Parents' expectations and their young adult children's gender-typed occupational choices. *Educational Research and Evaluation, 12*(4), 395–407. doi:10.1080/13803610600765851

Jacoby, B. (1996). Service-learning in higher education: concepts and practices. Jossey-Bass Publishers.

Jain, A. K., & Sullivan, S. (2019). An examination of the relationship between careerism and organizational commitment, satisfaction, and performance. *Personnel Review, 49*(8), 1553–1571. doi:10.1108/PR-05-2019-0280

Jakubczak, J. (2015). Youth entrepreneurship barriers and role of education in their overcoming-pilot study. *Managing Intellectual capital management, and innovation for sustainable knowledge and learning and inclusive society*, 1775-1782.

Jamil, M. I. M. (2019, November). The Factors influencing the Career Choice of University Students: A Descriptive Analysis of Pure Science and Social Science Students in Universiti Brunei Darussalam. In *Proceedings of the 1st International Conference on Business, Management and Information Systems 2019 (ICBMIS 2019)* (Vol. 1, pp. 566-588). Academic Press.

Jana, S. K., & Das, B. C. (2019). Women entrepreneurs in transitioning Indian economy. In Approaches to Sustainable Development. Renu Publishers.

Jana, S., Das, B. C., Manna, S. S., Payra, T., Maiti, A., & Paul, P. K. (2019). Women Entrepreneurship in Backward Region: A Study in Jhargram district of WB. *Asian Journal of Multidimensional Research, 8*(3). http://www.tarj.in

Jeong, J., & Choi, M. (2017). The expected job satisfaction affecting entrepreneurial intention as career choice in the cultural and artistic industry. *Sustainability, 9*(10), 1689. doi:10.3390u9101689

Jjuuko, R., Tukundane, C., & Zeelen, J. (2021). Reclaiming the educative power of vocational placements: Experiences from agriculture education practice in Uganda. *International Journal of Training and Development, 25*(2), 144–159. doi:10.1111/ijtd.12212

Johnson, M. K., & Mortimer, J. T. (2002). Career choice and development from a sociological perspective. *Career Choice and Development, 4*, 37-81.

Jones, B., & Iredale, N. (2010). Enterprise education as pedagogy. *Education + Training, 52*(1), 7–19. doi:10.1108/00400911011017654

Jungen, K. A. (2008). *Parental influence and career choice: How parents affect the career aspirations of their children*. Academic Press.

Kabay, S. (2021). *Access, Quality, and the Global Learning Crisis: Insights from Ugandan Primary Education*. Oxford University Press. doi:10.1093/oso/9780192896865.001.0001

Kabeer, N. (2016). Gender equality, economic growth, and women's agency: The "endless variety" and "monotonous similarity" of patriarchal constraints. *Feminist Economics*, *22*(1), 295–321. doi:10.1080/13545701.2015.1090009

Kabongo, J. D., & Okpara, J. O. (2010). Entrepreneurship education in sub-Saharan African universities. *International Journal of Entrepreneurial Behaviour & Research*, *16*(4), 296–308. doi:10.1108/13552551011054499

Kamberidou, I. (2020). "Distinguished" women entrepreneurs in the digital economy and the multitasking whirlpool. *Journal of Innovation and Entrepreneurship*, *9*(3), 3. doi:10.118613731-020-0114-y

Kariba, F. (2020, July 30). *The burgeoning Africa youth population: Potential or challenge?* Cities Alliance. Retrieved January 31, 2022, from https://www.citiesalliance.org/newsroom/news/cities-alliance-news/%C2%A0burgeoning-africa-youth-population-potential-or-challenge%C2%A0

Karimi, S., & Lans, T. (2018). Testing Relationship between Personality. *Characteristics Contextual Factors and Entrepreneurial Intentions in Developing Country*, *52*(3), 227–240. PMID:26334129

Kathuri-Ogola, L., VanLeeuwen, C., Kabaria-Muriithi, J., Weeks, L. E., Kieru, J., & Ndayala, P. (2015). Supervision challenges encountered during Kenyan university students' practicum attachment. *Journal of Education and Practice*, *6*(17), 111–117.

Kaviarasu, S. J., Ruban, A. H., & Dinesh, J. J. (2019). *Entrepreneurship as the better solution for unemployment of the people in India*. JETIR. www.jetir.org

Kenya Institute of Curriculum Development. (2017). *Basic education curriculum framework*. KICD.

Kenya Institute of Curriculum Development. (2019). *Popular sides on CBC*. https://kicd.ac.ke/cbc-materials/popular-slides-on-cbc/

Khavul, S. (2010). Microfinance: Creating opportunities for the poor? *The Academy of Management Perspectives*, *24*(3), 58–72. doi:10.5465/AMP.2010.52842951

Khazanah Research Institute. (2018). The School-to-Work Transition of Young Malaysians. Khazanah Research Institute. doi:10.4337/9781845421694.00018

Khazanah Research Institute. (2020). *Work in an Evolving Malaysia. The State of Households 2020 Part II*. http://krinstitute.org/assets/contentMS/img/template/editor/KRI - Full report- Work in an Evolving Malaysia - 20201103.pdf

Khoza, R. J. (2013). *Let Africa Lead: African Transformational Leadership for 21st Century Business*. Vezubuntu Publishing Ltd.

Kickul, J., & D'Intino, R. S. (2005). Measure for measure: Modelling entrepreneurial self-efficacy onto instrumental tasks within the new venture creation process. *New England Journal of Entrepreneurship*, *8*(2), 39–47. doi:10.1108/NEJE-08-02-2005-B005

Kickul, J., Wilson, F., Marlino, D., & Barbosa, S. D. (2008). Are misalignments of perceptions and self-efficacy causing gender gaps in entrepreneurial intentions among our nation's teens? *Journal of Small Business and Enterprise Development*, *15*(2), 321–335. doi:10.1108/14626000810871709

KIfPPRaA. (2017). Kenya Economic Report 2017" Sustaining Kenya's Economic Development by Deepening and Expanding Economic Integration in the Region. Kenya Institute for Public Policy Research and Analysis Nairobi.

Killingberg, N. M., Kubberød, E., & Blenker, P. (2020). Preparing for a future career through entrepreneurship education: Towards a research agenda. *Industry and Higher Education.*

Kim, B. P., McCleary, K. W., & Kaufman, T. (2010). The new generation in the industry: Hospitality/Tourism students' career preferences, sources of influence and career choice factors. *Journal of Hospitality & Tourism Education*, *22*(3), 5–11. doi:10.1080/10963758.2010.10696979

Kimiti, R. P., & Maria, M. M. (2012). *The dilemma of career choice: A case study of Kenyan secondary school students.* Academic Press.

Kim, M., Perrewé, P. L., Kim, Y. K., & Kim, A. C. H. (2017). Psychological capital in sport organizations: Hope, Efficacy, Resilience, and Optimism among Employees in Sport (HEROES). *European Sport Management Quarterly*, *17*(5), 659–680. doi:10.1080/16184742.2017.1344284

Kingma, B. (2014). Creating a dynamic campus–community entrepreneurial ecosystem: Key characteristics of success in academic entrepreneurship. *Emerald Group Publishing Limited*, *16*(August), 97–114.

Kinicki, A., & Fugate, M. (2017). *Loose Leaf for Organizational Behavior: A Practical, Problem-Solving Approach.* McGraw-Hill Education.

Kjeldsen, A. M., & Hansen, J. R. (2018). Sector differences in the public service motivation–job satisfaction relationship: Exploring the role of organizational characteristics. *Review of Public Personnel Administration*, *38*(1), 24–48. doi:10.1177/0734371X16631605

Klapper, L., Lewin, A., & Delgado, J. M. (2009). *The impact of the business environment on the business creation process* (Policy Research Working Paper 4937). Washington, DC: The World Bank.

KNBS. (2018). Economic survey 2018. *Kenya National Bureau of Statistics.*

KNBS. (2020, Nov.). *Quarterly Labour Force Report.* Author.

Kobia, M., & Sikalieh, D. (2010). Towards a search for the meaning of entrepreneurship. *Journal of European Industrial Training*, *34*(2), 110–127. doi:10.1108/03090591011023970

Kollmann, T., Stöckmann, C., & Kensbock, J. M. (2019). I can't get no sleep—The differential impact of entrepreneurial stressors on work-home interference and insomnia among experienced versus novice entrepreneurs. *Journal of Business Venturing*, *34*(4), 692–708. doi:10.1016/j.jbusvent.2018.08.001

Kolvereid, L. (1996). Prediction of employment status choice intentions. *Entrepreneurship Theory and Practice*, *21*(1), 47–57. doi:10.1177/104225879602100104

Kostal, J. W., & Wiernik, B. M. (2017). A meta-analytic investigation of demographic differences in protean, boundaryless, and proactive career orientations. *Career Development International*, *22*(5), 520–545. doi:10.1108/CDI-08-2017-0139

Kraaijenbrink, J., Bos, G., & Groen, A. (2009). What do students think of the entrepreneurial support given by heir universities? *International Journal of Entrepreneurship and Small Business*, *9*(1), 110–125. doi:10.1504/IJESB.2010.029512

Krafft, C., & Rizk, R. (2021). The promise and peril of youth entrepreneurship in the Middle East and North Africa. *International Journal of Manpower*, *42*(8), 1500–1526.

Krishna, K. S. R. (2020). Employability and entrepreneurship: issues and challenges for Indian Universities. In Reimagining Indian Universities. AIU.

Krueger, N. F. Jr, Reilly, M. D., & Carsrud, A. L. (2000). Competing models of entrepreneurial intensions. *Journal of Business Venturing*, *15*(5-6), 411–432. doi:10.1016/S0883-9026(98)00033-0

Krumboltz, J. D., Mitchell, A. M., & Jones, G. B. (1976). A social learning theory of career selection. *The Counseling Psychologist*, *6*(1), 71–81. doi:10.1177/001100007600600117

Krylova, O., & Shaposhnykov, K. (2020). Activation Of Innovative Entrepreneurship Development. *Three Seas Economic Journal*, *1*(1), 66–72. doi:10.30525/2661-5150/2020-1-18

Kumar, G., & Borbora, S. (2019). Institutional environment differences and their application for entrepreneurship development in India. *Journal of Entrepreneurship in Emerging Economies*, *11*(2), 177–199. doi:10.1108/JEEE-11-2017-0081

Kumar, S. (2016). Parental influence on career choice traditionalism among college students in selected cities in Ethiopia. *International Journal of Psychology and Educational Studies*, *3*(3), 23–30. doi:10.17220/ijpes.2016.03.003

Kundi, Y. M., Hollet-Haudebert, S., & Peterson, J. (2021). Linking protean and boundaryless career attitudes to subjective career success: A serial mediation model. *Journal of Career Assessment*, *29*(2), 263–282. doi:10.1177/1069072720959782

Kunnen, E. S. (2013). The effects of career choice guidance on identity development. *Education Research International*, *2013*, 2013. doi:10.1155/2013/901718

Kuratko, D. F. (2005). The emergence of entrepreneurship education: Development, trends, and challenges. *Entrepreneurship Theory and Practice*, *29*(5), 577–598. doi:10.1111/j.1540-6520.2005.00099.x

Kuratko, D. F. (2018). *Corporate Entrepreneurship: A Critical Challenge for Educators and Researchers*. SAGE Journal Author Gateway. doi:10.1177/2515127417737291

Kushida, K. (2015). *A Strategic Overview of the Silicon Valley Ecosystem: Towards Effectively "Harnessing" Silicon Valley*. https://fsi-live.s3.us-west-1.amazonaws.com/s3fs-public/strategic_overview_of_sv_ecosystems.pdf

Labour Market Dynamics. (2016). Labour market dynamics in South Africa. Statistics South Africa.

Lackeus, M. (2015). *Entrepreneurship in education: What, why, when, how.* Background paper.

Lanero, A., Vázquez, J. L., & Aza, C. L. (2016). Social cognitive determinants of entrepreneurial career choice in university students. *International Small Business Journal: Researching Entrepreneurship*, *34*(8), 1053–1075. doi:10.1177/0266242615612882

Laskovaia, A., Shirokova, G., & Morris, M. H. (2017). National culture, effectuation, and new venture performance: Global evidence from student entrepreneurs. *Small Business Economics*, *49*(3), 687–709. doi:10.100711187-017-9852-z

Lazear, E. (2005). Entrepreneurship. *Journal of Labor Economics*, *23*(4), 649–680. doi:10.1086/491605

Ldama, J., & Bazza, M. (2015). Effect of Training and Development on Employees' Retention in Selected Commercial Banks in Adamawa State-Nigeria. *European Journal of Business and Management*, *7*(36), 96–101.

Le Grange, L. (2007). The'theoretical foundations' of community service-learning: From taproots to rhizomes. *Education as Change*, *11*(3), 3–13. doi:10.1080/16823200709487174

Lee, S. M., Chang, D., & Lim, S.-B. (2005). Impact of entrepreneurship education: A comparative study of the U.S. and Korea. *The International Entrepreneurship and Management Journal*, *1*(1), 27–43. doi:10.100711365-005-6674-2

Lehrer, M., Nell, P., & Gaerber, L. (2009). A national system view of university entrepreneurism: Inferences from comparison of the German and US experience. *Research Policy*, *38*(2), 268–280. doi:10.1016/j.respol.2008.11.007

Lent, R. W., & Brown, S. D. (1996). Applying social cognitive theory to career counseling: An introduction. *The Career Development Quarterly*, *44*(4), 307–309. doi:10.1002/j.2161-0045.1996.tb00447.x

Leshilo, A., & Lethoko, M. (2017). The contribution of youth in Local Economic Development and entrepreneurship in Polokwane municipality, Limpopo Province. *Skills at Work: Theory and Practice Journal*, *8*(1), 45–58.

Levesque, M., & Minniti, M. (2006). The Effect of Aging on Entrepreneurial Behaviour. *Journal of Business Venturing*, *21*(2), 177–194. doi:10.1016/j.jbusvent.2005.04.003

Levkov, N., & Umpleby, S. (2009). *How Service Learning is Conducted in a School of Business*. CEA Journal of Economics.

Lex, M., Gielnik, M. M., Spitzmuller, M., Jacob, G. H., & Frese, M. (in press). How passion in entrepreneurship develops over time: A self-regulation perspective. *Entrepreneurship Theory and Practice*. doi:10.1177/1042258720929894

Linan, F. (2004). Intention-based models of entrepreneurship education. *Piccola Impresa/Small Business, 3*, 11-35.

Linan, F. (2008). Skill and value perceptions: How do they affect entrepreneurial intentions? *The International Entrepreneurship and Management Journal*, *4*(3), 257–272. doi:10.100711365-008-0093-0

Liñán, F., Rodríguez-Cohard, J. C., & Rueda-Cantuche, J. M. (2011). Factors affecting entrepreneurial intention levels: A role for education. *The International Entrepreneurship and Management Journal*, *7*(2), 195–218. doi:10.100711365-010-0154-z

Lombardi, R., Lardo, A., Cuozzo, B., & Trequattrini, R. (2017). Emerging trends in entrepreneurial universities within Mediterranean regions: An international comparison. *EuroMed Journal of Business*, *12*(2), 130–145. doi:10.1108/EMJB-10-2015-0052

Lombardi, R., Schimperna, F., & Marcello, R. (2021a). Human capital and smart tourism's development: Primary evidence. *International Journal of Digital Culture and Electronic Tourism*, *3*(3/4), 294–309. doi:10.1504/IJDCET.2021.116492

Luthans, F. (2002). The need for and meaning of positive organizational behavior. *Journal of Organizational Behavior: The International Journal of Industrial. Occupational and Organizational Psychology and Behavior*, *23*(6), 695–706. doi:10.1002/job.165

Luthans, F., Youssef, C. M., & Avolio, B. J. (2015). *Psychological capital and beyond*. Oxford University Press.

Luthans, K. W., Luthans, B. C., & Chaffin, T. D. (2019). Refining grit in academic performance: The mediational role of psychological capital. *Journal of Management Education*, *43*(1), 35–61. doi:10.1177/1052562918804282

Lüthje, C., & Franke, N. (2003). The "making" of an entrepreneur: Testing a model of entrepreneurial intent among engineering students at MIT. *R & D Management*, *33*(2), 135–147. doi:10.1111/1467-9310.00288

Lyons, S. T., Schweitzer, L., & Ng, E. S. (2015). How have careers changed? An investigation of changing career patterns across four generations. *Journal of Managerial Psychology*, *30*(1), 8–21. doi:10.1108/JMP-07-2014-0210

Mabasa, K., & Cawe, A. (2020). Introduction: The future of Black Empowerment and entrepreneurship. In Beyond Tenderpreneurship: Rethinking Black Business and Economic Empowerment (pp. 1-26). Johannesburg: Mapungubwe Institute for Strategic Reflection (MISTRA).

Macready, C., & Tucker, C. (2011). Who goes where and why: An overview and analysis of global educational mobility. In *IIE and AIFS Foundation*. Institute of International Education.

Mafema, E., & Tshishonga, N. (2010). Living on the margins: the effects of intergenerational poverty amongst youth at Cato Manor in Durban. In Contemporary Social Issues in Africa: Cases in Gaborone, Kampala and Durban (pp. 179-194). Pretoria: Africa Institute of South Africa.

Majurin, E. (2014). *Start and improve your business: Implementation guide*. ILO. https://www.ilo.org/wcmsp5/groups/public/---ed_emp/---emp_ent/---ifp_seed/documents/publication/wcms_315262.pdf

Makumbi, R. (2018). Uganda's national youth policy and job creation for youth. In S. Ayele, D. Glover, & M. Oosterom (Eds.), *Youth Employment and the Private Sector in Africa* (pp. 45–54). IDS Bulletin. doi:10.19088/1968-2018.173

Malaysia Ministry of Education. (2015). *Malaysia Education Blueprint 2015-2025 (Higher Education)*. Ministry of Education Malaysia. http://medcontent.metapress.com/index/A65RM03P4874243N.pdf

Mamabolo, A., & Myres, K. (2020). A systematic literature review of skills required in the different phases of the entrepreneurial process. *Small Enterprise Research*, *27*(1), 39–63. doi:10.1080/13215906.2020.1730230

Manjunatha, K. (2017). Entrepreneurship: A Scope for Employment in India. *Journal of Business Management*, *3*(12).

Manolova, T. S., Edelman, L. F., Shirokova, G., & Tsukanova, T. (2019). Youth entrepreneurship in emerging economies: Can family support help navigate institutional voids? *Journal of East-West Business*, *25*(4), 363–395.

Manyika, J., Chui, M., Miremadi, M., & Bughin, J. (2017). A future that works: AI, automation, employment, and productivity. *McKinsey Global Institute Research. Tech. Rep*, *60*, 1–135.

Maresch, D., Harms, R., Kailer, N., & Wimmer-Wurm, B. (2016). The impact of entrepreneurship education on the entrepreneurial intention of students in science and engineering versus business studies university programs. *Technological Forecasting and Social Change*, *104*, 172–179. doi:10.1016/j.techfore.2015.11.006

Marinas, L. E., Igret, R. S., Marinas, C. V., & Prioteasa, E. (2016). Factors influencing career choice: The Romanian business and administration students' experience. *European Journal of Sustainable Development*, *5*(3), 267–278.

Maritz, A. (2017). Illuminating the black box of entrepreneurship education programmes: Part 2. *Education + Training*, *59*(5), 471–482. doi:10.1108/ET-02-2017-0018

Martin, B. C., Mcnally, J. J., & Kay, M. J. (2013). Examining the formation of human capital in entrepreneurship: A meta-analysis of entrepreneurship education outcomes. *Journal of Business Venturing*, *28*(2), 211–224. doi:10.1016/j.jbusvent.2012.03.002

Mascarenhas, C., Marques, C. S., Galvão, A. R., & Santos, G. (2017). Entrepreneurial university: towards a better understanding of past trends and future directions. *Journal of Enterprising Communities: People and Places in the Global Economy*.

Matlay, H. (2008). The impact of entrepreneurship education on entrepreneurial outcomes. *Journal of Small Business and Enterprise Development*, *15*(2), 382–396. doi:10.1108/14626000810871745

Matt, M., & Schaeffer, V. (2018). Building entrepreneurial ecosystems conducive to student entrepreneurship: New challenges for universities. *Journal of Innovation Economics Management*, (1), 9–32. doi:10.3917/jie.025.0009

Mbuya, M. J. M. (2021). Youth Entrepreneurship in South Africa: A Progress Review. Academic Press.

McGee, J. E., & Peterson, M. (2019). The long-term impact of entrepreneurial self-efficacy and entrepreneurial orientation on venture performance. *Journal of Small Business Management*, *57*(3), 720–737. doi:10.1111/jsbm.12324

McGuinness, S., & Sloane, P. J. (2011). Labour market mismatch among UK graduates: An analysis using REFLEX data. *Economics of Education Review*, *30*(1), 130–145. Advance online publication. doi:10.1016/j.econedurev.2010.07.006

McIlveen, P., Morgan, T., & Bimrose, J. (2012). A longitudinal study of the experience of a career development program for rural school students. *Australian Journal of Career Development*, *21*(1), 22–30. doi:10.1177/103841621202100104

McKinsey Global Institute. (2013). *Disruptive technologies: Advances that will transform life, business, and the global economy*, Academic Press.

Megat Deraman, N. S. (2020, November 27). KPT-CAP beri sinar baharu buat graduan, tingkatkan kebolehpasaran. *The Malaya Post*. https://www.themalayapost.my/kpt-cap-beri-sinar-baharu-buat-graduan-tingkatkan-kebolehpasaran/

Mehrotra, S., & Parida, K. J. (2019). *India's Employment Crisis: Rising Education Levels and Falling Non-Agriculture Job Growth*. CSE Working Paper, Azim Premji University. cse.azimpremjiuniversity.edu.in

Melyoki, L. L., & Gielnik, M. M. (2020). How action-oriented entrepreneurship training transforms university students into entrepreneurs: Insights from a qualitative study. *Journal of Small Business and Entrepreneurship*, 1–28. doi:10.1080/08276331.2020.1832831

Meyer, D. F., & Mncayi, P. (2021). An Analysis of Underemployment among Young Graduates: The Case of a Higher Education Institution in South Africa. *Economies*, *9*(4), 196. doi:10.3390/economies9040196

Miller, D. J., & Acs, Z. (2017). The campus as entrepreneurial ecosystem: The University of Chicago. *Small Business Economics*, *49*(1), 75–95. doi:10.100711187-017-9868-4

Miller, T. L., Grimes, M. G., McMullen, J. S., & Vogus, T. J. (2012). Venturing for others with heart and head: How compassion encourages social entrepreneurship. *Academy of Management Review*, *37*(4), 616–640. doi:10.5465/amr.2010.0456

Ministry of Entrepreneur Development and Coorperatives. (2019). *National Entrepreneurship Policy Malaysia: An Outstanding Entrepreneurial Nation 2030*. https://www.medac.gov.my/admin/files/med/image/portal/NEP2030-Final.pdf

Ministry of Higher Education Malaysia. (2013). Malaysia Education Blueprint 2013 - 2025 (Pre-school to Post-Secondary Education). Ministry of Education Malaysia. doi:10.1016/j.tate.2010.08.007

Ministry of Higher Education Malaysia. (n.d.). *Graduate Tracer Study*. http://graduan.moe.gov.my/v/Penerbitan/terbitan.aspx

Minneci, F. (2015). If there were a "highly skilled red octopus"? The case of Italian highly skilled mobility at times of crisis. *Economia e Sociologia*, *8*(3), 170–182.

Minniti, M. (2008). The role of government policy on entrepreneurial activity: Productive, unproductive, or destructive? *Entrepreneurship Theory and Practice*, *32*(5), 779–790. doi:10.1111/j.1540-6520.2008.00255.x

Minniti, M., & Bygrave, W. (2001). A dynamic model of entrepreneurial learning. *Entrepreneurship Theory and Practice*, *25*(3), 5–16. doi:10.1177/104225870102500301

Minniti, M., & Nardone, C. (2007). Being in Someone Else's Shoes: Gender and Nascent Entrepreneurship. *Small Business Economics Journal*, *28*(2), 223–238. doi:10.100711187-006-9017-y

Minola, T., Donina, D., & Meoli, M. (2016). Students climbing the entrepreneurial ladder: Does university internationalization pay off? *Small Business Economics*, *47*(3), 565–587. doi:10.100711187-016-9758-1

Mlatsheni, C., & Leibbrandt, M. (2011). Youth unemployment in South Africa: Concepts, challenges and opportunities. *Journal of International Research and Development*, *14*, 118–126.

Moberg, K., Stenberg, E., & Vestergaard, L. (2012). *Impact of entrepreneurship education in Denmark*. The Danish Foundation for Entrepreneurship–Young Enterprise.

Moerane, P. (2016). *A study of graduates' experience of unemployment in Durban, South Africa* (Doctoral dissertation). University of Kwa-Zulu Natal.

Moerane, P. (2016). *A study of graduates' experience of unemployment in Durban, South Africa* (Doctoral dissertation). University Of Kwa-Zulu Natal.

Mohd Abdul Kadir, J., Naghavi, N., Subramaniam, G., & A'amilyn Abdul Halim, N. (2020). Unemployment among Graduates - Is there a Mismatch? *International Journal of Asian Social Science*, *10*(10), 583–592. doi:10.18488/journal.1.2020.1010.583.592

Molino, M., Dolce, V., Cortese, C. G., & Ghislieri, C. (2018). Personality and social support as determinants of entrepreneurial intention. gender differences in Italy. *PLoS One*, *13*(6), e0199924. doi:10.1371/journal.pone.0199924 PMID:29953517

Monsen, E., Mahagaonkar, P., & Dienes, C. (2010). *Entrepreneurship in India: The Question of occupational Transition. Schumpeter Discussion Papers, No. 2010-007.* Schumpeter School of Business and Economics, University of Wuppertal.

Monteiro, S., & Almeida, L. S. (2021). Employability of higher education graduates: Reflections and pedagogical implications. *Revista Lusófona de Educação*, *51*(51).

Moon, J. A. (2013). *A handbook of reflective and experiential learning: Theory and practice.* Routledge. doi:10.4324/9780203416150

Morgan, C., Isaac, J. D., & Sansone, C. (2001). The role of interest in understanding the career choices of female and male college students. *Sex Roles*, *44*(5), 295–320. doi:10.1023/A:1010929600004

Morris, E. (2006). *Globalization and its effects on youth employment trends in Asia.* Paper presented to the Regional Expert Group Meeting on Development challenges for young people, Bangkok, Thailand. Retrieved December 1, 2021, from https://www.un.org/esa/socdev/unyin/workshops/regm_ asia_ilo_elizabeth_morris_paper .pdf

Morris. (2017). Assessing the Impact of Entrepreneurship Education Programmes: A New Methodology. *Journal of European Industrial Training*, *30*(9).

Morris, M. H., Shirokova, G., & Tsukanova, T. (2017). Student entrepreneurship and the university ecosystem: A multi-country empirical exploration. *European Journal of International Management*, *11*(1), 65–85. doi:10.1504/EJIM.2017.081251

Mount Kenya University. (2021, July 2). *Linkages and partnership.* Mount Kenya University. Retrieved February 1, 2022, from https://www.mku.ac.ke/linkages-and-partnership/

Mtenga, V. D. (2013). *Empowering youth through entrepreneurship skills training: The case of Makangarawe ward* (Doctoral dissertation). The Open University of Tanzania.

Mukhwana, E., Oure, S., Too, J., & Some, D. K. (2016). *State of postgraduate research training in Kenya.* Commission for University Education. Discussion Paper 02.

Mulgan, R. (2000). Comparing accountability in the public and private sectors. *Australian Journal of Public Administration*, *59*(1), 87–97. doi:10.1111/1467-8500.00142

Munnell, A. H., & Fraenkel, R. C. (2013). Public sector workers and job security. *State and Local Pension Plans Issue in Brief, 31.*

Muñoz, P., & Cohen, B. (2018). Sustainable Entrepreneurship Research: Taking Stock and looking ahead. *Business Strategy and the Environment*, *27*(3), 300–322. doi:10.1002/bse.2000

Murage, G. (2018). *Effect of University Technology Business Incubator services on the performance of digital enterprises in Kenya* [Master's Thesis]. Strathmore University. Retrieved from https://su-plus.strathmore.edu/handle/11071/6016

Muscio, A., & Ramaciotti, L. (2019). How does academia influence Ph.D. entrepreneurship? New insights on the entrepreneurial university. *Technovation, 82–83*, 16–24. doi:10.1016/j.technovation.2019.02.003

Mwasalwiba, E. S. (2012). Entrepreneurship education: A review of its objectives, teaching methods, and impact indicators. *IEEE Engineering Management Review, 40*(2), 72–94. doi:10.1109/EMR.2012.6210519

Myburgh, J. E. (2005). An empirical analysis of career choice factors that influence first-year Accounting students at the University of Pretoria: A cross-racial study. *Meditari: Research Journal of the School of Accounting Sciences, 13*(2), 35–48. doi:10.1108/10222529200500011

Nabi, G., & Holden, R. (2008). Graduate entrepreneurship: Intentions, education, and training. *Education + Training, 50*(7), 545–551. doi:10.1108/00400910810909018

Nabi, G., & Linan, F. (2011). Graduate entrepreneurship in developing world: Intentions, education, and training. *Education + Training, 53*(5), 325–334. doi:10.1108/00400911111147668

Naong, M. (2011). Promotion of Entrepreneurship Education - A Remedy to Graduates and Youth Unemployment – A Theoretical Perspective. *Social Sciences*, 181–189.

National Youth Policy. (2015 – 2020). We are generation 2020. We don't want a hand-out, we want a hand up! #NYP2020.

Naude, W., Gries, T., Wood, E., & Meintjies, A. (2008). Regional determinants of entrepreneurial start-ups in a developing country. *Entrepreneurship and Regional Development, 20*(2), 111–124. doi:10.1080/08985620701631498

Nazlıer, E. (2022). Eğitim sistemi… *Evrensel Gazetesi*. Retrieved February 2, 2022, from https://www.evrensel.net/ haber/453888/egitim-sisteminin-son

Ndinga-Kanga, M., van der Merwe, H., & Hartford, D. (2020). Forging a resilient social contract in South Africa: States and societies sustaining peace in the post-apartheid era. *Journal of Intervention and Statebuilding, 14*(1), 22–41. doi:10.1080/17502977.2019.1706436

Neneh, N. B. (2017). *An Exploratory Study of Entrepreneurial Mindset in the Small and Medium Enterprise*. Department of Business Management, University of the Free State.

Nenzhelele, T. E., Moraka, N. V., & More, K. K. (2016). The impact of practical entrepreneurship project on future entrepreneurial intentions. *Problems and Perspectives in Management, 14*(4), 67–75. doi:10.21511/ppm.14(4).2016.08

Netshitenzhe, J. (2021). Beating the counter-revolutionaries: South Africa's people are the ultimate defenders of democracy. *Daily Maverick*. https://www.dailymaverick.co.za/article/2021-08-02-beating-the-counter-revolutionaries-south-africas-people-are-the-ultimate-defenders-of-democracy/

Netshitenzhe, J. (2021). *Beating the counter-revolutionaries: South Africa's people are the ultimate defenders of democracy*. South Africa. Daily Maverick. https://www.dailymaverick.co.za/article/2021-08-02-beating-the-counter-revolutionaries-south-africas-people-are-the-ultimate-defenders-of-democracy/

Neupert, K. E., & Baughn, C. C. (2013). Immigration, Education and Entrepreneurship in Developed Countries. *Journal of Enterprising Communities: People and Places in the Global Economy*, *7*(3), 293–310. doi:10.1108/JEC-12-2011-0033

New Straits Times. (2021, March 12). *Higher Education Ministry: Malaysian graduates' employability down to 84.4pc in 2020*. https://www.malaymail.com/news/malaysia/2021/03/12/higher-education-ministry-malaysian-graduates-employability-down-to-84.4pc/1957347

Ng, E. S., Burke, R. J., & Fiksenbaum, L. (2008). Career choice in management: Findings from US MBA students. *Career Development International*, *13*(4), 346–361. doi:10.1108/13620430810880835

Ng, E. S., & Parry, E. (2016). Multigenerational research in human resource management. In M. R. Buckley, J. R. B. Halbesleben, & A. R. Wheeler (Eds.), *Research in personnel and human resources management* (Vol. 34, pp. 1–41). Emerald Group.

Nguyen, T. T. (2020). Impact of entrepreneurship environmental support factors to university students' entrepreneurship self-efficacy. *Management Science Letters*, *10*, 1321–1328. doi:10.5267/j.msl.2019.11.026

Ntale, P. D., Ssempebwa, J., Musisi, B., Musoke, G. G., Joseph, K., Mugimu, C. B., Muhammed, N., & Ntayi, J. (2020). Gaps in the structuring of organizations in the graduate employment context in Uganda. *Journal of Organization Design*, *9*(1), 1–10. doi:10.118641469-020-0066-5

Ntale, P. D., Ssempebwa, J., Musisi, B., & Pope, H. C. (2019). Inter-agency collaboration for graduate employment opportunities in Uganda: A case for investigating the structure, social capital, and agency of organizations. *Journal of African American Studies*, *23*(1), 111–130. doi:10.100712111-019-09419-9

Nyamwange, J. (2016). Influence of Student's Interest on Career Choice among First Year University Students in Public and Private Universities in Kisii County, Kenya. *Journal of Education and Practice*, *7*(4), 96–102.

Odeh, M. A., & Okoye, C. O. (2014). Poverty reduction policy and youth unemployment in Nigeria. *Public Policy and Administration Research*, *3*(4), 92–103.

OECD & European Union. (2014). *Supporting Youth in Entrepreneurship.* Summary report of a policy development seminar organised by the OECD and the European Commission. Accessed from: http://www.oecd.org/cfe/leed/inclusive-entrepreneurship.htm

OECD. (2015). *OECD Skills strategy diagnostic report: Portugal 2015.* OECD Publishing.

OECD. (2015). *Strengthening public employment services.* https://www.oecd.org/employment/Strengthening-Public-Employment-Services.pdf

OECD. (2016). *Getting Skills Right: Anticipating and Responding to Changing Skill Needs.* OECD Publishing. doi:10.1787/9789264252073-en

OECD. (2017). *OECD Economic Surveys: Portugal.* OECD Publishing.

OECD. (2021). *Data: Unemployment rate by age group.* Retrieved August 31, 2021, from https://data.oecd.org/unemp/ unemployment-rate-by-age-group.htm#indicator-chart

Okafor, E. E. (2011). Youth unemployment and implications for stability of democracy in Nigeria. *Journal of Sustainable Development in Africa, 13*(1), 358–373.

Olaosebikan, O. I., & Olusakin, A. M. (2014). Effects of Parental Influence on Adolescents' Career Choice in Badagry Local Government Area of Lagos State, Nigeria. Academic Press.

Oleksii, S., Kharchenko, V., Sklyar, V., & Chris, P. (2015). *Hacking the innovations with university-industry Hackathon.* Academic Press.

OloweO. (2010). Graduate Unemployment and its Resultant Effects on Developing Economies. SSRN. doi:10.2139/ssrn.1457041

Olugbola, S. A. (2017). Exploring entrepreneurial readiness of youth and startup success components: Entrepreneurship training as a moderator. *Journal of Innovation & Knowledge, 2*(3), 155–171.

Olugbola, S. A. (2017). Exploring Entrepreneurial Readiness of Youth and Startup Success Components: Entrepreneurship Training as a Moderator. *Journal of Innovation and Knowledge, 2*(3), 155–171. doi:10.1016/j.jik.2016.12.004

Onyango, A., & Langat, D. (2019, July 2). *Community service learning.* Kenya News Agency. Retrieved February 1, 2022, from https://www.kenyanews.go.ke/community-service-learning/#:~:text=Kenya%20Institute%20of%20Curriculum%20Development,Based%20 Curriculum%20in%20secondary%20schools

Oosterbeek, H., Van Praag, M., & Ijsselstein, A. (2010). The impact of entrepreneurship education on entrepreneurship skills and motivation. *European Economic Review, 54*(3), 442–454. doi:10.1016/j.euroecorev.2009.08.002

Otto, L. B. (2000). Youth perspectives on parental career influence. *Journal of Career Development, 27*(2), 111–118. doi:10.1177/089484530002700205

Oviawe, J. I. (2010). Repositioning Nigerian youths for economic empowerment through entrepreneurship education. *European Journal of Educational Studies*, *2*(2), 113–118.

Oviawe, J. I. (2018). Revamping Technical Vocational Education and Training through Public-Private Partnerships for Skill Development. *Makerere Journal of Higher Education*, *10*(1), 73–91.

Oyugi, J. L. (2014). Effectiveness of the methods of teaching entrepreneurship courses to developing self-efficacy and intention among university students in Uganda. *International Journal of Social Sciences and Entrepreneurship*, *1*(11), 491–513.

Oyugi, J. L. (2021). From Ivory Tower to Entrepreneurial University: Agenda for Sustainable Job Creation among University Graduates in Uganda. *Journal of Education and Learning*, *15*(1), 127–134. doi:10.11591/edulearn.v15i1.15982

Özbilgin, M., Küskü, F., & Erdoğmuş, N. (2005). Explaining influences on career 'choice': The case of MBA students in comparative perspective. *International Journal of Human Resource Management*, *16*(11), 2000–2028. doi:10.1080/09585190500314797

Pacho, T. (2019). Service-learning: An innovative approach to education in Africa. *The good education and Africa's future: Concepts, issues and options*, 232-259

Paolillo, J. G., & Estes, R. W. (1982). An empirical analysis of career choice factors among accountants, attorneys, engineers, and physicians. *The Accounting Review*, 785–793.

Park, J. R., Coombs, C., Wilkinson, A. J., Loan-Clarke, J., Arnold, J., & Preston, D. (2003). Attractiveness of physiotherapy in the National Health Service as a career choice: Qualitative study. *Physiotherapy*, *89*(10), 575–583. doi:10.1016/S0031-9406(05)60056-9

Parsons, J. E., Adler, T., & Meece, J. L. (1984). Sex differences in achievement: A test of alternate theories. *Journal of Personality and Social Psychology*, *46*(1), 26–43. doi:10.1037/0022-3514.46.1.26

Pastore, F. (2019). Why so slow? The school-to-work transition in Italy. *Studies in Higher Education*, *44*(8), 1358–1371. doi:10.1080/03075079.2018.1437722

Pavan, R. (2011). Career choice and wage growth. *Journal of Labor Economics*, *29*(3), 549–587. doi:10.1086/659346

Pedroso, P. (2011). *Análise Prospectiva da Evolução Sectorial em Portugal*. ANESPO and ANQ.

Peng, T. N. (2020). The State of the Youth in Malaysia. In T. N. Peng, L. S. Li, & N. A. Ismail (Eds.), *Demographic Transition and Socio-Economic Development in Malaysia* (pp. 117–136). University of Malaya Press. doi:10.14425/9789674881368.117136

Perold, A. F. (2012). *Negative real interest rates: The conundrum for investment and spending policies*. Academic Press.

Peterson, C. (2006). *A primer in positive psychology*. Oxford university press.

Phan, P., Siegel, D. S., & Wright, M. (2005). Science parks and incubators: Observations, synthesis and future research. *Journal of Business Venturing, 20*(2), 165–182. doi:10.1016/j.jbusvent.2003.12.001

Pick, S., de Weiss, S. P., & Sirkin, J. (2010). *Breaking the poverty cycle: The human basis for sustainable development.* Oxford University Press. doi:10.1093/acprof:oso/9780195383164.001.0001

Pioch, S., & Dweck, C. S. (2017). Startup Intelligence: New Opportunities for Entrepreneurs of the Digital Economy Through Knowledge-Based Market Decisions. *Emerging Trends in Entrepreneurial Finance Conference.* 10.2139srn.2963682

Piperopoulos, P., & Dimov, D. (2015). Burst Bubbles or Build Steam? Entrepreneurship Education, Entrepreneurial Self-Efficacy, and Entrepreneurial Intentions. *Journal of Small Business Management, 53*(4), 970–985. doi:10.1111/jsbm.12116

Plattner, I. E., Lechaena, M., Mmolawa, W., & Mzingwane, B. (2009). Are university students psychologically ready for entrepreneurship? A Botswana study. *African Journal of Business Management, 3*(7), 305–310.

Pooe, T. K., Ngcaweni, W., & Zwane, N. (2020). "Lost in Transformation"? A case study of black youth entrepreneurship in post-apartheid South Africa. In Beyond Tenderpreneurship: Rethinking Black Business and Economic Empowerment (pp. 313-335). Johannesburg: Mapungubwe Institute for Strategic Reflection (MISTRA).

Poschke, M. (2013). Who becomes an entrepreneur? Labor market prospects and occupational choice. *Journal of Economic Dynamics & Control, 37*(3), 693–710. doi:10.1016/j.jedc.2012.11.003

Praskova, A., Creed, P. A., & Hood, M. (2015). Career identity and the complex mediating relationships between career preparatory actions and career progress markers. *Journal of Vocational Behavior, 87*, 145–153. doi:10.1016/j.jvb.2015.01.001

Prayag, G., Ozanne, L. K., & de Vries, H. (2020). Psychological capital, coping mechanisms and organizational resilience: Insights from the 2016 Kaikoura earthquake, New Zealand. *Tourism Management Perspectives, 34*, 100637. doi:10.1016/j.tmp.2020.100637

Preedy, S., & Jones, P. (2017). Student-led enterprise groups and entrepreneurial learning: A UK perspective. *Industry and Higher Education, 31*(2), 101–112. doi:10.1177/0950422216689349

Premand, P., Brodmann, S., Almeida, R., Grun, R., & Barouni, M. (2012). *Entrepreneurship training and self-employment among university graduates. Evidence from a randomized trial in Tunisia* (Research Working Paper 6285). Washington, DC: The World Bank.

Premand, P., Brodmann, S., Almeida, R., Grun, R., & Barouni, M. (2012). Entrepreneurship training and self-employment among university graduates: Evidence from a randomized trial in Tunisia. *World Bank Policy Research Working Paper*, (6285). https://www.econstor.eu/bitstream/10419/69343/1/733736653.pdf

Prencipe, A. (2016). Do University Incubators Stimulate Innovation of University Spin-Offs? An Analysis of Italian Firms. *International Journal of Business and Social Science*, *7*(7).

Pribbenow, D. A. (2005). The impact of service-learning pedagogy on faculty teaching and learning. *Michigan Journal of Community Service Learning*, *11*(2), 25–38.

Price, A. (2007). *Human resource management in a business context*. Cengage Learning EMEA.

Probst, L., & Scharff, C. (2019). *A strategy guide to upskilling. PwC's New World New Skills. Leadership, autumn 2019, 99.* https://www.strategy-business.com/feature/A-strategists-guide-to-upskilling?gko=0bb8b

Productivity Council. (2019). *A Produtividade da Economia Portuguesa*. Conselho da Produtividade.

QREN. (2012). *Relatório Estratégico 2012*. Observatório do QREN.

Qwesha, N. (2020, Dec. 22). The challenge of youth unemployment. *Daily News*, p. 6.

Rae, D. (2010). Universities and enterprise education: Responding to the challenges of the new era. *Journal of Small Business and Enterprise Development*, *17*(4), 591–606. doi:10.1108/14626001011088741

Rae, D., & Woodier-Harris, N. R. (2013). How does enterprise and entrepreneurship education influence postgraduate students' career intentions in the New Era economy? *Education + Training*, *55*(8/9), 926–948. doi:10.1108/ET-07-2013-0095

Rahim, H. L., & Chik, R. (2014). Graduate entrepreneurs creation: A case of Universiti Technologi MARA, Malaysia. *Australian Journal of Basic and Applied Sciences*, *8*(23), 15–20.

Rahim, H. L., Kadir, M. A. B. A., Abidin, Z. Z., Junid, J., Kamaruddin, L. M., Lajin, N. F. M., ... Bakri, A. A. (2015). Entrepreneurship education in Malaysia: A critical review. *Journal of Technology Management and Business*, *2*(2).

Rakib, Tawe, Azis, Syam, & Sanusi. (2020). Determinants of entrepreneurial intention: Empirical study of student entrepreneurs. *Academy of Entrepreneurship Journal, 26*, 1–12.

Ramphele, M. (2012). *Conservations with My Sons and Daughters*. Penguin Books.

Ramphele, M. (2012). *Conservations with My Sons and Daughters. Rosebank*. Penguin Books.

Rangarajan, C. (1980). *Innovations in Banking. Domestic Financial Study 63*. World Bank.

Raposo, M., & Armida, P. (2017). *Entrepreneurship Education: Relationship between Education Entrepreneurial Activity*. University of Beira Interior.

Rasmussen, E. A., & Sørheim, R. (2006). Action-based entrepreneurship education. *Technovation*, *26*(2), 185–194. doi:10.1016/j.technovation.2005.06.012

Rebmann, A., & Mickiewicz, T. (2020). Entrepreneurship as Trust. *Foundations and Trends in Entrepreneurship*, *16*(3), 244–309. doi:10.1561/0300000088

Rice, M. P., Fetters, M. L., & Greene, P. G. (2014). University-based entrepreneurship ecosystems: A global study of six educational institutions. *International Journal of Entrepreneurship and Innovation Management*, *18*(5/6), 481–501. doi:10.1504/IJEIM.2014.064722

Richert-Kazmierska, A., & Lechman, E. (2014). Creating entrepreneurial mind-set. *Innocase Project*, (2012-1).

Robb, A., Valerio, A., & Parton, B. (Eds.). (2014). Entrepreneurship education and training: insights from Ghana, Kenya, and Mozambique. The World Bank. doi:10.1596/978-1-4648-0278-2

Robles, N. (2017). *Development of university's business incubators in Panama* [Master Thesis]. Faculty of Engineering Economics and Management, Institute of Business, Riga Technical University.

Rodrigues, R., Butler, C. L., & Guest, D. (2019). Antecedents of protean and boundaryless career orientations: The role of core self-evaluations, perceived employability and social capital. *Journal of Vocational Behavior*, *110*, 1–11. doi:10.1016/j.jvb.2018.11.003

Ross, B. H. (1988). Public and Private Sectors—The Underlying Differences. *Management Review*, *77*(5), 28.

Roundy, P. T. (2017). Small town entrepreneurial ecosystems: Implications for developed and emerging economies. *Journal of Entrepreneurship in Emerging Economies*, *9*(3), 238–262. doi:10.1108/JEEE-09-2016-0040

Roura, J. C. (2015). Business incubation: Innovative services in an entrepreneurship ecosystem. *Service Industries Journal*, 1–18.

Ryan, R. M., & Deci, E. L. (2000). Intrinsic and extrinsic motivations: Classic definitions and new directions. *Contemporary Educational Psychology*, *25*(1), 54–67. doi:10.1006/ceps.1999.1020 PMID:10620381

Saeed, S., Yousafzai, S. Y., Yani-De-Soriano, M., & Muffatto, M. (2015). The role of perceived university support in the formation of students' entrepreneurial intention. *Journal of Small Business Management*, *53*(4), 1127–1145. doi:10.1111/jsbm.12090

Sajjad, M., & Mahboob, U. (2015). Improving workplace-based learning for undergraduate medical students. *Pakistan Journal of Medical Sciences*, *31*(5), 1272.

Salami, S. O. (2019). Examining the emerging entrepreneurial mindset in adolescence: A study in Nigeria. *International Journal of Psychology*, *2*(1), 431. doi:10.1002/ijop.12431 PMID:28493413

Salas-Velasco, M. (2021). Mapping the (mis)match of university degrees in the graduate labor market. *Journal for Labour Market Research*, *55*(1), 14. doi:10.118612651-021-00297-x

Samašonok, K., Išoraitė, M., & Žirnelė, L. (2020). Education of entrepreneurship by participation in a business simulation ˙ enterprise activities: Conditions of effectiveness and opportunities for improvement. *Entrepreneurship and Sustainability Issues*, *7*(4), 3122–3144. doi:10.9770/jesi.2020.7.4(36)

Sansone, G., Ughetto, E., & Landoni, P. (2021). Entrepreneurial intention: An analysis of the role of Student-Led Entrepreneurial Organizations. *Journal of International Entrepreneurship, 19*(3), 399–433. doi:10.100710843-021-00288-6

Santana, L. E., Feliciano, L., & Jimenez, A. B. (2016). Perceived family support and the life design of immigrant pupils in secondary education. *Review of Education, 372*, 35–62.

Sanyal, S., & Hisam, M. (2018). The role of business incubators in creating an entrepreneurial ecosystem: A study of the sultanate of Oman. *International Journal of Contemporary Research in Humanities and Social Sciences, 7*(1), 60–77.

Savickas, M. (2019). *Career counseling*. American Psychological Association. doi:10.1037/0000105-000

Savickas, M. L., Nota, L., Rossier, J., Dauwalder, J. P., Duarte, M. E., Guichard, J., Soresi, S., Van Esbroeck, R., & van Vianen, A. (2009). Life designing: A paradigm for career construction in the 21st century. *Journal of Vocational Behavior, 75*(3), 239–250. doi:10.1016/j.jvb.2009.04.004

Schimperna, F., Lombardi, R., & Belyaeva, Z. (2020). Technological transformation, culinary tourism and stakeholder engagement: Emerging trends from a systematic literature review. *Journal of Place Management and Development, 14*(1), 66–80. doi:10.1108/JPMD-03-2020-0028

Schoof, U. (2006). *Stimulating Youth Entrepreneurship: Barriers and incentives to enterprise start-ups by young people*. Youth and Entrepreneurship. http://search.ebscohost.com/login.aspx?direct=true&db=buh&AN=48077905&site=ehost-live

Schumpeter, J. A. (1942). *Capitalism, socialism and democracy* (3rd ed.). George Allen and Unwin. Retrieved from www.eet.pixel-online.org

Schwab, K. (2016). The Fourth Industrial Revolution: what it means, how to respond. *WeForum.* Retrieved from https://www.weforum.org/agenda/2016/01/the-fourth-industrial-revolution-what-it-means-and-how-to-respond/

Sehitoglu, Y., & Ozdemir, O. C. (2013). The impact of business incubation on firm performance during post graduation period - Turkey. *British Journal of Arts and Social Sciences, 12*(1), 171–190.

Selva, E., & Negro, F. (2021). *Youth employment in conflict and fragile settings.* ILO.

Sendouwa, R. H. E., Lonto, A. L., & Saroinsong, S. J. R. (2019). Entrepreneurship development program in the higher education in Indonesia. *International Journal of Recent Technology and Engineering, 8*, 1006–1010.

Setiawan, J. L. (2014). Examining entrepreneurial self-efficacy among students. *Procedia: Social and Behavioral Sciences, 115*, 235–242. doi:10.1016/j.sbspro.2014.02.431

Shane, S. (2012). Reflections on the 2010 AMR decade award: Delivering on the promise of entrepreneurship as a field of research. *Academy of Management Review, 37*(1), 10–20. doi:10.5465/amr.2011.0078

Shane, S., & Venkatarman, S. (2000). The promise of entrepreneurship as a field of research. *Academy of Management Review*, *25*(1), 217–226. doi:10.5465/amr.2000.2791611

Shaoul, J., Stafford, A., & Stapleton, P. (2012). Accountability and corporate governance of public private partnerships. *Critical Perspectives on Accounting*, *23*(3), 213–229. doi:10.1016/j.cpa.2011.12.006

Sharone, O. (2007). Constructing unemployed job seekers as professional workers: The depoliticizing work – game of job searching. *Qualitative Sociology*, *30*(4), 403–416. doi:10.100711133-007-9071-z

Shefiu, R. (2016). Youth empowerment leveraging on entrepreneurship. *Continental. Journal of Sustainable Development*, *7*(1), 45–60.

Shepherd, D. A., & Patzelt, H. (2018). Motivation and entrepreneurial cognition. In *Entrepreneurial Cognition* (pp. 51–103). Palgrave Macmillan. doi:10.1007/978-3-319-71782-1_3

Shi, L. P., Imdorf, C., Samuel, R., & Sacchi, S. (2018). How unemployment scarring affects skilled young workers: Evidence from a factorial survey of Swiss recruiters. *Journal for Labour Market Research*, *52*(1), 7. doi:10.118612651-018-0239-7 PMID:30046769

Shipp, V. H. (1999). Factors influencing the career choices of African American collegians: Implications for minority teacher recruitment. *The Journal of Negro Education*, *68*(3), 343–351. doi:10.2307/2668106

Shirokova, G., Osiyevskyy, O., & Bogatyreva, K. (2016). Exploring the intention–behavior link in student entrepreneurship: Moderating effects of individual and environmental characteristics. *European Management Journal*, *34*(4), 386–399. doi:10.1016/j.emj.2015.12.007

Shmatko, N. M., Pantelieiev, M. S., & Kurchenko, A. A. (2018). Creative Intelligence And Ideas Generation In The Context Of Strategic Management By Personnel. *Adaptive Management: Theory and Practice. Series Economics, 5*(10).

Shoffner, M. F., Newsome, D., Barrio Minton, C. A., & Wachter Morris, C. A. (2015). A qualitative exploration of the STEM career-related outcome expectations of young adolescents. *Journal of Career Development*, *42*(2), 102–116. doi:10.1177/0894845314544033

Sibanda, M. (2021). *Nuts & Bolts: Strengthening Africa's Innovation and Entrepreneurship Ecosystems*. Tracey McDonald Publishers.

Sibson, R. D. (2011). *Career choice perceptions of undergraduate event, sport and recreation management students: An Australian case study*. Academic Press.

Siivonen, P. T., Peura, K., Hytti, U., Kasanen, K., & Komulainen, K. (2019). The construction and regulation of collective entrepreneurial identity in student entrepreneurship societies. *International Journal of Entrepreneurial Behaviour & Research*, *26*(3), 521–538. doi:10.1108/IJEBR-09-2018-0615

Sika, N. (2017). *Youth Activism and Contentious Politics: Dynamics of Continuity and Change*. Cambridge University Press.

Simoes, N., Crespo, N., & Moreira, S. (2016). Individual determinants of self-employment entry: What do we really know? *Journal of Economic Surveys*, *30*(4), 783–806. doi:10.1111/joes.12111

Singaravelu, H. D., White, L. J., & Bringaze, T. B. (2005). Factors influencing international students' career choice: A comparative study. *Journal of Career Development*, *32*(1), 46–59. doi:10.1177/0894845305277043

Singh, B., Verma, P., & Rao, M. K. (2016). Influence of individual and socio-cultural factors on entrepreneurial intention. *South Asian Journal of Management*, *23*(1), 33.

Singh, G., & Verma, A. (2001). Is there life after career employment? Labour market experience of early retirees. In V. Marshall, W. Heinz, H. Kruegar, & A. Verma (Eds.), *Restructuring Work and the Life Course* (pp. 288–302). University of Toronto Press. doi:10.3138/9781442679290-019

Sitoula, T. (2015). *Challenges and Prospects of Youth Entrepreneurship in Kathmandu*. https://brage.bibsys.no/xmlui/bitstream/handle/11250/2385486/Sitoula.pdf?sequence=1

Slavtchev, V., Laspita, S., & Patzelt, H. (2012). Effects of entrepreneurship education at universities. *Jena Economic Research Papers*, *25*, 1–33.

SME Annual Report 2015–2016. (2016). SME Corp Malaysia. doi:10.5860/crln.77.11.9594

Smith, J. L., Sansone, C., & White, P. H. (2007). The stereotyped task engagement process: The role of interest and achievement motivation. *Journal of Educational Psychology*, *99*(1), 99–114. doi:10.1037/0022-0663.99.1.99

Smith, K., & Beasley, M. (2011). Graduate entrepreneurs: Intentions, barriers, and solutions. *Education + Training*, *53*(8/9), 722–740. doi:10.1108/00400911111185044

Souitaris, V., Zerbinati, S., & Al-Laham, A. (2007). Do entrepreneurship programmes raise entrepreneurial intention of science and engineering students? The effect of learning, inspiration and resources. *Journal of Business Venturing*, *22*(4), 566–591. doi:10.1016/j.jbusvent.2006.05.002

Spigel, B. (2017). The relational organization of entrepreneurial ecosystems. *Entrepreneurship Theory and Practice*, *41*(1), 49–72. doi:10.1111/etap.12167

Stam, E. (2014). The Dutch entrepreneurial ecosystem. SSRN *Electronic Journal*. doi:10.2139/ssrn.2473475

Stam, E. (2015). Entrepreneurial ecosystems and regional policy: A sympathetic critique. *European Planning Studies*, *23*(9), 1759–1769. doi:10.1080/09654313.2015.1061484

Standing, G. (2011). *The Precariat: The New Dangerous Class*. Bloomsbury Academic.

Statistics Portugal. (2020). *Enterprises in Portugal – 2018*. Statistics Portugal.

Statistics South Africa. (2021). *Quarterly Labour Force Survey: Quarter 1*. Statistics South Africa.

Stats, S A. (2020). Wholesale trade sales. *Statistical Release, 6141.*

Stats, S. A. (2019). *Youth graduate unemployment rate increases in Q1: 2019.* www.statssa.gov.za

Steenekamp, A. G., Van der Merwe, S. P., & Athayde, R. (2011). An investigation into youth entrepreneurship in selected South African secondary schools: An exploratory study. *Southern African Business Review, 15*(3), 46–75.

Sternberg, R. J. (2020). Creativity from start to finish: A "straight-A" model of creative process and its relation to intelligence. *The Journal of Creative Behavior, 54*(2), 229–241. doi:10.1002/jocb.223

Stewart, J. (2004). The meaning of strategy in the public sector. *Australian Journal of Public Administration, 63*(4), 16–21. doi:10.1111/j.1467-8500.2004.00409.x

Steyaert, C., & Katz, J. (2004). Reclaiming the space of entrepreneurship in society: Geographical, discursive and social dimensions. *Entrepreneurship and Regional Development, 16*(3), 179–196. doi:10.1080/0898562042000197135

Subramony, M., Segers, J., Chadwick, C., & Shyamsunder, A. (2018). Leadership development practice bundles and organizational performance: The mediating role of human capital and social capital. *Journal of Business Research, 83*, 120–129. doi:10.1016/j.jbusres.2017.09.044

Succi, C., & Canovi, M. (2020). Soft skills to enhance graduate employability: Comparing students and employers' perceptions. *Studies in Higher Education, 45*(9), 1834–1847. doi:10.1080/03075079.2019.1585420

Sultana, T., & Mahmud, M. K. (2020). Exploring the influential stimulators of career choice: An empirical assessment by exploratory factor analysis. *Asian Journal of Empirical Research, 10*(5), 137–149. doi:10.18488/journal.1007/2020.10.5/1007.5.137.149

TalentCorp & ILMIA. (2020). *Critical Occupations List 2019/2020 Technical Report.* https://www.talentcorp.com.my/clients/TalentCorp_2016_7A6571AE-D9D0-4175-B35D-99EC514F2D24/contentms/img/TalentCorp_CriticalOccupationsList_TechReport_2019-2020_Final.pdf

Taneja, B. (2021). The Digital Edge for M-Commerce to Replace E-Commerce. In *Emerging Challenges, Solutions and Best Practices for Digital Enterprises Transformation.* IGI Global.

Tarng, M. Y., Hsieh, C. H., & Deng, T. J. (2001). Personal background and reasons for choosing a career in policing: An empirical study of police students in Taiwan. *Journal of Criminal Justice, 29*(1), 45–56. doi:10.1016/S0047-2352(00)00075-1

TCMB. (2021). *İstatistikler.* Retrieved December 21, 2021, from https://www.tcmb.gov.tr/

Teijeiro, M., Rungo, P., & Freire, M. J. (2013). Graduate competencies and employability: The impact of matching firm's needs and personal attainments. *Economics of Education Review, 34*, 286–295. doi:10.1016/j.econedurev.2013.01.003

Tentama, F., & Yusantri, S. (2020). The Role of Entrepreneurial Intention in Predicting Vocational High School Students' Employability. *International Journal of Evaluation and Research in Education*, *9*(3), 558–563. doi:10.11591/ijere.v9i3.20580

Teo, H. A., & Poon, J. T. F. (1994). Career choice of undergraduates and SMEs in Singapore. *International Journal of Career Management*.

Terreblanche, S. (2012). *Lost in Transformation: South Africa's search for a New Future since 1986*. KMM Review Publishing Company.

The Innovation Hub. (n.d.). *Innovatively Working Together To Connect All of Us*. Accessed from: https://www.theinnovationhub.com/press-room-media/media/the-innovation-hub-celebrates-south-africas-innovators-and-entrepreneurs-during-global-entreprenuership-week-nws461

The Star. (2017, May 7). More student entrepreneurs by 2020. *The Star News Paper*, 5–8. https://www.thestar.com.my/news/education/2017/05/07/more-student-entrepreneurs-by-2020

The World Bank. (2021). *Youth Employment Transformation Initiative Project*. https://projects.world bank.org/en/projects-operations/project-detail/P160696

Thompson, E. R. (2019). Individual Entrepreneurial Intent. *Construct Classification and Development of an Internationally Reliable Metric*, *33*, 65–67.

Thunnissen, M., & Van Arensbergen, P. (2015). A multi-dimensional approach to talent. *Personnel Review*, *44*(2), 182–199.

Trivedi, R. (2016). Does university play significant role in shaping entrepreneurial intention? A cross-country comparative analysis. *Journal of Small Business and Enterprise Development*, *23*(3), 790–811. doi:10.1108/JSBED-10-2015-0149

Tshishonga, N. (2021). Economic survival: Towards balancing Financial and intellectual Act? In Higher Education, Community Engagement and Entrepreneurship in Southern Africa (pp. 66-95). Cambridge Scholars Publishing.

Tshishonga, N. (2019). The Effects of Intergenerational Poverty and Unemployment on South African Township Youth. In J. Kurebwa (Ed.), *Participation of Young People in Governance Processes in Africa* (pp. 1–21). IGI Global. doi:10.4018/978-1-5225-9388-1.ch001

Tshishonga, N., & Matsiliza, N. S. (2021). Addressing the Twin Challenges of Poverty and Unemployment through Community Work Programmes in South Africa. *African Journal of Development Studies*, *11*(2), 217–235.

TÜİK. (2021). *İşgücü İstatistikleri*. Haziran, No: 37482.

Turker, D., & Selcuk, S. S. (2009). Which factors affect entrepreneurial intention of university students? *Journal of European Industrial Training*, *33*(2), 142–159. doi:10.1108/03090590910939049

Türk-İş. (2021). *Açlık ve Yoksulluk Sınırı.* Temmuz. Retrieved November 3, 2021, from http://www.turkis.org.tr/TEMMUZ-2021-ACLIK-VE-YOKSULLUK-SINIRI-d542757#sthash.nmRDQCzT.dpuf

Tu, Y., & Wang, H. (2017). A study on the influence of college students' self-efficacy and creativity on entrepreneurial intention. *Journal of Higher Education (Columbus, Ohio)*, *3*, 95–100.

UNESCO. (2010). *World Conference on Higher Education 2009.* Final Report.

Unger, J. M., Rauch, A., Frese, M., & Rosenbusch, N. (2011). Human capital and entrepreneurial success: A meta-analytical review. *Journal of Business Venturing*, *26*(3), 341–358. doi:10.1016/j.jbusvent.2009.09.004

UNICEF. (2019). *Why India Should Worry About its Educated but Unemployed Youth.* https://gdc.unicef.org/resource/why-india-should-worry-about-its-educated-unemployed-youth

United Nations. (2015). *Transforming our world: the 2030 agenda for sustainable development.* New York: United Nations, Department of Economic and Social Affairs. Resolution adopted by the General Assembly on 25 September 2015. https://sustainabledevelopment.un.org/post2015/transformingourworld

United States Education: Statistical Profile. (2014). *Nation Master.* Retrieved from: https://www.nationmaster.com/country-info/profiles/UnitedStates/Education

Valerio, A., Parton, B., & Robb, A. (2014). *Entrepreneurship education and training programs around the world: Dimensions for success.* The World Bank. doi:10.1596/978-1-4648-0202-7

Vallerand, R. J., Blanchard, C., Mageau, G. A., Koestner, R., Ratelle, C., Léonard, M., Gagné, M., & Marsolais, J. (2003). Les passions de l'ame: On obsessive and harmonious passion. *Journal of Personality and Social Psychology*, *85*(4), 756–767. doi:10.1037/0022-3514.85.4.756 PMID:14561128

van der Heijde, C. M. (2014). Employability and self-regulation in contemporary careers. In *Psycho-social career meta-capacities* (pp. 7–17). Springer. doi:10.1007/978-3-319-00645-1_1

Van Der Heijden, B. I., Schalk, R., & Van Veldhoven, M. J. (2008). Ageing and careers: European research on long-term career development and early retirement. *Career Development International*, *13*(2), 85–94. doi:10.1108/13620430810860512

Van der Sluis, J., Van Praag, M., & Vijverberg, W. (2008). Education and entrepreneurship selection and performance: A review of the empirical literature. *Journal of Economic Surveys*, *22*(5), 795–841. doi:10.1111/j.1467-6419.2008.00550.x

Van Gelderen, M., Thurik, R., & Patel, P. (2011). Encountered Problems and Outcome Status in Nascent Entrepreneurship. *Journal of Small Business Management*, *49*(1), 71–91. doi:10.1111/j.1540-627X.2010.00315.x van Harten, J., De Cuyper, N., Guest, D., Fugate, M., Knies, E., & Forrier, A. (2020). Introduction to special issue on HRM and employability: mutual gains or conflicting outcomes? Vera, D., Samba, C., Kong, D. T., & Maldonado, T. (2020). Resilience as thriving: The role of positive leadership practices. *Organizational Dynamics*.

Van Praag, C. M., & Versloot, P. H. (2007). What is the value of entrepreneurship? A review of recent research. *Small Business Economics, 29*(4), 351–382. doi:10.100711187-007-9074-x

VanLeeuwen, C. A., Weeks, L. E., & Guo-Brennan, L. (2017). Indigenous perspectives on community service-learning in higher education: An examination of the Kenyan context. *The International Journal of Research on Service-Learning and Community Engagement, 5*(1), 129–143. doi:10.37333/001c.29769

Veiga, F., Alexandre, F., Silva, J., & Arezes, P. (2019). *Crescimento da Economia Portuguesa.* Associação Missão Crescimento.

Verd, J. M., Barranco, O., & Bolíbar, M. (2019). Youth unemployment and employment trajectories in Spain during the Great Recession: What are the determinants? *Journal for Labour Market Research, 53*(1), 4. doi:10.118612651-019-0254-3

Vesalainen, J., & Pihkala, T. (1999). *Motivation structure and entrepreneurial intentions.* Academic Press.

Voisey, P., Jones, P., & Thomas, B. (2013). The pre-incubator: A longitudinal study of 10 years of university pre-incubation in Wales. *Industry and Higher Education, 27*(5), 349–363. doi:10.5367/ihe.2013.0168

von Bloh, J., Mandakovic, V., Apablaza, M., Amorós, J., & Sternberg, R. (2020). Transnational entrepreneurs: Opportunity or necessity driven? Empirical evidence from two dynamic economies from Latin America and Europe. *Journal of Ethnic and Migration Studies, 46*(10), 2008–2026. doi:10.1080/1369183X.2018.1559996

Von Graevenitz, G., Harhoff, D., & Weber, R. (2010). The effects of entrepreneurship education. *Journal of Economic Behavior & Organization, 76*(1), 90–112. doi:10.1016/j.jebo.2010.02.015

Von Greiff, J. (2009). Displacement and self-employment entry. *Labour Economics, 16*(5), 556–565. doi:10.1016/j.labeco.2009.02.005

Vu. (2016). *Analysis of the influencing factors for choosing an entrepreneurial career among students in Finland.* Academic Press.

Walter, U. (2019). *Hackathon as a Formal Teaching Approach in Information Systems Capstone Courses.* Academic Press.

Weiss, E. M. (1999). Perceived workplace conditions and first-year teachers' morale, career choice commitment, and planned retention: A secondary analysis. *Teaching and Teacher Education, 15*(8), 861–879. doi:10.1016/S0742-051X(99)00040-2

Welter, F. (2011). Contextualizing entrepreneurship—Conceptual challenges and ways forward. *Entrepreneurship Theory and Practice*, *35*(1), 165–184. doi:10.1111/j.1540-6520.2010.00427.x

Wennekers, S., Van Stel, A., Carree, M., & Thurik, R. (2010). The Relationship between Entrepreneurship and Economic Development : Is It U-Shaped? *Foundations and Trends in Entrepreneurship*, *6*(3), 167–237. doi:10.1561/0300000023

What we do - Youth Business International. (n.d.). Retrieved September 22, 2021, from https://www.youthbusiness.org/what-we-do

Williams, C. C. (2008). Beyond necessity-driven versus opportunity-driven entrepreneurship: A study of informal entrepreneurs in England, Russia and Ukraine. *International Journal of Entrepreneurship and Innovation*, *9*(3), 157–165. doi:10.5367/000000008785096647

Wilson, F., Kickul, J., & Marlino, D. (2007). Gender, entrepreneurial self-efficacy, and entrepreneurial career intentions: Implications for entrepreneurship education. *Entrepreneurship Theory and Practice*, *31*(3), 387–406. doi:10.1111/j.1540-6520.2007.00179.x

Wong, P. K., Ho, Y. P., & Autio, E. (2005). Entrepreneurship, innovation and economic growth: Evidence from GEM data. *Small Business Economics, 24*(3), 335–350. doi:10.100711187-005-2000-1

Wong, I. A., Wan, Y. K. P., & Gao, J. H. (2017). How to attract and retain Generation Y employees? An exploration of career choice and the meaning of work. *Tourism Management Perspectives*, *23*, 140–150. doi:10.1016/j.tmp.2017.06.003

Wong, S. C. K., & Liu, G. J. (2010). Will parental influences affect career choice? Evidence from hospitality and tourism management students in China. *International Journal of Contemporary Hospitality Management*.

World Bank Group. (2017). *Harambee Youth Employment Accelerator: Solutions for Youth Employment*. https://www.s4ye.org/sites/default/files/S4YE%20Digital%20Jobs%20Case%20Study%20-%2012.%20Harambee%20Youth%20Employment%20Accelerator.pdf

World Bank Group. (2018). *An Incomplete Transition: Overcoming the Legacy of Exclusion in South Africa*. UCT Press.

World Bank. (2016). *Informal enterprises in Kenya*. World Bank.

World Bank. (2017). *Uganda Economic Update, December 2017: Accelerating Uganda's Development, Ending Child Marriage, Educating Girls*. World Bank.

World Bank. (2020). *Assessing the research institutions effectiveness of public research institutions*. http://bit.ly/WB_blogsMY

World Bank. (2020). *Kenya overview*. https://www.worldbank.org/

World Bank. (2021). *Tertiary Education Overview*. https://www.worldbank.org/en/topic/tertiaryeducation

World Bank. (2021, June 15). *Unemployment, total (% of total labor force) (modeled ILO estimate)*. International Labour Organization, ILOSTAT database. https://data.worldbank.org/indicator/SL.UEM.TOTL.ZS

World Economic Forum. (2016). *The Global Competitiveness Report 2016–2021*. Accessed from: https://www.weforum.org/reports/the-global-competitiveness-report-2016-2017

World Economic Forum. (2017). *The Future of Jobs and Skills in Africa Preparing the Region for the Fourth Industrial Revolution*. https://www3.weforum.org/docs/WEF_EGW_FOJ_Africa.pdf

World Economic Forum. (2020). *Towards a reskilling revolution: A future of jobs for all*. Accessed from: http://hdl.voced.edu.au/10707/448194

World Economic Forum. (2022). *The Global Risks Report 2022* (17th ed.). https://www3.weforum.org/docs/WEF_The_Global_Risks_Report_2022.pdf

Wright, M., Siegel, D. S., & Mustar, P. (2017). An emerging ecosystem for student start-ups. *The Journal of Technology Transfer*, *42*(4), 909–922. doi:10.100710961-017-9558-z

Wu, K. Y., & Eriksson Lantz, C. (2017). *Building and managing an innovation hub: A case study of the challenges and opportunities faced by a Northern Swedish innovation hub*. Academic Press.

Xavier, S. R., Guelich, U., Kew, P., Nawangpalupi, C., & Velasco, A. (2014). *Asean Regional Entrepreneurship Report 2014/2015. Policy Opportunities for inclusiveness and sustainable entrepreneurial growth*. The Global Entrepreneurship Monitor 2014 Global Report. https://www.academia.edu/28192121/ASEAN_REGIONAL_ENTREPRENEURSHIP_REPORT_2014_15_Driving_Asean_Entrepreneurship_Policy_Opportunities_for_Inclusiveness_and_Sustainable_Entrepreneurial_Growth

Xia, T., Gu, H., Huang, Y., Zhu, Q., & Cheng, Y. (2020). The relationship between career social support and employability of college students: A moderated mediation model. *Frontiers in Psychology*, *11*, 28. doi:10.3389/fpsyg.2020.00028 PMID:32047461

Xu, M. J. M., & Kim, S. H. (2018). The Fourth Industrial Revolution: Opportunities and Challenges. *International Journal of Financial Research, 9*(2).

Xu, Z., Lin, D., & Li, J. (2011). Graduate entrepreneurship in China. *Journal of Chinese Entrepreneurship*, *3*(3). Advance online publication. doi:10.1108/jce.2011.40503caa.001

Youndt, M. A., Subramaniam, M., & Snell, S. A. (2004). Intellectual capital profiles: An examination of investment and returns. *Journal of Management Studies*, *41*(2), 335–361. doi:10.1111/j.1467-6486.2004.00435.x

Young Entrepreneurs Mentoring Partnership. (n.d.). Retrieved September 22, 2021, from https://world-mentors.org/

Youssef, C. M., & Luthans, F. (2012). Positive global leadership. *Journal of World Business*, *47*(4), 539–547. doi:10.1016/j.jwb.2012.01.007

Zamberi Ahmad, S. (2011). Evidence of the characteristics of women entrepreneurs in the kingdom of Saudi Arabia: An empirical investigation. *International Journal of Gender and Entrepreneurship, 3*(2), 123–143. doi:10.1108/17566261111140206

Zeffane, R., & Bani Melhem, S. J. (2017). Trust, job satisfaction, perceived organizational performance and turnover intention: A public-private sector comparison in the United Arab Emirates. *Employee Relations, 39*(7), 1148–1167. doi:10.1108/ER-06-2017-0135

Zentner, S., Nagy, F., Götz, M., & Maiberg, H. (2011). *Lernen durch Engagement. service-learning in German schools. A promising way to get youth involved–in active learning and in civic engagement.* Weinheim: Freudenberg Foundation.

Zhang, L. (2018). What are the Causes and Consequences of Graduate Unemployment in China? *2nd International Conference on Modern Education and Information Technology (MEIT 2018).*

Zhang, M., Wang, F., Weng, H., Zhu, T., & Liu, H. (2021). Transformational leadership and perceived overqualification: A career development perspective. *Frontiers in Psychology, 12*, 12. doi:10.3389/fpsyg.2021.597821 PMID:33643130

Zhang, S.-N., Li, Y.-Q., Liu, C.-H., & Ruan, W.-Q. (2020). Critical factors identification and prediction of tourism and hospitality students' entrepreneurial intention. *Journal of Hospitality, Leisure, Sport and Tourism Education, 26*, 100234. doi:10.1016/j.jhlste.2019.100234

Zollo, L., Laudano, M. C., Ciappei, C., & Zampi, V. (2017). Factors affecting universities' ability to foster students' entrepreneurial behaviour: An empirical investigation. *Journal of Management Development, 36*(2), 268–285. doi:10.1108/JMD-06-2016-0093

About the Contributors

Isaac Wasswa Katono holds a BSc. (Agriculture) Rural Economy and a Masters in Business Administration (MBA) Marketing Option, both from Makerere University. He holds a PhD in Business Science (Entrepreneurship) of the University of Cape Town. Currently, he is a Senior Lecturer in the School of Business at Uganda Christian University. Prior to that, Isaac was the Associate Dean Faculty of Business and Administration, Uganda Christian University 2010 to 2016 as well as Head, Department of Management and Entrepreneurship 2012 to 2016. He participated in the development of modules for the Student Training in Entrepreneurship Promotion (STEP) project at the University of Giessen in 2008, and has since been a trainer in this program in Uganda and other countries since then to date. His research interest is Culture, Entrepreneurship, Management and Gender. Isaac is a reviewer for a number of international journals and is also a member of the European Association of Science Editors. He has attended and presented papers in several international conferences, and has published works in the area of Entrepreneurship and Management plus other related areas.

***

Diana Abdul Wahab is a Senior Lecturer at the Department of Applied Statistics, the Universiti Malaya in Kuala Lumpur, Malaysia. She completed her Doctorate at Leeds University Business School, Leeds, United Kingdom. Dr. Diana has been interested in applying statistical models to understand graduate labor market issues throughout her academic career, beginning at the Master's level when she collaborated with the Tracer Study Unit in the Ministry of Higher Education Malaysia. Her interest in the field has evolved to a deeper understanding of graduate employment issues including gender pay gap, first destination choices, and migration while developing her interest in the field of data science where she applies data science techniques in other areas of studies such as education and economy. She has published her paper in the Institutions and Economies and continues to write for other international academic journals. She has won a scholarship award to go to Kazakhstan to conduct a comparative analysis on the graduate employment issues between the two countries. She teaches Statistical

Computing and Business Analytics and planning to expand her research interest in the field of data science.

Mohd Amirul Rafiq Abu Rahim is a PhD candidate at Universiti Malaya. His research interest covers the statistical application of labour analysis which focus on skills mismatch and earning gaps among young people. With eight years of experience in policy-related research, he is currently working as Research Associate in Khazanah Research Institute, a research think tank in Kuala Lumpur since 2016. He started his early profession as a Statistician, with the National Population and Family Development Board (NPFDB) in 2012. In NPFDB, his area of research focuses on demographic and youth development issues.

Johnson Dare Adeeko is a Lecturer at the department of Entrepreneurial Studies, Bamidele Olumilua University of Education, Science and Technology, Ikere- Ekiti in Ekiti State, Nigeria. He is a graduate of Economics from the University of Ado-Ekiti in Ekiti state, Nigeria. He holds Master of Science in Entrepreneurship Education from the University of Ibadan in Oyo State, Nigeria and currently pursuing his PhD in Entrepreneurship at the University of Ibadan, Nigeria.

Nuno Crespo holds a PhD in Economics and a Master degree in International Economics. He is the Director of the MSc Business Economics and Competition. In the most recent years, Nuno Crespo was Vice-Rector of ISCTE-IUL and assumed several other positions such as Director of the Department of Economics, Scientific Commission of the Department of Economics, and the coordination of courses (MSc Portuguese Economy and International Integration and MSc Health Services Management). Researcher at Business Research Unit (BRU-ISCTE), he has several publications in scientific journals such as World Economy, World Development, Economics Letters, Review of World Economics, Journal of Common Market Studies, Journal of Economic Surveys, Empirical Economics, Papers in Regional Science, Tourism Analysis, Journal of Economics and Social Measurement, Telecommunications Policy, Journal of Informetrics, Scientometrics, and International Review of Applied Economics. Publications of books and book chapters in his areas of expertise. He is Co-Editor-in-Chief of the Academy of Entrepreneurship Journal and member of the editorial board of several international scientific journals (European Journal of International Management, International Journal of Trade and Global Markets, International Journal of Knowledge and Learning, Sustainability, and Tourism Analysis, among others). Editor of the MPRA. He integrates the board of the Portuguese Economists Association.

Badal Chandra Das is a Ph.D. student, Department of Economics with Rural Development, Vidyasagar University, Midnapore, West Bengal, India.

Arobindu Dash is a doctoral student at the Institute for Management & Organization (IMO), Leuphana University Lüneburg and also affiliated with Behavioral Science unit, World Bank. He was a visiting research fellow at Cambridge Judge Business School, University of Cambridge. Currently, he is doing research on job creation in developing countries through entrepreneurship education and training to tackle graduate youth unemployment. He holds a master's degree in Industrial/Organizational (I-O) Psychology and a bachelor's degree in Psychology from University of Dhaka, Bangladesh. He is interested in entrepreneurship education and training for social impact and value creation in global south.

Michael M. Gielnik is Professor of HR Development at the Leuphana University Lüneburg. He studied psychology at the University of Giessen and received his PhD from the Leuphana University Lüneburg. He was a Senior Research Fellow at the National University of Singapore Business School. He had research stays at the University of the Western Cape (South Africa) and the University of Sydney (Australia). His research focuses on the psychology of entrepreneurship, in particular cognitive and motivational success factors in entrepreneurship as well as entrepreneurship training and transfer. He is particularly interested in entrepreneurship in low and middle income countries. He has conducted several research and practice projects in different countries in sub-Saharan Africa, Asia, and Latin America.

Raj Karan Gupta is currently working as Assistant Professor (Senior Grade) in the area of General Management (Entrepreneurship) at School of Business Studies, Sharda University. Prior to joining Sharda University, he worked as an Assistant Prof. with Galgotias University and Galgotias Business School. He also worked as a Project Officer at Entrepreneurship Development Institute of India (EDII), Ahmedabad. He has completed his Doctor of Philosophy (D.Phil.) Degree in Commerce from University of Allahabad and also UGC-NET qualified. Also received MBA (Marketing) from Guru Jambheshwar University of Science & Technology (GJUS&T), Hisar, Haryana. He has 14 years' experience in Academics and Research. He has also been trained on Innovation and Technology Management from Indian Institute of Technology, Bombay (IIT-B) through MDP. He has several papers to his credit published in various National & International Journals / Conference Proceedings.

Haji Mohammad Izzuddin is currently a PhD Candidate at Universiti Brunei Darussalam, conducting research in the field of Business Management and Entrepreneurship. He received his Bachelor's Degree in Business Administration at Coventry University, United Kingdom, and Master's Degree in Management at Universiti Brunei Darussalam. He has also studied other courses including Software Engineering and Programming, Multimedia and Graphic Design. At Universiti Islam Sultan Sharif Ali, he studied Intermediate Level Arabic Language, Tadabbur Al-Quran programme and Pengurusan Jenazah Mazhab Syafi'i course. His industry experiences started when he first became a salesman and distributor, and has since worked in various industries including becoming a Tutor/Teacher, App Developer, Graphic Designer and Business Executive Officer. He is teaching in various academic branches in Entrepreneurship, Business Management, Financial and Management Accounting, Macroeconomics and Microeconomics, and Commerce. He has been involved in academic research for several years, and his research areas include Entrepreneurship, Growth and MSMEs.

Sebak Kumar Jana is a Professor of Economics, Department of Economics with Rural Development, Vidyasagar University, Midnapore, West Bengal, India.

Rohana Jani is a Senior Research Fellow at Ungku Aziz Center for Development Studies, Faculty of Economics and Administration, University of Malaya, Kuala Lumpur. She holds a BSc (Mathematics) from Ohio University, Athens, USA; MSc in Statistics from West Virginia University, USA and a Phd in Statistics from Macquarie University, Sydney, Australia. Her areas of expertise include Statistical Data Analysis using Multivariate Techniques, Quantitative Research Methodology, Market Research, Statistical Package for the Social Sciences (SPSS) applications. Migration of Human Capital (Brain-Drain); Capacity Building Among Youths: Development of A Smoke Free Generation Towards Smoke Free Malaysia 2045, Border Security: border security along the eastern coastal areas of Kudat and Sandakan Sabah, Malaysia; the Financial Adequacy and Well-Being of University Malaya Students, Graduates Unemployment in Malaysia, the Social and Economic Impact of COVID-19 on deaf community in Malaysia, are some of her current research projects.

İrfan Kalaycı received his BD in economics from Çukurova University (Adana), MSc and Ph.D in economics from İnönü University (Malatya), and associate professorship in macroeconomics from the TR Higher Education Institution-Inter Universities Board (Ankara). His main scientific studies are about economic policy, bioeconomics and Turkey - Europe - World - local economies. In addition to more than 100 articles and book chapters, he has 3 copyright books and 5 editorial books and 21 awards he received in various scientific and literary competitions. He is currently a professor of political economy at İnönü University.

Peter Dithan Ntale is a Deputy Director & a Research Fellow at Makerere University Business School, Faculty of Graduate Studies & Research in the Department of Doctoral Training. He holds a Master of Science in Marketing from Makerere University. Currently, Ntale is in advanced stages of his PhD studies from the East African School of Higher Education Studies & Development, College of Education and External Studies,

Makerere University. He holds a Bachelor of Business Administration (BBA) and a Post-graduate diploma in Marketing Management from Uganda Management Institute. He is a researcher in business related issues, higher education, employability, entrepreneurship and business psychology, entrepreneurial training and has widely published in international peer reviewed journals.

Oluwaseyitanfunmi Osunade is an Associate Professor of Computer Science at the University of Ibadan, Nigeria. His research covers data communications, educational technology, mobile agents, block chain and e-Health.Dr Osunade has designed and implemented several computer networks within and outside the University of Ibadan. His first network design was a 10-computer local area network for Computer Science Department, UI. He now designs optic fibre networks and IPv6 networks for institutions and organizations. Dr. Osunade jointly holds two patents for Radio Frequency Identification Smart Graduation Certification System and Accent based CAPTCHA System.

Nadia Simoes holds a PhD in Economics and a Master degree in Economics. Started teaching in the Economics Department of Iscte - Instituto Universitário de Lisboa in 2002. Director of the BSc Economics. Former Director of the MSc Business Economics and Competition. Researcher of the Economics Group of the Business Research Unit (BRU-ISCTE). Publications in several journals such as Economics Letters, Journal of Economic Surveys, Empirical Economics, Acta Oeconomica, International Review of Applied Economics, Telecommunications Policy, Panoeconomicus, International Journal of Social Economics. Associate Editor of the journal International Journal of Education Economics and Development (SCOPUS Q4) and Editor of the journal Cogent Economics & Finance (SCOPUS Q3). Member of the Editorial Board of the following journals: Entrepreneurship and Sustainability Issues (SCOPUS Q1); Journal of Entrepreneurship Education (SCOPUS Q2); Panoeconomicus (SCOPUS Q2); Journal of Entrepreneurship in Emerging Economies (SCOPUS Q2); Academy of Entrepreneurship Journal (SCOPUS Q3); and of the International Journal of Entrepreneurship (SCOPUS Q3). NEP Editor for the area of Education. She has participated in research national and international research projects financed by public institutions. Expert for different national and international institutions such as the European Employment Observatory (European Commission), ILO, Cedefop, Eurofound, Portuguese Labour Ministry, and Ministry of Education.

Bhavna Taneja has earned her Masters Degree in Business Administration with a specialization in Finance and Marketing. She has earned her Ph.D. in Management. She has an experience of 18 years of in the education sector and is currently an Assistant Professor at Amity University, Jharkhand. Her research interests are in the field of Entrepreneurship, Consumer behavior, and Finance.

Ndwakhulu Tshishonga is a Pan-Africanist Academic and Research Fellow in the School of Built Environment & Development Studies within Community Development Discipline at UKZN. He is the holder of BA, BA (Hons) in Development Studies (UNISA); an MA in Applied Anthropology (Goldsmith College, University of London), MM in Public Development and Management (WITS) and MPA-Public Administration (UWC), Advanced Diploma (UWC-Adult Education) and Social Reconstruction and Development Certificate (SADEP-UWC). His Academic Chores include Coordinating the Masters Programme and Post-Graduate Diploma in Community Development. He received the Golden Award for Best Student at UWC in 2002 and was awarded two awards by the University of KwaZulu-Natal for the new emerging and established scholar in 2018. Prior to joining UKZN in 2005, he worked for FAIRSHARE as a Political Economy Workshops Facilitator, Lecturer at both SADEP-UCT and PENTECK currently known as Cape Peninsula University of Technology (CPUT) as well as Community Development field worker in Limpopo Province. His interests are in Citizenship and Local government and Local governance, Intergovernmental Relations, Land reform issues, Scholarship in Higher Education and Community Engagement, etc. His teaching interests range from Alternative Models of Development, Project Management and Development Planning & Theories to Micro Level Strategies in Economic Development, Co-operatives and Research Methods and Public Administration.

Samuel Uwem Umoh holds PhD International Relations from the University of KwaZulu-Natal. He is also a field researcher at Tourism KwaZulu-Natal Province. He is a member of the Emerging Scholars Network, Australia. His research area teaching-learning, governance, social change, and migration He lectures at University of KwaZulu-Natal, Durban South Africa.

Henry K. Yatich is a Research Fellow in the School of Business and Economics, at Mount Kenya University, Thika, Kenya. His research FOCUS is on skill development in HEIs and TVET sector, in Kenya. He is also a member of the Diversity and Inclusion Steering Committee (AACSB), University-Business Linkages (UBL-ACCESS PROJECT with Leipzig University), and Steering Committee Member for the GOING GLOBAL-British Council Conference. He has consulted for Skills for Prosperity-UK (S4P-2019) and Department for International Trade (DIT-UK, 2021). He is the Founder and Director of StacVis Consulting-Kenya. Previously, he previously worked as a Faculty Dean, Director, ODeL (Content Development and Design), at Mount Kenya University.

Index

G

H

I

J

K

Y

www.ingramcontent.com/pod-product-compliance
Lightning Source LLC
LaVergne TN
LVHW080603300926
849162LV00005B/1036